Examining Reading

Research and practice in assessing second language reading

Also in this series:

Examining Reading

Research and practice in assessing second language reading

Hanan Khalifa
Assistant Director
University of Cambridge ESOL Examinations

and

Cyril J Weir
Powdrill Professor in English Language Acquisition
University of Bedfordshire

CAMBRIDGE
UNIVERSITY PRESS

CAMBRIDGE UNIVERSITY PRESS
Cambridge, New York, Melbourne, Madrid, Cape Town, Singapore, São Paulo, Delhi

Cambridge University Press
The Edinburgh Building, Cambridge CB2 8RU, UK

www.cambridge.org
Information on this title: www.cambridge.org/9780521736718

First published 2009

Printed in the United Kingdom at the University Press, Cambridge

A catalogue record for this publication is available from the British Library

Library of Congress Cataloging-in-Publication Data
Khalifa, Hanan.
  Examining reading : research and practice in assessing second language reading /
Hanan Khalifa and Cyril J. Weir.
    p. cm.
  Includes bibliographical references and indexes.
  ISBN 978-0-521-73671-8
  1. English language–Study and teaching–Foreign students–Evaluation.
2. Reading (Higher education)–Ability testing. 3. Second language acquisition–
Research. I. Weir, Cyril J. II. Title.
  PE1128.A2K418 2009
  428.0076--dc22

ISBN 9780521736718

Contents

Abbreviations

Adj	Adjective
AERA	American Educational Research Association
ALTE	Association of Language Testers in Europe
AOG	Assessment & Operations Group
APA	American Psychological Association
AWL	Academic Word List
BEC	Business English Certificates
BNC	British National Corpus
BULATS	Business Language Testing Service
CAE	Certificate in Advanced English
CB	Computer Based
CBT	Computer Based Testing
CEF	Common European Framework
CEFR	Common European Framework of Reference
CELS	Certificates in English Language Skills
CELTA	Certificate in English Language Teaching to Adults
CET	College English Test
CFA	Confirmatory Factor Analysis
CIS	Candidate Information Sheet
CLA	Communicative Language Ability
CLB	Canadian Language Benchmarks
CPE	Certificate of Proficiency in English
CRELLA	Centre for Research in English Language Learning and Assessment
CTT	Classical Test Theory
CUP	Cambridge University Press
DELTA	Diploma in English Language Teaching to Adults
DIALANG	Diagnostic Language (Assessment)
DIF	Differential Item Functioning
EAL	English as an Additional Language
EAP	English for Academic Purposes
EBAFLS	European Bank of Anchor Items for Foreign Language Skills
EFL	English as a Foreign Language
ELT	English Language Teaching
EPS	Examination Processing System
ESM	Electronic Script Management

ESOL	English for Speakers of Other Languages
ESP	English for Specific Purposes
ETS	Educational Testing Service
FCE	First Certificate in English
GEPT	General English Proficiency Test
GM	General marking
GPC	Grapheme–Phoneme Correspondence
GRE	Graduate Record Examination
IATM	Instrument for the Analysis of Textbook Materials
iBT TOEFL	Internet Based Test of English as a Foreign Language
ICFE	International Certificate in Financial English
ICR	Intelligent Character Recognition
IDP	International Development Program
IELTS	International English Language Testing System
IF	Item Facility
IIS	IELTS Impact Study
ILEC	International Legal English Certificate
ILTA	International Language Testing Association
IRT	Item Response Theory
ITC	International Test Commission
IW	Item Writer
IWGs	Item Writer Guidelines
KET	Key English Test
KR-20	Kuder-Richardson 20
L1	First Language
L2	Second Language
LCE	Lower Certificate in English
LIBS	Local Item Banking System
MCQ	Multiple Choice Questions
MQC	Marking-Quality Coordinator
N	Noun
NCME	National Council on Measurement in Education
OMR	Optical Mark Reader
PARA	Partnership for Accessible Reading Assessment
PB	Paper Based
PET	Preliminary English Test
PMS	Performance Management System
PRD	Project Research and Development
QMS	Quality Management System
QPP	Question Paper Production
QPT	Quick Placement Test
RITCME	Recruitment, Induction, Training, Co-ordination, Monitoring, Evaluation

Abbreviations

RNIB	Royal National Institute for the Blind
SAQ	Short Answer Questions
SD	Standard Deviation
SE	Standard Error
SEM	Standard Error of Measurement
SILT	Studies in Language Testing
SO	Subject Officer
SVO	Subject Verb Object order
TEEP	Test in English for Educational Purposes
TEFL	Teaching English as a Foreign Language
TESOL	Teaching English to Speakers of Other Languages
TKT	Teaching Knowledge Test
TLX	Task Load Index
TM	Test Method characteristics
TOEFL	Test of English as a Foreign Language
TOEIC	Test of English for International Communication
TTR	Type-Token Ratio
UAT	User Acceptance Test
UCLES	University of Cambridge Local Examinations Syndicate
UETESOL	University Entrance Test in English for Speakers of Other Languages
UN	United Nations
VDT	Visual Display Text
VDU	Visual Display Unit
VP	Vocabulary Profiler
VRIP	Validity, Reliability, Impact, Practicality
VSO	Verb Subject Object order
WPM	Words per minute
YLE	Young Learners English Tests

Series Editors' note

Examining Reading is the second volume in the Studies in Language Testing (SiLT) series that addresses the approach used by Cambridge ESOL in the assessment of language skills, the first being SiLT 26, *Examining Writing* by Shaw and Weir (2007). This volume sets out to describe and evaluate how Cambridge ESOL tests different levels of reading in English as a second language across the range of examinations it offers spanning the Reference Levels of the Common European Framework of Reference (CEFR) from A2 to C2, through focusing largely on the five examinations in the Cambridge ESOL Main Suite (KET, PET, FCE, CAE, CPE). As with *Examining Writing* (2007), it does so by presenting an explicit framework that structures the approach to validation according to a number of dimensions or parameters. It utilises the same theoretical framework as *Examining Writing* which was originally proposed by Weir (2005) and which seeks to take account of both the aspects of cognition, related to the mental processes the individual needs to engage in order to address a task, and the features of language use in context that affect the ways in which a task is addressed. The authors also look at the practical assessment issues related to the marking and scoring of reading tests. As with *Examining Writing* therefore, this volume explores the triangular relationship between three critical internal dimensions of language testing tasks – the test takers' *cognitive abilities*, the *context* in which the task is performed and the *scoring process*. Set alongside these are the twin external dimensions of consequential validity and criterion-related validity.

Cambridge ESOL has been involved in the assessment of reading skills ever since it launched its first English language examination in 1913. Since that time we have seen a significant development in our understanding of the reading construct from its early conceptualisation as an integrated skill, assessed largely by translation and even reading aloud tasks, through to the approaches documented in this volume.

When the CPE was introduced in 1913, reading as a skill in its own right did not feature explicitly among those to be examined. The history and most recent revision of CPE is well documented in SiLT 15, *Continuity and Innovation: Revising the Cambridge Proficiency in English Examination 1913–2002* (Weir and Milanovic 2003). The volume explains how the approach to the design of CPE in 1913 was based on *The Practical Study of Languages* (Sweet 1899) and candidates spent over twelve hours on a demanding set of activities that included translation to and from English, an essay on a topic such as Elizabethan travel and discovery, an English literature paper, English phonetics, dictation, reading aloud and conversation. While various reading skills were required throughout the examination, the skill itself was not singled out for particular attention as it would be today nor in the way that phonetics, grammar, reading aloud and conversation were singled out in the 1913 examination.

Little changed in relation to the assessment of reading for the 1938 version of CPE other than the introduction of an alternative to the English Literature paper focussing on General Economic and Commercial Knowledge. Candidates had to read extensively in order to engage with these papers but did so outside the context of the examination room, clearly extremely powerful with regard to the impact of the test on learning/teaching. Summarisation and explanation were required of candidates when tackling some of the questions in both of these papers. Typically, candidates had to choose between summarising a passage, which included defining the meaning of words and phrases in the text, and explaining a poem in detail including a focus on style and diction.

The Lower Certificate in English, introduced in 1939 and later known as the First Certificate in English (1975), tackled reading in a slightly different way. In its paper entitled Prescribed Texts, candidates had to read up to four prescribed texts typically taken from what we would today refer to as the classics of English literature but what would then have been closer to contemporary fiction. In the examination candidates had to answer questions on two of the texts. A short excerpt from each was presented and candidates were asked a number of open-ended questions, sometimes requiring close inspection of the text itself and sometimes a broader interpretation. In the Composition paper Part C was mandatory and required candidates to answer some short questions focusing on the meaning of vocabulary in a text, propose a title for it and summarise a part of it. Some of these activities would be familiar in reading tests today.

The 1955 variant of CPE introduced a Use of English paper and reading was tested both in this paper and in the English Language paper (introduced in the place of the Composition paper in 1945), though it was not referred to as reading in either. Short answer comprehension questions, summarisation and vocabulary questions were all used. From the 1940s to the mid 1970s relatively little changed on the surface but behind the scenes a revolution was taking place that would mark a radical shift in an approach that had been changing gradually since 1913.

There was much talk internally in the 1960s that the Cambridge approach lacked objectivity, that is, that it was in some way behind the times, that it needed to focus more explicitly on the four skills and that it was time to start making use of more 'scientific' methods of assessment, i.e. multiple choice questions, analysis, and, importantly, the demonstration of test reliability.

This affected CPE gradually at first in that multiple choice questions were introduced into the 1967 variant of the Use of English Paper. The focus was largely on vocabulary and the extent to which the questions were subjected to analysis was limited, but an important statement had been made. The 1975 release of both FCE and CPE made a much bolder statement. Cambridge exams now explicitly tested the four skills of Reading, Listening, Speaking and Writing. Both Listening and Reading were introduced in their own right. At the same time, the Use of English paper continued with its micro focus on grammatical and lexical knowledge. The reading construct, though not defined as such at this stage, involved reading a number of short passages and answering multiple-choice questions on them. The focus was on explicit and implicit meaning at both levels. There were also 25 discrete-point multiple-choice vocabulary questions. The reading construct appeared to reflect a combination of reading skills along with a knowledge of vocabulary, sometimes of a somewhat esoteric nature.

The FCE and CPE examinations changed relatively little in the next 21 years; however, as before, there was significant activity behind the scenes. The work of the Council of Europe in its Modern Languages programme, the emergence of the Threshold level, and the rise of the communicative language teaching movement all happened in the 1970s and 1980s and impacted on the Cambridge approach to language testing. In addition, an important study carried out in the late 1980s was to have quite a powerful influence on the shape of things to come. Bachman et al (1995) carried out a Cambridge-sponsored study entitled *An Investigation into the Comparability of Two Tests of English as a Foreign Language* (SiLT 1). While ostensibly looking at the comparison between FCE and TOEFL in order to establish an empirical link between the level systems of each examination, this study actually ended up providing an in-depth critique of the Cambridge approach with specific reference to the then well developed and documented psychometrically-oriented approach as demonstrated by the TOEFL. Significant issues in relation to reliability and validity emerged which were addressed vigorously with the 1996 release of the FCE and subsequent release of CPE in 2002. Apart from a range of measurement issues not particularly relevant to this discussion, a much sharper focus on test construct definition and validation emerged. Where test construct had had to be pieced together post hoc from test specifications in earlier releases of FCE and CPE, there were now explicit statements on test construct. The Reading paper in particular, underwent fairly radical revision and its construct was defined as 'Understanding the propositional, functional and sociolinguistic meanings at word, phrase, sentence or discourse levels and of reading outcomes relevant to FCE takers (i.e. gist, specific information, detail, main idea, deduced information).' Measures were put in place not only to develop test content with systematic reference to the underlying construct but also to validate the nature of that construct. It is this important step that has taken us to the work described in this volume and the others in this series. The volume on Writing assessment has already been published as SiLT 26, and parallel volumes on Speaking and Listening are currently in preparation for pubication over the next two years.

More recently, we have also seen the emergence of the Common European Framework of Reference for Learning, Teaching and Assessment (Council of Europe 2001) which encourages examination providers to map their certification to the Framework. Khalifa and Weir examine how Cambridge has approached this task in significant depth when exploring criterion-related validity. The approach taken by Cambridge seeks not only to establish the relationship with the Framework as a one-off study, but to deploy a methodology that ensures a long-term and continually verifiable relationship which is surely in the overall best interests of test users.

Skills assessment at Cambridge is now underpinned more formally than ever by a validation framework based on Weir (2005) and building on the work of Bachman (1989) which informed validation activities in the 1990s, as well as the VRIP approach developed by Cambridge in the 1990s. The approach outlined in this volume not only allows Cambridge to determine where current examinations are performing satisfactorily in relation to a range of relevant validity parameters, it also provides the basis for improvement and the construction of an ongoing research agenda. It provides an important benchmark against which test developers can evaluate the effectiveness of their respective approaches and it offers test users a model of what to expect from responsible examination providers.

Michael Milanovic and Cyril J Weir
Cambridge – April 2009

Acknowledgements

In bringing this volume to fruition, we are deeply indebted to a great number of colleagues. Their expertise, sound advice and collaboration have undoubtedly contributed to the quality of this volume.

We would like to thank Professor Eddie Williams (Bangor University) and Dr Roger Hawkey (University of Bedfordshire) for their many insightful comments when reviewing the whole manuscript. We wish to express special thanks to Dr Lynda Taylor for her painstaking reviews of, and thought-provoking comments on, the various drafts of the manuscript.

We are also grateful to a number of experts within the field of applied linguistics and language testing who provided valuable comments on individual chapters: Professor Antony Kunnan (UCLA) for his reflections on the test-taker characteristics chapter; Dr John Field (Reading University) whose views have been instrumental in shaping the chapter on cognitive validity; Dr Felicity O'Dell (Testing Consultant) and Dr Norbert Schmitt (Nottingham University) for their analysis of lexical, functional and structural resources in Main Suite reading papers; Dr Nick Saville and Dr Roger Hawkey for their valuable input to the chapter on consequential validity. Particular thanks go to the chairs of Main Suite Reading papers for their diligent and attentive reviews of text relating to their respective areas of interest: Sharon Ashton, Annette Capel, Anthea Bazin, Wendy Sharp and Judith Wilson.

Sincere thanks are due to three Cambridge ESOL colleagues who have read through the different manuscripts, judiciously reviewed them, provided insightful comments and sometimes heated discussions: Angela Ffrench (FCE/CAE/CPE Subject Manager), Mick Ashton (PET Subject Officer) and Glyn Hughes (FCE Subject Officer). We deeply appreciate their expertise and the time they have given us from their busy schedules.

This volume could not have been completed without the additional co-operation of numerous Cambridge ESOL personnel, many of whom enabled us to represent fully both the practitioner voice and the researcher voice. We would like to acknowledge here contributions made by members of the Assessment and Operations Group: Anne Gutch (Assistant Director), Edward Hackett (KET/PET Subject Manager), Margaret Cooze (KET Subject Officer), Helen Coward (CAE Subject Officer), Andrew Balch (CPE Subject Officer), Sharon Jordan (Computer Based Testing Subject Manager), Cris Betts (Senior Operations Manager), David Corkill (Use of English Subject Officer), Dr Rod Boroughs (IELTS Subject Officer) and Hugh

Bateman (BEC Subject Manager). We would also like to acknowledge contributions made by staff from the Research and Validation Group: Dr Neil Jones (Assistant Director), Dr Ardeshir Geranpayeh (Assistant Director), Dr Andrew Blackhurst (Senior Coordinator), Dr Andrew Somers (Main Suite Validation Officer), Dr Fiona Barker (Corpora Validation Officer), and Nick Beresford-Knox (Research Projects Assistant). Last but not least, we would like to thank Sonia Liddiard (Centre Manager) and Juliet Wilson (Assistant Director) for their contributions to Appendix C.

Finally, we would like to recognise the contribution of Dr Michael Milanovic (Cambridge ESOL Chief Executive) whose vision made the publication of the construct series a reality and whose willingness to support future research into issues raised in this volume makes this publication worthwhile.

To all of the above, and to others we have failed to mention, we offer our most sincere thanks and appreciation.

The publishers are grateful to the copyright holders for permission to use the copyright material reproduced in this book. Council of Europe and Cambridge University Press for Table 1.1, Table 1.2 and Table 4.7 from *Common European Framework of Reference for Languages: Learning, teaching, assessment,* 2001.

1 Introduction

This volume stands as the second in a series of volumes designed to explore the constructs underpinning the testing of English language skills. The specific focus here is on the testing of second language reading ability and the title is a companion to the first construct volume in the series, *Examining Writing*, by Shaw and Weir (2007). To some degree, *Examining Reading* covers ground already mapped out in the earlier publication in relation to testing second language writing. Where the concepts are identical there is inevitable overlap with that volume. For the most part, however, this volume reflects a novel updating of the theoretical framework for the validation of language examinations in relation to the testing of reading first outlined in Weir (2005). In addition, the volume examines the operationalisation of that framework by way of a critical evaluation of Cambridge ESOL examinations. This evaluation provides the context for the framework's exegesis as in each chapter Cambridge practice is reviewed in terms of the particular component of the framework under review.

Audience for the volume

This volume is aimed primarily at those working professionally in the field of language testing such as key personnel in examination agencies and those with an academic interest in language testing/examining. It is intended to provide a coherent account of the theoretical construct on which reading examinations should be based and of the rigorous procedures that need to be followed to provide evidence concerning the various components of a test's validity. As such it is hoped that it will offer other institutions a useful framework for reviewing their own examinations/tests.

However, some parts of the volume may also be of interest and relevance to anyone who is directly involved in reading assessment activity and/or Cambridge ESOL examinations in some way, e.g. reading curriculum and materials developers, or teachers preparing candidates for the Cambridge ESOL Reading tests.

Voices in the volume

As the reader progresses through the volume, it will become apparent that there are several 'voices' in the book, along with various styles of expression.

Firstly there is the voice of the wider academic community in Applied Linguistics and Language Testing which provides the theoretical foundation for the framework we have developed and the guiding principles on which we feel good practice should be based. In discussing each section of the framework an account is first given of contemporary thinking on the area under discussion. After we have addressed the current thinking on a particular element of the framework we examine it in detail in terms of Cambridge ESOL practice through the voice of the language testing practitioners within Cambridge ESOL who are responsible for developing, administering and validating versions of the tests. Alongside this may be detected the voice of the large community of external professionals who are actively associated with the production and delivery of Cambridge ESOL tests (e.g. test item writers, centre administrators, etc.). Sometimes the voice takes the form of case studies to exemplify particular issues; at other times it exists in quotations from or in references to external and internal documentation such as examination handbooks, item writer guidelines, examination and centre reports.

It will become clear that, in compiling the volume, we have drawn important material together from a variety of sources within the organisation relating to the operationalisation of Cambridge ESOL's examinations in relation to the theoretical framework; some of this information is extracted from previously internal and confidential documentation and is appearing in the public domain for the first time, for example see Appendices C, D and E. It reflects Cambridge ESOL's ongoing commitment to increasing transparency and accountability, and to sharing the organisation's knowledge, skills and experience with the wider language testing community.

The presence of multiple voices, together with the assembly of information from a wide variety of different documentary sources, inevitably means that differing styles of expression can be detected in certain parts of the volume. Apparent shifts in voice or style simply testify to the complex network of stakeholders which exists in relation to any large-scale testing practice and the fact that any large-scale testing enterprise constitutes a complex, and sometimes sensitive, environment.

Purpose of the volume

Language testing in Europe is faced with increasing demands for accountability in respect of all examinations offered to the public. Examination boards are increasingly being required by their own governments and by European authorities to demonstrate that the examinations they offer are well grounded in the language ability constructs they are attempting to measure. An explicit test validation framework is required which enables examination providers to furnish comprehensive evidence in support of any claims about the soundness of the theoretical basis of their tests.

Examination boards and other institutions offering high-stakes tests need to demonstrate how they are seeking to meet the demands of validity in their tests and, more specifically, how they actually operationalise criterial distinctions between the tests they offer at different levels on the proficiency continuum. This volume develops a theoretical framework for validating tests of second language reading ability which then informs an attempt to articulate the Cambridge ESOL approach to assessment at different proficiency levels in the skill area of reading. The perceived benefits of a clearly articulated theoretical and practical position for assessing reading skills in the context of Cambridge ESOL tests are essentially twofold:

- *Within Cambridge ESOL* – this articulated position will deepen understanding of the current theoretical basis upon which Cambridge ESOL assesses different levels of language proficiency across its range of products, and will inform current and future test development projects in the light of this analysis. It will thereby enhance the development of equivalent test versions and tasks.

- *Beyond Cambridge ESOL* – it will communicate in the public domain the theoretical basis for the tests and provide a more clearly understood rationale for the way in which Cambridge ESOL operationalises this in its tests. It will provide a framework for others interested in validating their own examinations and thereby offer a more principled basis for comparison of language examinations across the proficiency range than is currently available.

We build on Cambridge ESOL's existing approach to validating tests, namely the VRIP approach where the concern is with Validity (the conventional sources of validity evidence: construct, content, criterion), Reliability, Impact and Practicality. The early work of Bachman (1990) and Bachman and Palmer (1996) underpinned the adoption of the VRIP approach, as set out in Weir and Milanovic (2003), and found in various Cambridge ESOL internal documents on validity (e.g. Milanovic and Saville 1996).

We explore below how the socio-cognitive validity framework described in Weir's *Language Testing and Validation: an evidence-based approach* (2005) might contribute to an enhanced validation framework for use with Cambridge examinations. Weir's approach covers much of the same ground as VRIP but it attempts to reconfigure validity to show how its constituent parts (context, cognitive processing and scoring) might interact with each other. Reading, the construct of interest in this volume, is viewed as not just the underlying latent trait of reading ability but as the result of the constructed triangle of trait, context and score (including its interpretation). The approach adopted in this volume is therefore effectively an *interactionalist* position, which sees the reading construct as residing in the interactions between the underlying cognitive ability, the context of use and the process of scoring.

In addition, the approach conceptualises the validation process in a *temporal frame* thereby identifying the various types of validity evidence that need to be collected at each stage in the test development, monitoring and evaluation cycle. A further difference of the socio-cognitive approach as against traditional approaches is that the construct is now defined more specifically. Within each constituent part of the validation framework, criterial parameters for distinguishing between adjacent proficiency levels are identified. The approach, building on Weir (2005), is represented pictorially in Figure 1.1.

The framework is *socio-cognitive* in that the abilities to be tested are demonstrated by the *mental* processing of the candidate (the cognitive dimension); equally, the use of language in performing tasks is viewed as a *social* rather than a purely linguistic phenomenon. The framework represents a unified approach to establishing the overall validity of a test. The pictorial representation is intended to depict how the various validity components (the different types of validity evidence) fit together both temporally and conceptually. 'The arrows indicate the principal direction(s) of any hypothesised relationships: what has an effect on what, and the timeline runs from top to bottom: before the test is finalised, then administered and finally what happens after the test event' (Weir 2005:43). Conceptualising validity in terms of temporal sequencing is of value as it offers test developers a plan of what should be happening in relation to validation and when it should be happening.

The model represented in Figure 1.1 comprises both *a priori* (before-the-test event) validation components of context and cognitive validity and *a posteriori* (after-the-test event) components of scoring validity, consequential validity and criterion-related validity.

A number of critical questions will be addressed in applying this socio-cognitive validation framework to Cambridge ESOL examinations across the proficiency spectrum:

- How are the physical/physiological, psychological and experiential characteristics of candidates catered for by this test? (focus on the *Test taker* in Chapter 2)
- Are the cognitive processes required to complete the test tasks appropriate? (focus on *Cognitive validity* in Chapter 3)
- Are the characteristics of the test tasks and their administration appropriate and fair to the candidates who are taking them? (focus on *Context validity* in Chapter 4)
- How far can we depend on the scores which result from the test? (focus on *Scoring validity* in Chapter 5)
- What effects do the test and test scores have on various stakeholders? (focus on *Consequential validity* in Chapter 6)

Figure 1.1 A framework for conceptualising reading test validity
(adapted from Weir 2005)

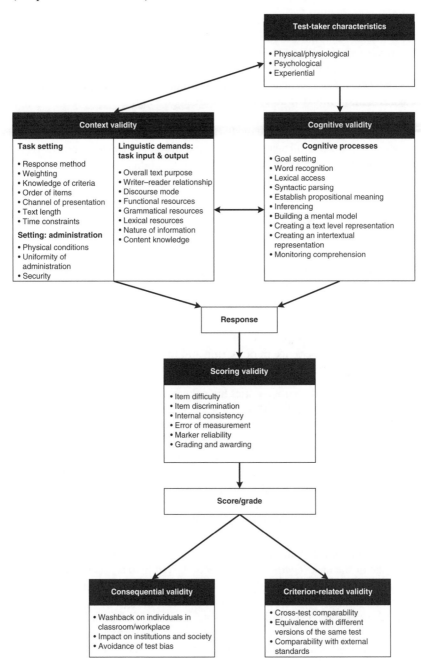

- What external evidence is there that the test is fair? (focus on *Criterion-related validity* in Chapter 7)

These are the types of critical questions that anyone intending to take a particular test or to use scores from that test would be advised to ask of the test developers in order to be confident that the nature and quality of the test matches their requirements.

The *Test-taker characteristics* box in Figure 1.1 connects directly to the cognitive and context validity boxes because 'these individual characteristics will directly impact on the way the individuals process the test task set up by the **context validity** box. Obviously, the tasks themselves will also be constructed with the overall test population and the target use situation clearly in mind as well as with concern for their cognitive validity' (Weir 2005:51).

Individual test-taker characteristics can be sub-divided into three main categories:

- *physical/physiological characteristics* – e.g. individuals may have special needs that must be accommodated such as partial sightedness or dyslexia
- *psychological characteristics* – e.g. a test taker's interest or motivation may affect the way a task is managed, or other factors such as preferred learning styles or personality type may have an influence on performance
- *experiential characteristics* – e.g. a test taker's educational and cultural background, experience in preparing and taking examinations as well as familiarity with a particular test may affect the way the task is managed.

All three types of characteristics have the potential to affect test performance (see Chapter 2 for detail).

Cognitive validity is established by *a priori* evidence on the cognitive processing activated by the test task before the live test event (e.g. through verbal reports from test takers), as well as through the more traditional *a posteriori* evidence on constructs measured involving statistical analysis of scores following test administration. Language test constructors need to be aware of the established theory relating to the cognitive processing that underpins equivalent operations in real-life language use (see Chapter 3 for detail).

The term content validity was traditionally used to refer to the content coverage of the task. *Context validity* is preferred here as the more inclusive superordinate which signals the need to consider not just linguistic content parameters, but also the social and cultural contexts in which the task is performed (see Chapter 4 for detail). Context validity for a reading task thus addresses the particular performance conditions, the setting under which it is to be performed (such as response method, time available, text length, order

of items as well as the linguistic demands inherent in the successful performance of the task) together with the actual examination conditions resulting
from the *administrative setting* (Weir 2005).

Scoring validity is linked directly to both context and cognitive validity
and is employed as a superordinate term for all aspects of reliability (see Weir
2005: Chapter 9, and Chapter 5 below for detail). Scoring validity accounts
for the extent to which test scores are arrived at through appropriate criteria in constructed response tasks and exhibit consensual agreement in their
marking, are as free as possible from measurement error, stable over time,
appropriate in terms of their content sampling and engender confidence as
reliable decision-making indicators.

Messick (1989) argued the case for also considering *Consequential Validity*
in judging the validity of scores on a test. From this point of view it is necessary in validity studies to ascertain whether the social consequences of test
interpretation support the intended testing purpose(s) and are consistent with
other social values (see Chapter 6 below for detail). There is also a concern
here with the washback of the test on the learning and teaching that precedes
it as well as with its impact on institutions and society more broadly. The
issue of test bias takes us back to the *test-taker characteristics* box. The evidence collected on the test-taker should be used to check that no unfair bias
has occurred for individuals as a result of decisions taken earlier with regard
to contextual features of the test.

Criterion-Related validity is a predominantly quantitative and *a posteriori* concept, concerned with the extent to which test scores correlate with
a suitable external criterion of performance with established properties
(see Anastasi 1988:145, Messick 1989:16 and Chapter 7 below for detail).
Evidence of criterion-related validity can come in three forms:

- Firstly if a relationship can be demonstrated between test scores and
  an external criterion which is believed to be a measure of the same
  ability. This type of criterion-related validity is subdivided into two
  forms: concurrent and predictive. Concurrent validity seeks an external
  indicator that has a proven track record of measuring the ability being
  tested (Bachman 1990:248). It involves the comparison of the test scores
  with this other measure for the same candidates taken at roughly the
  same time as the test. This other measure may consist of scores from
  some other reading tests, or ratings of the candidate by teachers, subject
  specialists, or other informants (Alderson, Clapham and Wall 1995).
  Predictive validity entails the comparison of test scores with another
  measure of the ability of interest for the same candidates taken some
  time after the test has been given (Alderson et al 1995).

- Demonstration of the qualitative and quantitative equivalence of
  different versions of the same test is a second source of evidence.

- A third source of evidence results from linking a test to an external standard such as the Common European Framework of Reference (CEFR) through the comprehensive and rigorous procedures of familiarisation, specification, standardisation and empirical validation (Council of Europe 2003).

Validity as a unitary concept

Although for descriptive purposes the various elements of the model in Figure 1.1 are presented as being separate from each other, undoubtedly a close relationship exists between these elements, for example between context validity and cognitive validity, which together with scoring validity constitute for us what is frequently referred to as *construct* validity. Decisions taken with regard to parameters in terms of task context will impact on the processing that takes place in task completion. The interactions between, and especially within, these aspects of validity may well eventually offer further insights into a closer definition of different levels of task difficulty. For the purposes of the present volume, however, the separability of the various aspects of validity will be maintained since they offer the reader a helpful descriptive route through the socio-cognitive validation framework and, more importantly, a clear and systematic perspective on the literature which informs it.

Focus of the volume

As a general principle, language tests should, as far as is practicable, place the same requirements on test-takers as are involved in communicative settings in non-test 'real-life' situations. This approach requires attention to both cognitive and social dimensions of communication.

A major focus of this volume is Cambridge ESOL's concern with *authenticity* which has been a dominant theme for adherents of the *communicative testing* approach as they attempt to develop tests that approximate to the 'reality' of non-test language use (real-life performance) (see Alderson 2000, Hawkey 2005, Morrow 1979, Weir 1983, 1990, 1993 and 2005). The 'real-life' approach (Bachman 1990:41), though initially the subject of much criticism in the USA, has proved useful as a means of guiding practical test development. It is particularly useful in situations in which the domain of language use is relatively homogeneous and identifiable (see O'Sullivan 2006 on the development of Cambridge's Business English examinations).

With regard to Cambridge ESOL examinations, authenticity is considered to have two characteristics. First, *interactional authenticity*, which is a feature of the cognitive activities of the test-taker in performing the test task (see Chapter 3 Cognitive validity below), and second, *situational authenticity,* which attempts to take into account the contextual requirements of the tasks (see Chapter 4 Context validity). Cambridge ESOL adopts an approach which recognises the importance of both situational and interactional authenticity (see Bachman and Palmer 1996 for discussion of these concepts).

Though full authenticity may be unattainable in the testing situation, as far as is possible, attempts should be made to use situations and tasks which are likely to be familiar and relevant to the intended test-taker. The concern with situational authenticity requires readers to respond to contexts which simulate 'real life' in terms of criterial contextual parameters without necessarily replicating it exactly. In this paradigm tests should be as direct as possible and, by employing tasks which activate the types of processing that characterise reading in the real life target situation, interactional authenticity is enhanced. The more features of real-life use of language, in this case of reading, that can be built into test tasks, the greater the potential for positive washback on the learning that precedes the test-taking experience and the easier it will be to extrapolate from the test to make statements about what students can or cannot do in real-life reading situations. If the purpose is to measure reading ability, examination boards should be employing reading tasks that encourage teachers to equip candidates with the reading abilities they will need for performing in a real-world context.

Cambridge ESOL's Main Suite examinations offer a picture of how reading ability is measured by the examination board across a broad language proficiency continuum. Its five levels correspond to equivalent levels of the Association of Language Testers in Europe (ALTE) and the Common European Framework of Reference (CEFR). These levels are compatible and correspond to the levels of language ability familiar to English language teachers around the world, i.e. from beginner to advanced. The relationship between Cambridge ESOL levels, ALTE levels and the CEFR levels is discussed in detail in Chapter 7. However, for initial orientation the reader is referred to Table 1.1 below for an overview of ALTE 'Can Do' statements and Table 1.2 which provides CEFR A2 to C2 illustrative scales for reading (see Jones 2002 and Chapter 7 for details of a Cambridge ESOL project which linked the ALTE levels to the CEFR). We then provide a description of Main Suite levels in terms of what materials successful candidates can handle and what they are expected to be able to do at each of the five levels (see Table 1.3).

When considering the ALTE Table (1.1) and the CEFR Table (1.2), the reader may feel that the distinctions between adjacent levels are not always clear and the characterisations on occasion imprecise. It is the intention of this volume to try and improve on these descriptions by clarifying the underlying theoretical construct of Reading at CEFR levels A2 to C2 and by a close examination of Cambridge ESOL practice to specify more precisely, where possible, any differences between adjacent levels in terms of a range of contextual and cognitive parameters.

Although the Main Suite, a set of General English examinations, forms

Table 1.1 ALTE 'Can Do' statements

ALTE Levels (CEFR Levels)	ALTE 'Can Do' Statements			
	Overall general ability	Social & Tourist typical abilities	Work typical abilities	Study typical abilities
ALTE Level 5 (C2: Mastery)	CAN understand documents, correspondence and reports, including the finer points of complex texts	CAN (when looking for accommodation) understand a tenancy agreement in detail, for example, technical details and the main legal implications	CAN understand reports and articles likely to be encountered during his/her work, including complex ideas expressed in complex languages	CAN access all sources of information quickly and reliably
ALTE Level 4 (C1: Effective Operational Proficiency)	CAN read quickly enough to cope with an academic course, to read the media for information or to understand non-standard correspondence	CAN understand complex opinions/ arguments as expressed in serious newspapers	CAN understand correspondence expressed in non-standard language	CAN read quickly enough to cope with the demands of an academic course
ALTE Level 3 (B2: Vantage)	CAN scan texts for relevant information, and understand details, instructions or advice	CAN understand detailed information, for example a wide range of culinary terms and abbreviations in accommodation advertisements	CAN understand most correspondence, reports and factual product literature he/she is likely to come across	CAN scan texts for relevant information and grasp main point of text
ALTE Level 2 (B1: Threshold)	CAN understand routine information and articles, and the general meaning of non-routine information within a familiar area	CAN understand factual articles in newspapers, routine letters from hotels and letters expressing personal opinions	CAN understand the general meaning of non-routine letters and theoretical articles within own work area	CAN understand basic instructions and messages, for example, computer library catalogues, with some help
ALTE Level 1 (A2: Waystage)	CAN understand straightforward information within a known area, such as on products and	CAN understand straightforward information, for example labels on food, standard menus,	CAN understand most short reports or manuals of a predictable nature within his/her own area	CAN understand the general meaning of a simplified textbook or article, reading very slowly

Table 1.1 (continued)

ALTE Levels (CEFR Levels)	ALTE 'Can Do' Statements			
	Overall general ability	Social & Tourist typical abilities	Work typical abilities	Study typical abilities
	signs and simple textbooks or reports on familiar matters	road signs and messages on automatic cash machines	of expertise, provided enough time is given	
ALTE Break-through Level (A1: Break-through)	CAN understand basic notices, instructions or information	CAN understand simple notices and information, for example in airports, on store guides and on menus. CAN understand simple instructions on medicines and simple directions to places	CAN understand short reports or product descriptions on familiar matters, if these are expressed in simple language and the contents are predictable	CAN read basic notices and instructions

Source: Common European Framework of Reference for Languages (Council of Europe 2001:251–256)

a major source of reference in this volume for illustrating how the reading construct differs from level to level in Cambridge ESOL examinations, we will also make reference to other reading papers from examinations in the Cambridge ESOL family such as the International English Language Testing System (IELTS) examination and the Business English Certificates (BEC) which cater for more specific EAP and ESP populations. This is intended to provide further clarification of how various performance parameters help establish distinctions between different levels of proficiency in reading. It will also demonstrate how research, though specifically conducted in relation to these examinations, has had wider effects throughout the range of examinations offered, for example in helping improve scoring validity. It is worth noting that non General English examinations are well documented in their own right in other volumes in the *Studies in Language Testing* series (see O'Sullivan 2006 for BEC and Davies 2008 for IELTS) and the reader is referred to these for comprehensive coverage of their history, operationalisation and validity.

BEC examinations are taken by those wishing to gain a qualification in Business English as a result of the growing internationalisation of business and the need for employees to interact in more than just a single language (see O'Sullivan 2006 for full details of this test). The IELTS Module on Academic English is principally used for admissions purposes into tertiary

Table 1.2 CEFR sample illustrative scales for reading

	C2	C1	B2	B1	A2	A1
OVERALL READING COMPRE-HENSION	*Can understand and interpret critically virtually all forms of the written language including abstract, grammatically complex, or highly colloquial literary and non-literary writings. Can understand a wide range of long and complex texts.*	*Can understand in detail lengthy, complex texts, whether or not they relate to his/ her own area of speciality, provided he/ she can reread difficult sections.*	*Can read with a large degree of independence, adapting style and speed of reading to different texts and purposes, and using appropriate reference sources selectively. Has a broad active reading vocabulary, but may experience some difficulty with low frequency idioms.*	*Can read straightforward factual texts on subjects related to his/her field and interest with a satisfactory level of comprehension.*	*Can understand short, simple texts on familiar matters of a concrete type which consist of high frequency everyday or job-related language. Can understand short, simple texts containing the highest frequency vocabulary, including a proportion of shared international vocabulary items.*	*Can understand very short, simple texts a single phrase at a time, picking up familiar names, words and basic phrases and rereading as required.*
READING FOR ORIENTA-TION	*As B2*	*As B2*	*Can scan quickly through long and complex texts, locating relevant details. Can quickly identify the content and relevance of news items, articles and reports on a wide range of professional topics, deciding whether closer study is worthwhile.*	*Can scan longer texts in order to locate desired information, and gather information from different parts of a text, or from different texts in order to fulfil a specific task. Can find and understand relevant information in everyday material, such as letters,*	*Can find specific, predictable information in simple everyday material such as advertisements, prospectuses, menus, reference lists and timetables. Can locate specific information in lists and isolate the information required (e.g. use the 'Yellow Pages' to find a service or tradesman). Can understand everyday signs and notices: in public*	*Can recognise familiar names, words and very basic phrases on simple notices in the most common everyday situations.*

READING FOR INFORMA-TION AND ARGUMENT	C2 *As C1*	C1 *Can understand in detail a wide range of lengthy, complex texts likely to be encountered in social, professional or academic life, identifying finer points of detail including attitudes and implied as well as stated opinions.*	B2 *Can obtain information, ideas and opinions from highly specialised sources within his/her field. Can understand specialised articles outside his/ her field, provided he/ she can use a dictionary occasionally to confirm his/her interpretation of terminology. Can understand articles and reports concerned with contemporary problems in which the writers adopt particular stances or viewpoints.*	B1 *Can identify the main conclusions in clearly signalled argumentative texts. Can recognise the line of argument in the treatment of the issue presented, though not necessarily in detail. Can recognise significant points in straightforward newspaper articles on familiar subjects.*	A2 *Can identify specific information in simpler written material he/ she encounters such as letters, brochures and short newspaper articles describing events.*	A1 *Can get an idea of the content of simpler informational material and short simple descriptions, especially if there is visual support.*
			brochures and short official documents.		*places, such as streets, restaurants, railway stations; in workplaces, such as directions, instructions, hazard warnings.*	

Source: Common European Framework of Reference (Council of Europe 2001:69–70)

Table 1.3 A description of Main Suite levels in terms of what materials candidates can handle and what they are expected to be able to do in Reading

CPE (C2)	CPE candidates are expected to be able to understand in detail a range of texts, both short and long, from the following sources: books (fiction and non-fiction); non-specialist articles from journals, magazines and newspapers; informational materials. They will be able to recognise the purpose and main ideas and details of the texts and the opinions and attitudes expressed in them. They will also recognise the structure of certain texts and be able to follow their development.
CAE (C1)	CAE candidates are expected to be able to deal with both short and long texts, from the following sources: newspapers and magazines; journals; books (fiction and non-fiction); promotional and informational materials. They will be able to understand the detail, tone, purpose, main idea and implication of the texts, and the opinions and attitudes expressed in them. They will recognise text organisation features such as exemplification, comparison and reference, and they will also understand how texts are structured and be able to follow text development.
FCE (B2)	FCE candidates are expected to be able to deal with both short and long texts, from the following sources: newspaper and magazine articles; reports; fiction; advertisements; correspondence; messages; informational materials. They will be able to locate specific information and detail and recognise opinion and attitude. They will also understand the purpose, main idea, tone and gist of the text, and be able to recognise the structure of a text and follow its development.
PET (B1)	PET candidates are expected to be able to understand public notices and signs; to read short texts of a factual nature and show understanding of the content; to demonstrate understanding of the structure of the language as it is used to express notions of relative time, space, possession, etc; to scan factual material for information in order to perform relevant tasks, disregarding redundant or irrelevant material; to read texts of an imaginative or emotional character and to appreciate the central sense of the text, the attitude of the writer to the material and the effect it is intended to have on the reader.
KET (A2)	KET candidates are expected to be able to understand the main message, and some detail, of a variety of short factual texts: for example, signs, notices, instructions, brochures, guides, personal correspondence and informative articles from newspapers and magazines. They should also have strategies for dealing with unfamiliar structures and vocabulary.

Source: University of Cambridge ESOL Examinations: Handbooks for teachers (2005, 2007, 2008) and personal communication with Main Suite Subject Managers

level institutions throughout the world (see Davies 2008 for a detailed history of the developments in EAP testing leading up to the current IELTS). Overviews of the reading elements of these examinations are shown in Tables 1.4 and 1.5 below for information and comparative purposes.

Table 1.4 A description of BEC levels in terms of what materials candidates are expected to be able to handle and what they are expected to be able to do in Reading

BEC Higher (C1)	BEC Higher candidates are expected to be able to deal with both short and long business-related texts from a variety of sources (e.g. business newspapers and magazines, books on business topics, company literature, job advertisements and websites). They will be able to understand the detail, purpose, main idea and inference in the texts and the opinions expressed in them. They will understand how texts are structured and be able to follow text development. They will also understand business lexis, and grammatical aspects of language. Typical candidates at BEC Higher level can understand the general meaning of more complex articles and can, within a reasonably short time, understand most reports that they are likely to come across.
BEC Vantage (B2)	BEC Vantage candidates are expected to be able to identify specific information and detail in informational texts e.g., newspapers, magazines and catalogues. They will be able to locate specific information and detail and recognise opinion. They will understand the purpose, main idea and gist of a business-related text, and be able to recognise its structure and follow its development. They will also understand business lexis. Typical candidates at BEC Vantage level can understand the general meaning of non-routine letters and can understand the general meaning of a report even if the topic isn't predictable.
BEC Preliminary (B1)	BEC Preliminary candidates are expected to be able to understand short real-world notices, messages, etc. They are able to interpret visual information and understand the language used to describe it, and to pick out salient points in a text and infer meaning where words in the text are unfamiliar. They are able to read for gist and detail, scan the text for specific information and understand the purpose of the writer and the audience for which the text is intended. They are able to extract relevant information and complete a form accurately. One part of the test has a predominantly grammatical focus and tests candidates' ability to analyse grammatical patterns. Typical candidates at BEC Preliminary level can understand the general meaning of non-routine letters within their own work area and can understand most short reports of a predictable nature.

Source: University of Cambridge ESOL Examinations: BEC Handbook for teachers (2005, 2008) and personal communication with BEC Subject Manager

The relationships between the above Reading tests in terms of level of proficiency is reviewed in Chapter 7 where research is reported on comparability studies of how the same candidates have performed on the different tests at particular proficiency levels.

Table 1.5 A description of IELTS (Academic Module) in terms of what materials candidates are expected to be able to handle and what they are expected to be able to do in Reading

---

Candidates for the IELTS Academic Reading test, which is a multi-level test, are expected to be able to understand three long texts (with a total word length of approximately 2400 words) which are appropriate for, and accessible to, candidates entering undergraduate or postgraduate courses or seeking professional registration. The texts, which are taken from books, journals and newspapers, are written for a non-specialist audience and do not favour candidates from any particular discipline. At least one of the texts contains a detailed logical argument. Texts may also include non-verbal materials such as diagrams, graphs or illustrations. Candidates will use a variety of reading skills, e.g. skimming, scanning, reading for detail, in order to understand the gist, main ideas, details and inferences of the texts, and recognise the opinions and attitudes expressed in them.

Source: University of Cambridge ESOL Examinations, British Council, IDP Australia: IELTS Handbook (2005, 2007) and personal communication with IELTS Subject Manager

Structure of the volume

The outline shape for *Examining Reading* closely follows the organisation of the framework described above in Figure 1.1 with its six component parts: *Test-taker characteristics; Cognitive validity; Context validity; Scoring validity; Consequential validity*; and *Criterion-related validity*. There is a separate chapter on each of these, which is organised so that a discussion of issues arising in the *research* literature on a topic is followed by consideration of Cambridge ESOL *practice* in the area.

Chapter 2 on *Test-taker characteristics* reviews the research literature in this area paying particular attention to research undertaken into Cambridge ESOL tests. The ways in which Cambridge ESOL tests take account of test-taker characteristics are then considered. This includes accommodations given to candidates with disabilities as well as the nature of the general candidature and how this is reflected in the tests at different levels.

Chapter 3 on *Cognitive validity* reviews the available research literature on the processing involved in real-life reading before examining in detail the cognitive processing involved in Cambridge Reading examinations at different levels.

The purpose of Chapter 4 on *Context validity* is to review the research literature on the impact of contextual variables on performance. The available research in this area relating to Cambridge ESOL Reading subtests is also explored. The chapter then examines the ways in which Cambridge ESOL Reading tests operationalise various contextual variables. Of particular interest here is the variation of parameters across tasks intended for test-takers at different levels of ability. The wider context of the physical conditions surrounding the delivery of the examinations is considered in Appendix C on *Administrative setting*.

Chapter 5 on *Scoring validity* looks at issues relating to the scoring of Reading tests. The available research literature is reviewed and research by Cambridge ESOL in this area is highlighted. The procedures developed by Cambridge ESOL in each of the elements of this part of the framework are exemplified (see also Appendix E on marking procedures).

In the penultimate chapters the value of the test score in terms of *Consequential validity* (Chapter 6) and *Criterion-related validity* (Chapter 7) is discussed. Again Cambridge ESOL Reading tests and research are the basis for the examples.

In the final Chapter 8 we summarise our findings from applying our validity framework to Cambridge Reading examinations. We indicate where the current tests embody and operationalise current knowledge and understanding about the reading ability construct. Where relevant, we also suggest improvements in terms of the various components of the socio-cognitive framework. Suggestions are also made for further research which might be of value to Cambridge ESOL as well as to the wider testing community.

Conclusion

This introductory chapter has argued that test developers should provide a clear definition of the ability constructs which underpin the tests they offer in the public domain; such an explication is increasingly necessary if claims about the validity of test score interpretation and use are to be supported both logically and with empirical evidence.

A test validation framework has been proposed which adopts a socio-cognitive perspective in terms of its underlying theory and which conceptualises validity as a unitary concept; at the same time the framework embraces six core components which reflect the practical nature and quality of an actual testing event. It is suggested that an understanding and analysis of the framework and its components in relation to specific tests can assist test developers to operationalise their tests more effectively, especially in relation to criterial distinctions across test levels.

The extent to which this volume is informed from multiple professional perspectives and how it draws on a wide variety of documentary and other sources in its attempt to communicate effectively to its intended audience has been explained.

In the following chapters the six components of our validation framework will be addressed in greater detail. The specific parameters which test developers need to take account of in developing their tests will be examined, beginning with test-taker characteristics in Chapter 2.

2 Test-taker characteristics

Introduction

As discussed in Chapter 1, real-life performance is increasingly seen as the criterion of choice against which test tasks are judged. However, it is important to remember that the test-taker, rather than the test task, is at the heart of the assessment event. The focus in this chapter is on the various characteristics of the test taker that have the potential to affect performance and the ways in which an examination board can take them into account in developing and administering examinations and interpreting test results, in as far as it is feasible and fair to do so.

Although success in language learning and assessment is mainly dependent on the individual's ability in the intended construct, variables which are related to personal characteristics may also impact on test performance. For example, Edgeworth (1888:615) makes reference to the affective domain; to 'the variation of the candidate's spirits'. Bachman (1990) refers to cognitive style, content knowledge, gender and first language (L1). O'Sullivan (2000), based on an extensive review of the literature, provides a useful categorisation of personal features which may affect performance (see Table 2.1 below).

Table 2.1 Categories of test-taker characteristics

Physical/Physiological	Psychological	Experiential
• Short-term ailments *(e.g. toothache, cold)* • Longer-term disabilities *(e.g. visual impairment)* • Age • Gender (originally sex)	• Personality • Memory • Cognitive style • Affective schemata • Concentration • Motivation • Emotional state	• Education • Examination preparedness • Examination experience • Communication experience • Target language country residence

Source: Based on O'Sullivan (2000:71–72)

A number of research studies have been conducted to investigate the effect of these variables on test performance. Geranpayeh and Kunnan (2007) looked at differential item functioning (DIF) with respect to age while Brown and Iwashita (1998) looked at it in terms of language background. Calver and

Khalifa (2008) investigated the effects of age, gender and L1 on performance in Reading papers in Cambridge Main Suite examinations. Purpura (1999) investigated learners' strategy use and subsequent performance on language tests. A number of researchers (Alderman and Holland 1981, Angoff and Sharon 1974, Oltman, Stricker and Barrows 1988, Swinton and Powers 1980) examined item performance on TOEFL across native language groups. All of these studies found significant variation among the groups examined and showed that personal characteristics can have an effect on test performance. Bachman (2004), however, rightly cautioned that the nature of the effect will always vary depending on the contextual parameters of the task and its demands on cognitive processing.

First we discuss the physical/physiological test-taker characteristics focusing mainly on longer term disabilities which require special modifications to be made to administrative arrangements or sometimes even to the tests themselves. Such characteristics have only recently come into prominence in the assessment literature and accordingly receive particular attention here.

Other characteristics under this heading such as age and gender are no less important but do not permit of specific action at the individual candidate level. They are relatively well understood in our field and are commonly taken account of in the test development cycle. We will meet these characteristics again in Chapter 4 when we discuss the specific mediating variables that need to be taken into account when selecting texts and designing tasks for different proficiency levels. For example, the analysis in Chapter 4 shows that texts at B1 level tend to be more suited to candidates who are in secondary schools and who are typically within the age range 13–16 years whereas texts at C1 level tend to be more suited to older candidates who are attending university and are typically within the age range 18–22 years.

The following section on physical and physiological differences accordingly focuses on issues related to the less well trodden area of assessing individual students with specific disabilities.

Physical/physiological characteristics

Assessing students with disabilities

Over the last decade increased attention has been given to issues of fairness in testing and test use, to the rights of test takers, to testing candidates with disabilities and to the responsibilities of producers and users of language examinations (see the Code of Practice and Quality Assurance Checklists set by the Association of Language Testers in Europe (ALTE), 1994; Standards for Educational and Psychological Testing set by the American Educational Research Association (AERA), American Psychological Association (APA) and National Council on Measurement in Education (NCME), 1999;

the Code of Ethics set by the International Language Testing Association (ILTA), 2000). According to these standards and codes, the offering of test accommodations, i.e. modifying the test or adjusting test administration conditions to accommodate the needs of test takers with disabilities, is usually perceived as promoting fair testing practice.

The International Test Commission (ITC) provides general guidelines on whether an assessment should be modified and how to carry out the modification. Essentially,

> disability may contribute no variance to test scores in which case no modifications are necessary; may contribute construct relevant variance where modifications to the test will affect the relevance of test scores; or may contribute to construct irrelevant variance in which case modifications should be aimed at removing the irrelevant source of variance by suitable modification of the test conditions or substitution of a more suitable test.
> (See ITC guidelines for test use version 2000 downloadable from www.intestcom.org).

ITC goes on to say that 'it is usually a matter of professional judgement as to whether it is better to use some alternative form of assessment, or to modify the test or its mode of administration' (see Appendix C, ITC guidelines for test use downloadable from www.intestcom.org). This view is not uncommon given the scarcity of information publicly available about the performance of candidates with disabilities on tests. Moreover, it is quite difficult to conduct research in this area and obtain consistent results. This is mainly due to the wide variety of accommodations, the various ways in which they are implemented and the heterogeneity of students to whom they are given.

Thurlow, Thompson and Lazarus (2006:658) summarise examples of accommodation policies in the United States according to five main categories. These are:

- presentation (visual, tactile, auditory, multi-modal), e.g., large print magnification devices, Braille, audio amplification devices, human readers, screen readers
- response, e.g., scribe, word processor, electronic text to speech conversion
- timing and scheduling, i.e., extended time, multiple/frequent breaks, change schedule or order of subtests
- setting, e.g., reducing distractions, availability of space for using special equipment
- linguistic, e.g., simplified English, responding in native language.

We will discuss below two of the most common types of accommodation which are relevant to assessing reading, that is, extended timing and use of Braille.

Extended time

Thompson, Blount and Thurlow (2002), summarising the results of several empirical research studies carried out between 1999 and 2001 on comparing scores from accommodated and non-accommodated test administrations, reported that extended time accommodation had a positive effect on student test scores in at least four studies. Similarly, Sireci, Scarpati and Li (2005) upon reviewing 21 experimental studies concluded that 'the accommodation of extended time improved the performance of students with disabilities more than it improved the performance of students without disabilities'. This 'consistent finding' highlights the controversy surrounding the use of test accommodations in terms of score interpretation and fairness to candidates with and without a disability. Another example which adds to this controversy is Schulte, Elliott and Kratchowill's (2001) findings. Their study showed that the effect of extended time on students with and without disabilities varied according to the response format used. When a selected response format was used, students with disabilities benefited slightly more from test accommodation than did those without disabilities. On the other hand, no differences were found in the two groups' performance when a constructed response format was used.

Use of Braille

As with extended time, researchers tend to ask whether students with and without visual impairments would demonstrate different cognitive processing when performing on reading tests. The Partnership for Accessible Reading Assessment (PARA) – a project funded by the United States Department of Education Office of Special Education – website draws attention to the fact that decoding an English Braille version of a text may not be comparable to decoding the same text in standard print. PARA's (2005) online publication on reading and students with visual impairments or blindness states:

> that English Braille uses contractions and other "shortcuts" might suggest that students have a short-cut version of text that would be easier to read. On the other hand, the complex use of the same cell to mean different things depending on the position within a word or sentence might suggest that students have a more complex decoding task than decoders of standard print. Other research has indicated that Braille reading demands a greater level of phonological awareness and memory than print reading.
> (www.readingassessment.info/resources/publications/ visualimpairment.htm)

Koenig's (1992) study showed that proficient readers with and without visual impairments use similar cognitive processes when decoding a reading text. They both resort to syntactic, semantic and contextual clues. Accordingly, visually impaired students may only face a barrier to accessing print. Pring (1994) found that students using Braille progressed through similar learning stages as students who learned to read print but they did not always develop awareness of whole word patterns. Pring (1994) also found that, on average, Braille readers in normal reading contexts read at about half the speed of print readers, at about 150 words per minute. Given the studies reported here, accommodation in terms of providing extra time can be seen as an attempt to make the reading experience fairer for Braille readers without biasing the test in their favour.

Physical/physiological characteristics: Cambridge ESOL practice

As an examination board, Cambridge ESOL is committed to ensuring that, as far as practicable, candidates are not excluded from taking an examination because of a disability or a learning difficulty, whether temporary or permanent. Special Arrangements are intended to facilitate attainment in the skill being assessed while at the same time ensuring that candidates with disabilities are not given an unfair advantage over other candidates and that the user of the test certificate is not misled about the candidate's attainment. The following description provides an account of provisions made by Cambridge ESOL for candidates with special needs who are sitting for Main Suite examinations (a multi-level assessment suite ranging from CEFR levels A2 to C2). Each of the five examinations assesses reading, writing, listening and speaking. At higher levels, i.e. B2 to C2, the examinations assess Use of English in a separate paper.

At the test pre-administration stage, information gathered on candidates sitting for the exam is used to provide test modification and accommodation as well as Special Arrangements for candidates with disabilities or short-term ailments.

As cited in the Cambridge ESOL *Handbook for Centres* (2008) and in Khalifa (2005), the most common provisions are:

1. **Additional time and/or supervised breaks.** Candidates may require extra time to read their papers and write their answers, for example, if they are dyslexic or have visual difficulties. For some candidates, supervised breaks may be appropriate instead of, or in addition to, the extra time allowance. An example would be a candidate who had difficulty concentrating for long periods of time and presented a medical record as evidence.

2. **Modified question papers.** Candidates may require modified papers if they have severe visual difficulties. These are available in either contracted Braille (where a single symbol may represent a group of

letters), or un-contracted Braille (where there is a separate Braille symbol for every letter); or enlarged print versions. In modifying question papers, assistance may be sought from nationally recognised organisations such as the Royal National Institute for the Blind (RNIB). The adapted versions, as far as possible, cover the same assessment objectives as their standard counterparts with minor changes to rubrics, layout and sometimes length. Braille versions of question papers are available on request for most examinations.

3. **Reading of question papers.** Usually candidates should be able to read the questions but exceptions may be made, for example for those with severe physical disabilities including those who are visually impaired but not proficient in Braille. In such cases the candidates are allowed to work with the aid of a Reader, that is, an independent person formally appointed to support the test taker by reading test materials aloud. The Reader is issued with a code of practice which provides a set of regulations to be followed during an examination. For example, a Reader must read accurately and must not advise on which questions to do or when to move on to the next question. The code of practice also informs the test centre of circumstances and conditions under which a Reader can be used so that the assessed construct is not undermined. For example, (a) candidates with dyslexia or other specific learning difficulties may not have a Reader; (b) the Reader may read out and repeat instructions, questions and rubrics but is not usually permitted to read texts to candidates; and (c) an invigilator must be present in addition to the Reader.

4. **The recording of answers.** Where the recording of answers is required, a variety of options are available for blind candidates, partially sighted candidates and candidates with physical writing disabilities. For example, they can dictate their answers to an Amanuensis, use a Braille machine alone or with assistance, use a typewriter or word processor or other forms of access technology, or use enlarged versions of machine scored answer sheets.

5. **Certificate endorsements.** Endorsements are added to test certificates where some of the objectives of the relevant examination have not been assessed on account of a particular disability of the candidate.

For an extensive description of these provisions and of rules and regulations set by Cambridge ESOL and followed by its certified centres worldwide, the reader is referred to the *Handbook for Centres* published annually by Cambridge ESOL and to the support page at www.CambridgeESOL.org

Tables 2.2 and 2.3 below show the number of applications made and provisions given for candidates taking Main Suite Reading papers over a five-year period (2002–2006).

Table 2.2 Applications for Special Arrangements for Main Suite candidates 2002–2006 (Reading papers only)

	2002	2003	2004	2005	2006
KET/PET candidates	46	146	180	172	225
FCE/CAE/CPE candidates	1,355	1,948	1,149	970	926

Table 2.3 Key categories of Special Arrangements for Main Suite candidates 2002–2006 (Reading papers only)

Categories	Exam	2002	2003	2004	2005	2006
Additional time OR	KET/PET	45	56	73	70	77
supervised breaks (Dyslexia only)	FCE/CAE/CPE	499	644	514	626	562
Modified question papers — Braille versions of paper	KET/PET	2	7	11	7	17
	FCE/CAE/CPE	31	21	20	12	11
Enlarged print versions	KET/PET	14	21	24	18	23
	FCE/CAE/CPE	52	50	41	60	56
Reading of question papers (Reader)	KET/PET	0	0	5	0	2
	FCE/CAE/CPE	1	5	4	4	6

Tables 2.2 and 2.3 highlight the volume of applications for Special Arrangements and the scope of work carried out by Cambridge ESOL accordingly. The number of provisions made fluctuates slightly from one year to another. Although the numbers may appear small in comparison to the total test-taking population (approximately half a million for Main Suite), it should be noted that all of the above provisions are dealt with on an individual basis. For example, a single candidate may require separate facilities for taking the examination, a specially modified question paper, a Reader and an invigilator, and extra time to complete his/her paper.

In order to ensure that candidates are indeed receiving the appropriate accommodation and to confirm and support the accommodations provided in Table 2.3 above, policy and practice in this area are kept under regular review and, as far as possible, are informed by internal research studies. Small scale research studies using qualitative methodologies, such as verbal protocols and observations, will be used to confirm that the tests are still valid, reliable and fair when accommodations are provided to test takers with certified disabilities.

A report on test accommodation is prepared on an annual basis providing a general survey of work carried out together with detailed statistical analysis of cases dealt with. A version of this report is updated and published annually on the Cambridge ESOL public website (see, for example, Gutteridge's 2006 report).

Psychological & experiential characteristics

This section addresses psychological and experiential characteristics which may affect test-taker performance.

Within a teaching and a learning context, it is critical to consider students' psychological characteristics in order to ensure a positive learning experience and subsequent successful outcomes. In a classroom setting teachers can observe the differences among students' styles and behaviours and adapt their teaching strategy and materials to help the underachievers and enhance the potential of successful ones. Among these 'learning style' characteristics are personality, cognitive traits, and affective factors which include motivation, anxiety and self confidence. The literature views these characteristics as 'relatively stable indicators of how learners perceive, interact with and respond to the learning environment' (Keefe and Monk 1986:16). Research studies such as De Bello's (1990), which compared 11 learning style models, showed that learning styles do have an effect on learning and on performance within a classroom environment. Dunn, Beaudry and Klavas' (1989) literature survey affirmed that teaching programmes which cater for appropriate learning styles statistically increase student language learning achievement.

It is difficult to see how such flexibility in catering for a plethora of individual learning styles can be addressed within an assessment context. It might be argued that the opportunity to select from a wide range of genres, rhetorical tasks and topics in the test event might cater for test takers' personal interests and motivation and enhance their test performance as a result. It might also be argued that the opportunity to select from a variety of tasks which elicit different components of cognitive processing would also address individual learning styles. However, offering a multiplicity of choice in tasks, topics and genres also raises serious issues for test sampling and comparability and may lead to problems in test equivalence (see Chapter 7).

Experiential characteristics as defined by O'Sullivan (2000) are those features related to the test taker's educational and cultural background, experience in preparing and taking exams, as well as knowledge of the demands of a particular exam. The AERA/APA/NCME standards (1999) advocate that test developers should provide the information and supporting evidence that test users need in order to select appropriate tests, and that test users should select tests that meet the intended purpose and that are appropriate for the intended test takers. Understanding the test taker's experiential characteristics helps test developers in creating tests that are appropriate to the targeted candidature.

In contrast to the provision made for individual physical disabilities, it may not be desirable or even possible to cater individually for the wide variety of psychological and experiential characteristics in a large test population. Shaw and Weir (2007:17) observe: 'it is often difficult for an exam provider to cater for individual variation across test takers and at the same time adhere to the requirement for test fairness'. Faced with a large heterogeneous population, the exam provider may be limited to reducing as far as possible the extent to which any candidate is disadvantaged in relation to other candidates by the cognitive, linguistic and/or cultural demands of the test.

Examination boards normally attempt to make test events as positive as possible in the full knowledge that some stress is probably unavoidable and may even be desirable, if it enhances performance. They try to put the candidates at their ease as far as is possible in a test situation (the discussion below on public access to information and exemplars of a test is relevant here).

Psychological & experiential characteristics: Cambridge ESOL practice

The description below provides an account of how Cambridge ESOL, as an examination board, takes into consideration the psychological and experiential aspects of test takers in its Main Suite examinations at all stages in the testing cycle. The Cambridge ESOL test development model (see Saville 2003 for details) is an iterative and cyclical one which starts with planning, moves on to designing and trialling, followed by administration, and finishes with monitoring and reviewing test performance which then feeds back to the planning phase.

The planning phase aims at establishing a clear picture of who the potential candidates are likely to be and who the users of the test results will be. Gathering information on the intended audience for the test is carried out through stakeholders' questionnaires and Candidate Information Sheets (see Appendix B for a sample).

Saville (2000) reports on research behind the development of a bank of language learning questionnaires to investigate the background characteristics of the ESOL candidature in relation to learning strategies and styles. The background factors are grouped as strategic, i.e., cognitive, metacognitive and communication strategies, and socio-psychological, i.e., attitudes, anxiety, motivation and effort. The questionnaires are intended to be used alongside examinations and tests in order to examine the relationships between test-taker strategies and styles and their performance on language tests and on self-assessment instruments (see Hawkey 2006 who reports on how this type of questionnaire has been used in a national project and how its results were used in learning, teaching and assessment practices).

The Candidate Information Sheet (CIS) is another valuable tool for generating data on test-taker characteristics. Table 2.4 below provides CIS information on the characteristics of test takers who took the various examination sessions in 2007.

Table 2.4 Test taker profile of Main Suite examinations

	L1 Top 10	Age	Gender	Educational level	Test preparation by attending classes	Reasons for taking Main Suite examination	Examination experience
CPE (C2)	• Greek: 13% • Spanish: 12% • German: 9% • Portuguese: 6% • Polish: 5% • French: 3% • Italian: 3% • Dutch: 2% • Romanian: 2% • Bulgarian: 1% • Blank response: 37% • Other L1s: 7%	• 15 or under: 6.5% • 16–18: 28% • 19–22: 27% • 23–30: 24% • 31 or above: 14% • Blank response: 0.5%	• Females: 62% • Males: 36% • Blank response: 2%	• College/ University: 30% • Secondary school: 18% • Primary school: 0% • Blank response: 52%	• Attended: 73% • Didn't attend: 26% • Blank response: 1%	• Further study of English/other subjects: 12.5% • Help career advancement: 20% • Personal interest: 9% • University recognition: 3% • Blank response: 55.5%	• Same exam: 0.5% • Other exams: 24.5% • Blank response: 75%
CAE (C1)	• German: 17% • Spanish: 16% • Polish: 11% • Romanian: 8% • Portuguese: 6% • French: 4% • Italian: 4% • Swedish: 3% • Czech: 2% • Bulgarian: 2% • Blank response: 13% • Other L1s: 14%	• 15 or under: 4% • 16–18: 37.5% • 19–22: 25% • 23–30: 22% • 31 or above: 11% • Blank response: 0.5%	• Females: 62% • Males: 36% • Blank response: 2%	• College/ University: 36% • Secondary school: 35% • Primary school: 0% • Blank response: 29%	• Attended: 83% • Didn't attend: 16% • Blank response: 1%	• Further study of English/other subjects: 21% • Help career advancement: 34% • Personal interest: 13% • University recognition: 5% • Blank response: 27%	• Same exam: 1% • Other exams: 22% • Blank response: 77%

Table 2.4 (continued)

	L1 Top 10	Age	Gender	Educational level	Test preparation by attending classes	Reasons for taking Main Suite examination	Examination experience
FCE (B2)	• Spanish: 24% • Italian: 10% • German: 10% • Polish: 7% • French: 5% • Portuguese: 5% • Greek: 4% • Czech: 3% • Catalan: 2% • Russian: 2% • Blank response: 20% • Other L1s: 8%	• 15 or under: 20% • 16–18: 42% • 19–22: 16% • 23–30: 15% • 31 or above: 6% • Blank response: 1%	• Females: 58% • Males: 40% • Blank response: 2%	• College/University: 27% • Secondary school: 45% • Primary school: 0.5% • Blank response: 27.5%	• Attended: 87% • Didn't attend: 11% • Blank response: 2%	• Further study of English/other subjects: 22% • Help career advancement: 34% • Personal interest: 12% • University recognition: 7% • Blank response: 25%	• Same exam: 1% • Other exams: 12% • Blank response: 87%
PET (B1)	• Italian: 31% • Spanish: 21% • German: 7% • Arabic: 5% • French: 4% • Greek: 3% • Portuguese: 3% • Chinese: 3% • Catalan: 2% • Czech: 2% • Blank response: 11% • Other L1s: 8%	• 12 or under: 5% • 13–14: 21% • 15–18: 52% • 19–22: 10% • 23 or above: 11% • Blank response: 1%	• Females: 56% • Males: 41% • Blank response: 3%	• College/University: 16% • Secondary school: 70% • Primary school: 6% • Blank response: 8%	• Attended: 87% • Didn't attend: 11% • Blank response: 2%	• Further study of English/other subjects: 27% • Help career advancement: 30% • Personal interest: 14% • University recognition: 12% • Blank response: 17%	• Same exam: 3% • Other exams: 12% • Blank response: 85%

KET (A2)						
• Italian: 25% • Spanish: 22% • Chinese: 8% • Greek: 5% • Portuguese: 4% • Turkish: 4% • French: 3% • Arabic: 3% • Catalan: 2% • Russian: 1% • Blank response: 11% • Other L1s: 12%	• 12 or under: 26% • 13–14: 48% • 15–18: 16% • 19–22: 2% • 23 or above: 7% • Blank response: 1%	• Females: 53% • Males: 43% • Blank response: 4%	• College/University: 6% • Secondary school: 64% • Primary school: 23% • Blank response: 7%	• Attended: 87% • Didn't attend: 11% • Blank response: 2%	• Further study of English/other subjects: 40% • Help career advancement: 22% • Personal interest: 13% • University recognition: 4% • Blank response: 21%	• Same exam: 7% • Other exams: 11% • Blank response: 82%

Source: Output data generated by Cognos software using CIS data from 2007 administration sessions

Table 2.4 reveals some interesting trends in the test-taker population across the proficiency levels:

- **First Language (L1).** Main Suite examinations are taken by candidates throughout the world with the majority of candidates in European and South American countries. Table 2.4 lists the top 10 L1s featuring in the 2007 administration (N.B. there are at least 100 L1s on an annual basis).

- **Age.** Candidates' age increases steadily across the levels from KET to CPE with younger candidates taking KET/PET and more mature or older candidates sitting for CAE/CPE.

- **Gender.** In general, more females than males take an examination. The proportion of female test takers increases steadily up the proficiency continuum from CEFR A2 level to C2 level (i.e. from KET to CPE).

- **Educational level.** The majority of candidates are in full-time education whether in schools or higher education. KET has the highest percentage (26%) of primary school candidates in the Suite. This may reflect the downward shift of English language teaching and learning into the primary school curriculum around the world, a growing trend noted by Graddol (2006). The proportion of secondary school candidates taking Main Suite examinations decreases as the proficiency level of the examination increases. As for candidates attending college or university, they represent at least one third of the candidature taking CAE or CPE. Their number is highest in CAE followed by CPE.

- **Preparation for an examination.** A large proportion of candidates undertake a preparatory course before taking an examination. This proportion slightly decreases from CAE upwards.

- **Reasons for taking an examination.** Candidates enter an examination for a variety of reasons: out of personal interest, to improve employment prospects, for further study or to fulfil an employer/university admission requirement. The most popular reasons are career advancement and further study.

- **Experience in taking examinations.** Candidates who responded to this question have previous test-taking experience, i.e., they are familiar with test-taking conditions, with similar test tasks, or with completion of similar answer sheets. Candidates at the lower levels, i.e., KET and PET tend to sit for the same exam more than once. This percentage decreases as the level of proficiency increases (see Appendix F for a discussion on experiential characteristics and paper-based versus computer-based tests).

At the test development stage steps are taken to reduce as far as possible the extent to which any candidate is disadvantaged in relation to other candidates by the content of the test. The information gathered on the candidature profile as exemplified in Table 2.4 is used for this purpose. Characteristics such as first language, age, gender, educational level, and reasons for taking an examination are considered when putting together new test specifications and when selecting texts for existing examinations. For example, Table 2.4 above shows that KET and PET candidates are different from FCE, CAE and CPE candidates at least in terms of age group and primary purpose for taking an examination. Thus, a topic on lifestyles and living conditions is typically more appropriate to the latter groups while a topic on hobbies and leisure is better suited to the former.

Being appropriate to a particular age group, not favouring one gender over the other, and not privileging a particular L1 or a specific culture are essential criteria to guide text selection and task construction. Specific guidelines are provided to item writers to ensure a balance is struck among these characteristics as far as is possible and practical. To ensure sample representation at the trialling stage, the use of CIS information is critical. Chapter 4 provides further discussion of these issues in relation to decisions on the contextual parameters of text selection.

Materials are pretested on a representative sample (usually candidates who are preparing to take an examination) in advance to confirm bias has not inadvertently occurred and to filter out any material which may be inaccessible/inappropriate. Feedback from candidates on the accessibility of topics and tasks is elicited at the pretesting stage (by means of a feedback questionnaire) and used in modifying materials where necessary. In addition to pretesting, the use of an item bank approach to test development ensures the comparability of the different versions of an examination not only in terms of content but also in terms of its measurement characteristics. The reader is referred to Chapter 7 which discusses Cambridge ESOL item banking methodology and pretesting procedures in detail (and Appendix D for question paper production process).

Providing adequate information on Cambridge ESOL examinations in the public domain, e.g., their purpose, content, candidature, development history, helps address test-taker characteristics such as anxiety and exam preparedness. It is important that this information is readily accessible, for example, through web-based information such as downloadable handbooks or through published materials such as past paper packs (see www.CambridgeESOL.org for exam-related handbooks, teacher seminars, examination reports, teaching resources). Public access to information about a test and the provision of exemplars of a test are in line with the ALTE Code of Practice (1994) which states that producers of language examinations must provide 'representative samples or complete copies of examination tasks, instructions, answer sheets, manuals and reports of results to users of language examinations' (www.alte.org/quality_assurance/code/part1.php). In fact any member of ALTE guarantees to provide examination users and takers with information 'to help them judge whether a particular examina-tion should be taken or if an available examination at a higher or lower level should be used' (www.alte.org/quality_assurance/code/part1.php). ALTE members also commit to providing candidates with the information they need in order 'to be familiar with the coverage of the examination, the types of task formats, the rubrics and other instructions and appropriate examina-tion-taking strategies' (www.alte.org/quality_assurance/code/part1.php).

At the post-administration stage, when test results are considered, CIS data is carefully examined in order to investigate, where necessary, factors which may have affected candidates' performance. Differential item func-tioning analysis is conducted (see Geranpayeh and Kunnan 2007) to check that no group bias has been inadvertently introduced into the test in respect of any group of test takers, which may affect test validity. Cambridge ESOL conducts bias studies and looks at DIF in terms of a number of experiential variables such as age and educational and cultural background (see Khalifa and Pike 2006, Khalifa, Robinson and Geranpayeh 2005 and Chapter 6 for further details on these studies).

The routine monitoring of the demographic make-up of the candidature of a given examination enables any changes in the test-taking population to be observed so that these can inform later review and revision of the test in ques-tion. Broadening the cultural context of Main Suite examinations in recent years has indeed been led by an awareness of the diversity of its candidature (Murray 2007). Similarly, changes over the years in the average age of test takers are reflected in the choice of the source material and in the provision of examinations more suited to the target age group, e.g. the newly developed KET for Schools and PET for Schools. Data which is gathered on candidates' experience in taking examinations and whether they have attended prepara-tion classes helps shape the support and information provided to candidates, for example, on the Cambridge ESOL website.

Conclusion

In a socio-cognitive framework of test development and validation, there are obvious links between test-taker characteristics and both cognitive validity and context validity. Personal characteristics will directly impact on the way an individual processes a test task and interacts with its contextual features. Test developers, therefore, need to ensure that, at the test development stage the targeted candidature is considered when decisions are made with regards to specific contextual parameters such as topic, text type, writer reader rela-tionship as well as the type of cognitive processing which is appropriate for the targeted candidature at a specific proficiency level.

The use of the demographic data gathered through CIS will provide test developers with knowledge of the test population and should help them to design tasks and select topics appropriately. Carrying out post-test analysis investigating DIF followed by content analysis would confirm that no psychological or experiential characteristics of the targeted candidature have been overlooked or are interacting adversely with the test tasks. It will also ensure that no bias is introduced to the test as a result of the contextual features of the task (see Chapter 4 for a discussion of these features).

In this chapter we also discussed assessing students with disabilities which may affect a relatively small population of candidates but so far has not been discussed in the test-taker literature as extensively as issues of gender or first language. It is seen as appropriate that provision is made on an individual basis to the extent that the validity of the resulting scores is not threatened.

The literature on the test taker is now growing as fair and ethical practices in assessment are gaining the recognition they deserve. On the other hand, interest in what happens cognitively when an individual processes a test task at a specific proficiency level remains a relatively under-researched area of validity in second language studies, and it is this area to which we turn our attention next in Chapter 3 on cognitive validity.

3 Cognitive validity

In this chapter the concern is with the cognitive validity of performances on Reading tests i.e. the extent to which the tasks we employ elicit the cognitive processing involved in target reading contexts beyond the test itself.

We first provide a brief review of psychometric attempts to establish the construct being measured by Reading tests and discuss some of the limitations of the *factorial approach* for our validation purpose. For many testers schooled in the American psychometric tradition this was, and for some still is, the method of choice for establishing construct validity in language testing.

We next look at the *reading subskills approach* which remains an important paradigm particularly in the teaching of L2 reading. This section addresses the contribution made by informed intuition to establishing the construct of reading in pedagogy and assessment, and discusses the limitations of an approach based largely on 'expert judgement' that takes insufficient account of the mental processes test takers actually employ.

We then focus in detail on a *cognitive processing approach* concerned with what readers actually do in real life when they engage in different types of reading. We will draw on external evidence from cognitive psychology concerning the nature of the expertise which we should aim to sample through test tasks. The principal concern is with the mental processes readers actually use in comprehending texts when engaging in different types of real-life reading. This approach appears to offer the most tenable and productive theoretical basis for establishing the construct validity of test instruments.

Finally we will apply our cognitive processing approach to the Main Suite Cambridge ESOL examinations to determine:

- the variety of the **reading types** demanded at each of the levels A2 (KET) to C2 (CPE)
- the comprehensiveness of the **cognitive processes** covered by each of the tests of the suite
- the cognitive demands imposed by relative **text complexity** in each of the tests of the suite
- whether the cognitive processes elicited by the tests of the suite resemble those of a reader in a non-test context.

A factorial approach to defining reading comprehension

From the 1960s onwards there has been a strong interest in the issue of the divisibility of reading for testing purposes. If reading is divisible, examination boards would need to consider the various *components* of this ability, and account for the potentially differing non-observable mental competencies of, for example, accessing knowledge of lexis and structure, textual inferencing, building a mental model, drawing on L1 resources or integrating information within or across texts. They would also need to cover the various *types of reading* that reflect different directly observable behavioural responses to texts, for example, search reading or scanning as against careful reading at the global level or careful reading at the local level. If reading were not a divisible construct, then examination boards might be encouraged to test only those components of reading that best met the criteria of practicality and scoring validity, for example knowledge of lexis and structure. The argument in the latter case would be that measuring any of the components of reading, given that the measures used were sufficiently reliable, would provide a valid prediction of a candidate's overall reading ability, concerns about washback validity (see Chapter 6) notwithstanding.

In pursuit of this divisibility hypothesis, testing researchers often adopted a purely quantitative approach to establishing what reading is by a *post hoc*, factorial analysis of candidate performances in reading tests. Fulcher (2003:203) has the following useful definition of this approach from Hinofotis, 1983 (p. 170):

> A data reduction procedure that allows researchers to collapse large numbers of variables into smaller, more meaningful underlying constructs. The procedure provides a means for conceptually related variables to cluster so that the researcher can come to a better understanding of the relationship among those variables.

This methodology tells us whether the different reading items we have included in our tests load on the same factor. It shows whether there are components that are shared in common by the tasks or whether different components underlie the variables under consideration.

Davis (1968) provides an early example of empirical research into the factors contributing to successful test performance. He employed two forms of a 96-item test, each comprising eight subtests designed to measure distinct operations. The tests were administered to 988 college students with English as an L1. Davis applied factor analysis to the data and found that five out of the eight factors showed appreciable percentages of unique variance and were consistent across the two test forms. This led him to conclude that he could reliably distinguish between five factors rather than eight. These were: recalling word meanings; drawing inferences about the content; recognising a writer's purpose, attitude, tone and mood; finding answers to questions asked explicitly or in paraphrase and following the structure of a passage. He argued that his results indicated that 'comprehension among mature readers is not a unitary mental skill or operation' (Davis 1968:542).

Using factor analysis on engineers' and technicians' reading performance on different types of reading, Guthrie and Kirsch (1987) identified two 'negligibly' correlated factors ($r = 0.20$): comprehension and locating information. Reading to comprehend, which involves reading carefully to understand the explicitly stated ideas (Kintsch and van Dijk 1978), was clearly differentiated from tasks involving reading to locate information which required selective sampling of text (see Weir, Yang and Jin (2000) for similar findings).

However, these findings in favour of divisibility of the reading construct are not shared by other researchers and there is considerable variation in findings concerning the number and nature of the components contributing to successful performance on the reading tests involved. Thorndike (1973), for example, questioned Davis's position and procedure and re-analysed his data. The analysis produced three factors: two of these did not admit of any clear-cut psychological interpretation and a third accounted for much of the greater portion of the covariance, which Thorndike identified as a 'word meaning' factor. This led him to conclude that the reading skills selected by Davis were not distinguishable.

The idea that reading is a monolithic entity and that it would be difficult to break it down for testing purposes is echoed in a number of other research findings based on factorial research. Rosenshine (1980), focusing on mental processes in reading comprehension, examined the results of previous correlational and factor analytic studies to seek empirical evidence for the distinctiveness of different reading comprehension skills. The review of these studies suggests that 'different analyses yielded different unique skills' (Rosenshine 1980:543). Even though some skills emerged as separate, the results were not consistent across the studies which led him to conclude his examination by saying 'at this point, there is simply no clear evidence to support the naming of discrete skills in reading comprehension' (1980:552).

Schedl, Gordon, Carey and Tang (1996) looked at the dimensionality of TOEFL reading items specifically in relation to 'reasoning' (analogy, extrapolation, organisation and logic and author's purpose/attitude) as against other types (primarily items testing vocabulary, syntax and explicitly stated information). Though their study did not support the hypothesis that the 'reasoning items' measured a separable ability factor, they remind us that this should not be taken as proof that separate skills do not exist in reading comprehension:

> Latent ability may be a composite of conceptually distinct subskills. Reasoning and non reasoning subskills may exist separately, as they do conceptually, but be so highly correlated in this data that they do not

define separate factors or dimensions. There may also be other subskills in reading that are not represented in this data set (1996:9).

The empirical evidence from these and other factorial studies provides evidence both for and against a multi-divisible view of reading. The separability and identification of the capabilities underlying performance in reading tests has not been clearly established and results appear to have been affected by:

- the population sampling
- the method of analysis of the data
- the tasks employed.

There would seem to be serious weaknesses in the assumptions which attend this method. The factorial approach focuses on the separability of the capabilities that a reader is assumed to need in tackling certain test items rather than the actual processes which a reader might be expected to apply in real-world reading for a variety of purposes. The concern in this psychometrically driven approach is thus not with the actual components of the reading *process* that are necessary for comprehension but with the factors which can be shown statistically to contribute to successful performance in the specific tests of reading under review. The approach might be described as focusing upon a product in the form of the outcome of a test rather than upon the process which gave rise to it. Thus the data examined is a measure not of successful reading *per se* but of successful performance in the test. The factors underlying the latter do not necessarily hold true for reading activities that take place in the real world.

Many of these *post hoc* quantitative studies are limited to the extent they do not test the range of *types of reading – careful* and *expeditious –* that we discuss below, nor do they consider the need to shape reading to the reader's goals, or the *level of cognitive demand* imposed on the reader by a particular task.

Given the aim of evaluating the cognitive validity of reading tests, an approach premised solely on a *post hoc* factorial analysis of reading tests seems problematic. Weir (2005) cautions against relying on this procedure for construct validation:

> There is a need for validation at the *a priori* stage of test development. The more fully and accurately we are able to describe the construct we are attempting to measure at the *a priori* stage, the more meaningful might be the statistical procedures contributing to construct validation that can subsequently be applied to the results of the test. Statistical data do not in themselves generate conceptual labels. We can never escape from the need to define what is being measured, just as we are obliged to investigate how adequate a test is in operation (Weir 2005:18).

Field (forthcoming) echoes this position, pointing to '. . . the dangers of relying exclusively on an approach that attempts to track back from a product or outcome to the process that gave rise to it'. Such analyses by their nature tell us little about what is actually happening when a reader processes text under test conditions. We need to go deeper and examine as far as is possible the nature of the reading activities in which we engage during a test in such a way as to enable comparison with the activities in which we engage during non-test reading. We argue below that in respect of cognitive validity we need to establish clearly the types of reading we wish to include and to ensure that the processing demands made are relevant to and appropriate for the level of the L2 candidates being assessed.

Informed intuition: A skills and strategies approach to defining reading

The kind of factorial approach described in the previous section emerged during a time when the climate of opinion in the methodology of teaching reading strongly favoured what was termed a skills or strategies approach with a clear focus on behavioural types of reading. This approach assumed that reading might be subdivided into competencies which the skilled reader is believed to have.

The development of the 'subskills' movement (Grellet 1987, Munby 1978, and Nuttall 1996) in L2 pedagogy aimed to break reading down into constituent competencies. Barr, Clegg and Wallace (1981) and Davies and Whitney (1981) provide two early examples of widely used and influential coursebooks for teaching reading 'skills/strategies'. The movement came about in large part from the need felt by teachers to provide more focused practice in these skills and strategies as an alternative to reading simply as 'language practice'. The approach also gave ideas for generating reading exercises other than 'reading comprehension questions' (see Williams and Moran 1989, section 4.3.6).

It may also have reflected the growing need at that time to develop communicatively oriented pedagogical syllabuses and curricula with 'bite-size' teaching/learning chunks. Previously the grammar/translation method of language teaching/learning could be conveniently broken down into a series of successive lessons on different structural features. Despite a move to communicative skills teaching, this approach still needed to be organised in some way for lesson planning and coursebook writing. The skills/strategies breakdown made this much easier (analogous to the list of structural features). So the earlier grammatical specification was complemented by the specification of skills/strategies and also by the specification of functions and notions derived from functional notional syllabuses (see Wilkins 1973 and 1976 for explication of the theoretical base for the latter). 'Tables of contents' with columns for grammar, function, skill/strategy, were generated for many EFL coursebooks and the practice has continued to this day.

The approach has mainly been based on informed intuition rather than empirical research but has been found to be useful by a generation of teachers. As a result it figured prominently in EFL reading materials for teaching purposes and test specification (for details see Williams and Moran 1989 and Urquhart and Weir 1998). It is widely accepted pedagogical practice in TEFL to break the reading process down and to address component skills and strategies separately.

However there was a disadvantage to this approach. It was more organisationally than theoretically driven and since Munby (1978) there has been much terminological overload and a good deal of inconsistency in the descriptors employed for describing various reading processes. The term 'subskill' has been used loosely to describe a wide variety of types of reading.

The distinction between reading 'skills' and reading 'strategies' has also been left unclear by many commentators. The term 'strategies' is used in this volume for purposeful, problem-solving activities, in other words exigencies to deal with immediate problems of communication and the term 'skills' for automaticised abilities performed largely subconsciously (Carrell and Grabe 2002, Cohen 2006, Cohen and Upton 2006, Phakiti 2003, Pressley and Afflerbach 1995, Urquhart and Weir 1998, Williams and Moran 1989). Grabe and Stoller (2002) caution that the distinction may sometimes become blurred as strategies become automatised in fluent readers and they therefore argue that 'strategies for definitional purposes are best defined as abilities that are potentially open to conscious reflection and use . . .' (2002:15–17).

In the field of testing, the subskills approach has given rise to the notion that it is possible to link particular types of item or task to specific subskills that they are said to tap into. Weir and Porter (1994:7) noted that 'a growing body of literature suggests that it is possible with clear specification of terms and appropriate methodology for testers to reach closer agreement on what subskills are being tested'. The body of literature the authors referred to includes Bachman, Kunnan, Vanniarajan and Lynch (1988), Teasdale (1989), Lumley (1993), and Weakley (1993). In the DIALANG project (Alderson 2005:125–137) individual items are viewed as testing identifiable subskills.

The value of this subskills approach for testing is contentious. Alderson (1990 and 1990a) threw doubt on the ability of item writers to determine with any precision what processes individual items will elicit. He presented the first pilot version of the reading module of the TEEP test (see Weir 1983 for details of the final test) to teachers to elicit expert opinion as to what each test item was measuring in terms of skills and asked them to categorise these skills into higher order and lower order skills. Alderson's study showed disagreement among these experts as to what skill each particular item tested, as well as a lack of relationship between the item statistics and the level of ability the item claimed to be testing.

If Alderson is correct, examination boards need to consider whether they are right to attempt to devise items that tap into a particular subskill or strategy or whether they should instead attempt to design the overall spread of items in a test in such a way as to cover the reading construct that is appropriate to reading purpose and target level of processing difficulty. Weir and Porter (1994:6) in fact state in relation to TEEP that: 'the pilot test items were not especially constructed to be discrete in terms of specific subskills but roughly to cover the range of identified skills in total'.

The jury is still out on whether it is possible for expert judges (including item writers and those involved in research and validation in examination boards) to be convincingly accurate in their predictions about what subskills individual items in a test are assessing. Given this uncertainty, those offering tests may be better served by identifying which types of reading are most appropriate to different levels of proficiency and attempting to ensure by the texts selected, the way items are constructed, and other salient performance conditions set, e.g. text length and time available (see Chapter 4 for details), that the cognitive processing demands to complete such tasks are commensurate with the skilled reading process as evidenced by research in cognitive psychology.

Informed intuitive approaches have been helpful in advancing our conceptualisation of what is involved in reading both for pedagogical and assessment purposes. The problem is that they often only represent the views of expert materials designers and setters as to what is actually being tested in terms of type of reading. In both the factorial approach to understanding reading and the informed intuition approach the central role of the *test taker* has been largely overlooked. The majority of the studies referred to in the two approaches discussed so far make little reference to the cognitive processing that might be necessary for L2 candidates to achieve the various types of reading initiated by the reading test tasks employed. To clearly establish the trait that has been measured we need to investigate the processing necessary for task fulfilment.

Alderson (2000:97) makes the point:

> The validity of a test relates to the interpretation of the correct responses to items, so what matters is not what the test constructors believe an item to be testing, but which responses are considered correct, and what process underlies them.

A cognitive processing model for reading comprehension

There is an oft-expressed concern over a mismatch between prevailing theories of reading comprehension and practice in the testing of reading comprehension dating back to Farr and Carey (1986), Bernhardt (1991), Anderson, Bachman, Perkins and Cohen (1991), Lipson and Wixson (1991), O'Malley and Valdez Pierce (1996), Engelhard (2001) and more recently Pollitt and Taylor (2006). In this section we examine various approaches to describing the reading process in an attempt to establish a suitable model of real-life reading which can then be applied to evaluate the reading tasks employed in tests and which may be used to develop tests in the future.

In attempting to understand what is involved in the process of reading comprehension, researchers over the years have proposed and developed various theories of reading (e.g. Goodman 1967, Gough 1972, Just and Carpenter 1980 and 1987, Kintsch and van Dijk 1978, LaBerge and Samuels 1974, Perfetti 1999, Rayner and Pollatsek 1989, Ruddell and Speaker 1985 and Stanovich 1980). These theorists all recognise the reading process as combining 'bottom-up' visual information with the 'top-down' world knowledge that the reader brings to the task; but they have diverged enormously in their accounts of the importance accorded to each and of the ways in which the two sources of information are combined by the reader.

Cohen and Upton (2006) describe bottom-up processes as employing linguistic knowledge to build smaller units into larger ones through several levels of processing: the orthographic, phonological, lexical, syntactic features of a text and then sentence meaning through to a representation of the whole text (see Birch 2007 for a complete treatment of this). In top-down processing larger units affect the way smaller units are perceived. Sources of information include context, where general and domain specific knowledge is used to enrich propositional meaning, and/or the developing *meaning representation of the text so far,* created in the act of reading a text.

There are two distinct uses for context: one to enrich propositional meaning extracted from a decoded text and the other to support decoding where it is inadequate. Stanovich (1980) argues that an interactive compensatory mechanism enables unskilled readers to compensate by resorting to top-down processing, for example by using contextual clues to *compensate* for slower lexical access due to inaccurate decoding. He suggests that skilled L1 readers employ context for enriching understanding rather than for supplementing partial or incomplete information as is the case for the poor reader. Perfetti (1985) also takes issue with the view that skilled readers made more use of context for word identification than poor readers. Jenkins, Fuchs, van den Broeck, Espin and Deno (2003) note research suggesting that skilled readers rarely depend on top-down prediction to identify words in context because they have rapid word identification skills which outstrip the rather slower hypothesis forming top-down processes, i.e. they already have automatic skills which do not make demands on working memory. The opposite is true for less skilled readers as their bottom-up processing of print is slower than top-down word prediction processes.

It is now generally accepted that we process at different levels simultaneously and draw on both bottom-up and top-down processes in establishing meaning. It is very unlikely that a reader (except perhaps an early novice L1 reader) would use one type of processing exclusively. Jenkins et al (2003) note that in Stanovich's interactive compensatory model both the bottom-up (text driven) and the top-down (meaning driven) processes operate at the same time. Similarly Faerch and Kasper (1986) argue that these processes do not operate in isolation from each other. 'Even in contexts where one processing direction is preferred, the other one is also operative typically, the various information sources interact, and outcomes of one operation are available as input for other types of processing' (Faerch and Kasper 1986: 264–265).

There will of course be some individual variation in cognitive processing but we need to consider whether there are any generic processes that we would want to sample in our Reading tests which would bring the process of comprehending in a test closer to what we might generally agree on as 'reading a text' in accordance with the different types of reading behaviour appropriate to different reading purposes. Pollitt and Ahmed (2000) describe such a 'cognitive psychology approach to construct validity', and generating validation evidence of generalised cognitive processes was advocated strongly by Messick (1989) as well as more recently by Weir (2005).

To examine further the nature of processing we consider below the predominantly L1 literature on processing in reading. We follow Field (forthcoming) in using L1 cognitive processing research to inform our understanding of decoding and building meaning in L2 reading tasks:

> . . . the premise is adopted that underlying the four language skills are certain established and shared routines which can be traced by examining and comparing the performance of expert language users. This assumption is supported by two lines of argument:
>
> a. *The universal argument.* All human brains are similarly configured. They can be assumed, at some level of generality, to share processing routines which are broadly similar in that they reflect the strengths and limitations of the organ and the means it adopts for transmitting information. These routines might be deemed to contribute not simply to the forms that language takes but also to the ways in which it is processed in performance.
> b. *The expertise argument.* A marked difference between an adult L1 speaker and an L2 learner lies in the fact that the former has had years of experience during which to develop the most rapid and most effective processing routines for dealing with the vagaries of the target language – and to develop them without competition from deeply ingrained routines associated with another language. An understanding of how such expert users perform should thus assist us in directing the development of novices.

The cognitive validity of a reading task is a measure of how closely it elicits the cognitive processing involved in contexts beyond the test itself, i.e.

in performing reading task(s) in real life. We will draw on the work of authors working within the field of cognitive psychology in order to devise a model of the L1 reading process – supported by empirical evidence – which can be treated as the goal towards which the L2 reader aspires.

The various types of reading and the cognitive processes they may give rise to that we have identified from the literature are represented in diagrammatic form in Figure 3.1 below and explained in the subsequent text. We will start in the left hand column with a brief description of the metacognitive activity of a *goal setter* because, in deciding what type of reading to employ when

Figure 3.1 A model of reading

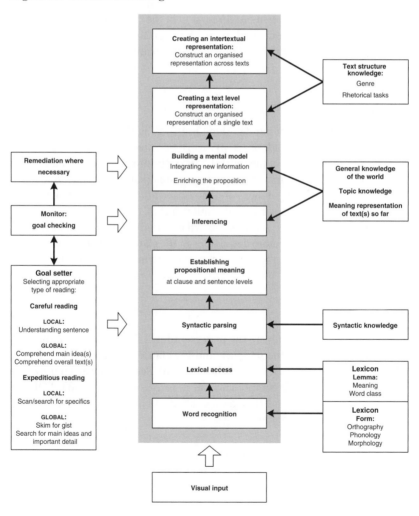

faced with a text or texts, critical decisions are taken which affect the level(s) of processing to be activated in the central core of our model. The various elements of this processing core in the middle column which might be initiated by decisions taken in the goal setter are then described individually. A discussion of the *monitor* then follows as this can be applied to each of the levels of processing that is activated in response to the goal setter's instructions.

We then return to the left-hand column and examine in more detail each of the *types of reading* we have listed under the goal setter. Having discussed the central processing core we will be better able to make links between the *components* of the reading process and the *type(s) of reading* selected to respond to a task. The knowledge base required for text comprehension in the right hand column is discussed in full detail in Chapter 4 and referred to briefly, where appropriate, in our discussion of the components in the central processing core and in our analysis of the cognitive load arising from the texts selected for Cambridge ESOL Main Suite examinations in the final part of the chapter.

The goal setter

The goal setter in the left hand column is critical in that the decisions taken on the purpose for the reading activity will determine the relative importance of some of the processes in the central core of the model. Urquhart and Weir (1998) provide an overview of the goals that are open to the reader and characterise reading as being either *careful* or *expeditious* or taking place at the *local* or *global* level. The various permutations of these two dimensions are listed in the model above and first described briefly. These *types of reading* will then be discussed in more detail later in the chapter when the processing elements of the model in the central core that are initiated after selecting the purpose for reading have been explained.

Local level

Local comprehension refers to the understanding of propositions at the level of micro-structure, i.e. the sentence and the clause. Enright, Grabe, Koda, Mosenthal, Mulcahy-Ernt and Schedl (2000) describe local comprehension as reading for basic comprehension. In respect of the new iBT TOEFL, Cohen and Upton (2006:17) suggest that local comprehension is strongly associated with linguistic knowledge:

> . . . according to the task specifications (ETS, 2003): Basic comprehension questions are used to assess lexical, syntactic, and semantic abilities and the ability to understand important information presented in sentence-level propositions.

Alderson (2000) makes a connection between local comprehension and test items which focus on understanding explicit information. In textually explicit questions, the information used in the question and the information required for the answer are usually in the same sentence (see Alderson 2000:87). In our model above, local comprehension is at the levels of *decoding (word recognition, lexical access* and *syntactic parsing)* and *establishing propositional meaning* at the sentence and clause level.

Global level

What Kintsch and van Dijk (1978:374) term macro-propositions contribute to the overall structure of the text. Global comprehension refers to the understanding of propositions beyond the level of micro-structure, that is, any macro-propositions including main ideas, the links between those macro-propositions and the way in which the micro-propositions elaborate upon them.

In reading at the macro-structure level of the text the main concern is with the relationships between ideas represented in complexes of propositions which tend to be logical or rhetorical (see Vipond 1980). Individual components of these complexes are often marked out by the writer by means of paragraphs. In *careful global reading* operations the reader is trying to identify the main idea(s) by establishing the macro-structure of a text: how the ideas in the whole text relate to each other and to the author's purpose.

Stromso and Braten (2002:212) argue that there is one further variety of careful global reading: '. . . research on the reading of multiple texts has indicated that this is an important part of normal reading, at least in higher education.' Where careful reading of more than one related text is involved, the macro-structure construction as suggested by Kintsch and van Dijk (1978) is only part of the processing required. Lacroix (1999) suggests that a further process of macro-structural organisation accounts for the connection of several text representations through higher-level semantic links.

Reading at the global level also occurs in *search reading global* where, in relation to previously identified needs, the reader is trying to gather macro-propositional information quickly and selectively through short cuts to save time. Global comprehension also includes *skimming* where the reader, through quick, selective sampling of the text, is trying to establish the overall discourse topic; the superordinate macro-proposition (see Kong 1996).

Careful reading

In the past, models of reading have usually been developed with *careful reading* in mind. Hoover and Tunmer (1993), for example, considered that their notion of reading:

> . . . assumes careful comprehension: comprehension that is intended to extract complete meanings from presented material as opposed to comprehension aimed at only extracting main ideas, skimming, or searching for particular details (p. 8).

Rayner and Pollatsek (1989:439) state that for most of their account of the reading process they are focusing on the skilled, adult reader carefully reading material of the textbook variety. They admit that careful reading models have little to tell us about how skilled readers can cope with other reading behaviours such as skimming for gist (Rayner and Pollatsek 1989: 477–478).

Careful reading is intended to extract complete meanings from presented material. As we have seen, this can take place at a local or a global level, i.e. within or beyond the sentence right up to the level of the complete text or texts. The approach to reading is based on slow, careful, linear, incremental reading for comprehension.

Expeditious reading

There seems to be also, as Carver (1992) found, a case for taking account of the speed of reading as well as comprehension. This is in line with Beard (1972), Weir (1983) and Weir et al (2000) whose studies into students' abilities indicate that 'for many readers reading quickly, selectively and efficiently posed greater problems than reading carefully and efficiently'. Urquhart and Weir (1998) refer to the former type as *expeditious reading*. Expeditious reading of continuous prose is difficult because it demands rapid recognition which is contingent upon sufficient practice in reading in the target language.

Expeditious reading involves quick, selective and efficient reading to access desired information in a text. *Expeditious reading* would appear likely to include *skimming, search reading,* and *scanning. Skimming* is generally defined (e.g. Munby 1978, Urquhart and Weir 1998, Weir 2005) as reading to obtain the gist, general impression and/or superordinate main idea of a text. For Urquhart and Weir (1998) *search reading* involves locating information on predetermined topics. The reader only wants information necessary to answer set questions or to provide data, for example in completing written assignments. Search reading differs from skimming in that the search for information is guided by predetermined topics so the reader does not necessarily have to establish a macro-propositional structure for the whole of the text.

Search reading can take place at both the local and global level. Where the desired information can be located within a single sentence it would be classified as local and where information has to be put together across sentences it would be seen as global. In both cases the search is for words in the same semantic field as the target information, unlike scanning where exact word matches are sought.

Scanning involves reading selectively, to achieve very specific reading goals, e.g. looking for specific words/phrases, figures/percentages, names, dates of particular events or specific items in an index, at the local word level.

The overriding attention paid to careful reading in the theoretical literature has meant that we have somewhat ignored expeditious reading strategies such as skimming, search reading and scanning (Hudson 1996 and Urquhart and Weir 1998) in both L1 and L2 teaching and testing of reading (see however Weir et al 2000 for a description of the Advanced English Reading Test in China; Zhou, Weir and Green 1998 for an account of the validation of the Test for English Majors, again in China; and Weir 2005 for an account of the GEPT in Taiwan.

We will return to these purposes for reading after we have discussed the central processing core of the model from the bottom level upwards, at which point we will be in a position to discuss the relationships between the intended purpose and the processing activity it elicits in this central core. The processes described below attempt to characterise the reading behaviours available to the competent L1 reader, which the L2 reader might be expected to approximate progressively as their proficiency level in L2 and exposure to reading in L2 improves. The knowledge base on the right hand side of the model is drawn upon by the central processing core in line with the intended purpose and the performance conditions established by the task.

Central processing core

Word recognition

Word recognition is concerned with matching the form of a word in a written text with a mental representation of the orthographic forms of the language. Field (2004:234) refers to this as 'the *perceptual* process of identifying the letters and words in a text'. Oakhill and Garnham (1988:10) note that the problem of word recognition is to decide which (if any) of all the words you know, the current visual pattern is an instance of. In the case of the less experienced L2 reader, the matching process is complicated by a more limited sight vocabulary in the target language, and by the fact that the reader does not make the automatic connection between written word and mental representation that an experienced reader would. The situation will be further complicated by the extent to which L1 and L2 scripts diverge.

Field (2004) cites Coltheart's (1978) dual route model of decoding which suggests that we process written words in two ways: 'A *lexical route* enables us to match whole words while a *sub-lexical* route permits us to identify words by means of grapheme–phoneme correspondence (GPC) rules which specify the relationship between spelling and sound. Though the sub-lexical route is slower it permits us to attribute a pronunciation to unfamiliar words'.

Readers in all languages where the script uses the alphabetic principle, rather than the ideographic principle appear to use both routes. The problem for the L2 reader of English is that it is much more difficult to match an unfamiliar written form to a known spoken one by means of the sub-lexical route or to internalise the spoken forms of written words. Much of the matching during the acquisition of L1 reading skills in English relies quite heavily on analogies between words with similar written forms (*light – fight – right*). L2 learners, with limited vocabulary and less automatic pattern recognition, are less able to apply these analogies. Rixon (2007:8) notes that the use of analogy and rhyme in teaching young EAL learners, though advantageous as compared to the grouping of words by initial letter, is rarely employed in young learner materials.

The opaque orthography of English may result in greater dependence on the lexical route and thereby increase the difficulty when unskilled L2 readers meet words in text which they have never encountered before in a written form. This may mean that examination boards need to ensure that at lower levels of proficiency the number of unknown words in a text needs to be controlled and the length of texts these candidates are exposed to will need to be shorter than those for skilled readers. L2 readers with L1 language backgrounds in which the orthographies are very dissimilar to that of English, e.g. in the script or direction of reading, will face additional problems at the decoding level (see Birch 2007).

The attentional resources of a reader are finite and, at least in the early stages of L2 development, one might expect a large part of those resources to be diverted towards more low-level considerations concerning the linguistic code. The effort of decoding makes considerable cognitive demands on the less skilled L2 reader and as a result decoding may become the principal focus of attention for many and prevent them transferring into L2 the kind of processing for building meaning that those literate in their L1 are able to apply.

The same point is made by Jenkins et al (2003) who note that less skilled readers are constrained by inefficient word recognition which requires attentional resources and uses up available working memory capacity that might otherwise be used for comprehension. In the skilled reader, efficient word recognition frees up attentional resources thereby increasing the capacity in working memory available for more complex operations (see Birch 2007).

Accuracy and automaticity of word recognition is critical for the skilled reader (Grabe 2004; Perfetti 1985, 1994, 1997; Stanovich 1991; Wagner and Stanovich 1996). Automaticity is the result of increasing experience in decoding and of the mind's orientation towards creating processes which are undemanding upon attention. Readers who can decode accurately and automatically will backtrack less often and have more attentional capacity available in working memory for comprehension, e.g. establishing propositional meaning, inferencing and building a mental model and integration of information across sentences.

Lexical access

This is described by Field (2004:151) as the 'retrieval of a lexical entry from the lexicon, containing stored information about a word's form and its meaning'. The form includes orthographic and phonological mental representations of a lexical item and possibly information on its morphology. The lemma (the meaning-related part of the lexical entry) includes information on word class and the syntactic structures in which the item can appear and on the range of possible senses for the word.

The orthographic form plays a part in what was described in the previous section as word recognition. Some accounts describe sets of visually similar words in the reader's mental vocabulary as being in competition with each other. Individual words are activated in relation to the extent to which they do or do not resemble a target word on the page. Finally, a point is reached where one word accumulates so much evidence that it is selected as the correct match.

Frequent words appear to be identified more quickly than infrequent ones because, according to serial models of lexical access, words are stored on this principle. Other theories such as parallel access indicate that words are *activated* in accordance with their frequency and the closest match to context (Field 2004:117, 151). This suggests that examination boards need to ensure that there is a suitable progression in terms of lexis from frequent words to those with less frequent coverage as one moves up the levels of proficiency in L2 reading examinations (see below and Chapter 4 for further discussion).

Syntactic parsing

In our view syntax is taken as synonymous with 'grammar' and therefore covers not only word order, but also word form (morphology) and structural elements (determiners, prepositions, auxiliary verbs etc.).

So called 'garden path' approaches commonly used in psycholinguistic research illustrate the importance of correct parsing to meaning making. A sentence such as '*The man who hunts ducks out at Xmas*' though grammatically correct may lead the reader to incorrect parsing. To make sense of the sentence it usually requires a second run-through with a different method of parsing.

Fluency in syntactic parsing is regarded as important in the comprehension process by a number of authorities (Perfetti 1997). Once the meaning of words is accessed, the reader has to group words into phrases, and into larger units at the clause and sentence level to understand the message of the text. Cromer (1970) illustrates the importance of competence in the syntax of the target language for deriving meaning from text. He demonstrates that good comprehenders use sentence structure as well as word identification to comprehend text (see also Haynes and Carr 1990).

Eddie Williams (personal communication) adds:

> The basic facts of English sentence structure (e.g. SVO order) may of themselves pose problems for learners whose languages operate VSO systems. Likewise the Adj + N order in English as opposed to N + Adj of many other languages. In addition the meanings of structural elements in English (e.g. determiners, and various forms of the verb phrase) can cause significant problems of comprehension.

Researchers like Alderson (1993), Weir (1983) and Shiotsu and Weir (2007) point out the strong positive correlations between test results in grammar and in reading. Bernhardt (2005) *inter alia* stresses the importance of L2 proficiency in reading L2.

It is clearly important that examination boards ensure that the syntactic categories appearing in texts employed at each level in their examinations are appropriate to the candidate's level of development (see below and Chapter 4 for further discussion).

Establishing propositional (core) meaning at the clause or sentence level

Field (2004:225) describes this as: 'An abstract representation of a single unit of meaning: a mental record of the core meaning of the sentence without any of the interpretative and associative factors which the reader might bring to bear upon it.'

Propositional meaning is a literal interpretation of what is on the page. The reader has to add external knowledge to it to turn it into a message that relates to the context in which it occurred.

Inferencing

Inferencing is necessary so the reader can go beyond explicitly stated ideas as the links between ideas in a passage are often left implicit (Oakhill and Garnham 1988:22). Inferencing in this sense is a creative process whereby the brain adds information which is not stated in a text in order to impose coherence. A text cannot include all the information that is necessary in order to make sense of it. Texts usually leave out knowledge that readers can be trusted to add for themselves. If there were no such thing as inferencing, writing a text which includes every piece of information would be extremely cumbersome and time consuming. Problems may of course arise where the assumed knowledge relates to that of the L1 host culture and such inferences are not possible for the L2 learner who lacks this knowledge. A rather difficult example is provided by a newspaper banner headline: Grayson 'shuts that door!' which referred to the rugby player who had kicked England to victory in a match against France the previous day, but also involves knowledge about the comedian Larry Grayson whose catchphrase was 'shut that door!'.

Inferencing may also take place at word level, when a word is ambiguous in its context or is a homograph. It may also involve guessing the meaning of unknown words in context.

Another type of inferential process is 'anaphor resolution' where pronouns and other referring items have to be linked by the reader to the entity that they refer to.

Hughes (1993) argues that we should replicate real-life processes and attempt to sample all types of inferencing ability in our tests with the caveat of being able to select texts which are close to the background and experience of the candidature. However, he admits that pragmatic inferencing questions (where the reader not only makes use of information in the text but also refers to their own world knowledge, i.e. non-linguistic knowledge from outside the text) may be problematic where candidates have very different knowledge, experience and opinions (see Chikalanga 1991 and 1992). Examination boards need to be conscious of this at the item writing stage to avoid penalising candidates who may lack particular world knowledge.

Pragmatic evaluative inferences may be particularly difficult to include in tests because of the marking problems associated with potential variability in answers. Even though the evidence available to the reader from the text is given, they will come to it with different perspectives and expectations. One man's terrorist is another man's freedom fighter.

Text-based inference which requires inference between parts of a text may be more amenable to inclusion within tests.

Building a mental model

Once the reader has processed the incoming sentence and *elaborated* it where necessary and possible through inferencing, the new information needs to be *integrated* into a mental representation of the text so far. Field (2004:241) notes:

> Incoming information has to be related to what has gone before, so as to ensure that it contributes to the developing representation of the text in a way that is consistent, meaningful and relevant. This process entails an ability to identify main ideas, to relate them to previous ideas,

distinguish between major and minor propositions and to impose a hierarchical structure on the information in the text.

Ongoing meaning representation is provisional and liable to revision as well as updating with new information from the text. *Selection* may occur whereby stored information is reduced to what is relative or important.

According to Kintsch and van Dijk (1978:374), the propositions representing the meaning of a text are linked together, usually by argument overlap, to form a hierarchical text base. Micro-structures are processed, converted into semantic propositions, and stored in the working memory, while the cohesion between them is established. As the process moves on, a macro-structure is built up. Background knowledge, stored in long-term memory, is utilised to supply an appropriate schema for the macro-structure, as well as to aid coherence detection in the construction of the micro-structure. Crucial information tends to be at the top levels of this hierarchy, while detailed information is at the lower levels.

Field (2004:174) refers to Gernsbacher's (1990) structure building framework:

> . . . the reader maps incoming information on to a current information substructure if it coheres with what is there. If it does not, the reader employs a *shifting process* which involves creating a new information substructure. Reading is normally supported by paragraphing which in well written texts helps the reader build a meaning structure of the text.

As we discuss below, while building a mental model there is a need to monitor comprehension to check the viability of the ongoing interpretation. Monitoring chiefly checks the consistency of incoming information against the meaning representation established so far. If the two conflict the reader regresses to check. World knowledge in the form of schemata in long-term memory plays an important part in judging the coherence and consistency of what has been understood when it is integrated into the ongoing meaning representation.

Creating a text level representation

Field (2004:225) notes how text structure is seen by some as 'a hierarchy of propositions; a set of prominent *macro-propositions*, beneath which (like subheadings in a table of contents) are grouped *micro-propositions* of diminishing degrees of importance'. We examined this distinction between global and local meaning in the discussion on the goal setter above.

At a final stage of processing, a discourse-level structure is created for the text as a whole. The skilled reader is able to recognise the hierarchical structure of the whole text and determines which items of information are central to the meaning of the text. The skilled reader determines how the different parts of the text fit together and which parts of the text are important to the writer or to reader purpose.

Enright, Grabe, Koda, Mosenthal, Mulcahy-Ernt and Schedl (2000:5–6) explain the text model as the representation of rhetorical structure(s) in a text:

> Constructing an organised representation of the text including main points and supporting detail; an integrated understanding of how supporting ideas and factual details of the text form a coherent whole . . .

Development of an accurate and reasonably complete text model of comprehension would seem to involve understanding:

- discourse structure: identifying macro level relationships between ideas
- which propositions are central to the goals of the text and which are of secondary importance: for example this might be signalled in a text through fore-grounding main information and back-grounding of secondary information, important information in first mention position, marking of thematic information with repetition (see Meyer 1975; McKoon 1977; Eamon 1978–79; Drum, Calfee and Cook 1981).

Creating an intertextual representation

Lacroix (1999) suggests that the comprehension of complex, multiple texts in a particular domain may require two distinct levels of macro-structural processing to ensure a coherent, condensed structuring of the multiple text information. She suggests that the process of macro-structure construction (extracting important information) outlined in Kintsch and van Dijk (1978), which involves identifying and establishing a hierarchy for units of information through the application of transformational macro rules of deletion, generalisation and integration, accounts well for the comprehension of a single text but may not be adequate to represent how mental representations are combined coherently across multiple texts. Lacroix suggests that the additional process of macro-structural organisation (structuring selected information) is necessary for the connection of several text representations through higher-level semantic links.

Stromso and Braten (2002:211) similarly argue that the 'discourse synthesis' of multiple texts in a specific domain involves 'composing a new text by selecting, organising and connecting content from more than one source text'. The need for an intertextual model, sometimes referred to as a 'documents model' (Perfetti, Rouet and Britt 1999) to account for the production of integrated representations of multiple texts is supported in the work of Britt and

Sommer (2004), Goldman (1997 and 2004), Hartman (1995), Perfetti (1997), Perfetti et al (1999), Spivey and King (1989), and Stahl, Hynd, Britton, McNish and Bosquet (1996). As Goldman (2004:344) succinctly puts it 'the information across texts is part of a larger whole not necessarily specified in any one of the texts'.

Britt and Aglinskas (2002) refer to the heuristics of corroboration, contextualisation and sourcing as being necessary in addition to information integration for document-level reading of multiple historical texts. It may be that future research will reveal further domain specific requirements for intertextuality.

Unaldi (forthcoming), in her investigation of what goes on beyond single text comprehension when readers read multiple texts, points to the higher cognitive demands of the latter: 'Since texts are not normally written to be read in conjunction with other texts, they lack explicit links to facilitate integration of information across texts, the demands on the reader to form a macrostructure are higher than when reading a single text with its own intratextual coherence.'

Processing in multiple text reading has clear resonances with the cognitive processing that takes place in knowledge transforming writing tasks (Scardamalia and Bereiter 1987) where the selecting, connecting and organisation of information from source texts constitute the first cognitive components in the writing process (see Shaw and Weir 2007: Chapter 3). Researchers such as Spivey and King (1989) have shown how competent students interweave texts in writing research papers by utilising source material deemed to have intertextual importance.

Stromso and Braten (2002) provide an interesting case study of students' intertextual linking activities in connection with learning from expository textual resources comprising civil law reading materials such as textbooks, a code of laws and legal cases. Hartman (1995) details a further interesting case study of students constructing a 'mosaic of intersecting texts' on the American Civil War. Both studies illustrate the additional processing required to produce an intertextual representation as compared to that of a single text.

The cognitive construction of intertextuality offers a useful heuristic for looking at reading into writing at an advanced level and it extends our view of reading beyond the act of comprehension of a single passage (Hartman 2005).

We have now looked at each of the levels of processing that may be brought into play as a result of metacognitive decisions taken in the goal setter. A further metacognitive activity may take place after activation of each level of the processing core: test takers are likely to check the effectiveness of their understanding (Sticht and James 1984). The *Monitor* is the mechanism that provides the reader with feedback about the success of the particular reading process (Urquhart and Weir 1998:105).

Monitoring

The nature of the monitoring is contingent on the type of reading, and therefore the monitor is activated in accordance with the original goals of the reader, who might even decide that they have adopted the wrong type of reading and change accordingly.

Self-monitoring is a complex operation which may occur at different stages of the process (after reading a word, a sentence, a paragraph or a complete text) and may relate to different levels of analysis. Pressley and Afflerbach (1995) provide a comprehensive review of monitoring strategies that help regulate comprehension and learning, and evaluating strategies whereby readers reflect or respond in some way to the text.

In decoding text, monitoring involves checking word recognition, lexical access, and syntactic parsing. Within meaning building it can involve determining the success with which you can extract the writer's intentions or the argument structure of the text.

Perfetti (1999:197) describes how comprehension monitoring has been found to be ineffective in less skilled readers in a number of studies. Oakhill and Garnham (1988:139–40) argue that the unskilled L1 reader often fails to monitor comprehension or at least makes less use of monitoring strategies, particularly at the comprehension level. Studies have shown that one of the hallmarks of a good reader is the ability to check the meaning representation for consistency. Skilled readers, on failing to understand a part of a text, will take action such as rereading to deal with the problem (see Hyona and Nurminen 2006).

The components of goal setter and monitor can be viewed as *metacognitive mechanisms* that mediate among different processing skills and knowledge sources available to a reader. Urquhart and Weir (1998) provide detailed explanations about how these metacognitive mechanisms enable a reader to activate different levels of strategies and skills to cope with different reading purposes. The reader may choose to skim, search read, scan, or read carefully, in response to the perceived demands of the test task. The level of processing required by the activity will relate closely to the demands set by the test task.

We are now in a position to examine in more detail the types of reading, discussed briefly above in the section on goal setting, which represent what reading might involve in real-life activities, and try to relate them more closely to the central core of the processing model we have just described.

Types of reading and the processing model

The goal setter part of the model in the left hand column of Figure 3.1 above is critical in that the decision taken on the purpose for the reading activity will determine the processing that is activated, mediated of course by any limitations in the L2 reader's competence and the cognitive load of text and task parameters.

Rothkopf (1982) illustrates how the purpose for reading a text determines what and how much the reader takes away from it. Once the readers have a clear idea of what they will be reading for, they can choose the most appropriate process(es) for extracting the information they need in the text (see Pressley and Afflerbach (1995) for a comprehensive review of planning processes). The goal setter determines the overall goal of the reading, and also selects the type of reading which is likely to achieve that goal.

Expeditious reading

The broad choices open to the reader as detailed in Urquhart and Weir's (1998) account of expeditious reading are skimming, search reading or scanning. These were briefly outlined in the section on the goal setter above. Now that we have discussed the central processing core in our model, we are able to deal more fully with the various component processes that are activated when a decision is made on which type(s) of reading to perform.

Skimming

For Urquhart and Weir (1998) the defining characteristics of skimming are (a) the reading is selective, with sections of the text either omitted or given very little attention; (b) an attempt is made to build up a macro-structure (the gist) on the basis of as few details from the text as possible. Skimming may help the reader decide quickly whether it is worthwhile to approach the text or parts of it again in a more careful fashion. Pugh (1978:54) adds that it may:

> . . . also be used to obtain an overall impression of features of a text. For example, it may be used to glean surface information, to check on a writer's tone, or to discover how a writer structures a chapter. Related to discovering the structure is a further use of skimming, where the reader seeks "advance organisation" of what he is subsequently to learn in detail.

Skimming is selective depending on how much information readers decide to process; they may access words and possibly process entire sentences. The reader will allocate his/her attention, focusing full attention on propositions that seem to be macro-propositional and reducing attention on others. They use knowledge of text and genre which indicates likely positions for macro-propositions, e.g. first sentence of paragraph.

Presumably, the *monitor* checks as to whether the material surveyed is appropriate or not; in this case, the amount processed may be quite substantial. The reader will pause at appropriate points to semantically process words, phrases and clauses. If skimming is equivalent to gist extraction, then presumably propositions are committed to the long-term memory on the hypothesis that they represent the macro-structure. That is, the process of debating whether a proposition is part of the macro-structure or not, which is assumed to take place during careful reading, is here replaced by a guess that it is usually supported by general knowledge of the world or domain knowledge.

The reader is trying to build up a macro-structure of the whole text (the gist) based on careful reading of as little of the text as possible. This is why skimming does not lend itself to the construction of numerous test items. A study of samples of EAP reading tests such as TEEP, or IELTS (see Weir et al 2000) reveals that skimming does not feature at all in items in those tests and when it does as in TOEFL (1991) and UETESOL (1996), it is realised in only a single item asking a question such as 'What is the main idea of this passage?'

Skimming requires the creation of a skeletal text level structure and in particular a decision as to the superordinate macro-proposition (Kintsch and van Dijk 1978) that encapsulates the meaning of a text. However, because of the rapid and selective nature of the processing involved it is unlikely to result in a detailed meaning representation of the whole text, a meaning representation that includes the relationships between all the macro-propositions and their relative importance. To arrive at a comprehensive and accurate text level structure, careful, rather than merely expeditious, global reading is necessary.

One can locate macro-propositions in two ways:

a. By selective eye movements which attempt to locate sentences within the text stating the major issues (beginning of paragraph, sections in bold type, etc.)

b. By evaluating propositions as they come in, in order to identify those which start a new meaning structure rather than those that are subservient to or supportive of an ongoing structure.

Skimming would seem to be heavily reliant on the first and careful reading (see below) on the second.

Search reading

Urquhart and Weir (1998) argue that in search reading, the reader is sampling the text, which can be words, topic sentences or important paragraphs, to extract information on a predetermined topic. The reader may draw on formal knowledge of text structure to assist in this search for information on pre-specified macro-propositions (Trabasso and Bouchard 2002).

Pugh (1978:53) states that in search reading:

> ... the reader is attempting to locate information on a topic when he is not certain of the precise form in which the information will appear ... the reader is not pursuing a simple visual matching task (as in scanning), but rather needs to remain alert to various words in a similar semantic field to the topic in which he is interested. It is true that the visual activity involved is similar to scanning in many ways. However, the periods of close attention to the text tend to be more frequent and of longer duration and, since information is more deeply embedded in the text, there is more observance of the way in which the author structures his subject matter and, hence, the linearity and sequencing. Information about the structure of the text may be used to assist in the search.

Pugh's definition is echoed in Guthrie and Mosenthal's (1987) model of search reading. Their model consists of five components: (1) 'goal formation' – this involves reading the question and encoding its features to guide the search; (2) 'category selection' – the reader selects suitable sections or subsections of the text for examination; (3) 'information extraction' – the reader, on extraction of information, makes a judgement as to whether it fulfils his/her search goal; (4) 'integration' – the reader integrates the extracted information with those parts previously examined or with his/her prior knowledge; (5) 'recycling' – the reader makes a judgement regarding the adequacy of the extracted information in fulfilling the search goal. If it does not, the reader recycles through the preceding processes until the search task is completed.

For Urquhart and Weir (1998) search reading involves locating information on predetermined topics so the reader does not have to establish an overall representation of the whole of the text as in skimming. The reader wants only the relevant information necessary to answer the set questions on a text in a test. In cognitive terms it represents a shift from generalised attention to more focused attention.

The start of the process is to look for related vocabulary in the semantic field indicated by the task/item. Once the required information to answer a question has been quickly and selectively located, careful reading will take over and this may involve establishing propositional meaning at the sentence level, enriching propositions through inferencing, and it may require the reader to integrate information across sentences. In the test situation the wording of the questions does not usually allow the candidate simply to match question prompts to text and so lexical access is more demanding than in scanning tasks.

Search reading involves the different aspects of meaning construction up to and including the level of building a mental model, but it does not require the creation of a text level structure. The relative importance of the information in the text (micro vs macro-proposition) is not an issue: all that matters is that the information has a bearing on the knowledge that is sought.

In a test where the information sought is gleaned from within a single sentence, this might be best described as search reading local. Where information from more than one sentence is required to produce an answer then it is best viewed as search reading global.

Scanning

Scanning involves reading selectively, to achieve very specific reading goals. It may involve looking for specific words/phrases, figures/percentages, names, dates of particular events or specific items in an index at the local word level. It is a perceptual recognition process which is form based and relies on accurate decoding of a word or string of words.

Rosenshine (1980) defines it as involving recognition and matching. The main feature of scanning is that any part of the text which does not contain the pre-selected word, symbol or group of words is passed over. A low level of attention is accorded until a match or approximate match is made. The reader will not necessarily observe the author's sequencing by following the text in a linear way.

Here, very few components of our model are involved. Suppose at the lowest level, the goal has been set as scanning a text to find a reference to a particular author. It is arguable that only a limited amount of lexical access is required. Presumably little or no syntactic processing needs to be involved; no checking of coherence is necessary and no attempt is made to build a macro-structure. There is usually no need even to complete the reading of the sentence, or to integrate the word into the structure of preceding text. As a result, scanning usually involves none of the different aspects of meaning building beyond the clause that we have identified in our model.

Careful reading

A brief description of careful reading at the local and global levels was provided when we discussed the goal setter earlier. We will focus here on the different aspects of meaning building upon which this reading type depends and will distinguish between processing that takes place at the local and at the global level.

Careful local reading

Careful local reading involves processing at the decoding level until the basic meaning of a proposition is established. Some local inferencing might be required to build a mental model at the enriched sentence level. However, it does not entail integrating each new piece of local information into a larger meaning representation.

Careful global reading

The defining features of careful global reading are that the reader attempts to handle the majority of information in the text; that the reader accepts the writer's organisation, including what the writer appears to consider to be important parts; and that the reader attempts to build up a macro-structure on the basis of the majority of the information received.

Careful global reading may draw upon most of the components of the model. The reader decides to read the text with a relatively high level of attention as for example for study of a chapter or chapters in a core textbook at undergraduate level or some similar purpose. The goal setter sets this attention level not just for the reading operation but also for the monitoring that accompanies it. The reader would normally begin at the beginning of the text and continue through to the end, employing the processes detailed in the central core of the model above: integrating new information into a mental model and perhaps finally creating a discourse level structure for the text where appropriate to the reader's purpose.

A more demanding level of processing in careful reading would be required when establishing how ideas and details relate to each other in the whole text. The reader not only has to understand the micro- and macro-propositions but also how they are interconnected. This will require close and careful reading and perhaps even a rereading of the whole text or at least those parts of it relevant to the purpose in hand. Most of the processing components listed in the central core of our model above will be required in this 'reading to learn' activity where there is new as well as given information to be understood.

Cohen and Upton (2006:17) describe this 'reading to learn' process. With reference to the new iBT TOEFL, they state that:

> . . . according to the task specifications (ETS, 2003): Reading to learn is seen as requiring additional abilities beyond those required for basic comprehension. Reading to learn questions assess specific abilities that contribute to learning including the ability to recognise the organisation and purpose of a text, to distinguish major from minor ideas and essential from nonessential information, to conceptualise and organise text information into a mental framework, and to understand rhetorical functions such as cause-effect relationships, compare-contrast relationships, arguments, and so on . . .

In the real world, the reader often has to combine and collate macro-propositional information from more than one text, for example in writing assignments in educational courses or writing an article for publication in a professional journal (Carson 2001). As we noted above in the section on *Creating an intertextual representation*, careful reading of several texts in a related field is likely to require additional processing beyond that required for understanding a single text in terms of macro-structural organisation (Lacroix 1999 and Unaldi forthcoming). The need to combine rhetorical and contextual information across texts would seem to place the greatest demands on processing of all our reading types. This view is supported by the work of Britt and Sommer (2004), Enright et al (2000), Goldman (1997), Perfetti (1997), Perfetti et al (1999), Spivey and King (1989), and Stahl et al (1996).

Leaving aside for the moment the cognitive load imposed by the complexity of the text(s) employed in the test, one might argue that difficulty in processing is in large part a function of which levels of processing in our model are required by a particular type of reading. This is an issue on which we do not have much empirical evidence (though see Ashton 1998).

The single weighting given to items testing expeditious local reading in the Cambridge Main Suite ESOL examinations would seem to accord with the idea that double weighted items which test global understanding of main ideas or text structure are usually more difficult in terms of processing and thus deserve the higher weighting (see Chapter 4 for details of weighting).

Rose (2006) conducted research during the review of FCE and CAE into the amount of time needed for candidates to complete a careful global reading multiple-choice item and an expeditious local multiple-matching item. She found that a careful reading MCQ needed more time to answer than an expeditious multiple-matching item, thus supporting the view that it was worth more than one mark because of the greater amount of processing time required.

The issue of interest for language testers is how these levels of processing and types of reading relate to different stages in language proficiency. This leads us back to a central concern: the identification of different stages of proficiency in L2 reading. We will next apply our model of reading types and associated cognitive processes to a selection of Reading papers from the Cambridge ESOL Main Suite examinations in English (see Appendix A for copies of the Reading test tasks). These cover a range of levels from A2 to C2. A retrospective analysis of such a set of examinations, which have a long pedigree and the support of considerable expertise and experience in pedagogy, is a good basis for attempting to ground our theory in practice.

Our findings must of course remain subjective judgements in that they are based only on the expertise and experience of the group of expert judges who examined these tasks. They need to be supplemented by an analysis of candidates' answers, and interviews with candidates – or ideally protocol analysis of students thinking aloud while doing the exam. The need for the latter to check the judgements of testing experts is clearly shown by the work of Weir, Green, Hawkey and Unaldi (2008) in their work on the cognitive processing involved in completing IELTS reading items and that of Cohen and Upton (2006) on the new TOEFL reading tasks.

Types of reading and cognitive processing: Cambridge ESOL practice

In relation to levels, Cambridge ESOL examinations are aligned with the Common European Framework of Reference for Languages (CEFR). Establishing this relationship is explored fully in Chapter 7 so we will content ourselves with a brief description here. The CEFR refers to six levels (Council of Europe 2001) for L2 learners of English. A1 and A2 levels describe the ability to read very slowly basic or straightforward information in a known area i.e., very simple sentences or very short predictable texts. B1 level describes the ability to comprehend texts that consist of familiar or high-frequency everyday language; 'understand routine information and articles, and the general meaning of non-routine information within a familiar area' and that scanning for specifics introduces a variety in reading purpose and style and speed of reading for the first time. At B2 level, readers start focusing on the content of texts (e.g. the ideas presented, the writer's attitude, etc.). From level B2 readers are also expected to be able to process text quickly as well as efficiently i.e. expeditious as well as careful reading is expected. C1 and C2 levels characterise more mature, proficient readers. Such readers are able to process more abstract texts with structurally and semantically complex language. At C2 the expectation is that candidates can understand everything they read 'including the finer points of complex texts . . . complex ideas expressed in complex language' (ALTE 'Can Do' statements, Council of Europe 2001:251–256).

In many ways these specifications are extremely limited in their characterisation of reading ability at the different levels and we need to be more explicit for testing purposes (see Weir 2005a). To extend understanding of these developmental stages, we will examine some examples of Reading papers in Cambridge ESOL Main Suite English examinations (see Appendix A for copies of these) from three perspectives:

- The types of reading demanded at each of the stages.
- How well calibrated the cognitive processing demands made upon candidates are in the design of the tasks and items. Is there a shift from tasks that focus on decoding to tasks that focus on meaning building?
- The cognitive load imposed by relative text complexity at each stage. In Chapter 4 we will provide a detailed analysis of this issue from the perspective of the contextual parameters that obtain at these levels but some reference will also be made in this chapter to these contextual parameters to the extent that they impact directly on our discussion of levels of cognitive processing.

The Cambridge ESOL Main Suite Reading papers used for the analyses in Tables 3.1 to 3.3 below are located at Appendix A and the reader is referred to them there to avoid unnecessary duplication. They are of course only a small sample and any conclusions drawn in the analysis below must be seen as tentative.

Additionally the analysis is based on the opinions of a group of expert judges only and findings will need to be more firmly grounded in the future by having students take the various Reading tests and complete verbal protocols on their experiences. An example of such research on IELTS is provided by Weir et al (2008) who comment also on the complexities and time consuming nature of such procedures.

Types of reading across Cambridge ESOL levels

Table 3.1 Types of reading tested at levels A2 to C2 in our examples of Cambridge ESOL Main Suite Reading papers

	KET A2	PET B1	FCE B2	CAE C1	CPE C2
Careful Reading Local Understanding propositional meaning at clause and sentence level	√	√	▓	▓	√
Careful Reading Global Comprehend across sentences Comprehend overall text Comprehend overall texts	√ ▓ ▓	√ ▓ ▓	√ (√) ▓	√ √ ▓	√ √ √
Expeditious Reading Local Scanning or search reading	▓	√	√	√	▓
Expeditious Reading Global Skim for gist Search reading	▓ ▓	▓ √	▓ (√)	▓ (√)	▓ ▓

√ *indicates a clear coverage of this type of reading*
(√) *indicates only a limited coverage of this type of reading (1 or 2 items per part)*
shaded area indicates non-coverage of this type of reading

KET

In **KET** most of the tasks require only careful reading at the local level to establish propositional meaning.

- Part 1: careful reading local: mainly matching similar words.
- Part 2: careful reading local: identifying appropriate lexical items.
- Part 3: careful reading local: Questions 11–15 involve matching sentences at the local level as each sentence is unrelated to the one before or the one that follows. Careful reading global: Questions 16–20

involve connecting one sentence to another; involve the candidate in ongoing mental representation of the text as this consists of a series of connected sentences. The candidate has to integrate the new pieces of local information into a larger meaning representation, and so this task extends into careful reading at the global level.

- Part 4: careful reading local: understanding a short article (occasional global items, for example item 24).
- Part 5: careful reading local: reading and identifying appropriate structural word.

In Part 4, there is an understanding between tester and candidate that the questions will follow the sequence of the text. Nevertheless, when candidates have to check on the 'doesn't say' answers, they may feel the need to read the whole of the text with a high level of attention. In seeking confirmation that the correct answer has been chosen, candidates may well resort to several readings of the whole text in order to reassure themselves that the question cannot be answered by information from anywhere in the text.

PET

In **PET** the candidate has to cope with a wider range of both expeditious and careful reading types at both the local and the global level.

- Part 1: careful reading local: reading real-world notices and other short texts.
- Part 2: expeditious reading global.
- Part 3: expeditious reading local.
- Part 4: careful reading global.
- Part 5: careful reading local.

Expeditious reading appears in Parts 2 and 3 with an emphasis on scanning which tends to be the least demanding cognitively of the reading types discussed above, but also some search reading is intended in Parts 2 and 3. Lack of control on time spent on each part, however, may mean that some candidates use careful reading rather than expeditious reading when completing these items. If we cannot control the time candidates spend on each part of the Reading paper, we cannot be sure how the candidate approaches the task (see discussion of expeditious reading in section on *Types of reading and the processing model* above).

FCE

In **FCE** the tasks focus on careful reading at the global level and expeditious reading mainly at the local level.

- Part 1: careful reading global: tests the candidate's ability to identify main points in a text, involving inferencing in a number of questions and one (item 8) relating to a large section of the text.
- Part 2: careful reading global: tests global comprehension and candidates' ability to follow text development usually within the paragraph.
- Part 3: expeditious local and occasional global reading: tests candidates' ability to locate specific information in a text or a group of texts.

Expeditious reading appears in Part 3, this time with a number of items focusing on more complex search reading rather than simply scanning. What makes this part more demanding cognitively is that items are not sequenced according to the presentation of information in the passage; thus more text needs to be processed than in the similar task in PET where the order of items matches the sequencing of information in the text.

Lack of control over the amount of time candidates spend on each part, however, may mean that some candidates are given the opportunity to use careful reading rather than expeditious reading in completing these items.

CAE

In **CAE** the tasks focus on global reading to comprehend main ideas and the overall text. Expeditious reading through searching (rather than scanning) is tested in Part 4 but the items are mainly set at the local level.

- Part 1: careful reading global: comprehend main ideas.
- Part 2: careful reading global: comprehend overall text.
- Part 3: careful reading global: comprehend main ideas.
- Part 4: expeditious local: search reading.

What puts clear water between this level and FCE is the need in CAE Part 2 to comprehend the information structure of the whole text. In the gapped task at FCE sentences only are deleted and only understanding of the immediate context is typically required to insert each sentence into the appropriate gap. The ability to comprehend the whole of the text in CAE and how its parts interrelate is seen to be more difficult than understanding individual propositions and their relationship to the immediate context. CAE Part 2 requires the candidate to apply the processes at the different levels shown in the model, to recognise macro- and micro-propositions, to establish the hierarchical links between a macro-proposition and the micros that depend upon it and to establish text structure on the basis of links between macro-propositions.

Gapped-text items in CAE and CPE (see Appendix A CAE paper Part 2 for an example of a whole text level task and CPE paper Part 3) are expected to require a substantial amount of processing by the candidates. Ashton (2003:128) notes '. . . the task has been designed to test a candidate's ability to understand text structure, and its successful completion is believed to involve candidates in performing at "whole text" level rather than processing identifiable chunks of text in order to answer each item in a set . . . The general perception among test users is that the gapped-text task type is more difficult than the other item types on the CAE Reading paper'. Candidate perceptions can be corroborated with empirical findings. Ashton (1998:98) notes in relation to testing at the whole text level: 'Rasch analysis applied to the six versions of the CAE reading subtest has revealed that the gapped-text task type is on average approximately one logit more difficult on the UCLES common scale than the other task types used in the test.'

In the expeditious reading task example we looked at (see Appendix A CAE Part 4), although the candidate has to search for the information rather than directly match through scanning, nearly all the answers are contained in single sentences with the possible exceptions of items 31 and 32. At this level, in an examination which can be used for university entrance purposes, the ability to locate global information expeditiously might be expected (see Weir, Devi, Green, Hawkey, Maniski, Unaldi and Zegarac 2006).

CPE

With the exception of the first task, **CPE** involves careful reading at the global level.

- Part 1: careful reading local: understand sentence.
- Part 2: careful reading global: comprehension of main ideas.
- Part 3: careful reading global: comprehension of overall text.
- Part 4: careful reading global: comprehension of main ideas.

The first task appears anomalous as the focus is restricted to the process of establishing meaning within the sentence which does not feature as a task focus in any of the other examinations after PET. Koda (2005) argues that processing at the lexical level predominates among low level proficiency learners whereas the reading of higher level learners is marked by information integration and conceptual manipulation. She notes the latter readers are sensitive to global text organisation whereas the former are sensitive to local linguistic constraints. Part 1 would appear to be somewhat anomalous at this level in terms of the processing demands it puts on candidates.

Despite concern over a potential lack of fit of these items with the construct of reading as measured by the rest of the paper, their popularity with teachers and the fact that the rest of the paper is machine scoreable led to their retention in a more contextualised form after the CPE revision in 2002. Ashton (2003:137) describes how:

> Feedback at all stages in the revision process had indicated that, despite the conflict with the construct of reading, items testing advanced lexical knowledge should be retained on the paper. The inclusion of discrete items testing lexical knowledge was endorsed by 96% of the participants in the first round of consultative seminars in autumn 1994.

This is a position examination boards are often likely to find themselves in as they try to achieve an acceptable balance between validity and practicality as well as addressing stakeholder wishes.

It is of course possible to establish high Rasch values for these items and so meet this requirement for C2 level items. Weir and Milanovic (2003:128) note: 'Generally speaking, items focusing on the same piece of text can be written to be easy or hard in multiple-matching and multiple-choice item sets.' This is often achieved through manipulating task difficulty by having candidates choose between two very close distractors in the multiple-choice items. The difficulty then lies in deciding between the options and not in the meaning of the word itself in the context.

Eddie Williams (personal communication) adds a note of caution from a language oriented as against a skills based perspective:

> . . . if such an item is linguistically difficult an argument may be made for retaining it. Given the uncertainty surrounding cognitive processes in reading, the Cambridge Main Suite examinations cannot be driven solely by levels of cognitive processing, with no attention to "levels of language". In the final analysis, these are language exams, not cognitive processing assessments.

There is no testing of expeditious global reading at CPE which, given its use for certification purposes in respect of university entry and the requirement of being able to read quickly and effectively for academic study, may need some attention.

Inclusion of expeditious items was seriously considered during the 2002 CPE revision but concerns were expressed about the practicality of having a separate section of the paper which would be performed under strict time constraints and employing a constructed response format.

The revision team concluded:

> Expeditious reading: skimming for gist, search reading or scanning for specifics are not catered for in the 2002 revision. Due consideration was given to the possibility of including items testing these strategies but it was not possible given the late introduction of these ideas into the revision process to investigate the possibility of testing expeditious reading empirically. Arguably it is these strategies that are critical for university and advanced study. Further research needs to be carried out into the possibilities of operationalising the testing of expeditious reading (Ashton 2003:146).

The CPE Reading paper contains no task which requires processing inter-textually, i.e. across multiple texts. However, there is a reading task currently located in the *Use of English paper*, where the candidate has to process and integrate information from two whole texts to form a summary of both (see Use of English paper Part 5 item 5 in Appendix A, CPE Handbook (UCLES 2008) and Weir and Milanovic 2003:251–260). Once again, the positioning of this task was considered at length in the 2002 revision but at the time the practicality of having all items on the Reading paper machine scoreable prevailed. Moving this task to the Reading paper and moving the selective deletion gap filling task (current Part 1) into the Use of English paper seems sensible and could be considered in a future revision. Comprehension and integration of main ideas across texts in the Reading paper would establish a clear distinction between CPE and CAE in this skill.

Summary: types of reading across Cambridge ESOL levels

There does seem to be a general progression of **careful reading** tasks in the Main Suite with careful local items only at KET and careful global items appearing for the first time at PET along with local items. At FCE, only careful global items are tested plus mainly local expeditious in one task. At CAE, as well as global items that require the identification of main ideas, candidates have to understand the whole of the text in one of the tasks. At CPE, Part 1 is somewhat of an anomaly as candidates are presented with 18 careful local items which appear to focus on accessing linguistic knowledge at the word and sentence level. The other three parts test careful global comprehension requiring integration of information and understanding at the whole text level.

Skilled readers are more likely to recognise changes of topic in a text; enrich their comprehension by bringing in general knowledge of the world or topic knowledge, and build meaning at global (text) level rather than just at local (sentence) level. It may be that from the C1 level upwards we should expect readers to be able to answer items which test understanding of how ideas in a text relate to each other. From the C2 level we should also be expecting candidates to integrate ideas from more than one text (see Weir et al 2006).

It is argued in the literature that unskilled poor L2 readers are unable to adjust their processing modes when confronted with different purposes for reading (Koda 2005). It thus seems appropriate that at KET level (A2) the reader only has to process information carefully. The high incidence of expeditious items at PET level (B1) might be of some concern at this early stage but with the complexity of text being relatively simple (see Table 3.3 below) it appears appropriate in terms of cognitive load for B1 level. Given the fact that no time limits are placed on individual tasks, the likelihood is that they may be processed carefully in any case.

Oakhill and Garnham (1988:6) view skilled readers as being able to adjust their types of reading in line with the text they have to process and with what they wish to get out of it, e.g. skimming a newspaper versus carefully processing a refereed journal article in your field of study. They note that skilled readers will do this 'efficiently'. Block (1986:465–6) notes that a number of studies suggest that skilled L2 readers are better able to monitor their comprehension and select appropriate strategies flexibly according to type of text and purpose. This suggests that requiring candidates to adjust modes from task to task is appropriate when testing more advanced L2 candidates.

In the CEFR there is no mention of different modes being applicable at levels A1–B1. However, the ALTE 'Can Do' specification (see Chapter 1) clearly states that at the B2 level readers are expected to be able to 'scan texts for relevant information, understand detailed information and grasp the main point of a text'. The expectation of a candidate at the C1 level is that they 'can read quickly enough to cope with an academic course', i.e. they can cope with expeditious global as well as careful global reading demands, adapting their reading style to meet different reading purposes. The absence in our examples (see Appendix A) of tasks which test expeditious global reading at CPE and the limited number of items of this type at CAE and FCE requires some attention.

Cognitive processing across Cambridge ESOL levels

We have examined the types of reading that are represented in the different stages of the Cambridge examinations. We will now turn to the central core of our model and look more closely at the level(s) of processing that appear to be necessary to cope with these types of reading in the various parts of each examination.

In Table 3.2 below we have attempted to summarise those parts of the central processing core that *appear* to be elicited by our sample of tasks from the Cambridge ESOL Main Suite examinations from KET (A2) to CPE (C2) (see Appendix A for copies of these tasks). These are of course only subjective judgements based on the expertise and experience of the group of expert judges who examined this sample of tasks. The need to verify these judgements by collecting verbal protocols of candidates taking these tasks is clearly shown by the work of Weir et al (2008) in their work on the cognitive processing involved in completing IELTS reading items and that of Cohen and Upton (2006) on the new TOEFL reading tasks.

Details of the progression in cognitive processing demands as one moves up the levels are indicated by our analysis of these levels in each of the parts of the tests below.

Table 3.2 Cognitive processing at A2 to C2 in our examples of Cambridge ESOL Main Suite Reading papers

	KET A2	PET B1	FCE B2	CAE C1	CPE C2
Word recognition	√	√	√	√	√
Lexical access	√	√	√	√	√
Parsing	√	√	√	√	√
Establishing propositional meaning	√	√	√	√	√
Inferencing	(√)	√	√	√	√
Building a mental model	(√)	√	√	√	√
Creating a text level structure				√	√
Creating an organised representation of several texts					√

√ indicates a whole task or numerous items in a task(s) elicit this type of processing
(√) indicates only a limited coverage of this level of processing
shading indicates this type of processing does not occur at all in a paper

KET

Most items are at the decoding level. Occasional inferencing and a few items (16–20) require integration of information across sentences.

- Part 1: Word recognition, lexical access and establishing propositional meaning at sentence level. The alternative options have to be read too – so there is an element of semantic matching. Sometimes the matching of similar words may require some local inferencing as is perhaps the case in Question 3, where an inference may be needed in order to link 'mechanic' with 'cars'.

- Part 2: Accessing word meaning as well as syntactic parsing and extracting propositional information. An element of ongoing mental representation may be present and may on occasion help candidates find the correct answer. In Question 8, for example, the overall context together with a degree of local inferencing will guide the candidate to option A.

- Part 3: Although functional appropriacy at the sentence level is the focus of these items, understanding of syntactic structure may help candidates eliminate the wrong options. Items 16–20 require integration of information across two options.

- Part 4: Establishing propositional meaning at the clause and sentence level. Inferences are sometimes required (see item 25).

- Part 5: Establishing propositional meaning at the clause and sentence level. Candidates will make use of syntactic parsing to establish basic meaning.

PET

- Part 1: Candidates establish propositional meaning at the sentence level in order to understand the meaning of a range of short, discrete texts. Inferences are sometimes required (see items 2 and 4).
- Part 2: Selective scrutiny of the text is involved for each item as the candidate looks for words in the same semantic field as those in the question. When a potential match to the item is located an ongoing meaning representation is required as successful matching is dependent on a configuration of requirements across sentences in a short paragraph. The information is for the most part explicitly stated, but because several pieces of information are being sought at one time to make a decision on the correct answer, considerable demands are made upon working memory, thus increasing task difficulty.
- Part 3: Implicit in the presentation of questions before the passage is an assumption by the testers that expeditious reading will be encouraged. The intention is not for students to read carefully, serially and incrementally, i.e. drawing on most elements of our processing model, although as the task is not constrained by time limits there is no guarantee that this does not happen. You do not have to read everything to answer the questions and this guidance is conveyed through exam reports, a teacher resources website, and teachers' seminars. Having the questions follow the order of the text makes the task easier as it assists the candidate in locating the necessary information more easily within the text and the candidate does not have to process text already covered in previous questions. The disadvantage of this is that it rather compromises cognitive validity (in the interests of making the task easier) in that in real life the points a reader wanted to check would not follow text order. Scanning is involved for exact matches in a number of items (e.g. items 14 and 16) but otherwise the reader has to look for equivalent words in the text, e.g. inexperienced writers – new writers, members of the Society – anyone belonging to the Society, regular events – monthly exhibitions. The task requires occasional inferences (see item 13 where candidates have to understand that 'to see a selection of articles . . . follow the links on this website' means that articles are available on the internet).
- Part 4: Building a mental model is usually required (see item 21) but some questions can be answered within a sentence. In the latter case, within-sentence processing is less demanding because there is no

necessity to make connections to build a wider meaning representation as happens in building a mental model. Items which focus on understanding attitude, opinion and writer purpose may require integrating information across longer stretches of the text. Item 25 requires candidates to choose one out of four possible summaries of the text. Item 21 refers to the purpose of the text so candidates should read through the whole text first before answering it.

- Part 5: Focus on lexical access and syntactic parsing. Establishing propositional meaning at the clause and sentence level.

In terms of processing there is an increase from KET in the number of items requiring integration of information across sentences and inferences are sometimes necessary to answer questions.

FCE

- Part 1: Usually requires integration of new information sometimes across large sections of the text (see item 8). Many of the answers require the reader to form inter-propositional connections (e.g. items 2, 3 & 5).
- Part 2: Requires integration of new information. No need to create a text level structure because sentences rather than paragraphs are being inserted. In order to complete the task successfully, candidates need to use the clues provided by, for example, discourse markers, understand how examples are introduced and changes of direction signalled. This often needs to be combined with inferencing, e.g. in item 10, where candidates need to realise that putting up tents in muddy fields is not seen as glamorous (see also items 9, 12, 13).
- Part 3: Mostly only requires understanding sentence level propositions to answer the questions once the information has been located (see however item 18). May involve inferencing in those items which test understanding of attitudes or opinions (see item 21).

In terms of processing there is a substantial increase over PET in the proportion of items dependent on the successful integration of information between sentences and many of these require inferencing.

CAE

- Part 1: Mostly integration of new information involved. A number of items require inferencing within (item 2) and between sentences (see items 3 and 4).
- Part 2: Candidates benefit from reading the whole of the text to see how it fits together. Involves integration of new information as well as establishing a text level representation. This latter level of processing is

the second highest in our model above. It is more difficult to understand the whole text and how its parts interrelate, than to just understand individual main ideas; rereading is likely to be required to complete the task. This example also involves reading to understand unknown information. At CAE/CPE, the ALTE specification for C1 upwards includes academic reading ability, hence texts need to contain new information in common with all texts used at university.

- Part 3: Tests candidates' detailed understanding of a text. Candidates may be able to answer some items by using propositional information at the sentence level only but others require the integration of information, especially those targeted at the opinions and attitudes expressed in a text. A number of items require inferencing (see item 16).

- Part 4: Tests candidates' ability to locate specific information in a text. Information to answer the question is usually located in a single sentence, so candidates only need to establish sentence level propositional meaning with the exception of items 31 and 32.

In terms of cognitive processing, the activities at CAE are in many parts similar to those at FCE. Both have a large number of items that require the reader to integrate information across sentences. The key difference is in Part 2 at CAE which is dedicated to building a text level representation. This level of processing is no longer required in the updated FCE (December 2008 onwards) where candidates are now only required to insert sentences, rather than paragraphs, into a gapped text.

CPE

- Part 1: Tests the candidates' sentence level processing abilities. Candidates at most only have to establish propositional meaning within the sentence where the lexical item has been deleted. The task appears to be somewhat anomalous in the highest level examination in the suite.

- Part 2: Tests the ability of the candidates to integrate information and select the relevant macro-propositional content from the text. Inferencing required within a sentence (see 21 & 22) and across sentences (e.g. 24) for a number of items.

- Part 3: Candidate benefits from reading the whole of the text to see how it fits together. The task involves integration of new information into an ongoing meaning representation as well as, albeit indirectly, establishing a text model. It also involves reading to learn unknown information with this particular example. At CAE/CPE reading to learn must be there, hence the need to expose candidates to new information they are unlikely to have previously encountered.

- Part 4: Tests candidates' ability to integrate information and select the relevant macro-propositional content from a longer text than used in

Part 2. The longer text is likely to place greater demands on the cognitive processing since more information will contribute to the mental model that the candidate has to carry forward and that information will be linked in more complex ways.

In terms of cognitive processing, the activities at CPE appear very similar to those at CAE. Both have a large number of items that require the reader to integrate information across sentences and also a part dedicated to building a text level structure.

As mentioned earlier, in the CPE *Use of English* paper there is a summary task where candidates have to integrate meaning across texts (see Appendix A for a sample task). Our earlier review of the literature on processing suggests that this is likely to require a higher level of processing than all the reading tasks we have reviewed so far.

Summary: cognitive processing across Cambridge ESOL levels

The cognitive psychology literature tends to focus on learners at two ends of a skilled and unskilled spectrum – but how does this help to define intervening levels in the CEFR? The literature would seem to suggest that in general there is a progression in ability to cope with lower to higher level processing in the central core of our model as L2 reading ability develops.

Examinations in the Main Suite would seem to follow the order of difficulty in cognitive processing that is suggested by our model and the literature. The attentional resources of a reader are finite and, in the early stages of L2 development (A2 level candidates), one might expect a large part of those resources to be diverted towards more low-level considerations concerning the linguistic code. No matter what the L1, decoding processes are reliant upon recognising not only letters but letter clusters, grapheme–phoneme correspondence (GPC) relationships and whole words. Decoding at the level of form is bound to be problematic for the low level L2 reader – only assisted by the extent to which there are cognates in L2. Whereas in L1 word recognition is usually highly automatic for practised readers, new form–meaning relationships need to be set up gradually for L2 and only slowly become automatised.

Eddie Williams (personal communication) adds a rider:

> There has been some debate about the L1/L2 distinction in recent years. Many people (especially in Africa and Asia) read little or nothing in their L1, and quite a lot, or even exclusively, in their L2. Furthermore, global mobility and migration means many people have "bilingualism as a first language". What is crucial in speed of word recognition is whether readers are highly practised in reading a particular language or not (and

this is a function of how much reading they do in that language, not necessarily whether it is their first language chronologically).

The effort of decoding makes considerable cognitive demands on the less skilled reader and as a result is likely to become the principal focus of attention for many up to the A2 level and the main focus for tests set at these levels. There is often a failure to employ comprehension processes (e.g. using contextual information to enrich comprehension or higher level meaning building) partly because of the demands of decoding and partly because of the unfamiliar situation of reading a text where there are gaps in understanding and words and phrases are perceptually unfamiliar (see Perfetti 1985).

Textually implicit questions require the reader to combine information across sentences in a text and such questions are generally more difficult than explicit items based on a single sentence given the additional processing that is required (see Davey and Lasasso 1984). Oakhill and Garnham (1988) suggest that the less skilled reader fails to make a range of inferences in comprehension, from local links between sentences, to the way(s) the ideas in the whole text are connected. Hosenfeld (1977) likewise shows that use of inferencing strategy can discriminate between good and poor readers (see also Chamot and El-Dinary 1999).

Inferencing makes an appearance at A2 and B1 level in a few items at the sentence level but it is only at FCE (B2) and above that it begins to be tested widely and across larger areas of text. From FCE onwards, certain question types require the candidate to report not on information contained in the text but upon what that information entails. Until learners have relatively automatic processes for dealing with word recognition, lexical access and syntactic parsing, meaning-making beyond dealing with sentence level propositions is restricted. This is usually well established by the B2 level, when there is more processing capacity available in working memory for making propositional inferences, building a mental model and integrating information. The cognitive demands made on the candidate need to vary between the reading tests set at different levels. It means that a task requiring understanding of text level representation may be less suitable below a C1 level in the CEFR, (CAE in Cambridge Main Suite examinations) because of the more demanding processing required for its successful completion. Thus the ability to cope with questions requiring the candidate to develop an overall text representation of argumentative texts only takes place on reaching the C1 (CAE) level.

The highest level of processing – that required to construct an intertextual representation of several texts – comes into play at the C2 (CPE) level albeit in the *Use of English* paper. In terms of our model presented in Figure 3.1 above, we would argue that the ability to engage in such higher level processing activities is appropriate at this level of language proficiency whereas a task demanding lower level processing skills only (i.e. Part 1 in CPE) is not.

Given the limited time and space available for testing reading skills and strategies and the necessity to establish clear water between proficiency levels, it might be prudent to ensure that a reading paper at the C2 level is eliciting data on the ability to cope with the higher level cognitive processes required in forming an intertextual representation.

Table 3.3 The cognitive demands imposed by relative text complexity at each stage in our examples of Cambridge ESOL Main Suite Reading papers

	Overall number of words	Time allowed	Lexis	Grammatical structure
KET (A2)	Approximately 740–800 words	35 items with a recommended 40 minutes	Restricted to common items which normally occur in the everyday vocabulary of native speakers.	Mainly simple sentences/single independent clauses, which contain a subject and a verb, and express a complete thought.
PET (B1)	Approximately 1,460–1,590 words	35 items with a recommended 50 minutes	General vocabulary sufficient for most topics in everyday life.	Mostly simple sentences but some use of relative and other subordinate clauses.
FCE (B2)	Approximately 2,000 words	30 items administered in 60 minutes	Good range of vocabulary. Topics are addressed in detail and with precision.	A range of sentence patterns – from the simple to the complex.
CAE (C1)	Approximately 3,000 words	34 items administered in 75 minutes	Broad range of vocabulary including idiomatic expressions and colloquialisms as well as language relating to opinion, persuasion and ideas.	This level is typified by: many complex sentences; frequent use of modals; some use of ellipsis; complex approaches to referencing; use of synonymy.
CPE (C2)	Approximately 3,000 words	40 items administered in 90 minutes	Very wide range of vocabulary including idiomatic expressions and colloquialisms as well as language relating to opinion, persuasion and abstract ideas.	Most sentences are long and complex. No restriction on the types of structure employed by the text. Many examples of structures typically used for effect in writing – sentences with several subordinate clauses, for example.

So far in the discussion we have said little about the performance conditions, the contextual parameters under which reading activities take place (see table 3.3). For example the length of a text and the vocabulary in a text will affect ease of reading. The complexity of the text is a function of how such contextual parameters are realised within it. Both individually and in combination they are likely to impact on the cognitive demands imposed upon the reader. A text with high-frequency lexis is likely to be easier to process than a text of the same length on the same topic with a large number of low frequency lexical items. A shorter text is likely to be easier to process than a significantly longer text *mutatis mutandis*. A full discussion of these parameters is presented in Chapter 4 but the calibration of a number of the key parameters affecting cognitive load across Main Suite levels is relevant here and is discussed next.

KET

The cognitive load imposed by the texts is relatively low, thanks to short sentence length, simple sentence structure, simple conceptual relationships within and between sentences and the familiar nature of the vocabulary used.

PET

Again lexis is familiar and structures mainly simple and easy to parse. Propositional load is quite low and inter-sentence relationships are quite simple.

FCE

The cognitive load is increased by the use of a broader range of vocabulary, some of which may be unknown to the candidate or less familiar, sentence structure and propositional content is more complex and text length is greater. The range of patterns from simple to complex at FCE as against mostly simple sentences at PET, and total text lengths amounting to 2,000 words as opposed to around 1,500 at PET add to the increase in cognitive demands between these two adjacent levels in the Main Suite.

CAE

The cognitive load in the parts testing careful reading for main ideas (Parts 1 and 3) is also increased by the use of more complex passages and a broader range of source materials than at FCE. This complexity is evidenced in:

- A broader range of vocabulary including idiomatic expressions and colloquialisms as well as language relating to opinion, persuasion and ideas, some of which may be unknown to the candidate or less familiar. There are also a number of quite low frequency words.
- The prevalence of more complex grammatical structures as opposed to a spread of patterns from simple to complex at FCE.
- Text lengths amounting to 3,000 words as opposed to 2,000 at FCE.

Changes in these parameters add to the increase in cognitive demands between these two adjacent levels in the Main Suite.

CPE

In terms of length both CPE and CAE texts are very similar. Vocabulary range is hard to distinguish between the two except perhaps for the treatment of abstract ideas at CPE, many examples of structures typically used for effect in writing, and occurrence of the language associated with conative purpose (see Chapter 4 for a more in-depth discussion). Sentence structure may be slightly more sophisticated at CPE and occasionally longer sentences may be used which may occasion slight differences in sentence complexity.

Summary: lexical development across Cambridge ESOL levels

There would seem to be four key points to notice with regard to lexical development throughout the Cambridge ESOL examinations.

- Inevitably, as candidates progress up the levels of the Main Suite examinations, the lexical demands that are put upon them are stronger. The amount of less frequent, less well known vocabulary increases. The number and complexity of the items that they are required to understand increases by level.
- Lexis at lower levels is restricted to everyday, literal and factual language. As students advance, they are gradually expected to deal with increasingly subtle uses of the language of feelings and ideas. The senses associated with the words are less concrete and issues of polysemy may arise. More abstract texts will not be presented to candidates until levels C1 and C2 (CAE and CPE).
- Fiction beyond that written especially for L1 children normally requires a broader receptive vocabulary and this is introduced from FCE (B2) onwards taking the vocabulary beyond the familiar everyday vocabulary found at KET (A2) and PET (B1).

- From FCE (B2) upwards the extent to which the text deals with or includes content and/or language extending beyond the knowledge or personal experience of the reader increases. By CPE (C2) the candidate may be exposed to texts on any subject (see discussion of content in Chapter 4).

Summary: grammatical structures across Cambridge ESOL levels

The key points which relate to the structural resources used in reading texts in Cambridge ESOL practice are:

- A survey of the papers across the five levels shows a very clear progression in terms of sentence structure from short, simple sentences to long, complex sentences. This is mirrored in the length of the texts used as very short texts are used at KET level (A2) and increasingly longer ones are employed at higher levels.
- This structural progression does not mean that some short sentences may not pose considerable difficulty and so still have a place in higher level texts. Ellipsis and colloquial use of language may make for short sentences that are hard to process and so only appropriate at more advanced levels.
- An increasing complexity of verb forms is also noticeable in texts as we move up the Cambridge ESOL levels. The use of modals, conditionals, inversion and other structures becomes more common as the texts used in the examinations become more concerned with conveying feelings and opinions, persuading and hypothesising rather than dealing simply with information as they do at lower levels.
- As well as sentence length and verb form, referencing is an aspect of structure that becomes noticeably complex in higher level texts where a reader needs to engage in quite complex anaphoric resolution and be aware of the contribution of synonyms to text coherence.

In addition, as one progresses up the levels propositional density and the complexity of relationship between propositions increases and adds to the cognitive load.

Conclusion

This validation exercise began by considering the types of reading that take place in real life and the cognitive processes they might elicit in non-test conditions. In terms of coverage, the analysis above indicates that, in general across the suite, the range of careful and expeditious *reading types* we established in our model are covered appropriately, although there are a few anomalies at CAE (C1) and CPE (C2) that may merit consideration.

The reading types can be roughly calibrated to reflect the demands they make upon the candidate in terms of the levels of language processing upon which they draw. The processing necessary for these reading activities can be seen as a cline from decoding through the various layers of meaning construction as we move upwards through the suite.

In grading the specifications for the five levels of the suite, careful thought has been given to the relative cognitive difficulty both of the tasks and of the texts employed. Text demands are increased only gradually; and the more demanding types of reading, for example reading to comprehend the whole text and integrate information across texts, are reserved for higher levels of the suite.

The qualitative analysis of reading tasks by a group of experienced judges reported in this chapter indicates that the Cambridge ESOL Main Suite examinations correspond closely to what we know of the cognitive processes involved in reading in real life reported in the cognitive psychology literature (as represented in Figure 3.1 above). The cognitive requirements have been adequately graded in relation to the different levels of the suite. Due consideration has been given both to task demands and to the types of processing that can be deemed to be representative of performance at different stages of proficiency.

This analysis of the Cambridge ESOL Main Suite examinations does not include research evidence of readers' views of their real-life reading, or of how students set about answering reading questions in examinations. Both sets of views depend on empirical evidence – obtainable through observation, survey and protocol analysis. Such research is necessary to provide further support for the relationship between the examination and real-life reading. Weir et al (2006 and 2008) demonstrate how this might be done in relation to reading at undergraduate level in the UK and how processing in real-life reading equates with the processing of reading items in IELTS.

Next in Chapter 4 we examine how decisions taken on *task setting*, and *linguistic demands: task input & output* affect the processing and resources required to successfully complete a test task.

4 Context validity

In Chapter 3 we focused on the levels of cognitive processing activated by different types of reading. We noted that this processing is mediated by the contextual parameters of the text and task in hand. Accordingly we referred briefly to a number of salient contextual parameters in terms of the cognitive load they might add to the processing initiated by a particular reading type.

Test task performance needs to be generalisable to the wider domain of real-world tasks that candidates may be exposed to. It is, therefore, important to be able to describe target reading activities in terms of their criterial parameters (context and cognitive) and to operationalise as many of these parameters as faithfully as possible in the test task(s). Examination boards should aim for both *situational* (contextual) and *interactional* (cognitive) authenticity (covered in Chapter 3 above) in their tests (see Bachman and Palmer 1996, Douglas 2000, and O'Sullivan 2006).

If the test tasks reflect real-life tasks in terms of important contextually appropriate conditions and operations, it is easier to state what a student can and cannot do through the medium of English, or another second language. Unless steps are taken to identify and incorporate such features, it would seem imprudent to make statements about a candidate's ability to function in typical conditions in his or her future target situation.

In this chapter we examine more comprehensively the contextual parameters that are likely to influence test task performance in reading. Context validity relates to the appropriateness of both the linguistic and content demands of the text to be processed, and the features of the task setting that impact on task completion.

Full situational authenticity/context validity is not attainable within the constraints of the testing situation. For example, the time that would normally be available for careful reading (and rereading) in real life has to be constrained in a test for reasons of practicality. However, the contextual parameters operationalised in a test should mirror the criterial features of the target situation activity as far as is possible.

In Figure 4.1 below, we draw on the contextual parameters suggested by Weir (2005) as being most likely to have an impact on reading test performance. Using this framework as our informing source, we will explore the task parameters of context validity in terms of *task setting* and *linguistic demands (task input and output)*. The subsequent text follows the ordering

Figure 4.1 Aspects of context validity for reading (adapted from Weir 2005)

Context validity	
Task setting	**Linguistic demands: task input and output**
• Response method • Weighting • Knowledge of criteria • Order of items • Channel of presentation • Text length • Time constraints	• Overall text purpose • Writer–reader relationship • Discourse mode • Functional resources • Grammatical resources • Lexical resources • Nature of information • Content knowledge

of the parameters in Figure 4.1. The wider context of the conditions surrounding exam delivery is considered in Appendix C on *Administrative setting.*

We first provide a brief review of the academic research and literature relating to each parameter in the framework above. We then exemplify each parameter in relation to Cambridge ESOL examinations at different levels by reference to the language testing practitioners within the Cambridge ESOL organisation who are responsible in their day-to-day work for developing, administering and validating versions of the tests and to the large community of external professionals who are actively associated with the production and delivery of Cambridge ESOL tests. At the end of the discussion on each parameter, we summarise how different levels of Cambridge examinations vary in respect of the parameter under review and attempt to establish where the critical differences are.

Task setting

Response method

Several research studies and a number of textbooks suggest that different test response methods seem to be measuring different aspects of language ability (e.g. Alderson et al 1995; Berry 1997; Graves, Prenn, Earle, Thompson, Johnson and Slater 1991; Kintsch and Yarborough 1982; Kobayashi 1995 and Spiegel and Fitzgerald 1990). We need to examine potential formats for testing reading in terms of the types of reading they are capable of assessing and the appropriateness of the level of cognitive processing they are likely to activate. We first discuss a range of formats that have shown themselves to be potentially valid and practical and then we examine Cambridge ESOL practice in this respect.

A recurring theme in this chapter will be the potential contribution, if any, of each of the contextual parameters in helping establish criterial differences between levels in reading examinations. The preliminary pilot version of the Manual for relating language examinations to the CEFR (Council of Europe 2003) has response method in its Form A1 checklist 'General examination description'. However, as Alderson, Figueras, Kuijper, Nold, Takala and Tardieu (2004:10) note there is nothing in the CEFR (Council of Europe 2001) about *response method* and there is no indication of how response method might be related to level. It will be necessary to look at examination board practice to determine the extent to which test format can help us in making clear distinctions between levels.

We have divided the discussion below according to whether the test format involves a *selected response* or a *constructed response*. In developing a typology of potential formats for testing reading this seemed to offer the clearest organising principle. In selected responses the candidate chooses the answer from a set of options provided at the word, phrase, sentence or paragraph level, and they identify the answer by, for example, lozenging a box or encircling the option on an answer sheet which is often capable of being electronically scanned. In constructed responses candidates have to produce the answer themselves, for example by writing a word, phrase, sentence, or even a short paragraph onto an answer sheet.

Selected response formats

Multiple-choice questions/items (MCQ)

Multiple-choice tests are often favoured by examination boards not least for their ease of marking and contribution to overall test reliability (in the form of internal consistency as well as marker reliability). Such items when well constructed tend to be good discriminators between strong and weak candidates and difficulty can be increased or lessened appropriate to level through careful selection of text and manipulation of the distractors.

Multiple-choice items are acknowledged to be an appropriate vehicle in large scale assessments for testing detailed understanding of the text. They are thought to allow more sophisticated elements of text content to be tested, e.g. opinion, inference, argument, in a more controlled way than is possible through open ended formats.

There is some concern, however, about the appropriateness of MCQ for activating the higher level processing required in constructing an organised representation of the text. For example, an empirical study by Rupp, Ferne and Choi (2006:468–469) questions their value 'as composite measures of higher order reading comprehension'; i.e. their usefulness for assessing comprehension of the macro-structure of a situation model. They conclude

(p. 469) that the format may involve the reader in 'response processes that deviate significantly from those predicted by a model of reading comprehension in a non-testing context' and they hypothesise (p. 454) that: '. . . responding to MC reading comprehension questions on many standardised reading comprehension tests is much more a problem-solving process relying heavily on verbal reasoning than a fluid process of integrating propositions to arrive at a connected mental representation of a text.'

There is also concern that the mental model which would normally be created in reading a text is affected if candidates try to incorporate all the options provided in an item into an ongoing text representation. The processing that takes place in working out which option fits and which does not would bear little resemblance to the way we process texts for information in any of the types of reading in the model we presented in Chapter 3 (see Farr, Pritchard and Smitten 1990; Nevo 1989; Rupp et al 2006; and Wu Yi'an 1998 for informed research studies on the process of taking multiple-choice tests).

However, the way the question is phrased and the way in which the candidate approaches the task will make a difference to the creation of the mental model. In the CAE Handbook for Teachers (2008:9), candidates are advised to read the question and establish which part of the text contains the answer, and only then go through the multiple-choice options to see which one is correct (as opposed to reading all the options first). The Rupp et al (2006:468) study itself showed that 'test-takers first tended to apply macro-level strategies in order to have an overall idea of what the given text and the related questions were about.'

There is some evidence too from classroom practice which indicates that candidates are trained to read the text first then look at the items. The presence of exercises in published textbooks focusing on Cambridge examinations, which train students to read the text before answering the questions, would support this. Also, the fact that Cambridge ESOL presents the text first in careful reading tasks encourages the student to read the text before the questions. Evidence from test takers themselves, on how they approach the tasks, would be the most convincing and research is needed on this.

Although the response required to provide an answer to an MC item may be seen as having little connection with real-life activity, this format may come closer to activating the natural processing for careful and expeditious reading discussed in Chapter 3 in items where students have to read the whole text or relevant parts of it in order to respond correctly.

True/false items

This can be seen as a variant of MCQ and is found at the lower levels in many examinations; for example, in PET (B1) candidates read 10 statements about a longer factual/informational text and decide whether they are true or false.

It has the usual objective format advantage of not involving the candidate in writing an answer. Additionally it allows the widest sampling of content per unit of testing time.

A particular problem, however, is that with only two choices it is easier to guess the right answer so overall scoring tends to be high and there may be less discrimination between candidates across the ability range. True/false tests are normally less reliable than multiple-choice tests unless relatively more test items are used.

Right/wrong/doesn't say items

This can also be regarded as a variant of MCQ, found in the Cambridge KET (A2) examination (see Appendix A). It is also found in IELTS where this task type has two forms; the candidate is given a number of statements and asked:

- 'Do the following statements agree with the views/claims of the writer?' or
- 'Do the following statements agree with the information in the text?'

In the first variation, candidates are asked to write 'yes', 'no' or 'not given' in the boxes on their answer sheet. In the second variation, candidates are asked to write 'true', 'false' or 'not given'. The first variation of this task type aims to test the candidate's ability to recognise opinions or ideas, and is thus often used with discursive or argumentative texts. The second variation tests the candidate's ability to recognise particular points of information conveyed in the passage. It can thus be used with more factual texts.

However, if the candidate cannot determine rightness/wrongness quickly from the way the text is structured, they may be forced to read long stretches of the text repeatedly to decide whether the text contains the information or not.

Matching

Matching is a variant on multiple choice and it can take a variety of forms, all of which can be scored objectively. A range of different matching methods can be found in the Cambridge ESOL examinations.

Multiple matching

In multiple-matching tasks, candidates are required to locate a section of text where an idea is expressed, discounting ideas in other sections which may appear similar but which do not reflect the whole of the question accurately. Some of the options may be correct for more than one question, and there may be more than one correct answer to some questions. If so, the instructions to the candidates will say this.

Multiple-matching tasks conform to one of two basic patterns:

- matching two lists, e.g. people to opinions expressed, companies to services offered
- matching a list to location in the text, e.g. matching statements to sections of text where they appear.

In PET (Part 2) candidates may, for example, have to match the preferences of a number of individuals with descriptions of attractions most suitable for them to visit. (See Appendix A for details of these tasks.) Further examples of multiple-matching tasks can be found in FCE (Part 3) and CAE (Part 4).

Gapped text

A gapped-text task consists of one text from which a number of sentences (e.g. FCE), or paragraphs (e.g. CAE), have been removed and placed in jumbled order after the text together with a further sentence or paragraph which does not fit in any of the gaps and functions as an additional distractor (see Appendix A for FCE Task 2 and CAE Task 2 for examples). Candidates are required to decide from where in the text each sentence or paragraph has been removed. Each sentence or paragraph may only be used once.

There is a strong argument for the use of such gapped text tasks as a response method, especially in terms of placing more demands on cognitive processing of a text at higher levels, to distinguish reading ability at these levels from that at lower levels, where other forms of matching may be used. In CAE, for example, the reader needs to understand the whole text in order to be sure of having completed the gapped-text task correctly. The testing focuses of text structure, text cohesion and coherence require the reader to select an option which fits the text both before and after the gap. This means that it should fit not only the immediate co-text but also fit so that the text after the gap follows on smoothly. Readers need to identify not only a wide range of linguistic devices which mark the logical and cohesive development of a text, but also to understand the development of ideas, opinion and events (over the whole text) rather than the recognition of individual words (and phrases). Finding which paragraph fits into which gap in a given text may require the reader to understand how the text develops from start to finish rather than just the section of text which occurs before and after the particular gap. Again it remains for empirical research to yield an evidence-based answer to this issue.

Cohen and Upton (2006:8) provide a further example of a matching task from the task specifications for new iBT TOEFL (ETS 2003): 'For the prose summary, test takers are asked to "complete a summary of a text, one or two sentences of which are provided" by selecting three additional sentences from a list of six that express the most important ideas in the passage . . .

Distractors include ideas that either are not presented in the passage or are deemed as minor ideas.'

To conclude, matching is less subject to guessing than MCQ as there are a greater number of options to choose from. The questions set in this technique normally try to cover the important information in a text: main ideas, gist and at higher levels text representation in careful reading (see gapped text tasks at CAE Part 2 and CPE Part 3 in Appendix A), and scanning for detail and search reading for main ideas in expeditious tasks (see Appendix A PET Part 2, FCE Part 3 and CAE Part 4).

Matching is a flexible and useful format as it allows the coverage of all the reading types described in our model in Chapter 3 and all of the levels of cognitive processing as appropriate to the level of candidates being assessed.

Constructed response formats

Short answer questions (SAQ)

Short answer questions are those which require the candidates to write down answers in spaces provided on the question paper. Length may vary but generally an attempt is made to restrict them, e.g. to three words in IELTS, for reasons of marker/scoring consistency. In addition to careful reading at both global and local levels this technique lends itself to testing skimming for gist, search reading for main ideas, scanning for specific information, the expeditious reading types we identified earlier as important in Chapter 3. Testing across the range of types of reading is not normally possible with restricted techniques such as single word gap filling.

Activities such as inference, recognition of a sequence, comparison and establishing the main idea of a text, normally require the relating of sentences in different parts of the text. This can be done effectively through short answer questions where the answer has to be sought rather than being one of those provided; if a student gets the answer right, one is more certain that this has not occurred for reasons other than comprehension of the text.

The main disadvantage of short answer questions is that they involve the candidate in some writing, and there is some concern that this interferes with the measurement of the intended construct. Care is needed in the setting of items to limit the range of possible acceptable responses and the extent of writing required, for example by using words from the text as keys.

In cases where there is more debate over the acceptability of an answer, in questions requiring inferencing skills, for example, there is a possibility that the variability of answers might lead to marker unreliability. Additionally the need to deal with a plethora of possible acceptable answers complicates the scoring procedure and has serious practical disadvantages. An examination board's preference for using MCQ in such cases is understandable.

In IELTS, item writers are advised to focus Short Answer Questions on factual information as otherwise the items end up too open to be workable. This also applies to other constructed response IELTS reading tasks such as completing gaps in notes, tables, flow-charts, sentences, or summaries using words from the reading text.

Information transfer

In an attempt to avoid this potential contamination of scores by candidates having to write, examination boards often include tasks where the information transmitted verbally is transferred to a non-verbal form, e.g. by labelling a diagram or completing a chart.

Information transfer involves the transfer of information from one type of layout to another, e.g. from connected text to a table, flow-chart, diagram, gapped notes or graph. The new format may still have a verbal element (e.g. labels on a diagram, words in a table, flow chart completion) but additional meaning is provided by the visual aspect. The candidate has to construct the response from the text provided.

However, there is some concern with potential bias associated with such tasks. Not all test takers are necessarily familiar/competent with diagrammatic representations such as flow-charts or graphs and tables. However, where such text and associated processing are typical of the real-world reading activities of the candidature, as perhaps in IELTS, then they may need to be considered.

Cohen and Upton (2006:8) describe an interesting computerised version of this task type at the text representation level:

> For the schematic table, test takers must click and move sentences or phrases into a table to complete a schematic representation [of the passage]. A correctly completed table should reveal an integrated mental model of how the two dimensions fit together conceptually based on the information in the text.

Random deletion cloze and selective deletion gap filling

There is some debate on what is being tested where only single word items are deleted as in cloze ('fixed ratio' or mechanical nth word deletion) or gap filling tests ('rational' or selective deletion by the item writer of individual words); in both cases the candidate has to supply the missing word (the technique becomes a selected response format if a pool of possible answers is provided as in CPE Part 1). Is it testing the ability to recognise which form of the word is required and/or lexical knowledge?

Read (2000:106–7) notes 'there has only been a small amount of research that has investigated the rational cloze in a systematic way with second language learners'. Such investigation may be difficult to conduct as, apart from the unconscious and interrelated nature of these aspects of processing, individuals may vary in the way they process deleted items.

In tests where only single lexical items are deleted real issues of content coverage also emerge. Critics raise the question of the extent to which we can generalise from the results on this task as to how candidates might cope with broader demands on their lexical knowledge. A 20 item test of any vocabulary would only sample one word in 500 from a 10,000 word vocabulary. Read (2000:247) does point out however, that:

> . . . computer corpus software allows us to calculate the frequency and range of particular lexical items in large sets of texts more efficiently than was possible in the past. Concordance programs can rapidly assemble multiple examples of a particular word or phrase, each in its linguistic context, so that we can see its typical meaning(s), its grammatical function(s), and the other words it collocates with and so on.

Such developments will improve the basis on which items can be selected but the generalisability issue still remains.

Kintsch and Yarborough (1982) suggest cloze tests are not sensitive to macro processes but related only to micro processes. Markham's (1985) study showed that cloze procedure does not provide an adequate assessment of inter-sentential comprehension (the ability to build an accurate mental model) which led him to conclude that 'cloze procedure may not yield a valid and reliable assessment of global comprehension in second language context' (Markham 1985:423). Kobayashi (1995) provided evidence that cloze tests are more likely to measure local comprehension whereas open-ended questions can more easily target global comprehension (see also Alderson 1978). In other words, whereas other constructed formats such as short answer questions can measure the reader's global comprehension of main ideas of the text and text structure, cloze tests or selective deletion gap filling do not necessarily reflect the reader's ability to comprehend beyond the sentence. Eddie Williams (personal communication) adds the caveat that much of course depends on the actual nature of the test item whether cloze or constructed and generalization at level of format is subject to this consideration.

Cloze or single item gap filling normally measure only a limited part of what might constitute reading proficiency in terms of the model we presented in Chapter 3, namely lexical access and syntactic parsing skills. It does not usually require the higher level of processing involved in text level reading or ongoing text representation (see, however, Bensoussan and Ramraz (1984) who proposed the deletion of phrases to try to test understanding of the functions of sentences and the structure of the text as a whole). Anecdotal evidence suggests that after many candidates take single word gap filling tasks they are often unable to say what the passage was about and so the candidate's knowledge of text representation or the integration of information would not seem amenable to investigation by this procedure.

The more restricted tasks are in terms of the level of processing required to complete them, the more difficult it is to generalise from scores on the test to statements about students' reading ability in terms of the model of reading types and cognitive processes outlined in Chapter 3. It is difficult to determine what the student would have to score on these tests to be deemed to have demonstrated adequate reading ability, and to be deemed a competent reader, since such tests normally only tell us about the processing involved in careful local reading to establish propositions at the sentence level. In addition, we have no data on the other levels of processing or types of reading on which we might premise a more grounded inference. On its own, therefore, a test of the ability to replace single words is likely to be an insufficient indicator of a candidate's reading ability because of the restricted processing involved. If the purpose of a test is to sample the range of our hypothesised components of reading including inferencing, mental model building and establishing a text representation, then additional techniques to gap filling are essential.

Reading into writing

Reading into writing activities are well supported in the current research literature on writing assessment (Grabe and Stoller 2002:14) and have been used in high-stakes writing tests around the world, for example, up to 1995 in IELTS, more recently in iBT TOEFL and since the 1980s in TEEP (see Weir 1983), and in CAE and CPE Part 5 in the Use of English paper. Pollitt and Taylor (2006) make a convincing argument for this type of task as does Hughes (2003).

There is obviously a good case for providing input in writing tests where provision of stimulus texts reflects the real-life situation (e.g. in response to an informal email from a friend at the lower levels, or the writing of university assignments at the higher levels). The highest level of processing in our model discussed in Chapter 3 is where students have to integrate information across texts to develop a combined representation of the texts they have read (see Weir et al 2006 for a detailed study of undergraduate reading habits and the relationship with the IELTS Reading test). Summary or an integrated reading into writing activity would seem to be the most appropriate techniques for doing this. Such an approach also helps ensure equal access to domain knowledge among candidates and reduces the potential bias that such internal knowledge can have.

The impact of background reading as task input on the quality of L2 written production has been investigated by Lewkowicz (1997). Whilst offering students a rich source of ideas, the provision of a background text did not appear to enhance quality of writing. Moreover, there was evidence of significant 'lifting' of the input task material by students (see also Shi 2004 for discussion of this issue). Weigle summarises the findings of the Lewkowicz study in the following way: 'writers who were given a text tended to develop their ideas less than students who were not given a text, and also tended to rely heavily on the language of the source text' (2002:68).

Integrating reading with writing activities not surprisingly presents problems for markers in making decisions about what level of borrowing from these texts is permissible and in being confident about what the candidate is capable of actually producing rather than just copying.

The extent of borrowing can be reduced by ensuring that the writing task demands a significant level of input language transformation from the candidate, i.e. the candidate has to do something more than simply lift input material. Additionally, it may be necessary to make clear to candidates what is not permissible in terms of borrowing from text provided and also limits may have to be set on how much text can be quoted as in real-life rules concerned with plagiarism.

Response method: Cambridge ESOL practice

Examples of the tasks used in each of the Main Suite examinations can be found in Appendix A and some reference has already been made to a number of these. Readers may find it useful to refer to Appendix A in following the discussion below, where the various formats employed are described. The response methods utilised in the Cambridge ESOL examinations are detailed in Table 4.1 below.

The reader will note that certain task types are introduced at certain levels in the suite of examinations. For example, Right/Wrong/Doesn't say occurs in KET and True/False in PET, gapped text at the sentence insertion level at FCE, and gapped text at the paragraph level in CAE and CPE. Though not in the Reading paper, there is a task in the Use of English paper at CPE which requires candidates to integrate information from across texts. The decision on which task type occurs at which level is based on the interplay between appropriate processing demands, text complexity, exam level, and intended audience. This decision is confirmed by expert judgement through the consultative stage of test development or revision (see Chapter 7 for discussion of the complex item production process). Information on candidates, taken from live administrations, is also taken into consideration at the materials writing stage.

Alderson et al (1995) have suggested that a test should include a range of

Table 4.1 Response methods in Main Suite Reading papers

Examination papers	Response method
KET (A2) Dec 05	Total of 35 questions. The Reading paper has 5 parts. 1. Multiple Matching (5 items): candidates match 5 sentences to the appropriate notice. 2. Multiple Choice – gap filling (5 items): 5 sentences all on the same topic. Candidates fill in the gap in each sentence using one of the three options provided. 3a. Multiple Choice (5 items): candidates complete 5 short conversational exchanges. 3b. Multiple Matching (5 items): candidates complete a continuous dialogue by selecting from a list of options. 4. Multiple Choice (7 items): a text followed by 3-option Right/wrong/doesn't say or traditional 4-option MCQ. 5. Multiple-Choice Cloze (8 items): a text from which individual words have been removed. Candidates fill in the gaps using one of the 3 options provided.
PET (B1) Dec 05	Total of 35 questions. The Reading paper has 5 parts. 1. Multiple Choice (5 items): candidates are given 5 short texts comprising public notices and personal messages and asked to choose the correct answer from a set of 3 options. 2. Multiple Matching (5 items): candidates match 5 short descriptions (of individuals or groups) to the appropriate short text from a set of 8 on the same theme. 3. True/False (10 items): candidates read 10 statements about a longer factual/informational text and decide whether they are true or false. 4. Multiple Choice (5 items): a text containing attitude/opinion followed by 4-option MCQs. 5. Multiple-Choice Cloze (10 items): candidates complete a text by choosing the correct word from 4 choices; 6 or 7 lexical items and 3 or 4 grammatical items.
FCE (B2) Dec 08	Total of 30 questions. The test paper has 3 parts. 1. Multiple Choice (8 items): a text followed by 4-option MCQs. 2. Gapped Text (7 items): a text from which sentences have been removed and placed in jumbled order after the text along with one distractor. Candidates must decide from where in text the sentences have been removed. 3. Multiple Matching (15 items): a text or several short texts preceded by questions. Candidates must match prompts to elements in the text.
CAE (C1) Dec 08	Total of 34 questions. The test paper has 4 parts. 1. Multiple Choice (6 items): 3 texts on one theme. Each text has two 4-option MCQs. 2. Gapped Text (6 items): a text from which paragraphs have been removed and placed in a jumbled order after the text along with one distractor. Candidates must decide from where in the text the paragraphs have been removed. 3. Multiple Choice (7 items): a text followed by 4-option MCQs. 4. Multiple Matching (15 items): a text or several short texts preceded by statements or questions. Candidates must match prompts to elements in the text.
CPE (C2) Jun 05	Total of 40 items. The test paper has 4 parts. 1. Multiple-Choice Lexical Cloze (18 items): 3 texts each containing 6 gaps. Each gap corresponds to a word or a phrase and candidates must select the word from the 4 options given.

Table 4.1 (continued)

Examination papers	Response method
	2. Multiple Choice (8 items): 4 texts on 1 theme. Each text has two 4-option MCQs. 3. Gapped Text (7 items): a text from which paragraphs have been removed and placed in jumbled order after the text along with one distractor. Candidates must decide from where in the text the paragraphs have been removed. 4. Multiple Choice (7 items): 1 text with 4-option MCQs.

Source: Examination handbooks (KET 2005, PET 2005, FCE 2007, CAE 2008, CPE 2005).

response methods in order to ensure that all candidates will have an opportunity to perform at their best and to reduce the possibility of construct irrelevant variance resulting from the use of a single method. Some readers may therefore query the predominant use of selected as against constructed response format in the Cambridge examinations. However, it should be noted that Cambridge ESOL uses variants of selected response formats at all levels, and these variants in themselves encourage a different approach to completing the different reading tasks. For example, as we saw in Chapter 3 completing a gapped-text task (CAE/CPE) involves different levels of processing than answering a set of multiple-choice questions that may only require processing information at the sentence or between sentence level.

As an examination board, Cambridge ESOL also uses constructed response types, e.g. in BULATS (Business English Language Testing Service) and IELTS. Where such a response type is used, a rigorous system is in place: a standardised marking scheme is used together with a rater-training manual, and an online service is set up to answer rater queries (see Chapter 5).

Cambridge ESOL's view is that the main advantage of using selected response formats is that it allows a broader range of test focuses than constructed response formats. Furthermore for examination boards like Cambridge ESOL who are engaged in large scale assessments worldwide, its scoring validity and the practicality of objectively scored formats are strong arguments in its favour. An argument can also be made that getting candidates to construct their own responses would muddy the measurement by involving the skill of writing. The additional cognitive processing required to formulate the answer in writing (see Shaw and Weir 2007 Chapter 3) might be additionally unfair on candidates with very different orthographies.

Reading into writing only appears on the *Writing* or the *Use of English* papers in the Main Suite examinations. For example, at CAE level (C1), comprehension and processing of the input text or texts is essential for successful completion of the Part 1 task in the Writing paper. In addition at CPE there is a summary task based on a number of texts in the *Use of English* paper.

Though not directly contributing to a profile of reading ability in terms of the Reading paper per se, it is part of the performance on the examination as a whole on which pass fail decisions are based.

It should of course be remembered that once questions are set on a text by someone other than the intended reader, normal cognitive processing must be affected to a certain extent. The very act of reading a question/item means that reading processes in a test can never be exactly the same for the individual as processing that text in a non-test situation. It would seem that employing either selected or constructed response in a test situation risks adding to and/or interfering with the normal processing load for reading that text. But such a risk is unavoidable and test formats can only be chosen in terms of their being the most suitable available for assessing the type of reading and level of processing that is desired.

Weighting

Weighting occurs when a different number of maximum points are assigned to a test item, task or component in order to change its score value in relation to other parts of a test. Weir (2005) points out that if different parts of the test are weighted differently then the timing or marks to be awarded should reflect this and any such differential weighting should be made clear to the test takers so that they can allocate their time accordingly in the *goal setting* phase of processing (see Chapter 3 for details of this).

It may well be possible to determine differential weighting at the task level; for example extracting the main ideas from a text is perhaps more important than finding specific details, and careful reading at the global level places far greater processing demands on candidates than scanning for specifics. The *weighting* of different parts of a reading test should always be based on a clearly defined rationale and reflect the perceived importance, or lack of importance of that aspect of the test in relation to other tasks. If any parts of the test are to receive differential weighting then candidates need to know this and allocate time and attention for monitoring their output accordingly.

Weighting: Cambridge ESOL practice

The weighting used in Cambridge ESOL examinations is detailed in table 4.2 below. In the cases where two marks are awarded for a correct response to a question/item, this is due to the linguistic and cognitive demands derived from the reading type and textual complexity. To illustrate, let us consider CPE Part 1 which is awarded one mark per question and CPE Part 3 where candidates receive two marks for each correct answer. Part 1 assesses the candidates' control and range of vocabulary including knowledge of collocation using three short texts with a maximum of 500 words in total. To answer

Table 4.2 Weighting in Main Suite Reading papers

KET (A2)	Equal weighting throughout the paper. Each correct answer receives one mark.
PET (B1)	Same as in KET.
FCE (B2)	Differential weighting: Parts 1 and 2 are weighted differently from Part 3. Each question in the former receives two marks whereas in the latter one mark only is awarded per question.
CAE (C1)	Differential weighting: Parts 1 to 3 are weighted differently from Part 4. Each question in the former receives two marks whereas in the latter one mark is awarded per question.
CPE (C2)	Differential weighting: Part 1 is weighted differently from all other parts. Each question in Part 1 receives one mark whereas in Parts 2 to 4, two marks are awarded per question.

Source: Examination handbooks (KET 2005, PET 2005, FCE 2007, CAE 2008, CPE 2005).

this part correctly, the candidate has to establish meaning at the propositional level only (see Figure 3.1 in Chapter 3). In contrast, Part 3 measures the ability to understand text structure and follow text development using one long text with a maximum of 1,100 words. The task purpose and the text demand more complex processing. Candidates have to read the whole text to determine how it fits together. This involves establishing a text level structure (see Figure 3.1 in Chapter 3).

During the update of FCE and CAE, Rose (2006) investigated the amount of time needed for candidates to complete a careful global reading multiple-choice item and an expeditious local multiple-matching item. She found that a careful global reading MCQ needed more time to answer than an expeditious local reading multiple-matching item, supporting the decision that it was worth more marks.

Knowledge of criteria

As well as having a clear idea of task purpose, candidates require a clear idea of how they will be judged; for example, if accuracy (spelling, punctuation, grammar) is to be taken account of in marking the answers to comprehension questions this must be made clear to candidates and their teachers prior to the examination. If responses are to be judged on anything other than semantic grounds this may well affect the construct that is being measured, i.e. in this case measurement of reading is muddied if the accuracy of writing is involved and rated.

The *Standards for Educational and Psychological Testing* (American Educational Research Association, American Psychological Association, National Council on Measurement in Education 1999:85) state that the higher the consequences of the test for the candidates, the more important it is that they are fully informed about the test process, the uses that will be made of results, the rating criteria, testing policy, and protection of confidentiality consistent with the need to obtain valid responses. These requirements are echoed in the *ETS Standards for Quality and Fairness* (2000:61) in terms of test-taker rights and responsibilities, which declare that candidates have a right to information about the nature and purpose of the test. Cambridge ESOL addresses this standard in its examinations, and regards the provision of such information as an important element of the validity of the test.

Knowledge of criteria: Cambridge ESOL practice

This parameter is less relevant to the Reading papers of Cambridge Main Suite examinations as the response type to date is a selected one. All answers are mechanically scanned and machine scored.

In other Cambridge ESOL Reading papers such as BEC and IELTS where the response type is a constructed one and in the Use of English papers in FCE, CAE and CPE, trained markers mark candidates' answers (see Chapter 5 on scoring validity). The handbooks inform candidates that, for example, when filling a gap with a word, or a short phrase, spelling should be correct and that answers should be in capital letters to ensure that the word is recognisable and unequivocally the one required. Examples are provided in the examination handbooks of what is expected of candidates in tasks requiring constructed response.

Order of items

According to our description of the careful global type of reading in Chapter 3, when people read a text they construct the referential representation incrementally. The text commonly unfolds by presenting new information that is then grounded in what has already been established. Readers construct a representation of each section of text and integrate this with their representation of what they have read up to that point. Thus, if careful reading is seen as a cumulative process, then setting the questions according to the order in which the answers are found in the text is consistent with this development, and does not interfere with the smoothness of the reading process. In fact, Hughes (1989/2003:130) states that 'not to do this introduces too much random variation and so lowers the test's reliability'. Weir (1993:96) agrees with this for careful reading and feels that such 'ordering of the questions helps bring the process of taking the test closer to the way readers would normally process that particular text'.

Where expeditious types of reading are the focus for test items, then this sequential approach may be less sacrosanct. Nuttall (1996) asks what should occur first in a reading test (presumably in relation to tests where different types and cognitive processing levels of reading are assessed on the same passage). Should it be those items that evoke top-down processes leading to a quick access to global understanding as in skimming, or items that evoke bottom-up processes leading to a gradual building up of the macro-propositional structure?

It is perhaps logical to assume that readers should understand the parts before the whole where careful types of reading are intended. However, in real life careful reading would often seem to be preceded by expeditious reading especially in an academic context (see Weir et al 2006 for an account of research into such reading activities at undergraduate level in the UK). Readers may interpret different parts of the text having already grasped the overall message through an expeditious skimming type of reading intended to generate a quick view of the macro-structure. This approach enables them to dismiss misinterpretations which do not fit in with the global meaning of the text, then go back to the words of the text to check their interpretation more carefully if necessary. This suggests that readers may begin by using a fast access to meaning top-down approach and later switch between the two approaches according to what they are trying to achieve when using a text (see Shih 1992 for evidence). Reading experts seem to advocate this in teaching practice. For example, Nuttall (1996) recommends that activities requiring thorough understanding (e.g. studying the development of an argument, analysing relationships between paragraphs) are best dealt with at the end, while tasks like skimming for overall gist ought to be performed at the beginning.

In search reading in real life the reader does not necessarily follow the author's sequence in a long text, and where test writers put such questions in the order in which the information occurs in the text, it may well make the processing associated with this reading type easier if candidates are aware of this (see Chapter 3 for details of the processing associated with the various types of reading).

In scanning, even less of the text needs to be processed and there is no reason for having the questions in the order the lexical items to be found appear. If questions are placed in order it diminishes incrementally the amount of processing necessary to find the particular lexical item.

Order of items: Cambridge ESOL practice

The order in which items appear in Cambridge ESOL Main Suite examinations can be found in Table 4.3 below.

Questions for careful reading are normally ordered according to the information in the text although questions addressing overall understanding of gist may occur in initial position and those testing development of an idea/attitude or summary in the text in final position. This explains the apparent anomalies in Table 4.3 below in a number of the careful reading tasks. In expeditious reading tasks, items are not usually in order (PET Part 3 is an

Table 4.3 Order of items in Main Suite Reading papers

Examination papers	Part	Items in sequence
KET (A2) Dec 05	Part 1 careful local	NO
	Part 2 careful local	YES
	Part 3 careful local careful global	NO, (Q16–20 jumbled)
	Part 4 careful local	YES
	Part 5 careful local	YES
PET (B1) Dec 05	Part 1 careful local	YES
	Part 2 expeditious global	NO
	Part 3 expeditious local	YES
	Part 4 careful global	NO. Q1 writer purpose, Q5 global
	Part 5 careful local	YES
FCE (B2) Dec 08	Part 1 careful global	YES
	Part 2 careful global	NO
	Part 3 expeditious local	NO
CAE (C1) Dec 08	Part 1 careful global	YES
	Part 2 careful global	NO
	Part 3 careful global	YES
	Part 4 expeditious local	NO
CPE (C2) Jun 05	Part 1 careful local	YES
	Part 2 careful global	YES
	Part 3 careful global	NO
	Part 4 careful global	YES

exception). Irrespective of how the items or parts are ordered, in a testing situation, candidates can attempt a task or a part in the order that best suits their own individual test-taking strategies.

Channel of presentation

A number of researchers have studied how text comprehension is influenced by the existence of non-verbal information as well as the interaction between text and diagrams, charts, graphs, tables, pictures, notices or illustrations (e.g. de Groot 1966; Hegarty and Just 1989; Holliday, Brunner and Donais 1977; Koran and Koran 1980). The studies suggest that the presentation of information in more than one form appears to help readers who have difficulty encoding information from either texts or diagrams alone. Hegarty, Carpenter and Just (1991:666) point out that in some cases 'the topic is sufficiently complex that the reader cannot visualise spatial representation of information without a diagram'.

One of the processes that candidates sitting for a reading paper may need to carry out in order to address inferential questions is relating the information presented in different parts of the text. 'Because working memory capacity is limited, this integration process may involve reactivating and integrating information that has been represented previously, but which is no longer in working memory' (Hegarty et al 1991:660). Presenting information in a non-verbal form can help this integration by reducing the search for information that has been represented previously. In fact, non-verbal presentation may allow more efficient search and visual comparisons than text since they have fewer inherent sequential constraints in their processing (see Larkin and Simon 1987).

Channel of presentation: Cambridge ESOL practice

Cambridge examinations present information verbally and non-verbally. Visuals are usually included in lower levels, i.e. KET and PET and to a lesser extent in FCE and CAE. They are not used in CPE. Consideration is also given to text layout so that it appears as authentic as possible.

Winn (1987) argues that some test takers tend to believe that they can get all the information they need from the text alone, and accordingly, they tend to disregard illustrations. As a result, Cambridge ESOL offers guidance on preparation for the reading components. In its handbooks, it points out that candidates should make use of the visuals. Visuals are used to support the text. So an article about dinosaurs at KET level might include a picture of a dinosaur as candidates would not be expected to know the word for dinosaur (British National Corpus 3,000 word level). Non-verbal clues are used in layout to support the candidate, e.g. in the PET Part 1 short texts or KET Part 1 notices tasks. Where non verbal information is included in FCE, CAE and CPE, it is similarly intended to provide support.

BEC Preliminary Part 3 and the IELTS Academic module have graphs and tables respectively which require interpretation by the reader.

Text length

Alderson et al (2004:127–8) note in relation to levels in the CEFR: 'There seems to be a progression in terms of overall number of words from lower to higher levels . . . number of words may prove useful to see whether length and difficulty level are related.'

When deciding on how long or short a text should be, we again need to bear in mind the operations a test intends to measure. Such a decision finds support in Alderson's (1996) and Nuttall's (1996) views concerning text length. The former argues that if candidates are to make judgements about relevance and irrelevance, or distinguish between main points and subsidiary detail, then a long text is needed for these operations to be truly realised. The latter argues that for certain operations such as skimming and search reading a long text is needed. Nuttall further states that 'short texts are frequently extracts: removing them from context robs them of important elements of meaning' (Nuttall 1996:174).

In addition, it seems that when candidates are given a short text, they may tend to employ a careful bottom-up approach to reading rather than expeditious if the time has not been constrained to prevent this.

A strong case can be made for the use of long texts in appropriate contexts on the grounds that these are more representative of required reading in the target situation, at least in terms of length and discourse type (Weir et al 2000). The beneficial washback effect of this on the teaching that precedes it cannot be ignored. At C1 (CAE) and C2 (CPE) levels tests are supposed to be able to determine whether candidates can cope with academic study and this means being able to deal with long texts expeditiously as well as being able to develop a mental model and text level representations (see Weir et al 2006). In terms of the reading model we presented in Chapter 3, the longer the text the more demands can be made on both lower and higher level processing and the more types of reading can be catered for.

The drawback of course is that including longer texts requires more time to be made available for reading, if the purpose of the task is to test careful global reading. This may mean that fewer texts can be included and the range of topics is diminished with possible implications for test bias. However, if the intention is to test skimming and search reading types then this would not be the case as reading in this mode is meant to be quick and selective.

Computer-based tests would enable the facilitation of timed tasks, appropriate for expeditious reading. However, with paper and pencil tests, separate papers would have to be produced to be able to control the amount of time given for doing the task. This also has implications for test security, uniformity of administration and increased cost of printing.

Cohen and Upton (2006:7) state that:

> ... according to the task specifications (ETS, 2003): The Reading section of iBT TOEFL incorporates fewer but longer (600–700 vs. 300–400 words) texts than used in previous TOEFL test designs (i.e., the traditional paper-based TOEFL and the newer, computer-based test, iBT TOEFL). The reasons given for this are that longer texts better represent the academic experiences of students and that they better facilitate the development of reading to learn purposes in the test design ...

Alderson et al (2004:12) point out that length is defined in the CEFR as 'short' or 'long', arguing that it is difficult for individuals to determine for themselves what is 'short' or 'long'. Text length potentially has an important effect in terms of the linguistic resources that will be called into play in cognitive processing. In general the longer the text candidates have to process, the greater the language and content knowledge required. Length of text will also affect the processing load involved in building a mental model and/or text representation. If short texts are not making the demands on these resources that occur in real-life situations, cognitive validity is compromised (see Skehan 1998).

Paradoxically, longer texts which mirror more the length of texts candidates are exposed to in real life often provide more contextual clues and more support for the reader than do short texts. Malvern and Richards (1997) note that because of the high frequency of some grammatical items (e.g. determiners), longer texts normally demonstrate lower type-token ratios (TTRs). This is also evidenced in recent studies (see Weir et al 2006) where it is clear that the TTRs of longer texts used at undergraduate level are noticeably lower than those of texts used in international high-stakes tests and accordingly, because of the lower proportion of different words, *mutatis mutandis,* they may be easier to process.

TTR is thus a useful statistic for examination providers as one facet of text difficulty. It is calculated by:

> . . . dividing the types (the total number of *different* words) occurring in a text or utterance by its tokens (the total number of words). A high TTR indicates a high degree of lexical variation while a low TTR indicates the opposite. The range falls between a theoretical zero (infinite repetition of a single type) and one (the complete non-repetition found in a concordance) (www.cels.bham.ac.uk/resources/essays/DaxThomas2005a.pdf).

TTR and length of text are not the sole determinants of text complexity. As we will see below, the degree of lexical and grammatical complexity as well as other factors such as the nature of the content will determine the overall level of difficulty of any given text.

Text length: Cambridge ESOL practice

In general, the length of the text increases as the examination level increases (see table 4.4 below). This is true for the following adjacent levels: KET/PET,

Table 4.4 Text length in Main Suite Reading papers

Examination	Overall number of words	Number of texts	Maximum for any single text
KET (A2)	Approximately 740–800 words	4	250
PET (B1)	Approximately 1,450–1,600 words	5	550
FCE (B2)	Approximately 2,000 words	3	700
CAE (C1)	Approximately 3,000 words	6	1,100
CPE (C2)	Approximately 3,000 words	9	1,100

Source: Item writer guidelines (KET 2006, PET 2006), Examination handbooks (FCE 2007, CAE 2008, CPE 2005) and Cambridge Main Suite examination papers 2004–6

PET/FCE, and FCE/CAE. There is no marked distinction between CAE/ CPE in terms of text length; however, CPE has a greater number of different texts normally with a wider coverage of genres.

Time constraints

Alderson (2000:30) notes that 'Speed should not be measured without reference to comprehension, but at present comprehension is all too often measured without reference to speed'.

Several researchers have investigated the question of reading speed. Fry (1963) suggests that a slow L1 reader reads at a rate of 150 words per minute (wpm), a fair reader at 250 wpm, and a good reader at 350 wpm. Taylor (1965) suggests 300 wpm for good readers. Carver (1985) suggests 300–600 wpm for very superior readers. Haynes and Carr (1990) conducted a study on adult Chinese L2 readers of English and reported that the mean reading speed was 86.5 wpm with a reading comprehension average of 63.5%. They compared this to their American subjects who had a mean reading speed of 254 wpm and a reading comprehension mean of 75.3%. Nuttall (1996) states that: 'university students in countries where English is a second language may read at about 200 wpm but have been found to study at rates as slow as 60 wpm; presumably the texts were difficult and had to be understood thoroughly . . . an L1 speaker of English of about average education and intelligence reads at about 300 wpm. The range among L1 speakers is wide: rates of up to 800 wpm and down to 140 wpm are not uncommon' (Nuttall, 1996:56).

Weir (2005:65) points out that:

> The time constraints for the processing of text and answering the items set on it will affect the nature of what is being tested. The test developer has to sequence the texts and tasks, and ensure there is enough time allowed for all activities; if time allotment is not carefully planned, it may result in unpredictable performance. If too much time is given in a reading test or is not strictly controlled per section, candidates may simply read a passage carefully and questions designed to test ability to process text expeditiously (i.e. selectively and quickly) to elicit specified information may no longer activate such operations (see Weir et al 2000 for an example of a research project where this happened). If time is more than sufficient in an expeditious reading task, then careful cumulative, linear processing rather than quick selective processing will result. Decisions relating to timing clearly impact on the processing and hence on the theory-based validity of our test tasks. Setting appropriate time limits is best done empirically.

Many exam boards have not sought to control the amount of time spent on individual parts of a reading test because of the practical difficulties of achieving this. The advent of computer-based testing may help here. Computer-based testing facilitates the accurate measuring of expeditious reading skills since it can be used to control the amount of time spent on each task by preventing candidates going back to earlier tasks or spending more than the suggested time on any one activity.

Decisions relating to timing clearly impact on the processing and hence on the cognitive validity of our test tasks. We noted in Chapter 3 that flexibility with regard to types of reading is the mark of a skilled reader. Similarly, processing speed is a mark of fluent readers as decoding, lexical access, syntactic parsing and establishing propositional meaning become automatised. At C1 and C2 levels candidates should be able to read quickly enough to cope with academic studies. This would seem to argue that a number of tasks at this level need to be performed under restricted time constraints to sample expeditious reading skills but as we will see below there are currently no such tasks at CAE or CPE.

Time constraints: Cambridge ESOL practice

Table 4.5 Time constraints in Main Suite Reading papers

Examination	Timing
KET (A2)	35 items with a recommended 40 minutes (N.B. reading and writing are administered together in one paper hence the recommended amount of time to spend on reading)
PET (B1)	35 items with a recommended 50 minutes (N.B. reading and writing are administered together in one paper hence the recommended amount of time to spend on reading)
FCE (B2)	30 items administered in 60 minutes
CAE (C1)	34 items administered in 75 minutes
CPE (C2)	40 items administered in 90 minutes

Source: Examination handbooks (KET 2005, PET 2005, FCE 2007, CAE 2008, CPE 2005).

The above table shows that the timing of Main Suite Reading papers varies across the five levels. The amount of time allocated to each level increases as the exam level increases. The allocation of time to any one paper is based on the task and text demands of that paper and includes transfer of answers to the answer sheet.

Cambridge ESOL specifies the total amount of time required for the Reading paper at the planning stage of test development. This specification is then monitored at the pretesting stage (through feedback forms taking account of candidature level) and confirmed prior to the first live administration stage of the test development cycle. Whenever a new task is introduced to a test paper, feedback is gathered on task suitability and on time allotment.

This is done via pretesting feedback forms or observation sheets given to centres where the task is being pretested (see Hawkey 2009 for details).

On the exam paper, time is specified for the whole paper rather than the parts. Ideally time constraints should be put on tasks to ensure as much as possible that candidates are using the intended reading strategies/skills whether it is careful or expeditious reading. Practically speaking (except in computer-based testing (CBT) mode), an examination board cannot easily force candidates to spend more or less time on a certain task. However there are cases, for example in China, where the exam board forces timings by sealing sections of the paper with 'stickers' and only allows candidates to break the seal for the next section at the appointed time.

As it stands there is no practical mechanism in place in Cambridge ESOL examinations to dictate the order in which candidates should attempt the tasks. Cambridge ESOL does not engineer a test to be speeded. However, the test may turn out to be speeded for a candidate who takes too much time on certain tasks.

What Cambridge ESOL does is provide candidates with guidelines on how they should approach a task and what reading type may be best suited to that task; such guidance is provided through examination reports or information in the handbooks and the websites for teachers and students. Cambridge ESOL practice is to present items in a way that suggests what is intended, e.g. by putting questions intended to test expeditious reading before the text, but this does not control whether students skim, search read, scan or read intensively in practice. The disadvantage of this non-interventionist approach is that items that are intended to test expeditious abilities such as search reading may for some candidates become solely careful reading activities and vice versa if time is running out for the candidate. With the onset of CBT this situation might be reviewed as it is a fairly simple procedure to control the time available for a task in a computerised mode. (See Appendix F for a discussion on paper versus computer-based testing).

Linguistic demands: task input and output

Our description of linguistic knowledge is based on a communicative approach to modelling language ability first appearing in Hymes (1972), extended by Canale and Swain (1980), and developed further by Canale (1983), Bachman (1990) and Bachman and Palmer (1996). Linguistic demands in a test need to be as similar as possible to those made by equivalent tasks in real-life language use at the level of performance which is being targeted if generalisations are to be made from test performance to language use in the future domain of interest.

Overall text purpose

Weigle (2002:10) provides a useful model of writing discourse, originally laid out by Vahapassi (1982), in which she presents text types 'categorised along two major dimensions: cognitive processing, and dominant intention or purpose' (2002:10). Weigle refers to a number of different dominant intentions or overall purposes which follow a scheme originally proposed by Jackobson (1960):

- *referential* (intended to inform)
- *conative* (intended to persuade or convince)
- *emotive* (intended to convey feelings or emotions)
- *poetic* (intended to entertain, delight, please)
- *phatic* (intended to keep in touch).

Written texts were commonly viewed as mainly referential and less frequently emotive or phatic (see Weigle 2002 for a discussion of these). It may be that nowadays there is more phatic (and emotive) written communication going on – chatrooms, text messages, blogs.

Overall text purpose: Cambridge ESOL practice

In looking at text purpose in Cambridge ESOL Main Suite examinations (see Table 4.6 below) it becomes apparent that at KET and PET levels, texts are aimed primarily at informing and are limited to the referential in terms of purpose with some emotive texts appearing at PET (see Part 4 in PET). At FCE level, texts with poetic purposes begin to be used; fictional sources begin to have some importance and their primary intentions could be said to be to convey feelings and to entertain. At CAE and CPE levels emotive and poetic language takes on a greater significance. Texts with overall conative purpose also start to be used at these levels. This coincides with the task purposes at CAE and CPE levels as well as the sources and topics used. For example, in CAE, a journal article on social trends where the author is presenting an argument for or against a particular trend may be suitable to assess candidates' understanding of attitude/opinion, text organisation, main idea, or implications.

Table 4.6 Text purpose in Main Suite Reading papers

Examination	Text Purpose
KET (A2) Dec 05	Mainly referential
PET (B1) Dec 05	Mainly referential, emotive
FCE (B2)	Referential, poetic, emotive
Sample Paper 07	
CAE (C1)	Referential, poetic, emotive, conative
Sample Paper 08	
CPE (C2) Jun 05	Referential, poetic, emotive, conative

Source: Appendix A

Writer–reader relationship:

Nystrand (1989:75) comments on writing as social interaction:

> The process of writing is a matter of elaborating text in accord with what the writer can reasonably assume that the reader knows and expects, and the process of reading is a matter of predicting text in accord with what the reader assumes about the writer's purpose. More fundamentally, each presupposes the sense-making capabilities of the other. As a result, written communication is predicated on what the writer/reader each assume the other will do/has done.

The reader or audience is, according to Grabe and Kaplan (1996:207), 'essential to the creation of text and the generation of meaning'. Ede and Lunsford (1984) describe two models of audience: *audience addressed* and *audience invoked*. Audience addressed refers to the real or intended readership definable by the writer that exists apart from the text. Audience invoked is a fictitious readership invoked by the writer for a rhetorical purpose.

Hyland (2002) notes that for a text to have an appropriate impact on the target reader the writer has to gauge accurately the reader's capacity for interpreting it and their probable reaction to it. It is clear that a notion of audience – the anticipated reader of the written text – will have a profound impact on the discourse of the written product.

The intended readership of a text will affect the amount of content knowledge that can be assumed by the writer of the text. Where the writer feels the audience is familiar with many of the concepts, e.g. in the case of a specialised text in an academic journal where an expert is writing for other experts, a good deal of inferencing and use of background knowledge may be necessary to develop the mental model. In addition domain-specific low-frequency lexis and more complex grammatical patterns may be used if they are the norm for that genre. All of this will make the text more complex for the reader who does not have the shared linguistic and content knowledge of that discourse community. The processing of text is not simply 'in the text' but depends crucially on all the knowledge that the reader possesses.

Writer–reader relationship: Cambridge ESOL practice

The audience for texts in examinations is disparate and it is difficult to make assumptions about what they might or might not know already. However, as we noted in Chapter 2, target age-ranges and various other background features are known for each examination level from the previous candidate information sheets (CIS). At the pre-editing stage, it is decided whether a text is suitable for the age range of the examination and the global market, and whether it is in accord with the item writer guidelines (IWGs). The text will be fine tuned at the editing stage and throughout the question paper production stage. A lot of work goes into ensuring the cultural context is as broad as possible and this is reflected in the whole process, from IWGs and pre-editing, through to test construction and overview.

In Cambridge ESOL practice, Main Suite exam texts are aimed at the general reader. No particular level of education or world knowledge is assumed at lower levels. At higher levels (CAE and CPE) texts assume a certain level of education and understanding of the world as well as of English. In general candidates are getting younger, so topics need to be more accessible and interesting to a lower age group too.

Discourse mode

Alderson (2000:39) argues that:

> Knowing how texts are organised – what sort of information to expect in what place – as well as knowing how information is signalled and how changes of content might be marked – has long been thought to be of importance in facilitating reading. For example, knowing where to look for the main idea in a paragraph, and being able to identify how subsidiary ideas are marked, ought in principle to help a reader process information.

Urquhart (1984) points out that there is evidence that rhetorical factors in the text as well as the more traditional intra-sentential linguistic factors should be considered in estimating text difficulty. This view was shared by Barnett (1989:56) who states that 'the fact that readers' formal schemata interact with texts substantiates the impact of text type or structure on the ease or difficulty with which readers understand written texts'.

Studies looking at the effects of text organisation on comprehension, for example those by Meyer and Freedle (1984), Carrell (1984) and Goh (1990), seem to suggest that certain types of rhetorical organisation enhance comprehension more than others. Meyer and Freedle's (1984) study is based on Meyer's (1975) classification of rhetorical organisation of expository prose into collection, description, causation, problem/solution, and comparison. Carrell's (1984) and Goh's (1990) studies are replications of Meyer and Freedle's (1984) study but within second language contexts. All three studies agree on the finding that problem/solution, comparison, and causation structures are better recalled than collection or description structures. In fact, they argue that comparison and problem/solution text types enhance comprehension more than other types of rhetorical organisation.

Alderson et al (2004:52) use the CEFR specification (Council of Europe 2001) to characterise text sources from the different domains, i.e., social, work related and study related (see table 4.7 below) and this bears a close similarity with Weigle's (2002) description of text genres that we use in our analysis of Cambridge ESOL examinations below.

Table 4.7 Text sources in the CEFR

Context of use			
Personal domain	**Public domain**	**Occupational domain**	**Educational domain**
• Teletext	• Public	• Business letters	• Textbooks, readers
• Guarantees	announcements &	• Reports, memos	• Reference books
• Recipes	notices	• Life & safety	• Blackboard text
• Instructional	• Labels &	notices	• Videotext
material	packaging	• Instructional	• Exercise materials
• Novels	• Leaflets, graffiti	manuals	• Journal articles
• Magazines	• Tickets, timetables	• Regulations	• Abstracts
• Newspapers	• Notices,	• Advertising	• Dictionaries
• Junk mail	regulations	material	
• Brochures	• Programmes	• Job description	
• Personal letters	• Contracts	• Signposting	
	• Menus		

Source: Council of Europe (2001:49)

Alderson et al (2004) highlight the difficulty in determining the types of written and spoken texts that might be appropriate for each level in the CEFR. Part of the problem in addressing this deficiency is the plethora of different schemes for analysing discourse. Alderson et al (2004:46) provide a useful classification of discourse types in Table 4.8.

Table 4.8 Alderson et al (2004:46) discourse types

Type	Subtype	Examples of discourse types
Descriptive	Impressionistic descriptions	Travel accounts, sports, commentaries
	Technical descriptions	Presentation of a product
Narrative	Stories, jokes, anecdotes	
	Reports	News reports, features, documentaries
Expository	Definitions	Brief definitions
	Explications	Broader accounts of abstract phenomena, e.g., lectures, talks
	Outlines	Programme listings on the radio, time-tables
	Summaries	An oral account of the plot of a book, summarising minutes of a meeting
	Interpretations	Describing a book, an article
Argumentative	Comments	By an individual in any situation
	Formal argumentation	Formal debate
Instructive	Personal instruction	Announcements, ads, propaganda, routine commands

Alderson et al (2004:127) record that: 'No set of specifications mentions a relation between text source and level.'

Cohen and Upton (2006:7) provide a useful description of the text types to be found in the new TOEFL examination:

... according to the task specifications (ETS, 2003): With regard to text type, previous TOEFL reading passages "consisted primarily of a particular type of expository text in which a number of discrete facts are loosely integrated and developed" (ETS, 2003, 1). Along with expanded length, the texts in the Reading section of the new TOEFL (each test has three texts on different general academic topics) include a broader selection of academic text types, classified by author purpose: (a) exposition, (b) argumentation, and (c) historical biographical/autobiographical narrative. Each of these has at least one structure, such as classification, comparison/contrast, cause/effect, and problem/solution, with information presented from more than one perspective or point of view (ETS, 2003).

Urquhart and Weir (1998:141 et seq) argued that test developers must generate evidence on which discourse modes are appropriate at each proficiency level. Investigating the nature and impact of discourse mode is however beset by two problems. Firstly, there is little agreement in the literature on the terminology that should be used to classify different texts and secondly the effect of texts on the difficulty level of the task is not particularly well researched at the moment.

We confine ourselves below to those descriptions of text that seem most helpful for analysing Cambridge examinations in accessible terms, and in particular we draw on the work of Weigle.

Discourse mode according to Weigle (2002:62) includes the categories of genre, rhetorical task, and patterns of exposition:

The genre refers to the expected form and communicative function of the written product; for example, a letter, an essay, or a laboratory report. The rhetorical task is broadly defined as one of the traditional discourse models of narration, description, exposition, and argument/persuasion, as specified in the prompt, while the pattern of exposition (Hale et al 1996) refers to subcategories of exposition or specific instructions to test takers to make comparisons, outline causes and effects and so on.

Discourse mode: Cambridge ESOL practice

Table 4.9 below illustrates types of discourse mode in relation to the levels of genre and rhetorical task across the Main Suite examinations. To comment meaningfully on patterns of exposition it is necessary to consider parts of specific individual texts as this category analyses tasks in detailed rather than general terms. Patterns of exposition are dealt with in the section below on functional resources and so this aspect of a task is not explored further in this section.

Table 4.9 Discourse mode in Main Suite Reading papers

Examination	Discourse mode
KET (A2)	**Genre:** public signs & notices, (such as those found on roads, at railway stations, airport); newspapers & magazines (e.g., reviews, letters, consumer information, advertisements); informational sources (e.g., encyclopaedias, leaflets, brochures) **Rhetorical Task:** Descriptive, narrative, instructive
PET (B1)	**Genre:** public signs & notices, (such as those found in shops, banks, restaurants); personal messages (text messages, notes, postcards, emails); newspapers & magazines (e.g., reviews, letters, consumer information, advertisements); informational sources (e.g., web pages, simple encyclopaedias, leaflets, brochures) **Rhetorical Task:** Descriptive, narrative, expository, instructive
FCE (B2)	**Genre:** newspapers & magazines (e.g., articles, reports), fiction books (extracts), informational sources (e.g., guides, manuals) **Rhetorical Task:** Descriptive, narrative, expository, argumentative, instructive
CAE (C1)	**Genre:** newspapers, magazines & journals (e.g., articles, reports), fiction & non-fiction books (extracts), promotional and informational sources (e.g., guides, manuals) **Rhetorical Task:** Descriptive, narrative, expository, argumentative, instructive
CPE (C2)	**Genre:** newspapers, magazines & journals (e.g., articles, reports, editorials), fiction & non-fiction books (extracts), promotional and informational sources (e.g., guides, manuals) **Rhetorical Task:** Descriptive, narrative, expository, argumentative, instructive

Source: Appendix A, examination handbooks (KET 2005, PET 2005, FCE 2007, CAE 2008, CPE 2005)

Authentic texts from a variety of sources are used throughout the Cambridge examinations. However, for assessment purposes text adaptation may sometimes be essential. Cambridge ESOL item writer guidelines 2006 for the Main Suite examinations list the following as potential amendments:

- cutting to make the text an appropriate length
- removing unsuitable content from otherwise inoffensive text
- cutting or amending to avoid candidates being able to get the correct answer simply by word spotting rather than by understanding the text
- glossing or removing cultural reference if appropriate especially where cultural assumptions might impede understanding
- deleting confusing or redundant references to other parts of the source
- amending complexity of language to the exam level especially at KET/PET levels, using a vocabulary list and checklist of structures
- rewording for clarity, e.g. replacing pronouns with names, especially at KET/PET

- glossing, amending or removing parts of the text which require experience or detailed understanding of a specific area especially at KET/PET/FCE.

The extent of text adaptation in the examinations decreases as the level of the examination increases. In general, as the exam level increases, more genres are used as well as a greater variety of rhetorical tasks.

The crucial factor in selecting a reading text is whether the text would allow the intended reading activities to be measured. For example, has the text got enough main ideas where extraction of these is the focus of the test or does it have pieces of information that can be linked together where inferencing is the focus of the item? Cambridge ESOL varies the criteria for selecting texts according to the test's intended audience and the test purpose (e.g. Academic English, Business English or General English). Guidelines to item writers include advice on selecting texts that are coherent, are clearly sequenced or have a clear line of argument running through them.

Functional resources

The solid foundations laid by Trim, Van Ek and Wilkins in their functional–notional analysis of English for the Council of Europe (Van Ek and Trim 1998, 1998a and 2001 and Wilkins 1973 and 1976), and the empirical work of North (2000) in calibrating functions onto a common scale, have resulted in functional requirements being fairly well defined at least for the A2 to B2 levels in the CEFR (though see Alderson n.d. for some reservations).

However, in response to the needs of language testers and teachers for a more comprehensive description of English across the CEFR levels, the English Profile programme is a long-term collaborative research project started in 2006 with the object of building on the work already undertaken by Trim and Van Ek (for A1, Breakthrough, A2, Waystage, B1, Threshold and B2, Vantage). English Profile is intended to provide an integrated, cumulative description of the communicative tasks learners can be expected to perform at each of the six levels of the CEFR; its goals are to assist English language teaching, learning and assessment through guiding curriculum development, teacher training, self-directed learning and language test development (www.englishprofile.org).

Although Van Ek and Trim (for A1, Breakthrough, A2, Waystage, B1, Threshold and B2, Vantage) produced a substantial body of work defining notional–functional progression across the CEFR levels A1 to B2, only limited work was carried out on the C levels.

A recent functional progression study for the English Profile programme carried out by CRELLA at the University of Bedfordshire (Green 2007a) focused on the C levels in the CEFR. Green (2007a) concludes that the CEFR suggests some qualitative change in the functions that characterise learner language between the A and B levels and the C level. Levels A and B appear to offer an expanding repertoire of communicative functionality reflected in expanding access to contexts for language use. Broadly:

- A1 is characterised by 'a very finite rehearsed, lexically organised repertoire of situation-specific phrases' for expressing personal information
- A2 by the expansion of 'social functions'
- B1 by 'the ability to maintain interaction and get across what you want to, in a range of contexts' and by increasing flexibility
- B2 is said to involve 'argument, effective social discourse and . . . language awareness' with conversation management, discourse skills and negotiation appearing at the B2+ level.

This suggests that, while the A1 learner is restricted in the contexts within which they can use language, the B2+ learner is capable of participating quite effectively in the public sphere in expressing points of view and putting forward arguments. The C level, on the other hand, appears to represent not so much an increase in functionality and in the range of contexts for use as increasing ease and subtlety of communication. At C1 there is, 'a deepening awareness of access to a broad range of language, which allows fluent, spontaneous communication' and, at C2, a level of 'precision, appropriateness and ease' in using the language. It is apparent in the CEFR that passing from B2 to the C level should enable the learner to access higher education, professional fields of employment and the literary culture associated with a language.

Green (2007a) carried out an empirical study to create a data base of the functions and 'Can Do' statements to be found in ESOL textbooks, tests, scales and syllabuses at the B2 to C levels. As many of the data sources did not distinguish between C1 and C2 they were treated as a composite C level for the purposes of Green's study.

A comparative analysis at the level of Wilkins' (1976) functional categories (Figure 4.2) across functions and 'Can Do' statements suggested that at the C level we see an increase in *argument, suasion* and *rational enquiry and exposition*. The proportion of functions is similar at the B2 and C levels for *emotional relations* while *judgement and evaluation* and, particularly, *personal emotions* seem to become less salient at the higher level.

The following of Wilkins' (1976) functions occurred only at the C level in the lists of functions. In this list Wilkins' superordinate categories of communicative function are given in parenthesis.

Acknowledgement (emotional relations); *disagree* (argument); *inform* (argument); *justification* (rational enquiry and exposition); *proposition* (rational enquiry and exposition); *recommend* (suasion); *threaten* (suasion).

Among the 'Can Do' statements, the following occur only at the C level:

Figure 4.2 Proportion of function words in Wilkins' (1976) categories found at the B2 and C level (functions and 'Can Do' lists) in the materials database

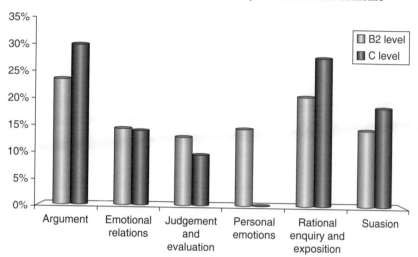

Advocate (argument); *assess* (judgement and evaluation); *demonstration* (rational enquiry and exposition); *illustration* (rational enquiry and exposition).

Clearly it would be wrong to infer from this comparison that none of the functions in these lists can occur at the B2 level. Taking the example of *inform*, synonyms such as *tell* or *give information* are found at B2 and below and so the choice of the word *inform* at the C level may suggest rather a subtle change of perspective. However, taken together, the pattern of function words emerging at the C level is suggestive of a shift in focus and points to *rational enquiry and exposition, argument* and *suasion* as being of particular relevance to the C level. A similar conclusion was reached by Shaw and Weir (2007) in their retrospective analysis of writing examinations at these levels.

Functional resources: Cambridge ESOL practice

A key aspect of a functional approach to language learning is that many functions can appropriately be tested at a range of levels. There are some basic functions which candidates may be expected to demonstrate an understanding of at any level – candidates from KET level upwards may be expected to understand simple opinions; this might, for example, involve an understanding of opinion in relation to likes and dislikes at KET or opinions in an argument at FCE. In such cases, learners show their level in part by their understanding of the range of exponents used for that function.

However, there are other functions which will not be encountered until the higher levels of examination. Hypothesising, for instance, is not a function which candidates at lower levels would be expected to be able to perform as the language used to realise it would be too high-level for the lower levels.

KET

The functions which candidates are expected to handle at KET level are listed in Waystage and in the KET Handbook (2005) under the following heading, *Inventory of Functions, Notions and Communicative Tasks*. Of course, at KET level the ways in which various functions such as giving advice and talking about feelings are expressed will be different from the ways in which those functions are expressed at other levels in the Main Suite examinations. Lexis and structure play their part in determining which exponents of any particular function are appropriate to any specific level (see KET wordlist on the following site: www.CambridgeESOL.org/teach/ket/index.htm).

PET

At PET level, too, a full list of language specifications is given in the handbook under *Inventory of Functions, Notions and Communicative Tasks* (2005). These reflect the functions outlined at the Threshold level of the CEFR. The essential changes at PET level, as far as functional resources are concerned, are that candidates are now expected to be able to understand more demanding genres. As well as the new functions indicated above, all the functions from the KET list are also included on the PET list (see also PET wordlist on the following site: www.CambridgeESOL.org/teach/pet/index.htm). At PET level candidates are expected to understand a wider range of lexico-grammatical exponents.

FCE

From FCE level upwards no list of specified functions is provided in the exam handbook. FCE, however, is at Vantage or B2 level and this determines the functions which learners at this level are expected to be able to handle. By this stage learners are considered to be 'independent users' able to operate in a wide range of personal and social situations in English.

CAE

A number of functions appear for the first time at this level; hypothesising, prioritising and summarising, for example, are functions that are not tested at lower levels. This is because these functions are most typical of text in an academic or professional context and so are typically found in some of the genres new at this level of the Main Suite.

Clearly, many of the other functions which are tested in the CAE Reading paper are also tested at lower levels. As far as the functional dimension is concerned, the difference at CAE level is that – once again – candidates are expected to cope with a richer variety of functional exponent. They are also expected to be developing the ability to appreciate a wider range of style and register and the ways in which functions are expressed in texts of different types.

CPE

By C2 level in the CEFR, learners have a very good appreciation of written English. They will be able to operate comfortably in most contexts of work and of higher education. The functions that are tested in CPE typically include those tested in CAE along with, additionally: presenting ideas, reporting, outlining, making proposals, judging priorities, analysing, drawing conclusions and making recommendations

The new functions that candidates are asked to comprehend typically include a degree of appreciation of style with regard to the description of people, places or events and the presentation of a point of view. Functions that relate to aspects of presenting a reasoned argument are key at this level. Candidates are expected to comprehend arguments for and against, even when these are presented indirectly.

Table 4.10 relating to functional resources in the Cambridge ESOL Main Suite examinations below indicates that there are only a few discernible differences in functions between the CPE and CAE examinations. The distinction lies more in the quality and range of writing that candidates are exposed to.

In Table 4.10 below we attempt to summarise the occurrence of functions across the Main Suite levels and in the final column, for illustrative purposes only, we have detailed the functions occurring in each of the sample papers located at Appendix A.

There are three key points to be borne in mind when considering Table 4.10. First the functions listed are not exhaustive. There are elements of other functions in most of the texts in the papers that were analysed. Secondly, at KET and PET levels the key functions noted are typical of most papers at their level. As we progress up the levels, however, there may be more variation as candidates are also expected to cope with all the functions from the lower levels albeit with more complex linguistic exponents. As more functions are available for testing at higher levels, so any one paper can only sample from the possible list. Lastly, although several of the functions such as describing people and giving information inevitably appear across the spectrum of the levels they are dealt with very differently at different levels. On the whole it

Table 4.10 Functions in Main Suite Reading papers

Exam	Overview of nature of functions	Functional resources		Exemplification
		Functional choices based on:		What this means in practice in one set of papers (see Appendix A). The writer is:
KET (A2)	Basic functions relating to personal information, everyday activities and social interaction, expressed in writing in a straightforward way	Waystage See *Waystage* (Van Ek & Trim 1998a) and Handbook for full listing of functions candidates are expected to be able to cope with at KET level.		• advising • warning • informing • describing activities • requesting and responding to requests • asking for and giving information • asking for and expressing preference • describing people and their lives • defining • expressing likes and dislikes
PET (B1)	As for KET • Also slightly more demanding understanding of functions is required in terms of: (a) length, (b) text type and (c) language complexity (d) complexity of exponents chosen.	Threshold See *Threshold* (Van Ek & Trim 1998) and Handbook for full listing of functions candidates are expected to be able to cope with at PET level.		• expressing likes and dislikes • describing experiences • stating rules and regulations • describing people • describing places • describing an organisation • giving instructions • giving factual information
FCE (B2)	As for PET • Also more demanding appreciation of functions is required in terms of: (a) variety of context, (b) text type and (c) language complexity.	Vantage See *Vantage* (Van Ek & Trim 2001) for full listing of functions candidates are expected to be able to cope with at FCE level.		• describing people • describing places in a literary way • describing experiences and events • narrating • describing objects • giving opinions

Candidates at this level are expected to be able not only to survive in an English-speaking environment but also to appreciate a degree of complexity and subtlety in functional use.

CAE (C1)	As for FCE • Also some more demanding functional appreciation required in terms of: (a) variety of context, (b) text type and (c) language complexity. Candidates at this level need to have an appreciation of register differences between different functional exponents. They should have an increasing awareness of how functions can be expressed in a range of stylistically differentiated ways.	Professional judgement of item writing team supported by information from pretesting.	• giving precise information • describing places in a literary way • presenting a reasoned argument • describing a situation in an entertaining way • narrating • giving an opinion in an entertaining way • describing people in an entertaining way • summarising • giving opinions
CPE (C2)	As for CAE • Also some more demanding functional appreciation required in terms of: (a) variety of context, (b) text type, and (c) language complexity. Candidates at this level need to have a deep appreciation of the full range of functional exponents. They should be able to appreciate language used in a sophisticated way for the full range of personal, literary and academic functions.	Professional judgement of item writing team supported by information from pretesting.	• giving precise information • comparing and contrasting • commenting on change • giving an opinion • describing a person's work in a literary style • criticising • describing a process • reviewing a work of art • praising • summarising

Source: *Appendix A, Examination handbooks (KET 2005, PET 2005, FCE 2007, CAE 2008, CPE 2005)*

could be said that it is the lexical and grammatical resources rather than function which are more significant in determining level in that it is the exponents used to express function that become more complex rather than the functions themselves.

There is a clear functional progression across the first three levels KET, PET and FCE in terms of complexity but also in the degree of precision in the grammatical exponents employed to fulfil the function(s). Functions associated with conative purposes and argumentative tasks for language appear at CAE although there are some elements of these at FCE. The functions at CAE and CPE are increasingly diverse and demanding and exhibit more complex grammatical structures, and more sophisticated use of lexis and collocation.

Grammatical resources

Alderson (2000:37) draws attention to the 'importance of knowledge of particular syntactic structures, or the ability to process them, to some aspects of second language reading . . . The ability to parse sentences into their correct syntactic structure appears to be an important element in understanding text'. Shiotsu (2003) investigated components most likely to affect performance in reading for Japanese undergraduates and established clearly the importance of syntactic knowledge. Shiotsu and Weir (2007) used structural equation modeling to demonstrate the relative superiority of syntactic knowledge over lexical knowledge in explaining variance in tests of reading administered to a variety of L2 participants.

Texts with less complex grammar on the whole tend to be easier than texts with more complex grammar. Berman (1984) investigated how opacity and heaviness of sentence structures could result in increased difficulty in processing.

However, as we noted earlier, text complexity is a balance, an inter-play of elements such as propositional content, discourse mode, lexis and sentence structure. Although longer complex sentences will often be harder than shorter simple ones, if the language used is very elliptical and the lexis used is highly colloquial, short simple sentences may actually be harder to understand than longer sentences. A tabloid newspaper article, for example, may be harder for the second language user than the grammatically more complex broadsheet newspaper article.

The CEFR (Council of Europe 2001) provides no guidance on the grammatical range candidates might be expected to cope with in reading tasks at various levels of ability. This is probably because the CEFR was not written as a language specific document but as one that would serve to guide the teaching and learning of a range of European languages. While the lexical domains and functions which the learner of, for example, English, Spanish,

Danish or Hungarian needs to acquire are likely to be comparable, the grammatical patterns which the learner has to master will inevitably vary from language to language.

This has consequences for the use of the CEFR in schools. Keddle (2004:43–44) noted that the CEFR did not measure grammar-based progression and this was problematic in relating the descriptors to the students' achievements. She argued that as a course designer she would have been happier if there were more explicit guidance in relation to grammatical appropriateness at the various levels.

Alderson et al (2004:49) provide four categories of grammatical complexity which can be mapped on to Cambridge ESOL Main Suite examinations as follows:

- only simple sentences   KET
- mostly simple sentences   PET
- frequent compound sentences   FCE
- many complex sentences   CAE and CPE

Alderson et al argue (2004:128) that '. . . these (categories) aim to provide a general and at the same time a standardised way of describing the grammar in input texts and seem sufficient for the purpose of helping identifying levels'.

Grammatical resources: Cambridge ESOL practice

The grammatical structures which learners need in order to cope appropriately with the functions identified at levels from A2 to B2 in the CEFR have been identified and are listed in the books describing the Waystage, Threshold and Vantage levels and in the handbooks for KET and PET. At higher levels in the CEFR there has as yet been no such systematic attempt to match structures with level.

By PET or B1 level, many of the basic structures of English have already been taught. B2 level students will have covered the full repertoire of verb forms and other key grammatical structures. Only a few major patterns – such as rhetorical uses of inversion or more sophisticated uses of modals remain. In terms of textual input learners at FCE level might be exposed to texts with higher level structures even if they are not expected to produce them themselves. Most of the rest of the grammar work to be done with C1 and C2 learners is a matter of recycling as it will focus on improving the learners' accuracy and confidence in handling the structures they were taught at lower levels.

Table 4.11 below attempts to summarise the occurrence of grammatical structures across the Main Suite examination levels and in the final column, for illustrative purposes only, we have detailed the functions occurring in each of the sample papers located at Appendix A.

Table 4.11 Grammatical structures in Main Suite Reading papers

Exam	Overview of grammatical structures available	Grammatical resources	What this means in practice: analysis of one set of papers (Appendix A)
		Grammatical resources based on:	
KET (A2)	Basic structures necessary to fulfil everyday needs.	Waystage 1990 See *Waystage* (Van Ek & Trim 1998a) and Handbook for full listing of grammatical structures candidates are expected to be able to cope with at KET level.	Normally simple sentences
PET (B1)	A wider range of structures are available than at KET level. Most verb forms will be understood although at this level candidates are not expected to have complete knowledge of passives, conditionals and modals, for example.	Threshold 1990 See *Threshold* (Van Ek & Trim 1998) and Handbook for full listing of structures candidates are expected to be able to cope with at PET level.	Mainly simple sentences but occasional use of relative and other subordinate clauses
FCE (B2)	Learners at this level are able to understand all the main tense forms and grammatical patterns of English. Complexity of grammatical structures used in any one text should not be so great that it impedes overall understanding or creates the impression of a task which is beyond the level.	Vantage See *Vantage* (Van Ek & Trim 2001) for full listing of structures candidates are expected to be able to cope with at FCE level.	A range of sentence patterns – from the simple to the complex. Frequent compound sentences
CAE (C1)	Complete range of structures available. Structures may be used for rhetorical effect as well as for conveying precise information.	Professional judgement of item writing team supported by information from pretesting.	Many complex sentences Frequent use of modals Some use of ellipsis Complex approaches to referencing – range of pronouns and adverbials, as well as use of synonymy

| CPE (C2) | Complete range of structures available. Structures may be used for rhetorical or literary effect and the conveying of opinion both directly and indirectly is focused on more than the conveying of information. | Professional judgement of item writing team supported by information from pretesting. | Sentences may be longer and more complex No restriction on the types of structure employed by the text Many examples of structures typically used for effect in writing e.g. sentences with several subordinate clauses |

Source: Appendix A. Examination handbooks (KET 2005, PET 2005, FCE 2007, CAE 2008, CPE 2005)

Sentence length in Cambridge ESOL Main Suite Reading texts

Average sentence length is often considered an approximate indication of text complexity. We examined average sentence length and range of sentence lengths in a small corpus of Main Suite texts created by the authors (143 texts in total) and these are listed in the table below:

Table 4.12 Sentence length in Main Suite Reading papers

Main Suite level	Average number of words per sentence	Range
KET (A2)	13.2	8–17
PET (B1)	14.9	10–20
FCE (B2)	18.4	11–25
CAE (C1)	18.6	13–27
CPE (C2)	19.6	13–30

There is a general upwards incline in sentence length as we move up the Cambridge levels though there can be considerable intra level variation.

A similar gradation in grammatical complexity can be seen in the average Flesch reading ease score and Flesch-Kincaid grade level estimates obtained for the texts in this small corpus listed in Table 4.13 below (see Gervasi and Ambriola 2002, Klare 1984 and Masi 2002 for discussion of the use of these formulae). Though often criticised as inadequate indices of text difficulty in themselves, these formulae still form the basic tools in recent and detailed analyses of textual complexity (Masi 2002). These two estimates of text complexity are largely based on average number of words in a sentence and average number of syllables per word. Again there is considerable intra text variation at each examination level. The low estimates for texts at CAE and CPE in Table 4.13 might be a cause for some concern as students at these levels should be capable of processing undergraduate level texts which Weir et al (2006) found to be at around 13.5 in terms of Flesch Kincaid estimates (see below). The narrowness of the gap between PET and FCE is also worthy of further investigation.

Table 4.13 Difficulty estimates in Main Suite Reading papers

Main Suite Level	Flesch reading ease score	Flesch-Kincaid grade level	Flesch Kincaid range
KET (A2)	78.3	5.5	2–7.4
PET (B1)	64.7	7.9	5–10.1
FCE (B2)	66.5	8.4	5–12.3
CAE (C1)	58.4	9.6	5.7–16
CPE (C2)	57.7	9.9	5.6–16.1

Weir et al (2006) in their study of the IELTS Reading test found that the IELTS texts (42 in total) in terms of both the Flesch reading ease and Flesch-Kincaid measures were significantly (p<.05) easier to read than (42) first year undergraduate texts. The difference between the means for IELTS and for undergraduate texts was five points on the 100-point Flesch reading ease scale or one year in terms of the Flesch-Kincaid grade levels (12.5 as against 13.5). However, as shown in Figure 4.3 below, the IELTS texts were generally of a similar level of readability to the undergraduate texts, falling within the range of undergraduate text readability. An implication here may be that using readability formulae could assist the IELTS test developers in identifying texts that might fall outside the range of readability typically found in university level texts.

It is also of interest that no IELTS text had an estimated grade level higher than 16, although undergraduate texts ranged as high as 18. This might be taken as a further indication that even the most difficult of the IELTS texts do not reflect the level of the most challenging of the texts that undergraduates might expect to encounter in their first year of study.

Figure 4.3 Flesch-Kincaid reading grade levels of IELTS and first year undergraduate core texts

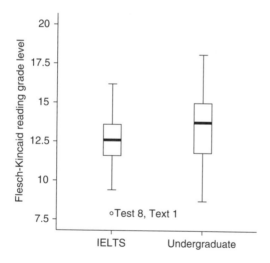

In general the grammatical structures used in the texts will be more complex than those used in the items as candidates are being tested on their understanding of the texts and not their understanding of the items.

The Main Suite examination papers across the five levels show a clear progression in terms of sentence structure from short, simple sentences to long, complex sentences, e.g. 'A new copywriter' text in CPE has a sentence of 235 words (see Appendix A). This is mirrored in the length of the texts used, as very short texts are used at KET level and increasingly longer ones are employed at higher levels. This progression does not mean that some short sentences may not pose considerable difficulty and so still have a place in higher level texts. As previously mentioned, ellipsis and colloquial use of language may make for short sentences that are hard to process and so only appropriate at more advanced levels.

An increasing complexity of verb forms is also noticeable in texts as we move up the Cambridge ESOL levels. The use of modals, conditionals, inversion and other grammatical structures becomes more common as the texts used in the examinations become more concerned with conveying feelings and opinions, persuading and hypothesising rather than dealing simply with information as they do at lower levels.

As well as sentence length and verb form, referencing is an aspect of grammatical structure that becomes noticeably complex in higher level texts where the successful reader needs to appreciate the use of synonymy and to have a full grasp of referencing pronouns and adverbials as well as sophisticated inferencing skills.

Lexical resources

A number of researchers and reading experts have identified potential sources of difficulty arising from the linguistic elements in a text (Nuttall 1996, Perera 1984, Urquhart 1984, Weir 1993). They suggest that lexical as well as grammatical difficulty strongly influence the ease with which a text can be read.

Weir (2005a:292–3) notes, however, that 'The CEFR provides little assistance in identifying the breadth and depth of productive or receptive lexis that might be needed to operate at the various levels'. Some general guidance is given on the learner's lexical resources for productive language use but as Huhta, Luoma, Oscarson, Sajavaara, Takala and Teasdale (2002:131) point out 'no examples of typical vocabulary or structures are included in the descriptors'. The argument that the CEFR 'is intended to be applicable to a wide range of different languages' (Weir 2005a) is used as an explanation, but this offers little comfort to the test writer who has to select texts or activities uncertain as to the lexical breadth or knowledge required at a particular level within the CEFR.

Alderson et al (2004:13) make a related point that many of the terms in the CEFR remain undefined. They cite the use of 'simple' in the scales and argue that difficulties arise in interpreting it because the CEFR has no advice on what this might mean for structures, lexis or any other linguistic feature. They suggest that for each language that is tested the CEFR would need to be supplemented with lists of grammatical structures and lexical items before terms like 'simple' are meaningful for those involved in item writing.

The generic function of the CEFR suggested above may mean that it cannot reasonably be expected to provide test writers with detailed guidelines on how lexical resources operate differentially at the various levels in their particular language; but test writers clearly require this sort of detailed guidance – usually in the form of wordlists – if they are to successfully create tests targeting specific levels of difficulty or covering particular domains.

Supplementary lists such as those suggested above by Alderson et al (2004) have been in existence for many years and have been used extensively in teaching and assessment; some lists (e.g. FCE and CPE in the 1980s were linked with the Cambridge English Lexicon created by Hindmarsh 1980). Some lists were developed more intuitively than empirically; others form part of a more functionally oriented specification (e.g. Waystage 1990 and Threshold 1990 levels) and later came to underpin some of the lower reference levels of the CEFR.

More recently, the development of corpora (i.e. computerised collections of written and spoken texts), both native speaker and L2 learner, and the application of corpus linguistics tools to these bodies of evidence, have made it easier to derive more empirically grounded wordlists for use in pedagogy and assessment contexts; these can be used to help validate and improve existing wordlists, as well as create new wordlists sometimes with a specific level/domain focus.

However, these wordlists have limitations which need to be understood. Most are based on frequency analyses, and thus are mainly useful for indicating whether particular words are common in language. Obviously, frequent words are more useful than non-frequent words, but this applies to language in general. The lower-level CEFR is largely based on a functional approach, and a frequency analysis does not indicate which particular words (or phrases) are linked to particular functions. Thus, although frequent words are useful in their own right, a list of frequent words does not necessarily cover all of the functions outlined in the CEFR. To provide true functional coverage, the wordlists would need to be developed by first identifying functional language use in the corpus (this would probably have to be done manually), and then tallying which words and phrases are realisations of the prescribed functions. Thus the lexical guidelines at these levels may or may not be accurate indications of the lexis learners actually need to know.

This being said, at the lower levels a list of frequent words is likely to cover many of the CEFR-mandated functions. The situation becomes more difficult at the higher levels. Because discussion can be on any topic, it becomes impossible to specify a particular set of vocabulary which would enable engagement with a wide variety of topics. Frequency research suggests that learning vocabulary up to about the 5,000 word family level provides rewards in the general ability to use English (this threshold may vary for other languages). Beyond the 5,000 level however, vocabulary becomes increasingly tied to specific topics and/or domains, and so the recommendation is for each learner to focus on their topic-specific technical vocabulary from this point onwards (Nation 2001). This is why the CEFR is so vague about the lexis required at these higher levels.

While it is difficult to specify *which* words are necessary for any particular language use context, vocabulary research has been more successful at specifying what size of vocabulary is necessary to achieve certain language aims. Around 2,000–3,000 word families should supply the bulk of the lexical resources required for basic everyday conversation (Adolphs and Schmitt 2003). About 3,000 word families is the threshold which should allow learners to begin to read authentic texts. Based partly on Laufer's (1988) research, it was formerly thought that knowledge of around 5,000 word families would provide enough vocabulary to enable learners to read authentic texts without lexical problems; however, this was based on 95% coverage of texts. Now the consensus is moving toward a view that closer to 98% coverage is necessary for ease of reading which would require a larger vocabulary: something in the area of 8,000–9,000 word families (Nation and Gu 2007). Of course many words will still be unknown, but this level of knowledge should allow learners to infer the meaning of many of the novel words from context, and to understand most of the communicative content of the text. Beyond this, for a wide L2 English vocabulary, a size of 10,000 word families is the figure most often cited (Hazenberg and Hulstijn 1996). It is important to note that these sizes are approximations, and ability in English also depends on many other factors, including speaking and reading skills, background knowledge, and strategy use. However the sizes do provide 'rules of thumb' which may prove useful for test developers to keep in mind.

Lexical resources: Cambridge ESOL practice

Over the past 10 years examination boards (e.g. Cambridge ESOL, ETS, Michigan) have been at the forefront of advances in the application of corpus findings not only to practical language test development but also in investigating the development of second language proficiency. Test developers, for example, can draw on native speaker corpora as an informing source for reading and listening tests, or as a means for checking the authentic features of specially written reading and listening texts. Such corpora can generate potential distractors for test tasks with a lexico-grammatical focus, e.g. multiple-choice gap filling. (See Taylor and Barker 2008 for an overview of the use of corpora in assessment, and Granger 2004 for a summary of learner corpora.)

Cambridge ESOL, for example, has in collaboration with Cambridge University Press been building corpora since the early 1990s and using outcomes from corpus studies to inform language test development and validation (see Barker 2004 for an overview) particularly with regard to lexical content. Corpus studies have been used to inform test revision projects (e.g. CPE, see Weir and Milanovic 2003), devise new test formats (Hargreaves 2000), and create or revise test writer and candidate wordlists (see Ball 2002, Barker 2004).

Cambridge ESOL's Local Item Banking System (LIBS) can also be considered as a type of corpus since it contains large quantities of tasks and items from Cambridge test versions delivered over the past 10 years or so (see Marshall 2006). In this way, LIBS functions as a powerful archive whose content is amenable to searching for particular lexical items or topics to check whether a word, phrase or structure has been tested before and in what contexts. The functionality of LIBS continues to be enhanced so that questions relating to features of test input at particular proficiency levels can be explored more closely.

The research literature indicates that receptive and productive vocabularies are typically of different sizes, and some scholars believe that differences between passive and active vocabulary size may increase as proficiency improves (e.g. Laufer 1998, Melka 1997), although this latter point is controversial and has not yet been empirically settled. Receptive vocabulary is widely accepted as being typically larger than productive vocabulary, and is assumed to encompass it, as well as to include words that are only partly known, low frequency words not readily available for use, and words that are avoided in active use. Productive and receptive vocabulary size are obviously interrelated but the size of one is unlikely to provide a definitive guide to the size of the other. Thus, an analysis of learner corpora based on written texts produced in examinations only, e.g. the Cambridge Learner Corpus, would be unsuitable as the only source for compiling a lexicon to guide the compilation of reading or listening papers.

An analysis of the lexical resources required by candidates to deal with Cambridge ESOL Main Suite examinations is provided in Table 4.14 below.

Invariably as candidates progress up the levels of the Main Suite examinations, the lexical demands that are put upon them are stronger. This shows itself primarily through the number and complexity of the lexical items that they are required to understand. Lexis at lower levels is restricted to everyday, literal and factual language. As students advance, they are gradually expected to deal with increasingly subtle uses of the language of feelings and ideas. More abstract texts will not be presented to candidates until level C1 (CAE) and used to a higher degree in C2 (CPE).

Fiction usually requires a broader receptive vocabulary and this is introduced from FCE onwards. This parallels the opportunity to work on a set text in order to be able to answer an optional task in FCE, CAE and CPE Paper 2 (Writing). Additionally, at higher levels candidates' ability is ascertained by requiring them to handle a larger number of texts in the exam than at lower levels covering a wider range of genres.

Table 4.14 Lexis in Main Suite Reading papers

Exam	Overview of nature of lexis	More specific aspects of lexis	Lexical Resources		Type of use	What this means in practice: analysis of one set of papers (Appendix A)
			Lexical resources based on:			
KET (A2)	Restricted to common items which normally occur in the everyday vocabulary of native speakers.	Lexis appropriate to simple personal requirements, e.g., nationalities, hobbies, likes and dislikes.	Waystage 1990 (Van Ek and Trim 1998a) and other high-frequency or otherwise words from corpus evidence.		Mainly literal use	• set of notices • set of sentences on theme of university life • two turn dialogues • longer dialogue: about renting a room • article about child violinist • factual article about badgers • vocabulary definitions relating to places in town
PET (B1)	General vocabulary sufficient for most topics in everyday life.	Lexis appropriate to personal requirements, e.g. nationalities, hobbies, likes and dislikes.	Threshold 1990 (Van Ek and Trim 1998) and other high-frequency or otherwise appropriate words from corpus evidence.		Mainly literal use	• set of notices, emails and memos • descriptions of people to match to descriptions of museums • informational text about Short Story Society • interview with new young TV star • encyclopaedic article about grass
FCE (B2)	Good range of vocabulary. Topics are addressed in detail and with precision.	General lexis as appropriate to specified topics relating to everyday life.	Vantage Van Ek and Trim 2001) and other high-frequency or otherwise appropriate words from corpus evidence.		Literal + some inferential evaluative/ synthesis/ analytical use Light fiction may be used	• popular fiction text – first person account of vet's life • piece of journalism – article about woman downhill mountain bike racer • 4 texts about collectors of different items

CAE (C1)	Broad range of vocabulary including idiomatic expressions and colloquialisms as well as language relating to opinion, persuasion and abstract ideas.	Candidates should be challenged by complexity of expression rather than arcane subject matter and specialist vocabulary.	Vocabulary appropriate to specific contexts demonstrating mastery of a particular domain. Lexical appropriacy determined by the professional judgement of item writing team supplemented by pre-testing information.	Literal/inferential evaluative/ synthesis/ analytical use Fiction may be used	• 3 texts relating to aspects of scientific research (competition instructions; extract from novel; opinion article) • magazine article on inter-species communication (how an East African bird communicates with members of a local tribe in order to gain access to food) • article about how people are taught to have good TV presence • number of reviews of crime novels
CPE (C2)	Very wide range of vocabulary including idiomatic expressions and colloquialisms as well as language relating to opinion, persuasion and abstract ideas.	Candidates should be challenged by complexity of expression rather than arcane or specialist lexis but at this level they are expected to be able to cope with the full range of general topics that might interest an educated native speaker.	As for CAE but with a range and appropriateness of vocabulary which an educated native-speaker might be expected to understand. Texts that can be understood in real-world professional contexts by native speakers.	Literal/inferential evaluative/ synthesis/ analytical use More complex fiction may be used	• 3 articles on different themes as basis for lexical items – (dealing with architecture, shopping in Europe and cosmetic dentistry) • 4 articles on aspects of advertising and publicity (articles from textbook, newspaper/magazine articles and a novel) • review of jazz album • comparison of US and UK weather forecasting (extract from book)

Source: Appendix A, *Examination handbooks (KET 2005, PET 2005, FCE 2007, CAE 2008, CPE 2005)*

At lower levels there are documents to help support decisions as to the appropriacy of specific lexical items, mainly based on *Waystage, Threshold,* and *Vantage* suggestions. The *Waystage* and *Threshold* lexical lists stem from a relatively constrained set of notions and functions, and so probably provide a coherent guideline to work from. However, the lexical exponents at the *Vantage* level are much less principled, and probably should be regarded as samples of appropriate lexis, rather than as specifications, as suggested in the *Vantage* document itself:

> The exponents listed here are not presented as a defined lexical syllabus, nor even as "recommended exponents". They represent stimuli which may be found useful by those involved in the development of theme-related ability to *Vantage*. Together with the common-core elements listed in Chapters 5 and 6 under "language functions" and "general notions", the lexicon contained in this appendix should provide learners with a significantly more advanced linguistic apparatus for dealing with the themes of most likely general interest to them than was available at *Threshold* level. In accordance with its intended role the list presented here is to a large extent open-ended. The majority of the lexical items contained in it are listed as members of open classes, to be reduced, expanded, or otherwise altered as may best suit the needs and interests of the learners (Van Ek and Trim 2001:120).

Thus, at the higher levels (FCE and above), the professional judgement of Cambridge ESOL staff and item writers plays the main role in informing decisions about lexical suitability. This judgement is supported by the use of corpora and of pretesting.

The lexical descriptors in the Type of use column in Table 4.14 above give guidance about *how* the words/phrases should be used (e.g. literal, evaluative), but give little indication of *which* words and phrases are appropriate for a particular suite level. The final column lists a set of topics from a sample of examinations. However, it is important to note that a different set of sample examinations would likely produce a completely different set of topics.

As part of the support provided to teachers and candidates, Cambridge ESOL publishes a guide to the vocabulary which can be tested in the KET and PET examination papers. This is available on the online teaching resources page at www.CambridgeESOL.org. The wordlists for KET and PET are updated on an annual basis by the addition and removal of words using a corpus-based approach. Suggested additions to the wordlists are collated and the frequency of these words is obtained by reference to established corpora. The corpora in question represent productive and receptive language in general contexts. The main corpora used for the validation of KET/PET vocabulary lists are the Cambridge Learner Corpus (part of the

Cambridge International Corpus) which includes over 30 million words of written learner English and the British National Corpus (BNC) which includes 100 million words of written and spoken native speaker data.

Unlike KET/PET, there are no wordlists for FCE, CAE and CPE. Item writers refer to the analyses of past papers as well as using their professional judgement and experience as to what candidates at these higher levels should be able to understand.

Analysis of Main Suite reading texts

Although our understanding of the nature of lexical resources in tests across different levels remains partial, it is nevertheless growing and investigative work is ongoing on a number of fronts. In order to gain a better understanding of lexical progression in the Cambridge Main Suite Reading examinations, and particularly what contributes to lexical difficulty, Cambridge ESOL commissioned a report from an acknowledged expert in the field of second language vocabulary and assessment at Nottingham University (UK), Norbert Schmitt. The findings from his lexical analysis of the Main Suite examinations are reported below with comment from the authors as relevant to our main theme; they are presented to illustrate the type of investigation which examination boards may wish to conduct if they are to gain a better understanding of test takers' lexical resources across the proficiency continuum.

To investigate whether there is lexical progression across the levels, a sample of 30 Reading papers was analysed by Schmitt using Wordsmith Tools and the Compleat Lexical Tutor (www.lextutor.ca/).

Lexical variation

Table 4.15 Summary of lexical differences in Main Suite Reading papers according to a 1,000/2,000/Academic Frequency Analysis

Lexical characteristic	KET (A2)	PET (B1)	FCE (B2)	CAE (C1)	CPE (C2)
Type-token Analysis					
Words in text (tokens)	1,310	3,962	17,332	21,895	19,601
Different words (types)	483	1,184	3,404	4,773	4,664
Type-token ratio	.37	.30	.20	.22	.24
Tokens per type	2.71	3.35	5.09	4.59	4.20
Lexical density (content words/total)	.51	.55	.50	.52	.52
Frequency Analysis (VP)					
(Frequency coverage in %)					
K1 Words (1–1,000)	86.95	81.22	82.24	77.67	77.98
K2 Words (1,001–2,000)	5.04	8.81	6.65	6.12	6.32
AWL Words (academic)	.61	2.45	3.30	4.58	4.33
Off-List Words	7.40	7.52	7.81	11.63	11.37

Table 4.15 lists type-token information, as calculated by the Vocabulary Profiler (VP) English version 2.6 software available on the Compleat Lexical Tutor website. This software is the latest version of the Vocabulary Profiler first developed by Paul Nation in the early 1990s (see Nation 2001).

The first thing to notice is that the total number of words at each of the KET and PET levels is far less than at the other three levels, and so they are not comparable either with each other or with the three other levels. Although type-token ratios are influenced by token size, the number of tokens in the FCE/CAE/CPE levels is close enough to make comparison reasonable. With this in mind, a number of points are worth noting:

- The ratio between types and tokens for FCE, CAE, and CPE is very similar. Across the examination readings sampled, each type was repeated between 4.2 and 5.1 times. Thus, in terms of how many different words (types) examinees must understand in the reading texts, there does not seem to be any progression through the upper end of the suite. Note that this is for a number of readings combined, and in any single examination, the repetition per reading would be less.
- The number of lexical (content) words in relation to function (grammatical) words appears to be constant, at about 50%. This mirrors the nature of language (a large percentage of function words is necessary to 'organise' language), and so it is not feasible to increase lexical difficulty by simply increasing the percentage of content words.

Frequency analysis (1,000/2,000 wordlists and academic vocabulary categories)

Table 4.15 also lists frequency information, as calculated by the VP English software. This VP version highlights high-frequency lexis, and so is useful in illustrating how the different suite levels differ in their concentrations of basic lexis.

- The KET level is clearly the easiest in that it has a high percentage of first 1,000 vocabulary (≈87%), and a relatively low percentage of off-list words (essentially >2,000 frequency band). The KET readings also have a very low percentage (<1%) of academic words (as defined by Coxhead's (2000) *Academic Word List*).
- PET is probably the next easiest, and although it has a slightly lower percentage of 1,000 word vocabulary than the FCE level, it has a higher percentage of 2,000 words. It also has a slightly lower percentage of off-list words than FCE. On balance, PET is slightly easier than FCE, but the margin is not great.

- Both CAE and CPE have fewer high-frequency words and more off-list words than FCE, making them more difficult. However, the VP analysis shows little difference between CAE and CPE levels.
- There is a fairly clear progression in the amount of academic vocabulary through the examination suite, with the exception of CAE and CPE, which have similar percentages of academic word list (AWL) vocabulary.
- Overall, there is a reasonably clear progression through the first four levels of the suite in terms of high-frequency/off-list/academic vocabulary, but not between CAE and CPE.

Frequency analysis (20 BNC frequency levels)

The frequency analysis tool with the finest degree of gradiance currently available is the BNC 20K software available on the Compleat Lexical Tutor web-site. It gives the percentage of occurrence of texts in each of the 20 most frequent 1,000 bands. The criterion corpus is the BNC, which is the best corpus of Main Suite openly available. Table 4.16 lists the results of this analysis.

Table 4.16 Summary of lexical differences in Main Suite Reading papers according to a 20-band frequency analysis based on BNC corpus data

Lexical characteristic	KET (A2)	PET (B1)	FCE (B2)	CAE (C1)	CPE (C2)
K1	89.30	84.73	84.17	78.67	78.95
K2	5.04	8.63	7.75	8.53	8.45
K3	.69	2.32	2.57	3.30	3.71
K4	1.22	.83	1.25	2.29	2.25
K5	.69	.43	.82	1.26	1.13
K6	.08	.08	.36	.85	.87
K7	.15	.05	.18	.67	.54
K8	0	.20	.28	.50	.45
K9	.08	.20	.09	.34	.36
K10	0	.10	.09	.32	.33
K11	0	.15	.05	.24	.31
K12	0	0	.08	.21	.22
K13	0	0	.07	.16	.21
K14	0	0	0	.11	.13
K15	0	0	.01	.04	.06
K16	0	0	0	.04	.04
K17	0	0	0	.01	.03
K18	0	0	.02	.03	.02
K19	0	0	0	.01	.05
K20	0	0	.01	0	.03
Off-list	2.75	2.27	2.19	2.42	1.88
Tokens per family (on-list)	3.54	4.66	8.42	7.45	6.65
Types per family (on-list)	1.28	1.37	1.59	1.56	1.53

Note that the different wordlists and word parsers underlying the VP, and BNC 20 (and WordSmith below) programs lead to slightly different coverage percentages being reported (e.g. the VP figure for KET 1,000 is 86.95%; the BNC 20 figure is 89.31%).

- At the K1 level (most frequent 1,000 word families in English), KET has the highest percentage, then PET and FCE with similar percentages, followed by CAE and CPE with similar percentages.
- At the K2 level, PET, CAE and CPE have similar percentages ($\approx 8.5\%$), with FCE and KET having lower percentages.
- At the K3 level, KET has dropped sharply to .69%, PET and FCE have about 2.5%, and CAE and CPE have 3.3% and 3.7% respectively.
- In terms of overall frequency, KET clearly has the highest percentage of high-frequency vocabulary. Mirroring the results from the VP analysis, PET and FCE readings have quite similar frequency distributions, and if anything, this finer analysis suggests that PET may even have marginally lower frequency vocabulary than FCE.
- CAE and CPE clearly have lower frequency vocabulary than FCE. However, the two levels have extremely similar distributions all the way down the frequency chart.
- The off-list percentages are similar among the five suite levels. However, given that the off-list words indicate a >20,000 frequency band in this analysis, they are largely made up of proper nouns, and so there is no real difference between the levels in this respect.

Perhaps an easier way to appreciate the vocabulary loads is to consider a cumulative chart. Table 4.17 is the cumulative version of Table 4.16. When interpreting this table, it is useful to note that even small differences in percentage coverage (e.g. the difference between 95% and 96% coverage) can make a big difference in ease of reading as this could involve exposure to words in the next one or two thousand word categories.

- KET has the highest percentage of K1 words, and since this is by far the best known band by learners, this indicates the relative lexical ease of the KET level. This advantage also obtains through the K2 level.
- If we include the K3 level, then PET and KET have similar percentages of coverage, and this does not change through the rest of the frequency bands. This means that examinees who know mainly words in the 0–2,000 frequency bands should find the KET readings easier than the PET readings, but if they know more vocabulary than this, they should find little difference in lexical difficulty between the two suite levels.
- A similar situation exists between the PET and FCE levels, but here the threshold of equal coverage occurs at about the 6,000 frequency band.

Table 4.17 Cumulative totals of Main Suite Reading Papers according to a 20-band frequency analysis based on BNC corpus data

Lexical characteristic	KET (A2)	PET (B1)	FCE (B2)	CAE (C1)	CPE (C2)
K1	89.30	84.73	84.17	78.67	78.95
K2	94.34	93.36	91.92	87.20	87.40
K3	95.03	95.68	94.49	90.50	91.11
K4	96.25	96.51	95.74	92.79	93.36
K5	96.94	96.94	96.56	94.05	94.49
K6	97.02	97.02	96.92	94.90	95.36
K7	97.17	97.07	97.10	95.57	95.90
K8	97.17	97.27	97.38	96.07	96.35
K9	97.25	97.47	97.47	96.41	96.71
K10	97.25	97.57	97.56	96.73	97.04
K11	97.25	97.72	97.61	96.97	97.35
K12	97.25	97.72	97.69	97.18	97.57
K13	97.25	97.72	97.77	97.34	97.78
K14	97.25	97.72	97.77	97.45	97.91
K15	97.25	97.72	97.78	97.49	97.97
K16	97.25	97.72	97.78	97.53	98.01
K17	97.25	97.72	97.78	97.54	98.04
K18	97.25	97.72	97.80	97.57	98.06
K19	97.25	97.72	97.80	97.58	98.11
K20	97.25	97.72	97.81	97.58	98.14
Off-list	100	100	100	100	100

- The cumulative coverage figures between the FCE and CAE levels show that learners must know words at the 10,000 frequency band or beyond for the readings to have similar coverage. As the 10,000 word families is considered a wide vocabulary, this will be stretching all but the highest proficiency learners. Thus, the CAE level seems clearly more difficult in terms of lexis than the FCE.

- Once again, the analysis shows the close similarity of lexis between the CAE and CPE.

- It is interesting to note what frequency level of vocabulary is necessary to reach the 95% coverage level suggested by Laufer (1988). This percentage Laufer suggests is necessary for learners to understand the gist of a text (and perhaps be able to inference the meaning of unknown words in the text). In the KET, PET and FCE levels, learners would need to know the words in the K1–K3 bands. For CAE and CPE this goes up to include the K4–K6 bands. This suggests that examinees will need knowledge of many more words to successfully engage with the CAE and CPE texts.

- If we use a higher criterion (97%) closer to that suggested by Nation and Gu (2007), we find that the KET and PET readings would require knowledge of words at the K5 level, moving up to the K6 level for the

FCE readings, and to the K10 level for the CAE and CPE readings. This suggests that for true ease in reading the passages (at least in lexical terms), examinees require a large vocabulary, even at the lower levels, but especially so at the higher levels.

The above analyses looked at pooled readings from a number of examinations. This gave a good impression of the general progression (or not) of the levels in the examination suite. However, this can be slightly misleading, because any particular examinee will not be exposed to numerous readings from a suite level, but will only have to engage with the readings in a single examination administration. Within each suite level, the individual passages vary widely in the amount of lexical variation (see Table 4.18).

Table 4.18 Analysis of individual reading passages

Suite level	Average type-token	Range of TTRs of individual passages
KET (A2)	27.37	19.12–30.59
PET (B1)	30.27	24.10–34.15
FCE (B2)	32.15	16.34–36.35
CAE (C1)	30.56	18.34–38.36
CPE (C2)	30.00	17.08–35.64

The above analysis, based on lexical frequency and lexical variation, goes some way towards indicating the lexical load of the various examination suite levels (see Alderson 2007). However, the limitations of such analysis methodologies are obvious. The crux of what makes vocabulary difficult for learners is its complexity, made up of a wide variety of factors, including but not limited to the following factors (see Laufer 1997):

- the similarity or dissimilarity to a learner's L1
- the morphological/phonological complexity
- regularity of spelling
- the number of words in the L2 which have similar spellings to the target word
- amount of register marking
- amount of polysemy
- whether lexemes are individual words or multi-word units (note that the analyses above describe only individual word forms).

Frequency of occurrence can only be an indirect indication of this complexity. What is needed is a direct measure of this complexity, but unfortunately such a standardised measure does not exist. There are many facets to knowing a word with any depth of knowledge, and it is not clear whether any single one can represent quality of word knowledge in isolation, or whether this requires a battery of tests to obtain a reliable measurement.

Word frequency is the best criterion of lexical complexity readily available at the moment, but this can only be a general guide. Hopefully further research into the depth of vocabulary knowledge will suggest the means to grade vocabulary in a contextualised manner, but this remains in the future.

Nature of information

Here the concern is with whether the information in the text is abstract, e.g. ethics, love etc. or concrete, e.g. description of the contents of a room. Both types may of course be present in the same text. Research indicates that abstract words are in general more difficult to understand than concrete words (Anderson 1974 and Corkill, Glover and Bruning 1988). It seems likely that concrete language is easier to process because it can draw upon the cognitive operations of both verbal and nonverbal (imagery) systems. In contrast abstract language is restricted to the verbal system.

Eddie Williams (personal communication 2008) comments that 'Concrete nouns are certainly easier to teach via ostensive definitions than abstract ones, but not necessarily easier to comprehend within text if the reader has not met them before.'

Alderson et al (2004:127) comment: 'This dimension, mentioned in the CEFR and also considered useful by the Project team, may prove useful to estimate the difficulty of the input text.'

Nature of information: Cambridge ESOL practice

In Cambridge ESOL practice the nature of the information provided at KET and PET levels is concrete. Texts tend to be factual, focusing on descriptions of people and places. They are frequently either simple biographical articles or extracts from simple encyclopaedia entries. At FCE level the texts are still primarily concrete and specific rather than abstract although they may deal with more complex expressions of opinion and feeling. It is at CAE and CPE levels where an abstract idea may be a main focus for a text. Some would argue that this adds a layer of difficulty that may be more than purely linguistic but this is appropriate at CAE and CPE level given the fact that these exams are used as evidence of sufficient language proficiency to enter higher education and given the descriptors of C1 and C2 reading levels in the CEFR.

Content knowledge

In our earlier discussion of processing (see Chapter 3) we discussed the focus of items in terms of the explicitness or implicitness of locating the requisite information in the text. Propositional inferencing was considered suitable but pragmatic inferencing was not. However, even if background knowledge is not tested directly per se, the relationship between the resources necessary to comprehend the text and those possessed by the candidates is an important one.

The relationship between the content of the text and the candidate's existing knowledge (see Douglas 2000) will affect the way it is dealt with. This interaction between the resources of the candidate and those demanded by the task emphasises the symbiotic nature of context and cognitive validity.

According to Hughes, in general testing (1989:93) 'the subject areas will have to be as "neutral" as possible, since the students are from a variety of disciplines'. This statement is also mirrored in Weir (1993:67): 'in those situations where we are writing tests for heterogeneous groups of students, we are by necessity forced to select texts with a wider appeal than is the case when we have a more homogeneous group.'

In an attempt to decide on how familiar test content is Tan (1990) and Clapham (1996) investigated the effect of content familiarity on candidates' performance. However, neither obtained significant results on the effect of familiarity on the test scores although Clapham does note an effect for very specific texts. Khalifa (1997) found that familiarity with the topic of text was a good predictor of performance in comprehending it.

Urquhart and Weir (1998:143) advise that:

> The content of a text should be sufficiently familiar so that candidates of a requisite level of ability have sufficiently developed schemata to enable them to process it. A text should not be so arcane or so unfamiliar as to make it incapable of being mapped onto a reader's existing schemata.

As Alderson (2000:29) argues: 'every attempt should be made to allow background knowledge to facilitate performance rather than allowing its absence to inhibit performance.' Neither should a text be too familiar as then there is a danger that the candidate will be able to answer questions without recourse to the text, what Buck (2001:126–7) calls the need for 'passage dependency'.

Enright et al (2000) make the point that if we are to include reading to learn activities at the text level then candidates need to be faced with texts that contain information that is new to them. Examinations at the C1 and C2 level are used to judge suitability to handle the language demands of university courses where it would be improbable that students were exposed to text that only contained information they already knew.

We next describe how Cambridge ESOL has addressed the parameter of topic at different levels in its own examinations.

Content knowledge: Cambridge ESOL practice

Given the powerful effect that topic may have on performance, candidates should perceive task topics as suitable, realistic, reasonably familiar and feasible (Hamp-Lyons 1990:53). In Cambridge ESOL examinations, the *sine qua non* is that candidates should have sufficient knowledge of the topic to allow normal processing to take place. This means avoiding arcane topics where candidates would be unlikely to possess the schemata necessary for processing them on a global level.

In the writing of tasks, Cambridge ESOL considers the following issues:

- Are the topics broadly appropriate for the level of candidature from most cultures, experiences and age groups?
- Is there any cultural/UK bias (urban/rural, boy/girl, etc.), i.e. does any task favour a candidate of a particular background, age or gender?
- Have any cultural knowledge assumptions been made in the treatment of the topic?
- Are potentially distressing topics avoided?
- Is each topic likely to appeal to a broad base of candidates?
- Will any topic 'date' too quickly?
- Is there a good range of options in terms of topic and functions?
- Are the topics likely to produce answers of the appropriate level and of the required length for the particular candidature, i.e. not too easy or too difficult?
- Will test takers have an existing schema, i.e. organised mental framework, to be able to access the topic?

In Cambridge ESOL examinations, every effort is made to ensure that test material does not contain anything that might offend or upset candidates, potentially affect their performance or distract them during the examination. Candidates who are angered, upset or mystified by a text are less likely to perform to their best or to provide a valid and reliable sample of their language skills in an examination situation. Thus the following topics are considered unsuitable for use in Cambridge ESOL examinations in general:

- war, politics, religion including aspects of daily life which are not acceptable to certain religions
- national standpoints, any historical references likely to offend certain nations or groups
- potentially distressing topics, e.g., examinations, death, terminal illness, severe family or social problems, natural disasters and the object of common phobias such as spiders or snakes, where the treatment might be distasteful

- sex, sexism, racism including clichés, stereotyping and what could be seen as patronising attitudes towards other countries, cultures or beliefs
- drugs, gambling.

Suitable topics are listed in Table 4.19.

Table 4.19 Topics in Main Suite Reading papers

KET & PET topics	FCE, CAE & CPE topics
• personal identification • personal feelings, opinions and experiences • hobbies and leisure • sport • travel and holidays • transport • health, medicine and exercise • shopping, clothes • services • language • house and home • daily life • entertainment and media • social interaction • school and study (education) • food and drink • people (relations with other people) • places and buildings • weather (environment) • the natural world • work and jobs	• business, commerce, industry • education, training, learning • entertainment, leisure • fashion • food, drink • health, fitness • history, archaeology • language, communication • lifestyles, living conditions • natural world, environment, wildlife • personal life, circumstances, experiences • places, architecture • psychology • relationships, family • science, technology • shopping, consumerism • social and national customs • social trends • sports • the arts • the media • travel, tourism, weather • work, jobs

Topics are chosen to be accessible and of interest to the broad range of candidates and are not intended to exclude any large group in terms of their standpoint or assumptions. Care is taken to ensure that candidates come to the text equally, no matter where they are from, how old they are, what their background is, and so on (as far as it is possible to control for this). Clearly, it is impossible to interest everybody, but subjects which appeal only to a minority are avoided. The topic should not be biased in favour of any particular section of the test population. Material must not favour candidates with specialised knowledge of a particular subject or have content that would be too specialised or technical for the majority of candidates. In those situations where tests are constructed for heterogeneous groups of students, there is a need to select texts with a wider appeal than may be the case when we have a more homogeneous group, for example, ESP tests. In the latter case, such as for the Cambridge Business English Certificate (BEC) examinations (see O'Sullivan 2006) it may be easier to select topics with narrower or more targeted appeal.

Nearly 80% of Main Suite candidates attend preparation classes where exam topics, text types and task types are covered. Candidates of a requisite level of ability should therefore have sufficient existing schemata to enable them to fulfil the requirements of the task. Cambridge ESOL attempts to identify and cover relevant content domains. Coverage of the appropriate domains of language use is attained through the employment of relevant topics, tasks, text types and contexts. The domains, therefore, need to be specified with reference to the characteristics of the test taker, and to the characteristics of the relevant language use contexts, as was discussed in some detail in Chapter 2.

Topics may not vary much between the levels in terms of familiarity but the treatment of the text in terms of text nature, source, length would certainly vary. For example, a Sports topic may be presented in KET and PET using a simple encyclopaedia entry while the same topic may be presented in FCE, CAE and CPE using a magazine article

At KET level candidates need to have the language to deal with personal and daily life: basic everyday situations and communication needs (see Van Ek and Trim 1998a). The focus tends to be on topics that are accessible to teenage candidates. AT PET level a broader range of general topics relating to the candidate's personal life and experience is covered; narrative topics also feature at PET level (see Van Ek and Trim 1998). FCE candidates may be expected to deal with a wide range of knowledge areas including any non-specialist topic that has relevance for candidates worldwide (see Van Ek and Trim 2001). CAE candidates are expected to be able to deal with topics that are more specialised and less personal than those that tend to feature at lower levels. The step up to CAE also involves coping with lexically and conceptually challenging treatment of topic areas. At CPE level more abstract and academic topics appear and the candidate may be expected to comprehend passages on any non-specialist topic. CPE candidates are expected to be able to operate confidently in a wide variety of social, work-related and study-related situations. At all levels topics that might offend or otherwise unfairly disadvantage any group of candidates are avoided.

Conclusion

In grading the specifications for the five levels of the Main Suite examinations, careful thought has been given to the relative complexity of the texts employed. Text demands are increased gradually as one progresses up the suite across the range of parameters identified as being likely to contribute to the processing load on the candidate. Due consideration has been given to the task demands that can be deemed to be representative of performance at different stages of proficiency.

Tasks which have generated adequate evidence of *a priori* validity according to expert scrutiny of their cognitive and context validity are then pretested on a representative group of candidates before administration proper (see Chapter 7 for details). Any final amendments are made with reference to the results and feedback from the pretesting. Live reading examinations are then constructed from such tasks.

We have now discussed all aspects of the *a priori* validation of test tasks in terms of their cognitive and context based validity. Once scores are available on operational tasks we enter the stage of *a posteriori* validation. The first crucial aspect of post test validation we will deal with is the aspect of *scoring validity*. We have already addressed the importance of candidates being aware of the criteria by which they will be assessed in those items where open constructed responses are required. In the next chapter we look at the issues relating to criteria in more detail and examine the whole rating process from appointment and training of examiners through to post examination adjustment procedures, all of which contribute to scoring validity and thereby to the overall validity of a test and its scores.

5 Scoring validity

In previous chapters we have looked at the test taker, at the cognitive and context validity of test tasks, and set out the various parameters that need to be addressed in a validity argument at the test design stage.

In this chapter we concentrate on the scoring process itself but earlier points made in relation to contextual parameters with the potential to affect test reliability, for example, the number and type of items in a task/paper, emphasise the interconnectedness of these validity components. Although for descriptive purposes the various elements of our socio-cognitive model have been presented separately, we have emphasised that there is a 'symbiotic' relationship between context validity, cognitive validity and scoring validity, which in our opinion together constitute what is frequently referred to as *construct* validity. Decisions taken with regard to parameters of task context will impact on the processing that takes place in task completion. Likewise, where scoring criteria are made known to candidates in advance they may, for example, choose to spend more or less time on a particular part of the reading test (see for example section on weighting in Chapter 4). The criteria for scoring are themselves an important part of the construct. One would not wish for example to see a mark scheme in a reading test which penalises mechanical aspects of a student's constructed responses. Our concern in a reading test should be whether the reader has understood the passage, not whether they have mastered the English spelling system.

Scoring validity is concerned with all aspects of the testing process that can impact on the reliability of test scores. It accounts for the extent to which test scores are based on appropriate criteria, exhibit consensual agreement in marking, are as free as possible from measurement error, are stable over time, and engender confidence as reliable decision-making indicators.

Scoring validity is important because if we cannot depend on the rating of student responses, it matters little that the tasks we develop are potentially valid in terms of both cognitive and contextual parameters. Faulty marking criteria, unsuitable rating procedures, lack of training and standardisation, poor or variable conditions for rating, and unsystematic or ill-conceived procedures for grading and awarding can all lead to a reduction in scoring validity and increase the risk of construct irrelevant variance. Deficiencies in scoring validity may vitiate the other work that has gone into creating a valid instrument (Alderson et al 1995:105). For these reasons, examination boards must devote attention and resources to all aspects of scoring validity.

In Figure 5.1 below, we draw on the scoring validity parameters suggested by Weir (2005) as being most likely to have an impact on reading test performance. The subsequent text follows the ordering of the parameters in Figure 5.1.

Figure 5.1 Scoring validity parameters

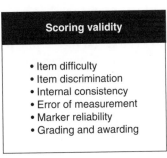

examination boards must devote attention and resources to all aspects of

Item difficulty and discrimination

Although Lado (1961:5) insisted that linguistic and not statistical analysis should determine the content of a test, he states that 'statistical treatment has its place in the refinement of the test'. Test items are usually analysed using classical test theory (CTT) or Item Response Theory (IRT) based statistics.

Classical item analysis considers item facility (IF), and item discrimination through point biserial correlations (r_{pbi}) in order to determine the suitability of each item for inclusion in the test. Henning (1987:49) states that difficulties with tests are often due 'to the misfit of item difficulty to person ability'. Basically, this means that the items are either too easy or too difficult for the learners. Item facility is calculated by finding the proportion of correct responses to a given test item using the formula:

$$IF = \frac{\Sigma C_r}{N}$$

Where, IF $\quad=$ item facility
$\Sigma C_r \quad=$ sum of correct responses
N $\quad=$ number of test takers

Items that prove to be too easy (i.e. IF 0.75 or above) or too difficult (i.e. IF 0.2 or below) are not very informative since they tell us little about the varying levels of ability and may create a floor or ceiling effect. The test designer needs to take a decision on their inclusion or exclusion from a test. If a wide spread of scores is required in a test, then the majority of items should be as near to a facility value of 0.5 as possible. Such items provide the widest scope for variation among the individual students (see Alderson et al 1995). Of course an item may prove difficult because as well as being an important part of the construct being measured, it is more cognitively demanding than other items set at this level. In this case it would be retained if it discriminated well. The problem with very easy items, though, is that so few people get them wrong that there is little or no difference between the strong and weak candidates so the discriminability figures will be adversely affected.

Discovering what the item facility is (the difficulty of an item for a specific population) does not really tell us enough. To discover how students of different ability levels cope with a particular item we must calculate that item's discriminability. An item discrimination index measures the extent to which the high-scoring group is getting an item right in relation to the low-scoring group.

Examination boards tend to employ a measure of discrimination called the point-biserial correlation (r_{pbi}), which looks at the correlation between two variables; one which is dichotomous (e.g. right or wrong) and the other is interval (such as scores in a test). In language tests, the dichotomous variable is the item response and the interval scale is the overall test score. The way the correlation works is to correlate an item with the total test score. This may lead to overestimating the discriminatory power of an item since that item's value is included in the total score. To counteract this problem, a corrected value is used. This value is the correlation between the item and the score on the whole test/subtest minus the score on that item. (r_{pbi}) is used to understand how well the item discriminates between the weak and strong candidates. In task-based items, a result of less than 0.25 means that the item doesn't discriminate well between high and low scoring groups as shown in Table 5.1 below.

Table 5.1 below contains data on two multiple-matching items testing reading comprehension, each with nine options (shown as letters in the Alt. column), i.e. it is a selected response item. The correct answer letter is in bold type, the rest are distractors. The point-biserial statistic is the main point of interest in this table. The table has been generated using ITEMAN – a classical item analysis software program.

Item 1, a relatively easy item (0.79), had an r_{pbi} of 0.18. The percentage of the less able candidates (Low) who answered the item correctly (i.e. selected C) is close to the percentage of the more able candidates (High) who got the item right (71% and 88%). In comparison, item 2 which is also a relatively easy item (0.85) had an r_{pbi} of 0.37 because more of the top group and a lower percentage of the bottom group got it right.

The main disadvantage of classical item analysis is that item statistics vary according to the level and spread of ability in a sample. The Item Response

Table 5.1 Example from FCE Reading with ITEMAN analysis

No	Item Statistics		Alt	Alternative Statistics			
Seq	Prop item Correct	Point Biserial		Prop Total	Low	High	Point Biserial
1 1–1	.79	.18	A	.00	.01	.00	−.07
			B	.15	.18	.10	−.08
			C	**.79**	**.71**	**.88**	**.18**
			D	.00	.01	.00	−.06
			E	.00	.00	.00	−.06
			F	.03	.04	.02	−.04
			G	.01	.02	.00	−.11
			H	.01	.03	.00	−.15
			I	.00	.00	.00	−.03
			Other	.00	.00	.00	−.02
2 1–2	.85	.37	A	.01	.03	.00	−.12
			B	.10	.19	.02	−.24
			C	.01	.02	.00	−.12
			D	.00	.01	.00	−.08
			E	.01	.02	.00	−.12
			F	.01	.03	.00	−.13
			G	**.85**	**.68**	**.98**	**.37**
			H	.01	.02	.00	−.11
			I	.00	.00	.00	−.02
			Other	.00	.00	.00	−.02

Theory measurement model, however, provides analysis of tests and test items that are not sample-dependent, that is, independent of the distribution characteristics of a sample (see Miller and Linn 1988). It allows us to see if an item is functioning in a predictable way, i.e. that it is not 'misfitting', and to relate the difficulty of any item to the ability of any test taker.

The various branches of IRT differ mainly

> ... 'in the number of item parameters (characteristics of the interaction between a test taker and a test item) being estimated in the analysis. Rasch analysis considers one parameter (item difficulty), while other models consider one or more additional parameters (item discrimination and a guessing factor). There is ongoing dispute over the relative merits of the two traditions, especially in relation to the analysis of dichotomous data' ... (Davies, Brown, Elder, Hill, Lumley and McNamara 1999:99).

Before using IRT, though, it is necessary for the data to meet the underlying assumptions of: uni-dimensionality (i.e. measuring a single trait); item-independence (i.e. responding to one item is not dependent on responding to a previous or a subsequent item); similar item discrimination indices; and sufficient allocation of time so that candidates can answer all the items (see Hambleton, Swaminathan and Rogers 1991).

The Rasch model provides the basis for constructing a measurement scale which is necessary for item banking and allows the linking of test versions (see Chapter 7 for fuller details of this and exam equating). Item banking involves assembling a bank of *calibrated* items, that is, items of known difficulty. Designs for collecting response data ensure a link across items at all levels (Bond and Fox 2001, Wright and Stone 1979).

Item difficulty and discrimination: Cambridge ESOL practice

Cambridge ESOL uses both Rasch-based and classical statistics to evaluate item suitability for use in test papers. Facility values, discrimination indices and Rasch values are generated using a number of in-house and third party applications routinely during the test development cycle. For example, at the pretesting stage where items are pretested on a representative sample of the targeted candidature (N.B. the sample is made up of candidates who are taking exam preparation courses), the statistics are scrutinised by the pretest review team and conventional ranges for these values are usually used, i.e., facility values between 0.33 and 0.67 or r_{pbi} of 0.25 or above. In the case of r_{pbi} the significance level of the estimate is examined and if it is less than 0.05 the indication is that the item may be acceptable. Items which have values outside of the predicted range are subjected to particular scrutiny. Often this allows the item-writing team to identify problems with the materials and will result in tasks or items being rejected or sent back to item writers for specific amendments. Exceptions are made, though, when items which test a specific aspect of language need to be included or starting a test with an easy item and ending a test with a difficult item is desired.

Cambridge ESOL uses the one parameter Rasch model for item calibration. Other Item Response Theory models are used from time to time for research purposes but do not form part of the routine procedures in the item banking system. The WINSTEPS analysis program (Linacre 2006), supplemented by Cambridge ESOL with in-house programs for formatting data and handling output, is used to produce a measurement scale known as the Cambridge Common Scale. It is this scale which underpins the Cambridge ESOL Local Item Banking System (LIBS). A full description of the item banking system in Cambridge ESOL examinations can be found in Chapter 7 where its use in developing equivalent forms of tests is described. Adopting a Rasch-based approach means that the inherent difficulty of the items in an examination can be estimated independently of the particular sample of pretest candidates who may, for different reasons, be higher or lower in ability than the live candidature. Item difficulty is looked at in terms of logits, i.e. the probability of a particular response. The logit scale not only tells us that one item is more difficult than another but how much more difficult it is. Within Cambridge ESOL, the Rasch logits are converted to a score of 0 to 100 on the Cambridge Common Scale. This is referred to as scaled Rasch.

When Reading Comprehension papers are constructed, every effort is made to ensure that in addition to content coverage, the mean difficulty of the paper is as close as possible to the target difficulty set for that paper. For example, a target difficulty of 62 scaled Rasch which is just above the mid point in the Cambridge ESOL Common Scale has been set for the construction of an FCE live Reading Comprehension paper. As of December 2008, there are 30 items in this paper that are allowed to vary in difficulty +/− 10 scaled Rasch. This is to make sure that a reasonable range of language ability within the B2 level is assessed in this paper. Because the items are weighted differently, these questions allow for a total raw score of 45 marks. Marks in each component are scaled out of 40 by means of linear algorithms, and summed to give a total for the whole examination of 200. Thus nominally Reading contributes 20% to a candidate's final result. The effective weighting actually differs slightly, depending on the standard deviation of marks in each component, which is not standardised in the current approach to mark aggregation.

As of December 2008 the raw mark out of a total 200 is converted for reporting purposes to a standardised score out of 100 and in the process the pass mark is set to a standard value of 60. This allows standardised scores to be reported which candidates can relate to grade boundaries, helping to meet a long-standing demand from exam users for such score-level information. Teachers want to know how many marks are needed to pass the exam, but in fact the pass mark varies slightly from session to session depending on the precise difficulty of the component papers (something which is nowadays well controlled for thanks to the item banking methodology used). This variation made it problematic to release raw marks, because they are not strictly comparable across sessions. The use of standardised scores addresses this problem. The pre-determined fixed ability level is based on various studies that were carried out when Cambridge ESOL's common scale was developed in the 1990s alongside the CEFR levels (see Chapter 7 for a full discussion of Cambridge ESOL's Common Scale and the CEFR levels).

Internal consistency

Three broad categories of instrument *reliability* have traditionally been recognised in the field:

a) alternate-form coefficients (derived from the administration of parallel forms in independent sessions)

b) test–retest coefficients

c) internal consistency coefficients.

Of these three, the use of internal consistency coefficients to estimate the reliability of objective tests, such as selected response reading or listening tests, is most common and to some extent this is taken as 'the industry standard' (e.g. use of Cronbach Alpha). The fact that these coefficients are relatively easy to calculate means that other, perhaps more appropriate, estimates are not used as commonly, e.g. test–retest estimates are less often reported because adequate data is difficult to obtain under operational conditions (see Chapter 7 on criterion-related validity for a discussion of the less commonly applied alternate form coefficient of a test's validity).

Popham (1990:55) defines internal consistency as the extent to which individual items are functioning in a similar fashion. Internal consistency is applicable to discrete item types, e.g. MCQ, and presumes that a test is *focused on just one ability or skill*. Where a test consists of items or groups of items which are intended to test different things, then they should never be analysed together when estimating internal consistency. The basic premise of internal consistency is that individual candidates will tend to perform in a similar way on items testing the same ability so the 'perfect' set of responses will consist only of all correct or all incorrect.

There are traditionally two methods used for calculating internal consistency: split half reliability estimates and estimates based on item variances. Split half estimates simply split the test into two halves typically taking the even numbered items and the odd numbered item and then correlating the two parts. The expected correlation coefficients are in the range of 0.8 to 0.9.

A flaw in the split-half reliability method is that the items in one half may not be equivalent to the items in the other half. It might be possible to split the test into two halves in other ways than that suggested above, but whichever way is chosen may suffer from lack of equivalence between the two halves. The solution to the problem of lack of equivalence between the two halves is to determine the mean of all possible split-half correlations. In this way the biases of any individual split-halves are substantially ironed out. Two simple formulae for estimating the mean of all possible split halves are Kuder-Richardson 20 and Cronbach Alpha. KR-20 can be used where items are simply right or wrong, and are scored 1 or 0. Cronbach Alpha can also be used where items are awarded scores on a range, e.g. 0, 1, or 2.

A Kuder-Richardson formula 20 can be calculated as follows:

$$r_{tt} = \frac{n}{(n-1)} \times \frac{(s_t^2 - \Sigma s_i^2)}{s_t^2}$$

Where, r_{tt} = KR-20 estimate of reliability
n = number of items in the test
s_t^2 = variance of the test scores (item variance)
Σs_i^2 = sum of the variances of all items (sometimes Σpq)

The minimum acceptable KR-20 estimate for a test is normally set at 0.7, though for a multi-item high-stakes test with a normally distributed population the acceptable standards are raised to 0.8 or 0.9 (for example for Cambridge ESOL and ETS). Bachman and Palmer (1996:135) advise that when setting 'the minimum acceptable level of reliability', test developers should consider 'the way the construct has been defined and the nature of the test tasks'. The narrower the definition is, the higher the expected level of reliability. Similarly, higher levels of reliability are expected if the features of the test tasks are 'relatively uniform' than if the test includes a 'wide variety of types of test tasks' (1996:135).

Estimates of reliability based on item variance are not without problems. The estimate will be affected by the number of items in the test: the more items, the higher the estimate will be. The other factor that can affect the estimate is the test population. Where the range of ability of the candidature is broad, with very weak to very strong candidates, the estimate has the potential to be high because of the wide range of ability. However, where there is a test population that is close in ability, i.e. a truncated population in a level-based test such as those in the Cambridge ESOL Main Suite, the estimate may be restricted. It is therefore of the greatest importance that the estimate of reliability is interpreted in terms of the range of ability tested.

Internal consistency coefficients have been historically reported for norm referenced measurement, based on classical test theory and with discrete items. Their use in examinations that are task-based may be misleading as they could underestimate the reliability of scores due to the fact that items are not interchangeable but are grouped together and in many cases are text/task-related. This may lead us to question whether we would want very high internal consistency estimates at all times. In the case of examinations which employ a wide variety of task-based materials and item types, a concern for context validity may mean that a high internal consistency might not be an appropriate aim (see Jones 2001).

Interestingly, internal consistency tells us retrospectively just as much about the construct we have measured as the dependability of the results. Though one might desire high internal consistency for a multiple-choice test of knowledge of structure or discrete lexical items, it might be rather naive to assume that constructs such as reading or listening are as unitary (see Chapter 3 above, Urquhart and Weir 1998, Grabe and Stoller 2002 and Weir 2005 where arguments are made for a partially divisible view of reading). If they are divisible, then presumably high internal consistency would not be expected when assessing these skills. It may well be the case that items in a reading test are clearly testing different aspects of reading ability, e.g. some may require text-level comprehension where other items are testing within sentence level comprehension. It may be that the focus is on expeditious versus careful reading comprehension abilities in different parts of the test (see Chapter 3 for theoretical support for this and Weir et al 2000 for empirical evidence of the differences).

Wood (1993:138–39) sums the matter up succinctly:

The plausibility of internal consistency estimates appears to be further compromised by the deliberate efforts made to introduce variety and heterogeneity into examinations. If the principle of inclusion in an examination is to mix modalities and skill requirements and contents so that individual opportunities to respond well are enhanced, why expect internal consistency?

Internal consistency: Cambridge ESOL practice

Saville (2003) points out that, in the case of Cambridge ESOL examinations, which employ a wide variety of task-based materials and item types, very high internal consistency may not be an appropriate aim. Task-based exercises, such as those now used in the Cambridge ESOL exams, have been gradually replacing discrete point multiple-choice items in order to provide far greater context and authenticity (both situational and interactional). A consequence of this is that the number of items in some papers might be limited to fit practical time constraints. This may bring about a small reduction in the estimated reliability using an internal consistency estimate when compared with longer tests using discrete point items. While this estimate might be regarded negatively as being on the low side, this may be an unwarranted conclusion when test validity, impact and practicality are taken into account.

Each Main Suite examination is benchmarked to a criterion level of proficiency, i.e. covers a restricted ability range within Cambridge ESOL's framework of criterion levels (see Chapter 7 below for further discussion of this). Candidates sitting for PET are expected to be at CEFR B1 level whereas those taking FCE are expected to be at CEFR B2 level. The truncation of the ability range is particularly true of the highest level (CPE–C2), where there is evidently an upper limit to the distribution of candidates' ability (see Weir and Milanovic 2003 Chapter 1 for a fuller discussion of this). Where the population of candidates is a truncated sample, tests will tend to produce lower reliability indices relative to tests which cater for a wider range of the ability continuum. Accordingly, each exam in the Main Suite is not likely to get the very high internal consistency figures seen in an examination like BULATS which examines a wider range of ability from CEFR level A1 to C2. BULATS is a multilevel examination designed to test the language of employees who need to use a foreign language in their work and for students and employees on language courses or on professional/business courses where foreign language ability is an important element of the course.

While a reliability estimate is considered to be useful as evidence in the investigation of test quality, it is used with caution for several reasons. Strictly speaking, the estimated reliability is not a feature of the test itself, but rather of the results of administration of the test to a given group of examinees. This is precisely why Sawilowsky (2000) warns that reliability indices of tests should not be compared devoid of the context in which they were collected. 'Statements about the reliability of a certain test must be accompanied by an explanation of what type of reliability was estimated, how it was calculated, and under what conditions or for which sample characteristics the result was obtained' (Sawilowsky 2000:157–73).

Even though Main Suite examinations will be affected by the format and a truncated population, Cambridge ESOL has attempted to apply variance-based estimates to its different papers. It routinely calculates Cronbach Alpha when item analysis is carried out at the pretesting stage and after live test administration use. The statistic is scrutinised by subject officers and chairs of the examination papers as one indicator of the quality of the test (see Chapter 7 for further details of the pretesting stage). A lower than expected alpha, at the pretesting stage, leads to further investigation and a subsequent course of action. For example, it may reveal a problem with the way the data was collected, e.g. lack of variance in the sample, or a specific flaw in the test materials, e.g. poorly functioning distractors.

In recent years Cambridge ESOL has set target internal consistency estimates for the item-based components of the Main Suite examinations – Paper 1 (Reading), Paper 4 (Listening) and, where applicable, Paper 3 (Use of English). These target levels are routinely used in the test construction procedures and the predicted operational reliability for each paper is based on the type and quality of the tasks that are chosen according to the test specifications. The information used includes the Rasch-based difficulty estimates and other data obtained during the item writing and pretesting processes such as feedback from test centres. In practice this means that the estimates which are obtained operationally in 'live' test administrations typically fall between an acceptable minimum value and the intended target value (which is also sometimes exceeded).

In Main Suite examinations, the expected range of alphas for a Reading paper such as CPE with 40 items ranges from 0.80 to 0.85. The alphas do vary according to the length of the test paper in terms of number of items. Better reliability scores are obtained if the test has more items. Geranpayeh (2004) reported 0.84 as an average reliability figure for 2002/2003 FCE Reading papers which had 35 items, all of which are based on communicative tasks (Weir and Milanovic 2003:107–108). Similar levels of reliability are reported by O'Sullivan for the three levels of the Business English Certificates (BEC) examinations (O'Sullivan 2006: 99–100).

Table 5.2 reports the reliability figures for FCE over a number of sessions. On average the reliability of the Reading paper is 0.84 which, as mentioned earlier, is a respectable index for a test with 35 items.

Table 5.3 reports figures for IELTS and indicates the expected levels of reliability for task-based tests containing 40 items.

In addition to Cronbach's Alpha, Cambridge ESOL uses other approaches

Table 5.2 Alpha across FCE versions

Year	Session	Version	Alpha by version
2005	June	1	0.85
	June	2	0.81
	Dec	1	0.83
	Dec	2	0.83
2006	June	1	0.85
	June	2	0.85
	Dec	1	0.84
	Dec	2	0.84
2007	June	1	0.86
	June	2	0.85
	Dec	1	0.84
	Dec	2	0.85

Source: Cambridge Local Item Banking System

Table 5.3 Alpha across IELTS Academic Reading versions in 2007

Average alpha across versions	Alpha by version
version 310	0.85
version 311	0.85
version 312	0.87
version 313	0.87
version 314	0.84
version 315	0.85
version 316	0.88
version 317	0.85
version 318	0.83
version 319	0.90
version 320	0.87
version 321	0.88
version 322	0.89
version 323	0.84
version 324	0.84
version 325	0.90
Average alpha across versions	**0.86**

Source: www.ielts.org/teachers_and_researchers/analysis_of_test_data/test_ performance_2007.aspx

to estimating and reporting on the reliability of the examinations and their components which are appropriate to a level-based system of examinations. For example, Bachman et al's 1996 study made use of Generalisability theory. In this multi-faceted Generalisability-study design, content analysis of test method characteristics (TM) and components of communicative language ability (CLA) was carried out by five raters using six versions of the FCE Reading paper. To investigate raters' consistency of content ratings, variance components were estimated for all six forms using the Genova software program for generalisability analyses (Crick and Brennan 1983). Results showed that 'for the CLA ratings, the five raters agreed on about 64% of their ratings. For the TM ratings, however, the agreement was closer to 75%' (p.134). According to the researchers, the lower agreement percentage on CLA demonstrated a need for further rater training and a better definition of the components of CLA. It should be noted that TM characteristics comprised of facets of the testing environment and test input such as nature of language and channel of presentation whereas CLA looked at grammatical, textual, illocutionary, sociolinguistic and strategic facets of communicative competence.

Standard error of measurement

Standard Error of Measurement is a useful measure of test consistency as it incorporates not only the internal consistency of the test but also the variation in test scores. For Bachman (1990:161), reliability is concerned with minimising the effects of measurement error. No test is likely to be totally accurate. All will have a 'grey' area around the score. The test taker's ability lies somewhere near the score they achieve in a test. The SEM is an indication of the range, on either side of the test score, in which the test taker's ability might actually lie. We can use the SEM to calculate a confidence interval which Bachman (2004:196) describes as: 'the score range within which a given test taker's "domain score" is likely to fall.'

Luoma (2004:183), in one of the clearest accounts of SEM, describes how the SEM shows the degree of confidence we should place in a reported score. This can be important especially if individuals are compared on the basis of their scores. If one has a score of 28 and the other a score of 31, the SEM can indicate whether the difference between them is as clear as it may seem.

To calculate the SEM, we use the following formula:

$$SEM = SD\sqrt{1 - r}$$

Where SEM = Standard error of measurement
     SD   = Standard deviation
     r   = Internal consistency

It should be noted that this formula makes use of internal consistency or other reliability estimates, and the higher this is the lower the SEM, which is therefore likely to be subject to the same limitations as were discussed in the previous section.

Hughes (2003:42) points out that using Item Response Theory provides an even better estimate of probable error in a student's score. In classical analysis, as described above, we have only a single estimate of SEM for all candidates whereas . . .'IRT gives an estimate for each individual, basing this estimate on the individual's performance on each test item'.

Standard error of measurement: Cambridge ESOL practice

Table 5.4 presents the SEM figures for FCE Reading papers over recent years.

Table 5.4 SEM across FCE versions

Year	Session	Version	Alpha by version	SEM	SD
2005	June	1	0.85	2.30	5.95
	June	2	0.81	2.39	5.50
	Dec	1	0.83	2.43	5.91
	Dec	2	0.83	2.31	5.57
2006	June	1	0.85	2.38	6.10
	June	2	0.85	2.44	6.23
	Dec	1	0.84	2.30	5.74
	Dec	2	0.84	2.42	6.14
2007	June	1	0.86	2.34	6.14
	June	2	0.85	2.45	6.26
	Dec	1	0.84	2.40	5.95
	Dec	2	0.85	2.41	6.24

Source: Cambridge Local Item Banking System

The above table shows that the SEM is within an acceptable range and has been stable across the different sessions.

Average SEM figures for IELTS Academic and General Training Reading papers used in 2007 are shown in Table 5.5.

Table 5.5 Mean, standard deviation and standard error of measurement of Listening and Reading

	Mean band score	Standard deviation	SEM
Academic Reading	5.98	1.06	0.39
General Training Reading	5.59	1.26	0.41

Source: www.ielts.org/teachers_and_researchers/analysis_of_test_data/test_performance_2007.aspx

For IELTS, the SEM should be interpreted in terms of the final band scores reported for Reading modules on a scale of 0–9.

Weir and Milanovic (2003 Chapter 8) advise that in constructed response items, when taking decisions on pass or fail, consideration should be given to double marking at least those candidates who fall within one standard error of the pass/fail boundary. Hughes (2003:42) in a similar vein argues that we should be: 'very cautious about making important decisions on the basis of the test scores of candidates whose actual scores place them close to the cut-off point.'

Marker reliability

Rater reliability makes an important contribution to overall test reliability. If we have different markers for a constructed response reading test (i.e. where responses are produced by candidates rather than being selected), will they arrive at the same results? What steps can we take to ensure that different markers will give the same picture of somebody's ability and that they can maintain consistency in their own standards of marking from the first to last answer sheet? The closer the agreement in these matters, the more reliable a test.

Error variance can also result from the performance of the scorers involved in the marking process. If two people are marking the same constructed responses in a reading test we would want to know to what extent they are:

- in overall agreement
- ranking a group of students in the same order
- rating individuals at the same level of accuracy
- consistent in their own judgements during the whole marking process.

When we are concerned with tests in which responses are produced by candidates rather than being selected, the consistency of the markers needs to be estimated. Markers need to be consistent in two ways: they need to be consistent within themselves (*intra-rater reliability*), i.e. given a particular quality of performance, they need to award the same mark whenever this quality appears; and there needs to be consistency of marking between markers (*inter-rater reliability*), i.e. one marker will award the same mark as another when confronted with a performance of the same quality.

In cases where two raters are used, inter-rater reliability is established via correlation, perfect agreement being indicated by a correlation of 1.0. A correlation of 0.9 or above is where we might start to feel comfortable that two markers are rating in a similar fashion.

If the test consists of selected response items, and is machine scored, we can expect a high degree of reliability of marking. An Optical Mark Reader (OMR) form which is accurately designed and printed, and properly filled out and handled will read with 100% accuracy. Where marking is done by hand (often using a transparent plastic key) there is likely to be a lowering of the reliability due to manual human error. This, for example, can occur from faulty application of the marking key to errors occasioned by transferring scores to a spreadsheet programme (like Excel). In high-stakes tests, this manual transfer process is done twice and the two data sets compared for accuracy. Ensuring the accuracy of transferring this data is crucial because unless individual item data is collected accurately, we can never properly analyse a test.

Marker reliability: Cambridge ESOL practice

The Reading component of Main Suite examinations is objectively marked. Candidates shade their answers on OMR forms. Examples of these forms with explanations on how to fill in the responses are provided in the handbooks for teachers and candidates. The OMR forms are automatically scanned using optical mark reading scanners. The data is captured in an electronic file held on the OMR application server. Error-free forms are batched together into groups and are stored on the Cambridge Assessment Exam Processing System (EPS). Figure 5.2 below provides an overview of the process.

Any forms that contain data errors are automatically sorted by the scanning machine for error correction. The type of errors that may occur are either lozenging errors, e.g. missing responses/multiple responses where a single one is required, or failure of the encoded data to be read accurately by the scanning equipment, e.g. misreading of centre number. Every batch of errors has an equivalent electronic file. This data error file is then amended manually, checked and, upon completion, the corrected file is uploaded onto EPS.

OMR scanning lends itself to the automatic marking of selected responses which take the form of numbers or letters. However, in other Cambridge ESOL examinations such as BULATS or BEC involving the construction of short answers, the marking of the Reading papers requires the use of human raters (see Appendix E for a comprehensive description of General marking: performance management). A well-trained team of markers checks candidates' answers against a list of appropriate responses. To ensure the accuracy of this process, a comprehensive and robust programme of recruitment, induction, training, co-ordination, monitoring and evaluation of general markers is in place. The programme starts with assessing an applicant's suitability taking into account the applicant's educational standard and work experience. Once short-listed, applicants take a 15-minute language test which evaluates their skills in error correction and use of English, as well as an interview which explores the extent to which candidates are able to work in a team environment and their level of attention to detail. Those recruited sign a confidentiality undertaking and then undergo face-to-face training using General Marking Training materials which include both general and version-specific elements (i.e. co-ordination in the application of the relevant mark scheme). Here, extensive marking guidelines are provided for each part of the Reading paper giving detailed standardised procedures for dealing

Figure 5.2 OMR process

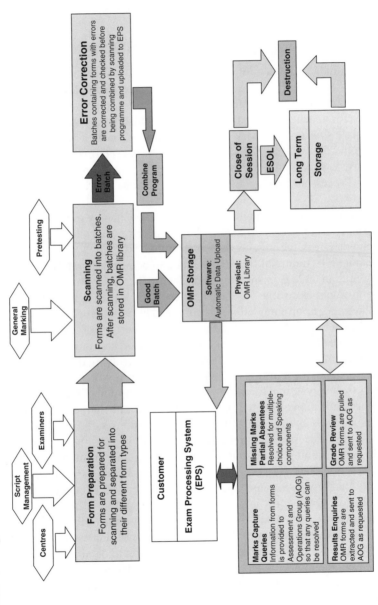

with candidates' responses, as well as instructions for atypical responses (including legibility issues and the use of brackets by candidates).

In the case of IELTS, general markers have no contractual relationship with Cambridge ESOL but are instead engaged by individual IELTS test centres. All general markers for IELTS must be certificated. Certification is based on an assessment of performance following training and standardisation. Trainees are given two attempts at certification. Failure to reach the required standard on the second attempt results in permanent rejection. Successful trainees sign a code of practice which makes them eligible to start working as general markers.

In mainstream general marking at Cambridge ESOL, all general markers are trained and co-ordinated each administrative session. Co-ordination means version-specific training, where general markers are familiarised with both the generic test (e.g. FCE) and the specific test version (e.g. FCE, Dec 2008) they are going to mark. This includes item-types, particular tasks and items and the mark scheme, and is conducted by the Marking Quality Co-ordinator (MQC), a suitably qualified external ELT professional. Though the behaviour of individual items is to some extent predicted by pretesting, this co-ordination process allows general markers to be warned of items where the key may be more flexible than is normally the case, and where, as a result, extra vigilance is required in order to bring potentially correct candidate responses to the attention of the MQC.

Throughout the marking period, which takes place on-site, general marking instructions are provided and the MQC is always available to answer queries. The general marking teams are also monitored on an ongoing basis and the Monitor, who is a highly trained rater, provides feedback to markers and alerts the Marking Quality Co-ordinator and the administrative team which manages marker performance with regard to any markers whose accuracy rate may give cause for concern. Accuracy rates are recorded by Monitors on an ongoing basis and performance below standard is discussed and corrected by retraining and remarking of scripts before results are released. Performance is regarded as satisfactory where 99.9% of items have been marked correctly.

As part of Cambridge ESOL's commitment to quality control, it investigates the degree of general markers' accuracy and consistency and determines follow-up actions. Training and monitoring records are kept for evaluation purposes. All general markers undergo a performance review at the end of each administration session using Cambridge ESOL's standard Performance Management System (PMS) ratings. The PMS considers the principal accountabilities of a job and the performance objectives related to these accountabilities. When performance is reviewed against the set objectives, one of the following ratings is awarded: incomplete, acceptable, good, high, exceptional. The rating 'incomplete' is defined as someone who is not learning the job as expected, has not met the agreed objectives and who has not responded to feedback (see Appendix E for further information on Cambridge ESOL Marking Procedures).

Research is carried out to investigate the effectiveness of training and standardisation. For example, Thighe's (2002) study of IELTS general marking led to the development of the IELTS general marking standardisation manual. Blackhurst and Cope (2007) investigated the effectiveness of this manual through examining the accuracy and consistency of general markers. OMRs from the IELTS Academic Reading paper were re-marked for this study. The centres chosen for the study were selected randomly worldwide. The researchers found that there had been a noticeable improvement in the marking accuracy of the Reading paper. The results of the 2007 study led them to conclude that the introduction of the manual has contributed to an increase in marker reliability. The accuracy of general markers continues to be monitored and similar studies will take place in future. All IELTS examination data is collected and stored electronically, both for immediate grading purposes and for post-test analysis and for future research and validation purposes. For IELTS Reading, response data is collected and stored at item level. This means that item analysis and other statistical procedures can be used to investigate the validity and reliability of the papers. The data can also be matched with information about the candidates' background so that issues such as differential functioning of items and other forms of bias can be investigated (see Chapter 6 below).

Routine analysis is carried out on all Cambridge ESOL papers and reports are produced which are used in the Grading and Awards process (see below), as well as to feed into the ongoing refinement of test production procedures. The aim is to ensure that the awarding of grades for the examination at each level is as fair as possible and that the examinations continue to be improved over time.

Grading and awarding

> The reliability of grades is, in an important sense, the bottom line of the examining system . . .There exist direct relationships between the reliability of the examination, which usually means the reliability of the overall marks, the number of grades on the scale, the reliability of the grades and the severity of the consequences of misclassification (Wood 1993:134).

Exam providers need to be certain that the pass/fail boundary is the same for different versions of a test. The most effective way of achieving this is by IRT (see below); other ways would involve standard setting methodology, for example, using a version of the Angoff method, with a group of experts setting the pass/fail boundary based on their understanding of the test items and of the typical population.

Grading and awarding: Cambridge ESOL practice

Grading is the process of setting cut-off scores for various grades. The Cambridge ESOL approach to *Grading* the examinations allows candidates' results to be compared from session to session and from year to year to ensure that grades in a particular examination remain constant. This aspect of fairness is of particular importance, not only to the candidates themselves, but also to universities and employers looking to recruit people with a specific level of language ability which they can rely on.

The details of scoring vary across exams, but the general picture is as follows. Skill papers contain different numbers of items, but the marks are usually equally weighted. The revised CPE for example, has five papers *weighted* to 40 marks each, the marks being summed to an exam score out of 200. Mark distributions are not scaled to have an equal standard deviation (although linear scaling may be used in the case of differential version difficulty in the case of the Listening paper). The papers are graded in such a way that the marks indicating a satisfactory level of performance in each paper sum to a passing grade in the exam (Grade C).

This begs the question of how the expected levels of performance are defined for each level of Cambridge ESOL examinations. The approach has *normative* as well as criterion-related features. In criterion terms, each exam level can be seen as representing a level of proficiency characterised by particular abilities to use English to some purpose (see Chapters 3 and 4 on context and cognitive validity). The normative aspect relates to the way that the target difficulty of each component paper is set, with the aim of making each paper in an exam of similar difficulty for the 'typical' candidate. A mean facility of about 60% is the test construction target for exams at the three upper levels, i.e. FCE, CAE, CPE (B2 to C2) which should indicate a satisfactory level of performance for the criterion level if repeated across all papers.

The candidates' response data from a live reading examination is captured for analysis before the grading event. Using anchoring techniques the difficulty of live test items is adjusted and new values are loaded onto the Cambridge ESOL Local Item Banking System (LIBS). A conversion table is constructed to link the weighted raw scores (1–40) to various language ability levels on the common scale. Table 5.6 shows a typical ability–raw marks conversion table. The fixed criterion ability indicates a satisfactory level of performance for each paper. In criterion terms, each exam level can be seen as representing a level of proficiency characterised by particular abilities to use English to some purpose. The pre-determined fixed ability level is based on various studies that were carried out when Cambridge ESOL's common scale was developed in the 1990s alongside the CEFR levels (see Chapter 7 for a full discussion of Cambridge ESOL's common scale and the CEFR levels).

Once a conversion table such as the one below is constructed using a

Cambridge ESOL in-house statistical programme, the weighted raw score representing the criterion ability is identified. For example, in Table 5.6 below, a weighted raw score of 25 represents a scaled ability of 67 which is used as a cut-off score for a certain grade (N.B. scaled logits in Table 5.6 below are logits anchored to the Cambridge ESOL Common Scale which ranges from 0 to 100). Such values are examined against the picture of the same paper in previous sessions. In other words, candidates' ability and paper difficulty for the current session will be compared with the previous sessions (12 recent sessions at each comparison). The purpose of this comparison is to fine-tune the ability estimates and adjust the cut-off score (criterion-referenced) to reflect the relative difficulty of the paper and candidates' ability. This cut-off score assumes an expected adequate performance for a successful candidate on the Reading paper.

The performance of large groups of candidates or cohorts is compared with cohorts from previous years, and performance is also compared by country, by first language, by age and a number of other factors, to ensure that the standards being applied are consistently fair to all candidates, and that a particular grade 'means' the same thing from year to year and throughout the world. Any requests for special consideration are reviewed at this stage, together with any reports from centres about specific problems that may have arisen during the examination (see Chapter 2).

Table 5.6 An extract from a conversion table

Weighted raw score	% of weighted total	Ability Scaled logits	Error scaled	Scores in SE range			
				−2	−1	+1	+2
39	98	97	7.71	35	38	40	40
38	95	91	5.56	34	37	39	39
37	93	87	4.63	33	35	38	39
. . . .							
29	73	72	2.81	24	27	31	33
28	70	70	2.74	23	26	30	32
27	68	69	2.68	22	25	29	31
26	65	68	2.64	21	23	28	30
25	63	67	2.60	20	22	27	30
24	60	66	2.57	19	21	26	29
23	58	65	2.55	18	20	25	28
22	55	64	2.53	17	19	24	27
. . . .							
4	10	41	4.07	2	3	6	8
3	8	38	4.62	1	2	5	7
2	5	34	5.55	1	1	3	6
1	3	27	7.70	0	0	2	5

Source: Cambridge in-house software program

In practice, candidates will not pass or fail an individual skill paper within a Main Suite examination. An overall grade is provided to show how a candidate has performed on the whole examination. Several steps are taken to arrive at the overall grade. The cut-off raw score on the Reading paper is added to the cut-off scores on other objectively scored papers, i.e. Listening and Use of English, and to the criterion-referenced adequate performance on Writing and Speaking papers to form an aggregate pass score. At this stage various other considerations such as examiner reports, relative performance of big cohorts and candidates' overall language ability may adjust the final cut-off score for passing the examination.

A system of graphical profiling provides information to show how close a candidate's marks on each component of the assessment, e.g. Reading, was compared to the average performance of other candidates in that paper (see the following section on reporting results for further discussion).

After the grading meeting, results in terms of grades are generated. At this stage a procedure known as Awards is carried out to ensure the fairness of the final results before they are issued to candidates. As part of this procedure an Awards Committee looks particularly closely at the performance of candidates who are close to the grade boundaries – particularly the pass/fail boundary.

Reporting results and certification

Once the Awards procedure is complete, test centres are sent a statement of provisional results, along with individual results slips for each candidate. These results are known as provisional results because they are still subject to a final quality check, e.g. to ensure that the candidate's name is spelled in the correct or preferred way before examination certificates are printed.

The results slip provides the candidates with a 'graphical profile' which shows the profile of their performance across the various components of the exam. Approximately three months after the examination, certificates are issued (via the centre) to successful candidates. These documents incorporate a number of security features to make them extremely difficult to forge. Cambridge ESOL keeps detailed records of the certificates awarded to candidates (additionally score data is stored for an indefinite period) so that it can if necessary verify at a later date any claim about which an employer or university is dubious.

Main Suite certificates do not have a fixed 'shelf-life' and do not expire. They attest to the fact that at the time of the examination, the candidate had achieved and demonstrated a specified level of English. The length of time since the certificate was obtained is a factor that potential employers or universities need to take into account.

While the users of the Cambridge ESOL Main Suite examinations are overwhelmingly in favour of the current approach to grading, with a single exam grade, there is at the same time a demand for more information concerning the way the grade was arrived at. This largely reflects the pedagogical context in which Cambridge ESOL examinations are generally taken – feedback on performance in each paper is seen as a useful guide for further study, particularly in the case of failing candidates who may wish to re-take the exam.

For this reason, Statements of Results containing a graphical profile of the candidates' performance were introduced in 2000. The following explanatory notes were issued to explain how the information should be interpreted.

> Every candidate is provided with a Statement of Results which includes a graphical display of the candidate's performance in each component. These are shown against the scale Exceptional – Good – Borderline – Weak and indicate the candidate's relative performance in each paper.
>
> In looking at this graphical display it is important to remember that the candidates are NOT required to reach a specific level in any component, i.e. there are NO pass/fail levels in individual components. Thus different strengths and weaknesses may add up to the same overall result.
>
> We recommend that fail candidates planning to resit an examination, or pass candidates who plan to continue their studies, do not focus only on those areas where they have a performance which is less than Borderline, but try to improve their general level of English across all language skills.
>
> The profile indicates a candidate's performance on the specific occasion when they sat the exam – this may be influenced by a number of different factors, and candidates can find that they have a somewhat different profile on another occasion. Evidence of candidates who resit exams indicates that in some cases performance declines overall and in other cases declines in some papers while improving in others (Saville 2003:104).

The purpose of the profiled result slips is to give useful information about performance in each paper. What are plotted in the result slips are not candidates' raw marks, but marks which are scaled to implement the normative frame of reference which has been presented above. The candidate with a borderline pass, if their skills profile were completely flat, would be shown as having all papers just above the 'Borderline' boundary. A very good candidate, achieving an A grade, would most probably have at least one paper in the 'Exceptional' band. In each paper a similar proportion of candidates fall in the 'Exceptional' and 'Weak' bands.

The profiled result slips attempt to achieve a balance between the need to provide more information about performance in components, and a full-blown system of component-level grading. This latter option, as explained above, is not wholly appropriate for the construct of English language proficiency embodied in the Cambridge ESOL Main Suite examinations. Feedback from consultative exercises with stakeholders on the use of these result slips has generally been extremely positive as shown by questionnaire data gathered from a number of test centres worldwide. In Greece, for example, in a total of 97 responses 98% of the respondents thought that the Statement of Results with graphical profiling is better than the older one, 87% found the graphical display easy to interpret, 93% reported that it helped them explain the results to their stakeholders, 97% found it useful in guiding their students' further study and 86% reported that their students liked it (internal report from Greece Centre Examinations Manager).

In an attempt to further improve on the Statement of Results, Cambridge ESOL introduced another feature in December 2008, namely, the reporting of a standardised score on a scale from 0 to 100 (see Fig. 5.3 below).

Figure 5.3 Statement of Results for the First Certificate in English (FCE)

Statement of Results
ENGLISH FOR SPEAKERS OF OTHER LANGUAGES

Session

Reference No:

Candidate Name

(To be quoted on all correspondence)

Place of Entry

Qualification

Score   Grade   Result

Candidate Profile

Exceptional

Speaking

Good

Writing   Listening   Reading

Borderline

Weak

The **First Certificate in English** (FCE) is a general proficiency examination at Level B2 in the Common European Framework of Reference (CEFR). It is at Level 1 in the UK National Qualifications Framework (NQF).

CEFR Level	Examination
C2	Certificate of Proficiency in English (CPE)
C1	Certificate in Advanced English (CAE)
B2	First Certificate in English (FCE)
B1	Preliminary English Test (PET)
A2	Key English Test (KET)
A1	

Passing Grades	Score
A	80 to 100
B	75 to 79
C	60 to 74

Failing Grade	
D	55 to 59
E	00 to 54

Other

Interpretation of overall grades

Grade C covers the range of ability from a borderline pass to good achievement at the level. Grade B indicates the range of good achievement up to Grade A, which indicates a very strong performance at the level. Grade D is a narrow fail.

The total number of marks available in the examination is 200. Marks out of 200 are converted to a standardised score out of 100.

X – The candidate was absent from part of the examination
Z – The candidate was absent from all parts of the examination
Pending – A result cannot be issued at present, but will follow in due course
Withheld – The candidate should contact their centre for information

The following explanatory notes will accompany the new Statement of Results and will be available on the Cambridge ESOL website.

Your Statement of Results gives you three pieces of information:

1. Your grade: This is the most important piece of information. If you pass the exam, you will get a certificate with your grade on it. Or you could have one of these on your Statement of Results:

X (you were absent from part of the exam)
Z (you were absent from the whole of the exam)
Pending (your result is not ready yet)
Withheld (you need to contact your centre)

2. Your score: This is your score for the exam. You can see whether your score is near the top of the grade, in the middle or near the bottom. Your score is shown as a number between 0 and 100, which is converted from the total number of marks available in the exam. It is converted so that the score you need for each grade is the same every time the exam is taken. This is called a 'standardised score'. Your score will not be shown on your certificate.

3. Your 'candidate profile': This shows you how you performed on each of the papers in the exam. For each paper it shows how you performed compared to the standard of all the other candidates taking that paper at the same time. If you did not get the grade you wanted, it will help you to decide which skills you need to improve. N.B.: the bands on the 'Candidate Profile' do not correspond to grades.

Once again, a questionnaire was sent out to test centres (in 2007) to gather feedback on the introduction of a standardised score on the Statement of

Results. A total of 256 centres from the top 15 countries for Main Suite and BEC entries were contacted to complete the questionnaire. Positive feedback was received, e.g., 90% and above of the respondents agreed that giving a score out of a 100 is useful for both candidates and test centres respectively and provides clear information for other stakeholders.

Post-exam analysis

Cambridge ESOL recognises the need to provide end users with sound and transparent evidence for the quality and fairness of their exams and a wide range of statistical measures and techniques are used to estimate the reliability of test scores and the examination results (as discussed above).

As results are reported as a single overall grade, whether it is a passing grade such as A, B or C for FCE, CAE, CPE, or pass and pass with merit for KET and PET, the reliability of the examination can be estimated as a composite (as discussed in Feldt and Brennan 1989:116–117 and Crocker and Algina 1986:119–121). The typical composite reliability of the Cambridge ESOL exams is generally considered acceptable. For example, for an examination like FCE which has five papers assessing reading, listening, speaking, writing and use of English, reliability is estimated at 0.94.

This is acceptable given the fact that the construct of overall English language proficiency operationalised is heterogeneous (see Geranpayeh 2007 for empirical evidence of this), reflecting the view that a candidate's aggregate score over the whole range of language skills is the most appropriate measure of ability for exams of this type and purpose. While these skills can be related to the underlying model in terms of overall ability, they are not highly inter-correlated; this has the effect of setting practical limits on the possible composite reliability of the exam, although this is higher than for any single component alone.

The IELTS exam contains four components, including reading, upon which an overall band score is awarded. Composite reliability estimates were carried out from the period 1 January to 20 December 2004. To generate an appropriately cautious estimate, minimum alpha values were used for the objectively marked papers, and g-coefficients for the single rater condition on subjectively marked scores. The composite reliability estimate for the Academic module was 0.95 and produced a composite SEM of 0.21. This finding shows a 95% probability for a candidate's true score to fall within less than half a band (0.41) of the observed score. For General Training the composite reliability was 0.95 with an SEM of 0.23. If average, rather than minimum, values are used for the objective paper alphas, the reliability for both Academic and General Training versions improves slightly to 0.96.

Conclusion

Post-examination analysis reveals that acceptable levels of reliability are being met for reading and other test components and provides the input to ongoing attempts to enhance this aspect of the examinations. As mentioned earlier, feedback from the users of Cambridge ESOL examinations reveals that they are largely happy with the notion of examination grades and the fairness of the assessment system as it now operates. While the assessment of each component is made as reliable as possible, the overall reliability of the grade awarded in Main Suite examinations is based on the overall assessment made across all five papers (i.e. in over 5 hours of tests) and on the rigour of the procedures used to set and monitor the grade boundaries. The aim is to achieve a fair outcome for all candidates.

So far we have looked at those 'internal' elements of our validity framework that affect the candidates, the test task and the raters, and which make a direct contribution to the construct validity of our tests.

The other elements of validity we now turn to are 'external' to the test process itself; they relate to the effects and impact of test scores, and how these scores compare with other measures of the same construct in the world external to the test. We start by considering the consequential validity of a test in the next chapter.

6 Consequential validity

Messick (1989) argues that it is necessary in test validation studies to ascertain whether the social consequences of test use and interpretation support the intended testing purpose(s) and are consistent with other social values. Messick emphasises that the appropriateness, meaningfulness, and usefulness of score-based inferences are a function of the external social consequences of the testing.

In this chapter we consider three important aspects of the effects of a test which are each now seen as part of its *consequential validity*. Figure 6.1 identifies the aspects of consequential validity in our validation framework.

Figure 6.1 Aspects of consequential validity

Consequential validity
• Impact on institutions and society • Washback on individuals in classroom/workplace • Avoidance of test bias

We examine these three aspects of consequential validity, first through recourse to the theory and practice emerging from the literature, and then by examining relevant Cambridge ESOL principles and practices.

Impact and washback

Theory and definitions

We note that consequential validity includes both 'impact' and 'washback'. It is perhaps also important to point out that these terms have themselves been defined in various and sometimes overlapping ways, and that the concepts they represent have evolved in recent years.

Bachman and Palmer (1996:29) saw impact as operating on two levels:

(i) 'a socio-cultural level, in terms of educational systems and society in general' (macro level)

(ii) 'a local and personal level, in terms of the people who are directly affected by tests and their results' (micro level).

Wall (1997) views impact as: 'any of the effects that a test may have on individuals, policies or practices, within the classroom, the school, the educational system or society as a whole' (p. 291). In the same vein, Hamp-Lyons (1997) defines impact as that which pertains to high-stakes tests whose influence extends to the school, educational systems, and society. High-stakes tests are so called because they are employed to determine admission or otherwise of candidates to programmes of study, professions or social contexts (e.g. access to citizenship within a nation state). They are also instrumental in shaping educational goals and processes, and society generally. However, in a more recent re-interpretation of the notion some authors question whether in fact all tests are not high-stakes to some degree, depending on the individuals concerned (e.g. Oates 2006). Even a 'low-stakes' test may be high-stakes for a test taker if their low performance on the test proves to have a demotivating or other negative effect on them and on their future learning trajectory.

Alderson and Wall (1993:121) suggest that the term 'washback' should be limited to the influences the test might have on teaching, teachers, and learning (including curriculum and materials) and this seems now to be generally accepted.

Wall's (1997) and Hamp-Lyons' (1997) concept of impact appears to reflect Bachman and Palmer's (1996) (i) plus (ii) above, namely test effects on 'educational systems and society in general' as well as 'the local and personal level'. Alderson and Wall's (1997) 'washback' may be closer to Bachman and Palmer's (ii), that is, effects at 'a local and personal level' on people 'directly affected by tests and their results'. Impact can thus be seen as a superordinate which subsumes washback. Impact is concerned with 'wider influences', with the macro contexts in society, as well as with the micro contexts of the classroom and the school whereas washback focuses rather more narrowly on the latter (see Hawkey 2006 and Hamp-Lyons 2000).

Saville (2009) reminds us of the inevitable complexity and interplay of impact:washback relationships:

> This distinction is useful for conceptualising the notion of impact, but it does not, of course, imply that the levels are unconnected. On the contrary, the potentially complex relationships between individuals, the institutions to which they belong, and broader systems in society are clearly of crucial importance in reaching an understanding of what impact is and how it works.

In Weir's (2005) framework, *test bias* is also included within consequential validity. Following the AERA/APA/NCME definition, bias can result from either *construct under-representation* or the inclusion of *construct-irrelevant* components of test scores that differentially affect the performance of different groups of test takers (American Educational Research Association et al 1999). Such bias effects can have negative consequences for individual test takers and adversely affect the use of test results for decision making. In the interests of test fairness we need to assure ourselves that the test is performing in the same manner for each group of examinees who take it (Zumbo 2007). Differential Item Functioning (DIF) is now seen as the method of choice for investigating test bias (see Camilli and Shepard 1994, Chen and Henning 1985, Ferne and Rupp 2007, Geranpayeh 2001, Kim 2001, Kunnan 1990, 1994, 1995, for examples of studies in this area and suggested methodologies for carrying out such studies). In the final section of this chapter, we pursue further Cambridge ESOL's use of DIF in the treatment of test bias.

A brief overview of the research

Until the early 1990s, there was little research in the language testing literature on washback or impact. The 1990s saw a growing interest and awareness of these concepts and a growing body of research starting with a focus on washback and moving on to a greater emphasis on impact in the broader sense. The works of Alderson and Wall (1993), Hughes (1993) and Bailey (1996) were influential in helping researchers to conceptualise washback and to develop washback hypotheses.

Alderson and Wall (1993) state 15 washback hypotheses, covering a test's influence on: the teacher, the learner, what and how teachers teach and learners learn the rate and sequence of learning, and attitudes to teaching and learning methods. Given the number of potential intervening variables between a test and its washback, it is obviously difficult to establish clear-cut causes and effects between a test and developments apparently associated with it.

Examples of early washback research include Yang and Weir (1998) who describe a comprehensive validation study of the College English Test (CET) in China and detail how one examination board attempted to generate empirical evidence on the value of its tests as perceived by a variety of its stakeholders, e.g. end users of test results in universities and the business world (see also Weir et al 2000). Other early studies compared test preparation and general English courses (for example see Alderson and Hamp-Lyons 1996).

More recently, Cheng and Watanabe (2004) draw attention to the fact that test washback and impact have now become a central area of concern in educational research. Eight new projects are described in their volume including Saville and Hawkey's (2004) account of the IELTS Textbook Washback Study conducted for Cambridge ESOL (see below for details). The centrality of test washback and impact in language testing is also reflected in the publication of several recent titles in the *Studies in Language Testing* (SILT) series published jointly by Cambridge ESOL and Cambridge University

Press (CUP). Between 2005 and 2007 four new volumes appeared focusing on major washback and impact studies carried out by Cheng (2005), Wall (2005), Hawkey (2006) and Green (2007).

Green (2007: Chapter 1), provides a comprehensive review of the interpretations of washback in the language testing literature:

> Washback is broadly defined as "the effect of a test on teaching" (Richards, Platt and Platt, 1992) and often also on learning (Hughes, 2003; Shohamy, 2001). It has also been variously associated with effects on teachers, learners (Buck, 1988; Messick, 1994; Shohamy, 2001), parents (Pearson, 1988), administrators, textbook writers (Hughes, 2003), instruction (Bachman, 1990; Chapelle and Douglas, 1993; Weigle, 2002), the classroom (Buck, 1988), classroom practice (Berry, 1995), educational practices and beliefs (Cohen, 1994) and curricula (Cheng, 1997; Weigle, 2002), although for Hughes (2003) and Bailey (1999), the ultimate effects on learning outcomes are of primary concern.
>
> . . . There is now a clear consensus on the need for concern with, if not agreement on, the effects of what has been termed "washback/backwash". Washback is considered a "neutral" term (Alderson and Wall, 1993 and 1996) which may refer to both (intended) positive (Bachman and Palmer, 1996; Davies et al. 1999) or beneficial (Buck, 1988; Hughes, 2003) effects and to (unintended) harmful (Buck, 1988) or negative effects (Bachman and Palmer, 1996; Davies et al. 1999; Hughes, 2003) (Green 2007:2).

Green's model of washback is arguably the most comprehensive to date. Green (2007) proposed the predictive model of test washback set out in Figure 6.2. He argues (personal communication 2008):

> The model starts from test design characteristics and related validity issues of construct representation identified with washback by Messick (1996) and encapsulated in Resnick and Resnick's (1992) formulation of overlap, or the extent of congruence between test design and skills developed by a curriculum or required in a target language use domain. Test design issues are most closely identified with the direction of washback – whether effects are likely to be judged beneficial or damaging to teaching and learning.
>
> The model relates design issues to contexts of test use, including the extent to which participants (including material writers, teachers, learners, and course providers) are aware of and are equipped to address the demands of the test and are willing to embrace beliefs about learning embodied therein. These features are most closely related to washback variability (differences between participants in how they are affected by a test) and washback intensity. Washback will be most intense – have the most powerful effects on teaching and learning behaviours – where participants see the test as challenging and the results as important (perhaps because they are associated with high stakes decisions, such as university entrance).

Figure 6.2 A model of washback

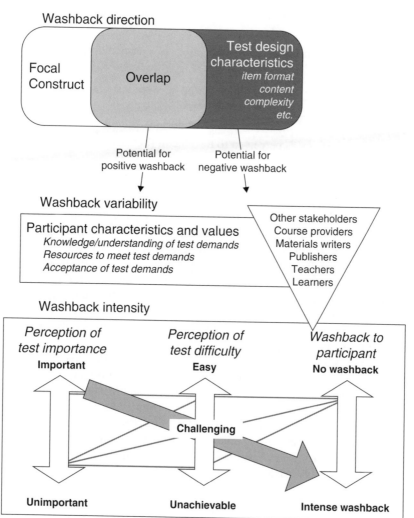

Source: Green (2007)

Some researchers have focused proactively on how tests might become instruments of desirable positive change. Hughes (2003) offers some suggestions for achieving *beneficial* backwash:

- test the abilities whose development you want to encourage
- sample widely and unpredictably
- use direct testing

- make the testing criterion-referenced
- ensure the test is known and understood by students and teachers
- where necessary provide assistance to teachers.

Green (2007) adds aspects and perceptions of a particular test that need to be in place for positive washback:

- there needs to be a considerable overlap between test and target situation demands on language abilities
- success on the test is perceived to be important
- success on the test is perceived to be difficult (but both attainable and amenable to preparation)
- candidates operate in a context where these perceptions are shared by other participants.

Weir (2005) emphasises that the major washback research studies carried out by Wall (2005) and Cheng (2005) argue for the centrality of Hughes' criterion of necessary provision of assistance to teachers if *beneficial* washback is to occur through testing innovations. Training teachers in the new content and methodology required for a revised high-stakes test is essential. If teachers are untrained in the new knowledge, skills and attitudes required for effective teaching towards the examination, why should we expect positive backwash? Support in the forms of appropriate teaching materials must also be readily available.

A limited number of the early studies also examined the wider impact of testing in the context of educational reforms and innovations (Wall 1997 and 2005 and Cheng 1997 and 2005). Hawkey (2006) and Milanovic and Saville (1996: 2) again stress the scope and intricacy of the washback and impact concepts, including as they do the complex interactions between the factors which make up the teaching/learning context (including the individual learner, the teacher, the classroom environment, the choice and use of materials etc.) and the relationship between local contexts and the broader socio-cultural milieu.

Thus, in recent years there has been a growing concern for the social dimension of assessment and this has led to research into complex relationships between more localised assessment contexts and society as a whole. This is consistent with Messick's (1989) 'social consequences of test use' and the need for assessment purposes to be consistent with other 'social values' (see above).

Post-modernism, ethics and the 'critical language testers'

The increasing focus on the washback concept has led to post-modernist and 'critical' views of assessment being introduced into the debate.

Spolsky (1981) was one of the first testing specialists to encourage us to consider carefully the use of language tests for 'momentous decisions affecting individuals' and, later, to make explicit connection between post-modernist views and test ethics:

> Post-modern testing adds a sincere, ethically driven, consideration of the potentially deleterious effects of testing on the test taker, on the instructional process, and on other facets of the social context in which we test (1995:354–7).

Saville and Hawkey (2004:75) note in a similar vein: 'in tune with increasing individual and societal expectations of good value and accountability, testers are expected to adhere to codes of professionally and socially responsible practice'. They argue that this: 'tends to increase the concern of high-stakes exam providers with the ethics of language testing. Such codes (for example, of the International Language Testing Association (ILTA), or the Association of Language Testers in Europe (ALTE), were intended to improve test development rigour and probity.'

From the 'critical testing' perspective a test is potentially an instrument of power and control in society. Shohamy (2001) argues that we need to include within the validation process probing studies of the use made of tests. For Shohamy, tests are:

> ... powerful because they lead to momentous decisions affecting individuals and programs ... They are conducted by authoritative and unquestioning judges or are backed by the language of science and number ... Critical testing refers to the need to examine the use of tests within a broader social and political critique of aspects of testing as a social and institutional practice. (2001:714).

Shohamy was referring to the high-stakes status of some tests, where people's lives were affected by the decisions made on the basis of the results, and raising the question of ethicality in contexts of test use related to 'gate keeping' for migration and citizenship.

Several other researchers have attempted to address such concerns by suggesting ways in which the potential negative effects can be avoided. For example, Kunnan's work on test fairness lays out a comprehensive agenda for achieving fairness, equity and social justice (Kunnan 2000, 2004, 2008). See also Chapter 2 above for details of some Cambridge ESOL practices designed to promote fairness.

The widening debate on the social impact of assessment has given rise to a number of potential dilemmas for test developers. One such dilemma relates to how individual test takers' needs can be effectively catered for while also providing assessments that are suitable for high-stakes decision making in society. Another dilemma concerns the limits of a test developer's responsibility for the consequences of the test.

A post-modernist view will be critical of standardised testing, absolute measurement, and a focus on the product of learning for accountability purposes. Assessment which is focused on the individual, is learning-based, and has a formative function might be considered an alternative approach with fewer negative effects (see Weir 2001 for a discussion of formative versus summative assessment). But how can this approach be reconciled with the need for accountability which society often demands? Davies (1997:335), whilst agreeing that we need to ensure the validity/ethicality of our tests, recognises that there are limits to this:

> An ethical perspective for a language tester is, I have argued, necessary. But I have also urged the need in all professional statements of morality for a limit on what is achievable or even perhaps desirable. In my view, therefore, the apparent open-ended offer of consequential validity goes too far. I maintain that it is not possible for a tester as a member of a profession to take account of all possible social consequences.

Impact (by design) and washback: Cambridge ESOL practice

1996 saw the first explicit policy statement of the Cambridge ESOL approach in 'working for positive impact' and 'limiting negative consequences'. Central to this were the four maxims from Milanovic and Saville (1996) which are now part of ESOL standard procedures. The maxims were related to work conducted in collaboration with the Association of Language Testers in Europe (ALTE) on content analysis, 'Can Do' statements, a glossary of terms etc., as described by Saville (2003). The maxims themselves were as follows and remain relevant to ESOL's current approach:

Maxim 1 PLAN
Use a rational and explicit approach to *test development*
Maxim 2 SUPPORT
Support *stakeholders* in the testing process
Maxim 3 COMMUNICATE
Provide comprehensive, useful and *transparent information*
Maxim 4 MONITOR and EVALUATE
Collect all relevant *data and analyse* as required

Cambridge ESOL fully recognises that, as a central part of the test validation process, there is a need for extensive research to be undertaken into the washback and impact of high-stakes tests on stakeholders. As an examination board it regards itself as answerable to a broad range of stakeholders, from test takers and their parents, test-preparation teachers, to test centre administrators, education policy makers, as well as receiving institutions and employers (see, for example, Taylor 2000, Weir and Milanovic 2003 and Hawkey 2006 and 2009).

Figure 6.3 below provides an overview of the various stakeholders with an interest in Cambridge ESOL examinations both at the development stage of the test and *a posteriori* in relation to the use made of the test results.

Figure 6.3 Stakeholders in the testing community

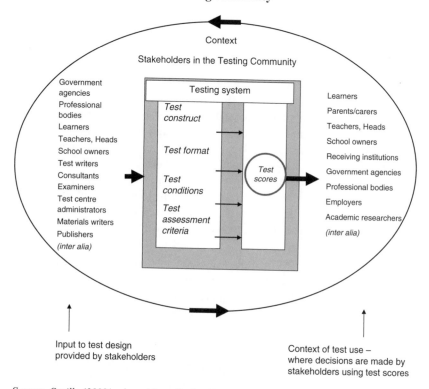

Source: Saville (2009) adapted from Taylor (2000).

Taylor (2000:2) notes: 'Some of the stakeholders (e.g. examiners and materials writers) are likely to have more interest in the "front end" of a test, i.e. the test assessment criteria or test format. Others may see their stake as being primarily concerned with the test score. Some stakeholders, such as learners and teachers, will naturally have an interest in all aspects of the test.'

Notice, in the light of our impact:washback distinctions above, that those stakeholders who are more likely to be influenced by the nature of the front end of a test, to use Taylor's description above, may, in the main, be more concerned with test washback, while those using the scores of a test for their decision-making will be concerned with its impact. There are, however, as Taylor notes, stakeholders with involvement on both sides of the stakeholder community.

Saville (2003:60) argues that such a 'taxonomy of stakeholders' demands of an exam provider such as Cambridge ESOL systems that ensure that it can 'review and change what it does in the light of findings on how the stakeholders use the exams and what they think about them'. The views of the stakeholders concerned can be taken into account along with other impact data, in decisions on test revision or renewal (see Weir and Milanovic 2003, Hawkey 2004, 2006 and 2009).

Saville (2009) argues that the 'impact by design' approach now espoused by Cambridge ESOL builds on Messick's 1996 concept of what might be termed 'washback by design' (seeking validity by design as the basis for positive washback); it also formalises the earlier maxims within a paradigm which conceptualises impact appropriately within the work of an examinations board and allows for planned and well-managed actions to be based on this.

Saville notes that unlike much of the research in the literature to date which has been conducted *post hoc* by external researchers (e.g. many of the contributors to Cheng and Watanabe 2004), the Cambridge ESOL approach builds in impact considerations from the start, and seeks to anticipate potential effects and consequences with a commitment to monitoring and changing things as required ('anticipatory impact research').

Saville (2009) itemises the necessary conditions for the Cambridge ESOL approach:

- a commitment to assessment as a potentially positive component within dynamic educational and societal processes
- an understanding of context within educational systems – a multi-level approach with unpredictable interactions between the wider milieu and local contexts/individuals
- a socio-cognitive approach to learning and assessment
- an explicit and evidence focused approach to construct definition (cf. the importance of the construct in washback research – e.g. Green 2007)
- a test development and validation model which allows for the planning of activities over time (cyclical and iterative) and for changes/ innovations to be implemented when necessary (a systematic plan, cf. maxim 1)
- a commitment to ongoing improvements within a QMS (Quality Management System) approach

- a well-developed view of the constituency of stakeholders and how to involve them effectively in the development and validation of the exams
- anticipation of potential impacts (positive/negative) at various levels (micro/macro) i.e. impact hypotheses
- enhanced methods for 'finding out' and communicating with stakeholders
- collection of adequate data and appropriate analyses – both routine and as part of specific instrumental projects to find out what is happening (c.f. maxim 4)
- use of mixed method approaches (quasi experimental and constructivist models of research)
- development of a 'toolkit' for making data collection more routine and easier to manage – including storage and analysis of qualitative data such as videos
- a 'theory of action' – the ability to deal with change and innovation based on the evidence collected and an understanding of what needs to be done to make things better.

Saville argues that within the complex, dynamic systems of education in which language assessment plays an important part, the validity of the testing system is 'latent' at the start of an innovative process of test development. The evidence to support validity claims 'emerges' as the process proceeds over time; in this sense validity can be seen as an 'emergent' property of the system as a whole.

To help ground this impact by design approach a Cambridge ESOL Stakeholder Relations and Legal Affairs Division has been created charged with establishing and monitoring stakeholder relationships, with a clear focus on matters germane to the washback and impact of its exams. This group complements the work of the Research and Validation Division which is responsible for conceptualising and planning impact validation and impact-related research projects and for carrying out the data collection, storage and analysis.

The importance ascribed by Cambridge ESOL to the study of the impact of its exams is well documented (e.g. Weir and Milanovic 2003 and Hawkey 2006). Saville (2003) describes the procedures that need to be put into place after a Cambridge examination becomes operational to collect information that allows impact to be estimated. This should involve collecting data on the following:

- who is taking the examination (i.e. a profile of the candidates)
- who is using the examination results and for what purpose
- who is teaching towards the examination and under what circumstances
- what kinds of courses and materials are being designed and used to prepare candidates

- what effect the examination has on public perceptions generally (e.g. regarding educational standards)
- how the examination is viewed by those directly involved in educational processes (e.g. by students, examination takers, teachers, parents, etc.)
- how the examination is viewed by members of society outside education (e.g. by politicians, businessmen etc.).

The need to monitor the test's effects on language materials and on classroom activity (see, for example, Hawkey 2004, 2006 and Green 2007), as well as to seek information on and views of a full range of stakeholders (see Taylor 2000 above) is now accepted by most serious examination boards and it has been the hallmark of Cambridge examinations since the modern revisions commenced in the 1980s.

In fact the interest in washback and impact in Cambridge goes back a lot longer. Weir (2003) notes:

> In one of the very first references to the concept of washback validity Roach questioned how far examinations act as a stimulus and a focusing point for both teachers and taught, and thereby promote the expansion of the studies that they are designed to test (Roach 1944:36).

In the CPE 2002 revision project conscious efforts were made to elicit feedback on the existing test from participants and a wide variety of stakeholders contributed to the decisions that were taken concerning changes in the examination (see Weir and Milanovic 2003 for a full account of stakeholder involvement in the CPE revision project). Along similar lines, Taylor (2000) reports on the stakeholder consultation activity which underpinned the 1996 FCE revision and Hawkey (2004) describes this within the CELS examination change process. A similar process of extensive stakeholder consultation forms part of the 2004–08 FCE/CAE modifications project and Hawkey (2009) traces the recurring theme of consultation with stakeholder groups such as teachers, applied linguists, British Council staff, etc. throughout the various revision projects for CAE and FCE which took place during the 20th century. Recent work done by Cambridge ESOL on recognition and currency issues with stakeholders and other test users (e.g. higher education institutions, employers) constitutes another strand related to consequential validity matters and reflects the functional real-world orientation of Cambridge ESOL examinations.

As part of its interaction and responsibility for communication with stakeholders Cambridge ESOL has an interest in promoting 'assessment literacy', to help ensure that information, exemplification and, where appropriate, training are available to key front and consumer end stakeholders. Examples of this principle in practice in relation to its General English and other examinations are:

- the Cambridge ESOL teacher seminar programme described by Taylor (2000)
- the Cambridge ESOL Teaching Resources website pages (www.CambridgeESOL.org/teach)
- the teacher training and professional development channels, for example the content of the teacher education and certification programmes CELTA and DELTA described in Cambridge ESOL *Research Notes*, Issue 29, Aug 2007 (www.CambridgeESOL.org/rs_notes/rs_nts29.pdf)
- the handbooks available for Cambridge ESOL examinations, which provide a clear specification of test content, teaching suggestions and sample tests for teachers
- the public availability of specimen papers for all examinations and the wide range of appropriate exam specific coursebooks and exam preparation materials published by Cambridge University Press.

These activities demonstrate awareness that tests function within a broad and complex system or 'ecology' and that their developers recognise a responsibility to the educational stakeholder sectors of teachers and teacher trainers. They also take us back to Chapter 2, where we identified the importance of *experiential* characteristics of the test taker. We noted how a test taker's familiarity with a particular test may affect the way the task is managed. The greater the assessment literacy of both teacher and student the less we need to worry about potential bias from this source. Indeed Taylor (2009) comments that, as assessment practices assume an increasingly influential position in education and society, there is an urgent need to promote better assessment literacy among teachers, students, and wider society if tests and test scores are to be responsibly and appropriately used; and she suggests that examination boards have a key role to play in achieving this.

Some case studies

Concomitant with the growing importance of high-stakes language tests is the increasing demand for preparation courses for international English language tests, and for accompanying coursebooks and associated materials. As candidature rises for language tests such as those in and beyond the Cambridge Main Suite, so does the importance of the study of the textbooks designed for use on such courses (Saville and Hawkey 2004, Hawkey 2004, 2004a and 2009, and Smith 2004) and of the washback of preparation courses for international English language tests. The CPE Textbook Washback Study is a good example of an exam board's concern for the effect that changes in an examination might have on the textbooks used in preparation for the test (Hawkey 2004 and 2004a). Green's IELTS Washback Study

(2007) compares practices and outcomes on IELTS examination preparation courses with EAP courses such as university pre-sessional courses.

Brief descriptions of two particular washback and impact case studies are given below as examples of the sort of empirical investigations that can be undertaken, especially with regard to the research questions to be addressed and the methodologies to be employed.

The CPE Textbook Washback Study

The principal objective of the CPE Textbook study was to test the hypothesis that the constructs and content of a test have washback effects on test preparation textbooks. The primary research questions which the study sought to explore included:

- to what extent did the revision of the CPE examination in 2002 impact on textbooks designed for use with CPE students?
- in what way were the changes in the exam reflected in the textbooks?

Ten CPE-related textbooks were identified as being suitable for the study. They included four books written for the preparation of CPE candidates prior to 2002, four books revised for the post revision CPE exam, and two totally new CPE-oriented books. Each of the 10 chosen books was independently assessed by two language-teaching specialists, selected on the basis of their background with the CPE exam and other relevant experience. In total, 20 textbook evaluations were produced.

The instrument used for making evaluations was the Instrument for the Analysis of Textbook Materials (IATM). This particular instrument had its origins in an initial version developed by Bonkowski (1996) and had previously been refined and used in the study of IELTS impact described below (Saville and Hawkey 2004, and Hawkey 2006). The IATM was further adapted – from suggestions made by members of the Cambridge ESOL Main Suite team – to make it suitable for the CPE washback investigation. The IATM gathers both quantitative and qualitative information on: the evaluator; the evaluator's view of the CPE exam; textbook type; units of organisation; language features; enabling skills; task types; genre; media; communicative activities and opportunities; text topics; text and task authenticity. The instrument further elicits qualitative comment on a textbook's treatment of language skills and use of English, the overall quality of the textbook, and its relationship with the CPE exam.

The hypothesis that the pre-revision and revised CPE exams strongly influenced the evaluated textbooks in their respective treatment of English language skills, micro-skills, task types, language elements and topics was supported by the study. Other main conclusions gleaned from the data are that:

- evaluators deem it appropriate that the textbooks concerned reflect the content (text topics), approaches (enabling skills), activities and tasks of the exam directly, but consider that
- the textbooks should additionally offer opportunities and materials to aid the development of learners to enhance their overall language knowledge and ability
- both the revised and new versions of course preparation books do mirror significantly the changes in the revised CPE exam.

The IELTS Impact Study

The IELTS Impact Study constitutes a major long-term programme of research by Cambridge ESOL into the impact of IELTS, one of the most widely used language tests for those needing to study or train in the medium of English. The IELTS Impact projects from 1995 onwards were important in developing Cambridge ESOL's methodology and instrumentation for carrying out impact research and validation activities.

Describing the study from its inception in 1995, Saville (2001:5) remarks: 'It was agreed that procedures would be developed to monitor the impact of the test and to contribute to the next revision cycle'. He explains the rationale for this study as follows:

In order to understand the test impact better and to conduct effective surveys to monitor it, it was decided that a range of standardised instruments and procedures should be developed to focus on the following aspects of the test:

- the content and nature of classroom activity in IELTS-related classes
- the content and nature of IELTS teaching materials, including textbooks
- the views and attitudes of user groups towards IELTS
- the IELTS test-taking population and the use of results.

The first two of these points concern washback in the sense accepted above, (i.e. the effect of the test on teaching and learning). The second two are administrative and academic contexts of the tests, and on the attitudes and behaviour of the stakeholders in these contexts.

The study included three phases: identification of areas to be targeted and the development of instrumentation to collect information which allows impact to be measured (Phase 1); validation of the instruments prior to full-scale implementation (Phase 2); and implementation of the instruments as part of a major survey (Phase 3).

Phase 1 was undertaken by Alderson and his research team at the University of Lancaster (see Alderson and Banerjee 1996; Banerjee 1996; Bonkowski 1996; Herington 1996; Horak 1996; Winetroube 1997; Yue 1997).

Phase 2 entailed analyses and pretesting of the draft data collection instruments by the Research and Validation Group (Cambridge ESOL) in conjunction with external consultants including Purpura (Teachers College Columbia), Kunnan (UCLA) and Hawkey (University of Bedfordshire).

Phase 3 streamlined to five the original 13 data collection instruments:

- a modular student questionnaire on pre- and post-IELTS candidate language learning background, objectives and strategies
- a language teacher questionnaire embracing teacher background and experience, attitudes towards IELTS, experience of and ideas on IELTS preparation programmes
- an instrument for the evaluation of IELTS-related textbooks and other materials (the IATM described above)
- a classroom observation instrument for the analysis of IELTS preparation lessons
- a pro forma for receiving information from IELTS administrators on their IELTS experiences and attitudes.

For a comprehensive, reflective account of the complete study the reader is referred to Hawkey (2006) in this series. We restrict our focus in this volume to reporting a number of the findings that came out of the IELTS Impact Study (IIS) which are directly relevant to the assessment of second language reading.

Some findings in relation to the IELTS Reading module

Very similar perceptions of the relative difficulties of the IELTS macro skill modules (Reading, Writing, Speaking, and Listening) were held by both teachers and candidates in the study.

Table 6.1 Student and teacher perceptions of IELTS module difficulty

	Most difficult IELTS module? (%)	
	Students	Teachers
Reading	49	45
Writing	24	26
Listening	18	20
Speaking	9	9

Source: Hawkey (2006)

The Reading module is seen as clearly the most difficult of the four IELTS test modules across the candidate and preparation course teacher participants. However, it is interesting to note that the Reading test did not appear in the top five reasons given by the 28% of IELTS candidates who felt IELTS was unfair.

The inter-relationships between perceived difficulties emerging from the questionnaire data were investigated further by Hawkey through *second-level* analysis to discover whether there was a correlation between the perceived most difficult test skill, reading, and other factors perceived as affecting candidates' performance, in particular, *time*, which was also frequently mentioned as a significant cause of worry for candidates. Table 6.2 emphasises the dominance of the Reading test module as the most difficult according to IIS test takers and of time pressure as the most prominent problem with the Reading test.

Table 6.2 Relationship between perceived skill difficulty and other factors perceived as affecting candidate test performance

	Difficulty of language	Difficulty of questions	Unfamiliarity of topics	Time pressure	Fear of tests	Others	Total
Listening	4	7	6	16	4	1	38
Reading	13	20	28	51	14	2	128
Writing	10	10	19	26	8	0	73
Speaking	2	4	6	9	3	1	25

Source: Hawkey (2006)

For Hawkey his impact findings here raised a number of important issues for future research on the IELTS Reading module:

> The perception of the reading module as more difficult than the other IELTS test modules, and of time pressure as affecting all modules, may be seen as test validity concerns (i.e. relating to cognitive validity in particular in our terms). One might ask, for example, whether the reading expected of post-IELTS test-takers in their target higher education domain is more 'difficult' than their writing, listening and speaking activities in that domain. Such a question would be part of a set of questions about how the IELTS test modules compare with the skills, macro and micro, that they purport to be testing. Should the reading module focus more on expeditious reading skills (e.g. Skimming, search reading, scanning) rather than or as well as narrower, specific micro-skills? And is time such a pressure on those skills in the real higher educational life that candidates are preparing to face? (Hawkey 2006:124)

At the conclusion of his review of IELTS Impact Studies Hawkey (2006) calls for further . . . IELTS impact studies linking test impact and test *performance*, for example:

- given evidence of the need for further investigation of the validity of IELTS Reading and Writing tasks, research involving receiving institution subject lecturers, into the nature of reading and writing activities in a range of higher education courses, linked, perhaps, to
- an investigation of candidate reading and writing performances on different reading and writing test tasks based on the initial enquiry. (Hawkey 2005:163)

Hawkey's recommendations were taken up by the IELTS research programme funded by the British Council and IDP Australia. Two research studies, one on the relationship between the academic reading construct as measured by IELTS and the reading experiences of students in the first year of their courses at a British university, and one on the cognitive processes underlying the academic reading construct as measured by IELTS were carried out in 2006–08 (See Weir et al 2008).

Examination boards could usefully consider replicating this sort of washback/impact-related research for other tests and test levels, using the research questions and methodological approaches described above, as part of their study into the washback and impact of their assessment products.

Avoidance of test bias

Geranpayeh and Kunnan (2007:1) provide a useful overview of DIF, seen above as a key method of choice for investigating test bias:

When standardized English-language tests are administered to test takers worldwide, the test-taking population could be varied on a number of personal and educational characteristics such as age, gender, first language, and academic discipline. As test tasks and test items may not always be prepared keeping this diversity of characteristics in mind, it is essential for test developers to continuously monitor their tests in terms of whether all test takers are receiving a fair test . . . One approach to this problem has been to examine test scores from a pilot group or, if the test has already been launched, to examine test scores from a large sample of test takers and detect items that function differently for different test taking groups and to investigate the source of this difference. This approach is called differential item functioning (DIF), and it has been popular since the 1980s.

The aim of such DIF/test bias analysis is to help us to understand better what the test is measuring and make us aware, with particular reference to our consequential validation of a test, of the influence of construct irrelevant factors. DIF analysis should contribute to test equity or fairness by statistically flagging items which present evidence of DIF.

Chen and Henning (1985), Geranpayeh (2001), Kim (2001), Kunnan

(1990, 1994, 1995), Pae (2004) and Ryan and Bachman (1992) looked at DIF/ test bias in relation to various background variables. Ferne and Rupp (2007) synthesised 27 studies covering 15 years of research on DIF with the aim of improving the design, analysis, and reporting of results of DIF research in the language testing literature (see also Camilli and Shepard 1994 on how to do DIF analysis).

However, if due care and attention is paid to the test taker at the design and development stage the chance of serious bias is in all likelihood reduced. It is interesting to note the conclusion of Geranpayeh and Kunnan (2007) after a review of the relevant research literature that: 'no clear and definitive findings regarding DIF in tests based on test taker characteristics have emerged as yet.' A similar conclusion is reached by Ferne and Rupp (2007:145) in their major review of the literature:

'Despite the laudable attempts to account for causes for DIF, the methodological heterogeneity of studies along with the general lack of explanatory power of predictor variables has made the practical utility of many DIF studies for item revision and development questionable. In other words, it is very difficult to say what conclusions can be reliably drawn from 15 years of research on DIF in language testing for the future construction of tests that measure a specific ability.'

Such conclusions do not, however, absolve examination boards from checking on this aspect of test fairness however rigorous their item writing guidelines. Following Bachman (1990) they need to consider four potential sources of test bias:

• cultural background
• background knowledge
• cognitive characteristics
• native language/ethnicity/age and gender.

Examination boards have to take steps to ensure that potential sources of DIF/test bias suggested by Bachman are guarded against. It is, however, necessary to remember Bachman's (1990:278) caveat that group differences must be treated with some caution as they may be an indication of differences in actual language ability rather than an indication of bias. Zumbo (2007:224) points out:

... the introduction of the term differential item functioning (to replace item bias) allowed one to distinguish item impact from item bias. Item impact described the situation in which DIF exists, because there were true differences between the groups in the underlying ability of interest being measured by the item. Item bias described the situations in which there is DIF because of some characteristic of the test item that is not relevant to the underlying ability of interest (and hence the test purpose).

Despite the methodological and construct-predictive problems of DIF (see Ferne and Rupp 2007, above), its use in the investigation of the test bias element of consequential validation must continue.

Avoidance of test bias: Cambridge ESOL practice

We noted in Chapter 2 in relation to the test taker that, before a test is administered, it is obviously necessary to establish evidence of the context and cognitive validity of test tasks to try and ensure that no potential sources of bias are allowed to interfere with measurement. The avoidance of bias is sought through the careful item writing and test production process, i.e. Item Writer (IW) guidelines, IW recruitment, induction, training, co-ordination, moderation and evaluation, and the whole item/test development process through various stages of monitored writing, editing, revising, within expert teams (see Chapter 7 for details of the item writing process).

Striving to avoid bias is thus not simply about checking, by means of DIF, whether or not you can identify bias after the event (through research-oriented investigations and studies), but building test production and delivery systems that aim to systematically embody consequential validity at all points, i.e. embed it within the whole system.

A final statistical check on potential item bias is made against candidate bio data as collected by Cambridge ESOL at the time of test administration on the Candidate Information Sheets (CIS) which are routinely completed by all ESOL candidates enabling Cambridge ESOL to gather demographic data such as age, gender, nationality, first language etc. for research purposes (see Chapter 2). An example of the CIS form is supplied in Appendix B. Such candidate information is valuable as it can be collected and electronically recorded and later compared with test scores. Saville (2003:103) describes how at Cambridge ESOL Grade Review and Awards meetings:

> The performance of large groups of candidates (or cohorts) is compared with cohorts from previous years, and performance is also compared by country, by first language, by age and a number of other factors, to ensure that the standards being applied are consistently fair to all candidates, and that a particular grade 'means' the same thing from year to year and throughout the world.

Geranpayeh and Kunnan (2007) point out that age is a particularly important concern in the Cambridge General English examinations, as there has been a shift in the traditional test population with test takers of many age groups now taking cognitively challenging tests. They argue that 'Anecdotal historical observations have indicated that if there were going to be any DIF in these examinations, it was likely to impact mainly listening items. Banks

(1999) and Geranpayeh (2001) examined the country and age bias in examinations such as the First Certificate in English and Preliminary English Test and recommended further investigation into DIF of listening item types' (Geranpayeh and Kunnan, 2007:193).

As there had been no empirical research in this area Geranpayeh and Kunnan (2007:1) describe how they 'investigated whether the test items on the listening section of the Certificate in Advanced English examination functioned differently for test takers from three different age groups. The main results showed that although statistical and content analysis procedures detected differential item functioning in a few items, expert judges could not clearly identify the sources of differential item functioning for the items.

Conclusion

In this chapter we have argued that three parameters in consequential validity need to be addressed in considering a test's validity:

- evidence that the impact on society, individuals and institutions, is beneficial
- evidence that the washback effects of the test on learning and teaching are positive
- evidence that bias has been avoided, using DIF studies.

We have examined some of the empirical research carried out by Cambridge ESOL in each of these three aspects. We next turn to the final set of parameters that exam boards need to consider in generating evidence on the validity of their tests, namely those of *criterion-related validity*.

7 Criterion-related validity

The ALTE *Multilingual Glossary of Language Testing Terms* notes that a 'test is said to have criterion-related validity if a relationship can be demonstrated between test scores and some external criterion which is believed to be a measure of the same ability' (ALTE 1998a:140).

As the importance attached by test users to test comparability information has increased in recent years, test providers have had to pay greater attention to issues of *cross-test comparability* – both in terms of the relationships between their own tests and with those offered by other examination boards. The ability to relate different tests to one another in meaningful ways provides testers with criterion-related evidence to use for comparability purposes.

When new versions of an examination are produced, there is limited public evidence that examination boards compare empirically the statistical properties of alternative forms of their exams. As well as ensuring equivalence in terms of the cognitive and contextual features of reading examinations, examination boards need to adopt an item banking approach underpinned by Item Response Theory (IRT) if they are to demonstrate acceptable *equivalence with different versions of the same test*.

Additionally, there is a growing interest worldwide in *comparability with external standards* such as the Common European Framework of Reference (CEFR). These standards tend to be influential as they provide policy makers with tools that can be used for gathering baseline data, for benchmarking and for evaluating current practices. External standards are of particular benefit to governments which have educational or test reform initiatives.

We will examine criterion-related validity in detail from the three perspectives listed in Figure 7.1 below.

Figure 7.1 Parameters of criterion-related validity

Criterion-related validity
• Cross-test comparability • Equivalence with different versions of the same test • Comparability with external standards

Cross-test comparability

Taylor (2004:2) argues that test users want to know how one test compares with other available tests which claim to perform a similar function. University admissions officers want to know how to deal with students who present them with TOEFL, IELTS, CAE or CPE scores; employers need to know how to equate different language qualifications presented by job applicants; educational institutions, teachers and students have to choose which test to take from those on offer.

Taylor (2004a) points out that there have always been informal as well as formal attempts to compare language proficiency measures; traditionally, comparisons have tended to focus on whether the scores or grades from two different tests are comparable with one another (see further discussion of this in the section below on the empirical stage of linking examinations to the CEFR). Bachman, Davidson, Ryan and Choi (1995) emphasised that any comparability study needed to take account of more than just score equivalences. They point out that it must also investigate comparability of test content and performance, a point which we will return to below.

Cross-test comparability: Cambridge ESOL practice

Taylor (2004a:2) describes how: '. . . in 1998 and 1999 internal studies examined the relationship between IELTS and the Cambridge Main Suite Examinations, specifically CAE (C1 level) and FCE (B2 level). Under test conditions, candidates took experimental reading examinations containing both IELTS and CAE or FCE tasks. Although the studies were limited in scope, results indicated that a candidate who achieves a Band 6.5 in IELTS would be likely to achieve a passing grade at CAE (C1 level). Further research was conducted in 2000 as part of the ALTE Can Do Project (see below) in which Can Do responses by IELTS candidates were collected over the year and matched to grades; this enabled Can Do self-ratings of IELTS and Main Suite candidates to be compared. The results, in terms of mean "Can Do self-ratings", further supported placing IELTS Band 6.5 at the C1 level of the CEFR alongside CAE.'

The conceptual framework mapping exams onto a comparison scale presented by Taylor in *Research Notes* 15 (Taylor 2004) describes the links between Cambridge ESOL suites of level-based examinations or syllabuses, i.e. Main Suite, BEC, and YLE (Young Learners English). These suites are targeted at similar ability levels as defined by a common measurement scale based on latent trait methods (see below for a discussion of Cambridge ESOL item banking system); many are also similar in terms of examination content and design (multiple skills components, and similar task/item-types).

The 2004 conceptual framework was subsequently revised to accommodate IELTS more closely within its frame of reference. Figure 7.2 illustrates how, based on the evidence available at that time, the IELTS band scores, Main Suite, BEC and BULATS examinations were believed to align with one another and with the levels of the CEFR. Note that the IELTS band scores are the overall scores, not the individual module scores (an issue we return to below).

Figure 7.2   Alignment of IELTS, Main Suite, BEC, YLE , ILEC, ICFE and BULATS examinations with the Common European Framework

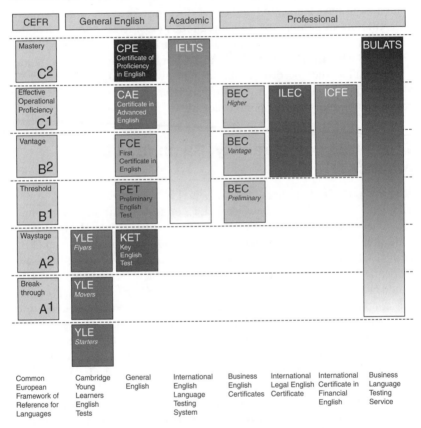

Source: www.CambridgeESOL.org/exams/exams-info/cefr.html

Lynda Taylor (personal communication 2008) notes that: 'this alignment between examinations is based not only on the internal research at Cambridge ESOL referred to above, but also the long established experience of examination use within education and society, as well as feedback from a range of examination stakeholders regarding the uses of examination results for particular purposes.' It will continue to be refined as further evidence is generated.

Equivalence with different versions of the same test

Test equivalence is established if 'a relationship can be demonstrated between test scores obtained from different versions of a test administered to the same candidates under the same conditions on two different occasions' (Weir 2005:208. See also Mislevy 1992 for a comprehensive discussion of this area). The ALTE *Multilingual Glossary of Language Testing Terms* (1998a:144) offers the following definition of equivalence in test forms:

> Different versions of the same test, which are regarded as equivalent to each other in that they are based on the same specifications and measure the same competence. To meet the strict requirements of equivalence under classical test theory, different forms of a test must have the same mean difficulty, variance, and co-variance, when administered to the same persons.

The American Educational Research Association et al (1999) further refine the test equivalence definition. It distinguishes between: *parallel* forms, which should demonstrate equivalence in raw score means, standard deviations, and correlations with other measures for a stated population; *equivalent* forms, where score conversion techniques or 'form-specific norm tables' are used to compensate for differences in raw score statistics between test versions; and *comparable* forms, which are very close in terms of content but where the extent of statistical similarity remains unproven. For test providers, of course, it is vital to achieve as complete as possible equivalence across alternate forms of the same test which are produced on different session dates to meet the needs of test users.

Lynda Taylor (2004:2) notes that:

> '. . . Cambridge ESOL produces different versions – also known as "alternate" or "parallel" forms – of the same examination to be taken on different session dates throughout the year; examinations must clearly be equivalent from session to session in terms of their content coverage and measurement characteristics. The multilingual glossary (ALTE 1998[a]) notes that equivalence is very difficult to achieve in practice and that considerable effort and expertise goes into ensuring examination equivalence through the implementation of a comprehensive set of standard procedures applied at each stage of examination production (see Saville 2003).'

The *Dictionary of Language Testing* by Davies et al (1999) offers a similar definition for equivalence to the one given above and goes on to mention the increasingly common use of IRT analysis and item banking to help with the process of creating equivalent forms: the method employed by Cambridge ESOL.

Equivalence with different versions of the same test: Cambridge ESOL practice

In this section, we will examine how Cambridge ESOL attempts to achieve version equivalence through establishing a common measurement scale, its item banking system and its item writing and pretesting procedures. For discussion of how it attempts to achieve equivalence between paper-based and computer-based versions of its tests (e.g. PET) see Appendix F.

Item banking and the Cambridge ESOL Common Scale

In Cambridge ESOL Reading papers, question paper production is based on the Local Item Banking System (LIBS), which is a computer-based management and analysis tool developed by Cambridge ESOL to handle the entire production cycle. LIBS contains a large bank of materials for use in the examinations (more than 100,000 items) which have all been fully edited and pretested according to the procedures described below.

Item banking is an application of Item Response Theory (IRT) (Bond and Fox 2001, Wright and Stone 1979). It involves assembling a bank of *calibrated* items – that is, items of known difficulty. Designs employed for collecting response data ensure a link across items at all levels. The Cambridge ESOL Common Scale, a single measurement scale covering all Cambridge ESOL levels, has been constructed with reference to these objective items. The Cambridge ESOL Common Scale relates different testing events within a single frame of reference, greatly facilitating the development and consistent application of standards.

For most routine analysis, Cambridge ESOL uses the BIGSTEPS analysis program supplemented by in-house programmes for formatting data and handling the output. Items are pretested in specially constructed papers which include *anchor items*. Because the anchor items are of known difficulty, the analysis that is carried out on the pretest responses allows the new items to be calibrated on a logit scale. This scale produced by BIGSTEPS is rescaled to produce a conventional ESOL scale, which is used for examination construction purposes. It is this scale which underpins the Local Item Banking System (LIBS). Examinations are constructed from the calibrated tasks in the item bank. Each task, therefore, consists of items of measured (Rasch) difficulty, which are selected from within a specified range to determine the mean difficulty of the task.

In this context it is worth pointing out that the logit intervals which define the Common Scale cannot be compared with the logit values provided for the CEFR reference levels as defined by the illustrative scales (North 2002a). This is because they have been derived in completely different ways: the Common Scale from learners' responses to objective test tasks, vertically anchored across five exam levels; the CEFR scales from teacher ratings of learners' observed behaviour. But if the scales are not comparable, neither are they contradictory. Both refer to the same broad conceptual framework of language proficiency levels.

Figure 7.3 shows how constructing a single measurement scale requires all the item response data to be linked in some way. Two ways of achieving this are *common person* linking, where a group of learners might, for, example take examination papers at two different levels, and *common item* linking, where different examinations contain some items in common. The latter is the basic approach used in pretesting, where each pretest is administered together with an anchor test of already calibrated material.

Figure 7.3 Item banking approach to scale construction

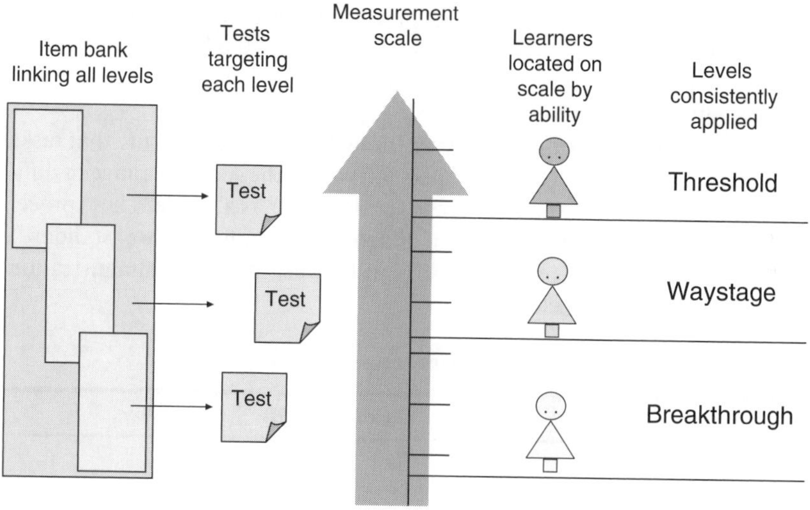

Source: www.cambridgeesol.org

Figure 7.3 pictorially represents the basis for the construction of parallel forms of the examinations at the different levels of the system. The common scale which underpins the item bank is based on Rasch scaling, which means that the paper construction must hit a target for the average difficulty of the paper using the difficulty estimates obtained from pretesting.

In operational test production new items are pretested in specially constructed papers which include anchor items. Because the anchor items are of known difficulty, the analysis that is carried out on the pretest responses allows the new items to be calibrated and linked to the common scale. Using this approach to model the predicted facility of new items, the test construction team is able to make a judgement on how examination tasks are likely to perform under live examination conditions. It also allows for a comparison between the 'live' values and those modelled, at the time when analysis takes place for grading the examination (see Table 7.1 below).

Table 7.1 Mean difficulty of Reading paper in 2005 sessions

	Exam/Session	At test construction	At live test/grading
KET (A2)	Dec	41	40
PET (B1)	Dec	55	55
FCE (B2)	June	62	62
CAE (C1)	June	70	71
CPE (C2)	June	78	77

The above table shows no or slight variation between the difficulty of the Reading paper at the test construction stage and at the live administration stage which is an outcome of the rigorous procedures in place to ensure stability of difficulty levels at these stages.

The standard operating procedures for test construction ensure that tasks selected for Main Suite Reading papers fall within the specified range of difficulty and achieve the targeted average for the paper as a whole. These procedures help to ensure comparability of difficulty and maintenance of standards across different versions of the paper and between different administration sessions (see Table 7.2 below).

Table 7.2 Stability of Reading papers across sessions in 2005

	June (Session A)	June (Session B)	December
KET (A2)	41	39	40
PET (B1)	56	56	55
FCE (B2)	62		62
CAE (C1)	71	not applicable	71
CPE (C2)	77		79

The overall targeted difficulty values for Main Suite Reading papers on the Cambridge ESOL Common Scale are: 41 for KET, 56 for PET, 62 for FCE, 71 for CAE and 78 for CPE. The above table shows that the difficulty of the Reading papers administered for each Main Suite examination over a period of two sessions in 2005 remained within an acceptable range of variation, i.e. one to two points on either side of the difficulty point on the scale.

Following our discussion of cognitive and context aspects of validity in Chapters 3 and 4 above, it must be stressed that high indices of alternate-form reliability alone do not necessarily yield a significant meaning unless supported by evidence of comparability in other aspects of validity as well. For example, inconsistent context validity across examination forms may influence examination scores, resulting in bias against particular cohorts as a consequence and affecting examination fairness.

Weir and Wu (2006) attempted to measure a number of aspects of the parallel-form reliability of three trial proficiency speaking test forms both quantitatively at the form and task level and qualitatively at the task level. Apart from measuring parallel form reliability statistically in a conventional quantitative way, the assistance of raters' judgements also helped to investigate such parallelness qualitatively. The Weir and Wu study employed the use of checklists to investigate the parallelness of content of the three trial forms from the viewpoints of raters. An individual checklist was specifically developed for each of the three task types in which potential variables affecting difficulty of the task were detailed for raters' judgements.

Weir and Wu's study sounds a warning for all those involved in intra-task variability research and producing equivalent forms. The results show that without taking the necessary steps to control context variables affecting test difficulty, test quality may fluctuate over tasks in different test forms. They argue that high correlations in themselves do not provide sufficient evidence that two tests are equivalent in validity. When evidence of context comparability in both test forms is also provided, this still only constitutes a partial equivalence argument. We need further evidence of their cognitive validity to be confident of the equivalence of the test forms.

Item writing

The *item writing* process and subsequent *pretesting* play an important part in ensuring equivalence across forms. The procedures followed by Cambridge ESOL in respect of these are outlined briefly below. A fuller description of the standard procedures for the production of examination material is provided in Appendix D.

The item writing process plays an important role in achieving equivalence between different versions of an examination particularly in relation to context and cognitive validity. Item writers, who are all external consultants engaged in teaching and/or writing materials for the target candidature, are commissioned to produce a range of tasks for a particular examination based on a specially adapted version of the Examination Specifications, i.e. item writer guidelines (IWGs). They follow the IWGs which specify the task type and focuses required for each part of the paper. The IWGs also offer advice on how to select appropriate texts and how to exploit the texts to provide the required number of items from them. This constitutes the first stage of the question paper production (QPP) process (see Appendix D).

Following receipt of the commissioned materials, a pre-editing meeting is held. The pre-editing team comprises the subject officer (SO) and chair of the paper together with a third independent consultant who has experience of producing similar materials, either by skill or by level. The commissioned materials are scrutinised to ensure they meet the specifications laid down in the IWGs (topic suitability/testing focuses/anticipated item difficulty/length of texts) and are either accepted or rejected. Successful writers will have selected texts appropriate for the target candidature and which provide the range of testing focuses required across a range of items. The texts they have selected will not favour candidates with specialised knowledge of a particular subject nor have content that would be too specialised or technical for the majority of candidates (see Chapter 4 for further detail on this). The texts will have been drawn from as wide a range of sources as possible and authentic textual features such as headlines may have been amended to help the candidates understand what is in the body of the text. Successful writers will avoid texts that have a short shelf-life, i.e. those that make reference to contemporary public figures whose fortunes may change before the examination takes place, or texts that refer to recent changes in technology which may have been superseded.

Materials which successfully pass the pre-editing stage are loaded into LIBS and are submitted for editing. At this stage, the original item writers, together with the SO and chair, are involved in re-checking the quality of the materials against the specifications, and making changes as necessary. These are kept to a minimum in order to preserve the authenticity of the original texts, but may include, for example: finding synonyms for words that are crucial to items but are likely to be unknown to FCE-level candidates; removing unsuitable content from an otherwise inoffensive text; cutting to satisfy the overall length as laid down in the specifications.

Lynda Taylor (personal communication 2008) points to '. . . the critical importance of developing a common professional testing culture within a testing organisation'. The Question Paper Production referred to above depends heavily upon a team approach involving a number of different individuals. All those involved, whether they are working internally for Cambridge ESOL or externally as independent consultants, bring their professional expertise and experience to bear on the process and its outcomes. Members of the item-writing team typically have a background in applied linguistics and/or language education and they receive specific training for their test development role. For item writers, many of whom are already teachers or materials writers, this is achieved through Cambridge ESOL's training and development framework structured around a set of procedures referred to by the acronym RITCME: Recruitment (R), Induction (I), Training (T),

Co-ordination (C), Monitoring (M) and Evaluation (E). The RIT part of the system ensures that item writers have a suitable professional background and are given appropriate training in the skills needed as well as information on the processes involved. The CME procedures allow for ongoing professional development, through standardisation, monitoring and evaluation in the longer term, including the monitoring of item writing acceptance rates and the evaluation of the item writing team's success on each paper. (For more details of how this system works in practice, see Ingham 2008 and Appendix E).

Lynda Taylor (personal communication 2008) also observes that

> 'this team approach resonates with the notion of "communities of practice" which has emerged and gained ground in recent years, in relation to how learning and organisational development take place. Communities of practice constitute groups of people that develop over time through the sustained pursuit of some shared enterprise; in the course of this, such "communities" develop a set of common practices including resources such as tools, documents, routines and even a vocabulary that in some way embody the knowledge of the community (see Lave and Wenger 1991, Wenger 1999)'.

For Cambridge ESOL, there are a number of distinct advantages to this 'communities of practice' approach: it provides a powerful and sustainable mechanism for the large-scale production of high-quality test material; it creates a learning and development context into which new writers can be introduced and in which established writers can take on new responsibilities (e.g. the role of a chair); and it offers regular and direct opportunities for two-way dialogue between Cambridge ESOL and the item writing consultants, thus maintaining contact with a key sector of the larger stakeholder constituency for the Cambridge examinations.

Pretesting

The outcome of the pre-editing and editing stages should be the production of materials which appear to be of an acceptable standard for inclusion in a live examination. In order to confirm this, Cambridge ESOL uses the process of pretesting on volunteer candidates. A range of age and nationality groups is represented in the pretest population which roughly corresponds to that of the live candidature.

Every year, around 20,000 candidates are involved in the pretesting of Cambridge ESOL examinations. Almost all of them are learners who are preparing for or have recently taken a Cambridge ESOL examination. They take the pretest under examination conditions, and their answers are assessed in the same way as 'live' examinations. The materials used in these pretests do not appear in live examinations in the short term, and never in the combinations in which they are presented so that pretest candidates are not unfairly advantaged in any way by taking part, although of course the extra practice in taking examinations can be extremely valuable. Each edited item is pretested on a representative sample of candidates, usually involving around 200 learners who are about to take one of the live examinations, so that data can be statistically analysed. Caution is exercised when selecting the pretest sample to avoid bias, e.g. in terms of L1 or age group or gender. In this way pretesting plays an important role in achieving reliability in terms of parallel forms of the tests.

Pretested materials are subject to statistical analysis at task and item level using both classical item analysis to establish that items are discriminating, and Rasch analysis to determine the level of difficulty. All the materials which are pretested can be related to the underlying scale of difficulty in the item bank by the use of 'anchor' items; as discussed above, these are items with known measurement characteristics which provide the basis for calculating the difficulty of the new items to go into the bank.

After pretesting, a meeting is held to review the results of the pretests and evaluate the measurement characteristics of tasks and items. Tasks which are approved at the pretest review are those which satisfy the requirements of the paper in terms of difficulty, at item and task level, and which discriminate appropriately between the more and less able candidates. Those which do not are both rewritten and sent back for re-pretesting, or are rejected. This procedure ensures, as far as possible, that no editing will need to take place at the paper construction stage.

Until this stage, all items, whether discrete or text based, are kept separately in LIBS. Now items are combined to form complete papers according to established procedures, using LIBS as an examination construction tool. Paper construction normally takes place about two years before the date of the live examination. The chair of the paper selects material for a first draft of the question paper and a team comprising the SO, chair and experienced external consultant meets to review this first draft.

LIBS can store information about each of the items/questions/tasks, including such things as statistical data from pretesting (Rasch difficulty, facility, and discrimination), text type, item type, text length, topic, and answer key. Constructing papers in LIBS is an efficient and accurate way of ensuring the correct balance of all these attributes is satisfied within the paper and, additionally, that equivalence of versions across sessions is achieved. When the first draft of a new paper has been constructed, reports can be generated from LIBS which show all of this information. If the examination construction team wishes to make adjustments by selecting materials with different characteristics this process can be repeated several times until a suitable version of the paper is constructed, meeting both content and difficulty criteria. This method provides a prediction of how difficult the paper will be when it is used under live conditions.

One further check is made before a paper is approved to be passed into the question paper production (QPP) process, where further quality checks are made to the content and presentation of the paper. All of the papers for a given examination are scrutinised by the team of SOs responsible for the examination: this ensures that there is no overlap of topic within the examination, with previous examinations at the same level, or with examinations at adjacent levels.

After the examination has been administered and scored, a series of checks is carried out to ensure that all candidates have been assessed accurately and to the same standards. These include a review of the item analysis and descriptive statistics, which enables the SOs to confirm whether the examination materials 'performed' as predicted by the pretesting activities. This process provides additional confirmation of the difficulty of the paper and allows for adjustments to be made if necessary in order to maintain a consistent standard across different versions.

The subject officers and subject manager meet to review all the information available and to make a recommendation for where the grade boundaries should be set, according to the performance criteria defined for that grade (see Chapter 5 for a detailed discussion of this). Certificated exams report results as passing and failing grades, rather than a score on a continuous scale. Grading is therefore a process of setting the cut-off score for the various grades: A, B, C (passing) D, E (failing). At the grading meeting, reports and analyses which have been carried out on the score data (the way the examination materials have worked in practice) and in relation to various groups of candidates are reviewed according to an established procedure. These recommendations are then presented to senior management for approval before being finally signed off.

In terms of establishing equivalence between different versions of the same Reading test the procedures adopted by Cambridge ESOL are rigorous and extensive.

Comparability with external standards

At the moment, there seems to be increasing pressure on test providers and examination boards to link their examinations to a particular external standard, namely the CEFR. Indeed, within a relatively short period of time the CEFR has become highly influential in Europe and beyond.

Let us consider the European context first. In France, secondary school students are expected to achieve B1 in their first foreign language and A2 in their second. In fact, the French Ministry of Education in its objectives for languages across the curriculum for the academic year 2007–8 onwards links achievement to the levels of the CEFR (Martyniuk 2008). National reading tests for school children in Norway are based on the CEFR levels and their results are reported as a CEFR level (Moe 2008). In Finland school assessments have been linked to the CEFR (Tuokko 2008). The same is true in Hungary with regard to examination reform initiatives (David 2007, Szabo 2007); in Germany the national standards for languages; in England the 'languages ladder', i.e. the national language strategy; and in the Netherlands curriculum reform and examinations (North 2008). The European Survey on Language Competence Project (SurveyLang) refers to the CEFR levels and will report achievement levels of 15–16 year old school students across Europe for the two most widely taught foreign languages in each European Union country. If we look at different domains there is also a CEFR impact. For example, the language requirements in relation to immigration and citizenship in Europe are increasingly couched in terms of CEFR levels. In Germany and Denmark a B1 level is currently required for citizenship, in Austria and Finland an A2 level is preferred. So it is clear that the influence and power of the CEFR is already widespread in Europe and it will increase.

Beyond Europe, Education Ministries and other national agencies are increasingly preoccupied with international benchmarking. In Taiwan, for example, the Ministry of Education in 2005 set about establishing a common standard of English proficiency through the adoption of the CEFR. The CEFR is now the external benchmark for its English language examinations and it is compulsory for agencies offering such examinations to provide evidence of linking to the CEFR (see Wu and Wu 2007). Public English language examinations in Chile, China, Colombia, Korea and Japan are investigating similar linking procedures. The United Nations have adopted the CEFR levels for training purposes at UN institutions around the world. In Canada the CEFR has been adopted for national standards in foreign languages, alongside the indigenous framework of the Canadian Language Benchmarks (CLB).

For examination providers it is thus increasingly necessary to make the case that their exams are aligned to the CEFR. Examination boards in the UK offering TESOL examinations (Cambridge ESOL, Trinity College, London English Examinations and City and Guilds) are all involved at various stages in the linking processes. ETS in respect of TOEFL and TOEIC is similarly involved in the USA. Publishers are also concerned to lay claim to linkages for their ESOL textbooks at various CEFR levels.

The Council of Europe has attempted to facilitate the alignment process by providing a toolkit of resources, including a draft pilot Manual for relating language examinations to the CEFR and a technical reference supplement to this (Council of Europe 2003, 2004) and by providing fora where practitioners share their reflections on the use of the Manual and their experience in using the different linking stages as suggested in the Manual. Examples of such fora include a seminar entitled 'Reflections on the use of the Draft Manual for Relating Language Examinations to the CEFR: Insights from

Case Studies, Pilots and other projects' held in Cambridge in December 2007 (see Taylor 2008) and a pre-conference research colloquium, entitled 'Standard Setting Research and its Relevance to the CEFR' (Athens, May 2008). In these fora representatives from bodies offering examinations in France, Germany, Greece, Hungary, Italy, Netherlands, Norway, Finland, Japan, Slovenia, UK and Turkey presented data concerning their progress to date in linking a whole range of language examinations to the CEFR.

Comparability with external standards: Cambridge ESOL practice

In this section, we will focus on the relationship between Cambridge ESOL Main Suite examinations and the CEFR as an external standard. The relationship has its roots in their shared purposes; in the way both the examinations and the framework have influenced each other's evolution; in the anchoring of the ALTE 'Can Do' statements to the CEFR; and in the embodiment of the *Manual* (Council of Europe 2003) procedures for relating examinations to the CEFR in the Cambridge test development cycle.

Both Cambridge ESOL and the CEFR provide a learning ladder and proficiency framework. The CEFR sets learning objectives as part of its aim to be 'a comprehensive, transparent and coherent framework for language learning and teaching and assessment' (Council of Europe 2001:9) and the examinations assess the outcomes through defining levels of proficiency which allow learners' progress to be measured at each stage of learning and on a life-long basis. The Main Suite examinations were all designed to offer learners and teachers useful curriculum and assessment levels.

A synergistic evolution

Taylor and Jones (2006) stated that much of the evidence linking the examinations to the CEFR is conceptual, theoretical and derives from the historical context in which the examinations developed in terms of linguistics and pedagogy. They went on to explain that during the late 1980s, various stakeholders (Cambridge ESOL included) helped fund and provided professional input to the revision of the linguistic and functional level descriptions Threshold and Waystage (Van Ek and Trim 1998). This was a natural extension of earlier level specification work initiated by the Council of Europe in the 1970s. The updated *Threshold 1990* and *Waystage 1990* underpinned the revised examination specifications for PET and the new design of KET, strongly defining their lexico-grammatical and functional/notional content, as well as the selection of texts and tasks for language ability assessment. Work to develop the third level *Vantage* drew strongly on the existing FCE examination (B2) and received financial and professional support from Cambridge and the ALTE partners (Van Ek and Trim 2001). From these three level specifications which were already closely linked to the three Main Suite examinations KET, PET and FCE, the CEFR began to emerge.

North (2008) also attests to this unique relationship by stating that 'the process of defining CEF levels started in 1913 with the Cambridge Proficiency exam (CPE) that defines a practical mastery of the language as a non-native speaker. This level has become C2 . . . The existence of LCE (later FCE) since 1939 also helped in defining B2 level'.

Figure 7.4 below provides a pictorial representation of the evolution and development of Main Suite examinations in relation to the CEFR levels

Figure 7.4 Historical development of Main Suite levels and the CEFR

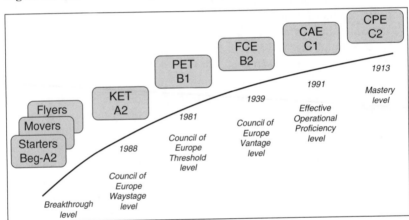

Source: Figure by Neil Jones www.CambridgeESOL.org

Figure 7.4 indicates that there has always been a close relationship between developments in Cambridge's General English examinations and the definition of language levels in the CEFR. The close involvement of language teachers with the development of both helps explain this.

ALTE/Cambridge ESOL 5-level Framework and the CEFR

During the 1990s, the Association of Language Testers in Europe (ALTE) with Cambridge ESOL as a founding member was engaged in the development and validation of the 5-level ALTE Framework. This project aimed at establishing common levels of proficiency to aid transnational recognition of language certification in Europe. Assessment was to be carried out at a variety of different criterion levels, from the level of beginner up to the level of a highly proficient user, with a series of intermediate levels in between.

The ALTE scale of levels provided a set of common standards and was the basis of a *criterion-referenced approach* to the interpretation of examination results. In particular it required the *vertical* mapping of the continuum of language ability from low to high; and the detailed specification of examination content at each criterion level together with examples of criterion performance in terms of candidates' performance in speech and writing (i.e. the *horizontal* dimension). Each Cambridge ESOL examination was benchmarked to a specific criterion level and could be interpreted within the context of the ALTE overall framework of levels.

The ALTE 'Can Do' scales provided criterion-related statements at each of the five levels in relation to the specified domains, which are covered in the examinations. The criterion scale and the 'Can Do' descriptors provided representations of the external reality, which helped to ensure that the examination results were relevant and meaningful to the key stakeholders, e.g. the candidates, their sponsors and other users of examination results. The 'Can Do' scales consisted of about 400 statements, organised into three general areas: Social and Tourist, Work, and Study. These are the three main areas of interest for most language learners. Each includes a number of more particular areas, e.g. the Social and Tourist area has sections on Shopping, Eating out, and Accommodation etc. Each of these includes up to three scales, for the skills of Listening/Speaking, Reading and Writing. Each such scale includes statements covering a range of levels. Some scales cover only a part of the proficiency range, as there are many situations of use, which require only basic proficiency to deal with successfully.

The scales were subjected to an extended process of empirical validation aimed at transforming the 'Can Do' statements from an essentially subjective set of level descriptions into a calibrated measuring instrument. Data collection has been based chiefly on self-report; the 'Can Do' scales being presented to respondents (approx. 10,000) as a set of linked questionnaires. It is these response patterns which define the meaning of a given level in 'Can Do' terms. In other words, the definition of a level is not based on *a priori* prescriptive, absolute criteria, but is rather descriptive of the experience of a large number of foreign language users.

After the release of the first draft of the CEFR in 1997, ALTE conducted several studies to verify the alignment of the ALTE Framework with the CEFR (for a discussion of this see Chapter 9 and Appendix D in Council of Europe 2001) and a major project was carried out in 1999–2000 using the ALTE 'Can Do' scales providing an empirical link between examination performance and perceived real-world language skills, as well as between the ALTE Framework and the CEFR scales (Jones 2000, 2001, 2002, Jones and Hirtzel 2001).

At that time, data was collected to link ALTE 'Can Do' self-ratings to grades achieved in Main Suite and BEC examinations at different levels.

A clear relationship was found, making it possible to begin to describe the meaning of an examination grade in terms of typical profiles of 'Can Do' ability. Candidates achieving an ordinary pass in an ALTE examination at a given level should have an 80% chance of succeeding on tasks identified as describing that level. Data collected on Main Suite and BEC candidates indicated that this figure accorded well with their average probability of endorsing 'Can Do' statements at the relevant level. This relationship was found to be fairly constant across examination levels. By defining 'Can Do' explicitly in this way a basis for interpreting particular ALTE levels in terms of 'Can Do' skills was established.

The two frameworks ALTE and the CEFR had entirely complementary aims, and thus, following the publication of the CEFR in 2001, ALTE members adopted the CEFR levels ranging from A1 to C2. The CEFR level system now provides an interpretative frame of reference for all Cambridge ESOL examinations. Such a criterion-referenced approach, whether it is the ALTE Framework or the CEFR, allows individual results on any one examination to be situated in relation to the total 'criterion space', i.e. the much wider continuum of ability. These European levels have the advantage of according with what Peter Hargreaves (the late Chief Executive of the then UCLES EFL) termed the 'natural' proficiency levels familiar to teachers. They are supported by the work of the Council of Europe over at least the last three decades which is based on a consensus view that adequate coverage is afforded by these broad levels for the purposes of organising language teaching and learning in the European Community (Council of Europe 2001).

The CEFR is the best descriptive framework available to us at the moment of what learners 'Can Do' in the target language in several domains of reference at each of six proficiency levels (see North 2000 for a description of how these levels of performance were empirically derived). It gives us a useful if indirect external operationalisation of the criterion of 'real life' that we advocated as a benchmark in the earlier chapters of this book for establishing the internal validity of our test tasks.

It is difficult to see what other external comparisons with real life could be employed by examination boards. Tracer studies following up students in 'real life' after their examinations to see whether they exhibit similar performances may be fine in conception but would be very difficult in practice. A predictive validity study where performance on the language test is compared with an external criterion such as later degree results is again problematic not least because of the intervening variables that may intrude. To compare our tests with performance in the real world we are forced to rely on a set of procedures available to examination boards for linking their examinations to the external criterion of the CEFR. These procedures are described below and those of *standard setting* and *empirical validation* are particularly germane to our advocacy of the CEFR as an external point of reference for establishing criterion-related validity.

Manual procedures and Cambridge ESOL practice

Cambridge ESOL has embarked on a systematic, ongoing and long-term programme of activities for relating its examinations to the CEFR as recommended by the Language Policy Division of the Council of Europe in its *Manual for Relating Language Examinations to the Common European Framework of Reference for Languages: Learning, Teaching, Assessment* (Council of Europe 2003). This work can be classified under the recommended sets of procedures outlined in the Manual, i.e. *familiarisation* with the CEFR, *specification* of the content and purposes of an examination, *standardisation* of interpretation of CEFR levels and *empirical validation* studies.

In Table 7.3 below, drawing upon the Manual, we summarise the steps in the first three of these stages that are currently recommended for linking examinations to the CEFR. This is inevitably a long-term agenda as the breadth and depth of the procedures below attest.

Table 7.3 Overview of Manual procedures for linking examinations to the CEFR

Familiarisation
1.1 Familiarisation with the CEFR. Review the: • CEFR   • Manual for relating examinations to the CEFR   • reference supplement to the manual   • 'linking' studies to date   • reported problems in the linking procedures   2.1 Design familiarisation procedures   • identifying the group profile   • gather baseline data on familiarity with CEFR   • determining the number of sessions needed   • establish familiarisation instruments   • designing workshops   • documentation of the changes made to the procedures suggested in the linking manual together with the rationales for doing so   • select tasks   • identifying the statistical tools to be used in the sessions   • gather information on how the CEFR descriptors/scales work for the context in question   • identify the problems (if any) with the descriptors   • explore ways of improving and/or adapting the descriptors/scales for the context in question
Specifications
3.1 Fill in the CEFR general specifications document for the examination; identify the level of the examination in relation to the CEFR with a team   3.2 Fill in the CEFR specifications documents for each paper of the examination, identify the level of the papers in relation to the CEFR with a team

Table 7.3 *cont.*

3.3 Send the examination test specifications and a sample exam to a team of external experts to fill in the CEFR specifications
• analyse the specifications filled in internally and externally
• identify areas of disagreement
• identify level of agreement
• discuss with the external expert areas of disagreement
• explore reasons of disagreement
• develop strategies for reducing these disagreements

Standardisation

4.1 Choose and invite c20 inside/outside experts (a range of stakeholders including educators, users of the examination results and academics) to participate in the standardisation

4.2 Choose a standard setting method
- a literature review of commonly used standard setting methods
- analysis of strengths and weaknesses of commonly used standard setting methods
- identifying the most suitable standard setting method for the given context

4.3 Standardise participants (local and external) using CEFR sample test items for each sub-test
- getting participants to identify the level of standardised items
- carrying out statistical analysis of judgements on calibrated items (calculating intra-rater and inter-rater reliability (calculating mean for each item; comparison of the judgements made by the local experts and the external experts; calculating the reliability of any cut points emerging from the process)
- discussion as a group (local experts and external experts all together)

4.4 Benchmarking
- getting participants to benchmark local test items
- analysing the judgement data

4.5 Standard setting
- establishing cut-off points for particular subtests
- establishing cut-off points for the exam as a whole

It is important to make the point that the alignment of tests to the CEFR should not be seen, as it often is, as a one-off exercise. To be fully effective diachronically it must be embedded as appropriate into each stage of the testing process as is now occurring in the Cambridge ESOL Test Development Cycle (for a full discussion of the cycle see Weir and Milanovic 2003) from planning and design to development and administration to monitoring and evaluation and back to planning again where revisions may be necessary. The ongoing and iterative nature of the cycle allows for changes in learning, pedagogy and assessment trends as well as in the targeted candidature to be incorporated into an examination. We will provide below an account of how the Manual procedures are integrated with Cambridge ESOL practice.

Figure 7.5 below provides an overview of the linking procedures and how they are embedded in Cambridge ESOL standard procedures.

Figure 7.5 Manual procedures and Cambridge ESOL test cycle

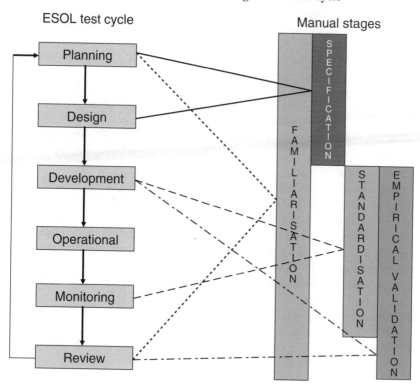

Familiarisation

The Manual perceives the familiarisation procedure as an 'indispensable starting point' before a linking exercise to the CEFR can be carried out effectively. It goes on to say that 'an account of activities taken and results obtained is an essential component of the validation report'. It advocates that 'participants in the linking process [should] have detailed knowledge of the CEFR' (Council of Europe 2003:1).

Before embarking on a familiarisation activity, Cambridge ESOL addressed several issues: who are these participants, how many, how familiar are they with the CEFR on a familiarity–unfamiliarity continuum, should their assessment experience be considered or should a zero baseline of knowledge be the starting point? The picture gets complicated when the participants involved in ensuring that an examination is related to the CEFR span across the organisation and beyond.

Experienced members of this large community certainly have a close understanding of Cambridge ESOL levels. For example, item writers providing materials for a particular examination are familiar with how to interpret the level, e.g. in terms of text difficulty, linguistic features, genre choice etc.

Item writer guidelines and examination handbooks provide detailed information on text selection and item writing at a certain level. Through their work with a certain proficiency level, many will also be familiar with the ALTE 'Can-Dos' and, of course, have come into contact with the CEFR. For Cambridge ESOL, then, familiarisation with the CEFR is at times seen as a part of consolidating and building on existing knowledge.

At the same time the prominence of the CEFR raises the need for a more general awareness-raising, of particular importance for staff just entering the organisation. Staff or external experts, whose current frame of reference may not extend beyond the Cambridge levels, or whose daily duties do not require them to look at developments further afield, also benefit from a better understanding of the CEFR.

Using activities and materials described in Chapter 3 of the Manual, a set of familiarisation procedures is made available to internal staff and to the network and are being implemented as applicable. Examples include induction worksheets, face-to-face workshops, and presentations at annual team meetings. The purpose of these familiarisation activities is to foster a common understanding of the aims and aspirations of the CEFR and its descriptive scheme; develop a broad awareness of the nature of the relationship between Cambridge ESOL examinations and the CEFR; build a shared knowledge of differentiating features across certain level thresholds, i.e. B1/B2 and B2/C1, to enable the rating of tasks and performances across these levels; produce an action plan for cascading the knowledge gained as a result of this familiarisation activity to other members of staff and the network.

Specification

Specification involves 'mapping the coverage of the examination in relation to the categories of the CEFR' (Council of Europe 2003:6). Cambridge ESOL's participants in this phase are subject officers, exam managers, validation officers, and a network of chairs, item writing teams, examiners, and academic consultants.

In the design phase of the test development cycle, test specifications are produced. Decisions are made with regards to item types, text features, range of topics etc. Sample materials are written and stakeholders' feedback is sought. Task design and scale construction for performance tests include explicit CEFR reference. This is documented in research publications (see for example Galaczi and Ffrench 2007). The objectives and the content of the examination are described in the publicly available handbooks (e.g. PET Handbook) and internal documents such as item writer guidelines. The internally and publicly available documentation specifies and operationalises exam constructs and levels and makes use of many things now incorporated into the CEFR which were familiar for many years to exam boards – the Waystage and Threshold specifications, for example.

The move towards further clarifying how Main Suite examinations define and operationalise reading, listening, speaking and writing constructs in terms of a socio-cognitive framework at each of the CEFR levels is currently being documented in a series of *Studies in Language Testing* volumes (see for example Shaw and Weir 2007 and this volume). The approach maps exam specifications onto the CEFR both in terms of cognitive and contextual parameters elicited by the given tasks. Projects such as these permit close investigation and analysis of content of examination items/tasks in different exams; they contribute to a better understanding of the criterial parameters which distinguish one proficiency level from another and thus provide valuable evidence in support of claims about CEFR alignment that may be made at the specification stage.

Standardisation

Standardisation involves 'achieving and implementing a common understanding of the meaning of the CEFR levels' (Council of Europe 2003:7). The Manual states that this involves: (a) *Training* professionals in a common interpretation of the CEFR levels using productive skills samples and receptive skills calibrated items which are already standardised to the CEFR; (b) *Benchmarking* where the agreement reached at *Training* is applied to the assessment of local performance samples; (c) *Standard-setting* where the cut-off scores for the examination CEFR level(s) are set.

These correspond closely to processes at different stages of the Cambridge ESOL test development cycle. For objectively marked skills, the stability of the measurement scale to which all exam levels relate is achieved by an item banking methodology that is employed in the development phase where new items are pretested and calibrated using anchor items to monitor exam difficulty. As we noted above, the calibrated items are then stored in the Cambridge ESOL Local Item Banking System (LIBS) where each item has a known difficulty and accordingly examination papers are constructed to a target difficulty on the CEFR A2–C2 continuum and can be graded accordingly to a high degree of precision. This is better described as *standard-maintaining* rather than *standard setting*, given that the standard is a stable one which is carried forward. The current rationale for the standard of the objective papers owes something to an essentially normative view of skill profiles in a European context (as, probably, does the CEFR), and something to the progression depicted by the common measurement scale, which can be represented as a rational 'ladder' of learning objectives.

Empirical validation

In the past shared understanding enabled the CEFR concept to function quite well without extensive underpinning from measurement theory and statistics. However, measurement theory became increasingly important as attempts were made to validate aspects of the CEFR empirically (North and Schneider 1998, North 2000a) and to link assessments more rigorously to it (North 2000a and Kaftandjieva 2004). Claims of linkage or alignment needed to be examined more carefully; simply to assert that an examination is aligned with a particular CEFR level does not necessarily make it so, even if assertion is based on intuitive or reasoned subjective judgement. To some extent, alignment can be achieved historically and conceptually as we have seen above, but empirical alignment requires more systematic analytical approaches. Appropriate evidence needs to be accumulated and scrutinised to ensure that the results produced by the examination relate to the levels of the CEFR in the way predicted.

However, empirical validation of the linking process is still in its infancy worldwide. To date there are no published studies on this. Studies have in large part focused on the specification and standardisation stages only (Tannenbaum and Wylie 2004, Alderson et al 2006, Noijons and Kuijper 2006, and Wu and Wu 2007). According to the Manual for relating examinations to the CEFR, empirical validation of linkage claims will involve the collection and analysis of data on (a) task performance and item characteristics, (b) test quality, (c) learner performance and test scores, (d) rater behaviour and (e) the adequacy of the standards set. Empirical validation takes place on two levels:

1. Internal validation

This involves the collection of traditional validation data of the kind collected by most reputable test providers in support of score interpretation (for example see Weir 2005 and Shaw and Weir 2007) and is well covered by the ongoing operational Cambridge ESOL procedures and related research programmes.

2. External validation

This involves independent corroboration of the standards set in the examination. Again two routes are recommended: i) anchor tests and ii) judgements made by teachers well trained in the CEFR (i.e. those who have already undergone familiarisation and standardisation). The Manual makes the following suggestions for external validation projects.

a) The test score route: correlating test results to tests that have already been calibrated in a valid and reliable fashion to the CEFR then using regression to relate test scores to CEFR levels.

b) The 'Can Do' route: correlating teacher ratings of students against 'Can Do' descriptors that have already been calibrated to the CEFR (e.g. the CEFR and ALTE 'Can Do' statements) then using regression to relate the students' test scores to CEFR levels.

The objective of the exercise is to generate graphics showing the nature and strength of the empirical relationship of the examination to the CEFR following a standard format and a descriptive report providing information about how the study was conducted with details of: data collection design, number of subjects, analysis methods, problems encountered and solutions adopted, results obtained and interpretation of results.

It should be feasible for Cambridge ESOL to pursue both avenues of empirical validation by inviting Cambridge ESOL candidates to take anchor tests based on material from previously calibrated English language tests and by administering CEFR based 'Can Do' questionnaires to Cambridge ESOL preparation teachers whose students are entering for the test. Both routes raise challenges, but these are not insuperable.

The Test Score route: potential research activities

Other tests of English previously mapped to the CEFR (though not as yet through empirical external procedures) include London Tests of English, Trinity College, City and Guilds, GEPT, TOEIC, TOEFL, DIALANG and Finnish national tests of English. If contextually and cognitively appropriate material which has been successfully calibrated at relevant levels can be sourced, this would serve the purpose well, although obtaining such material may prove difficult. A test based on these could be administered alongside the Cambridge ESOL tests to support the empirical validation, although this inevitably raises issues of response validity as the reference test may not be taken as seriously by the test takers as the Cambridge ESOL test or they may not be familiar with it or have prepared for it in the same way. Many test takers follow a preparation course for Cambridge tests – the exams are heavily pedagogically embedded and this may not be the case with regard to the external criterion test.

Ways to address some of these problems might include using material from the external criterion test embedded in practice Cambridge ESOL material so that test takers cannot readily notice which material is authentically part of Cambridge ESOL and which is not. However, large-scale test providers today tend to control their test formats, making them as familiar and predictable as possible for students and for reasons of accessibility and standardisation; this enterprise is underpinned by extensive test documentation plus commercial test preparation materials/courses which build up around the test. A key issue is how far can/should the external criterion test material be something 'different' or something 'similar'?

Participants at each level would need to represent both successful and unsuccessful test takers and provide sufficient numbers to support Rasch analysis – this suggests a minimum of perhaps around 250 test takers per level, although it would be preferable to use more. Achieving such a sample may be problematic, however, as Cambridge Main Suite ESOL examinations are designed to be level-based, where candidates are encouraged to enter when they are 'ready' and have a good chance of succeeding. This normally means the candidates represent a naturally truncated sample. So what may be desirable in measurement terms may conflict with sound pedagogical practice the examinations are premised on.

Jones and Saville (2008) refer to a current European Commission-sponsored project *Building a European Bank of Anchor Items for Foreign Language Skills (EBAFLS)* which can be seen to fall within this approach. The problem they note is whether tasks can be identified which function adequately as anchor items across a range of contexts.

The 'Can do' statements route: potential research activities

Jones and Saville (2008) consider that the 'Can do' approach is a promising one which was successfully employed in the construction of the CEFR descriptor scales, and in the ALTE 'Can Do' project (Jones 2002) which related exam performance to candidates' self ratings of ability.

Here the major challenge is essentially logistic: a matter of tracking test takers and their teachers and ensuring that data from the two sources can be linked and reconciled. Once a suitable data set is obtained the analysis is similar to that for test material although the added dimension of rater harshness needs to be taken into account. Again similar numbers of student participants would be needed, ideally with ratings from more than one teacher for each student participant and with overlapping groups of teachers so that the harshness of their ratings could be compared: T1 rates S1, S2 and S3; T2 rates S3, S4 and S5; T3 rates S5, S6 and S7 etc.

Lynda Taylor (personal communication 2008) feels that this approach to empirical validation:

> ... would be consistent with and supportive of the notion of the CEFR as a "framework of reference" for language teaching, learning and assessment, rather than seeing it primarily as a measurement framework with strictly defined and calibrated scales which can be reconciled to one another and to which other things can be attached in a definitive way, cf. a measurement framework with a set of scales for recording and reporting physical temperature. Do we risk treating the CEFR levels too strongly as a measurement construct rather than as a social construct?

Caveat

The purpose of any linking exercise is to provide a framework of how tests and levels relate to each other in broad terms within a common frame of reference. As Taylor (2004a) emphasises, comparative frameworks are primarily designed to function as communicative tools, summarising in an accessible and transparent manner those features which two or more tests are considered to share.

They do not, for the most part, represent strong claims about exact equivalence between exam performances since, even though two different test scores may be used in a similar way, the actual content, length, format, availability, etc. of two tests may be different in ways that are significant. Conceptually it may be possible and even desirable to be able to co-locate different tests at shared proficiency levels (e.g. B2 on the CEFR) or along common dimensions (e.g. social and tourist, study, work) but of course the different design, purpose, intended audience, methods of assessing language traits, mark schemes and formats of examinations under review make it difficult to give exact comparisons across tests and test scores. As we have noted, where tests differ in terms of the contextual or cognitive parameters operationalised, differences in performance are likely.

In this respect it is also important to distinguish the activity of comparing across skills-focused subtests or components (e.g. a writing or a reading paper) either from the same test or from different tests, and the activity of comparing at least two different whole tests. The issue is seldom discussed in the linking literature (see however Bachman et al 1995) as to whether we should be focusing on skills based proficiency links or overall language proficiency. The fundamental touchstone of any linking process is an explicit specification of the construct being measured and evidence of its successful operationalisation in the methods or scale under comparison. Credible linking is only possible if this condition is met.

The challenge of this task for linking even one skill is illustrated in the multiplicity of descriptive parameters addressed by Shaw and Weir (2007) in their volume in this series *Examining Writing*. A similar extended process involving numerous participants has been necessary to produce the explication of construct in this volume on reading. The magnitude of linking to the CEFR is also illustrated by the Dutch Construct Project (see Alderson et al 2006). The Dutch Ministry of Education funded a comprehensive project from 2003 to 2005 which in part was intended to establish a better means of specifying the reading construct (than was currently available in the CEFR) to facilitate linking between reading tests and the CEFR.

Attempts to link examinations to the CEFR in terms of overall proficiency might even be seen as 'adventurous' as such proficiency is even less well defined conjunctively than are the separate skills in the CEFR as it currently exists. It is noticeable that current attempts at linking are in the main confined to single skills, e.g. reading in the General English Proficiency Test (GEPT) in Taiwan (Wu and Wu 2007). Aligning skills against each other in the linking process would seem to be problematic and further compensatory issues come into play.

Conclusion

Taylor (2004:3) advises for a cautious approach in general in using any comparative framework. She argues that:

> . . . while they promise certain benefits they can also carry inherent risks. This is because all frameworks, by definition, seek to summarise and simplify, highlighting those features which are held in common across tests in order to provide a convenient point of reference for users and situations of use. Since the driving motivation behind them is usefulness or ease of interpretation, comparative frameworks cannot easily accommodate the multidimensional complexity of a thorough comparative analysis; the framework will focus on shared elements but may have to ignore significant differentiating features. The result is that while a framework can look elegant and convincing, it may fail to communicate some key differences between the elements co-located within it. The result is likely to be an over simplification and may even encourage misinterpretation on the part of users about the relative merits or value of different exams.

Taylor (2004:4) concludes that:

> . . . there is no doubt that comparative frameworks can serve a useful function for a wide variety of test stakeholders: for test users – such as admissions officers, employers, teachers, learners – frameworks make it easier to understand the range of assessment options available and help users to make appropriate choices for their needs; for applied linguists and language testers frameworks can help define a research agenda and identify research hypotheses for investigation; for test providers frameworks not only help with product definition and promotion, but also with planning for future test design and development. However, we need to understand that they have their limitations too: they risk masking significant differentiating features, they tend to encourage oversimplification and misinterpretation, and there is always a danger that they are adopted as prescriptive rather than informative tools. They need to come with the appropriate health warnings!

We have now looked at all the parameters examination boards need to consider in generating evidence on the validity of their reading tests. In the final chapter we attempt to summarise our findings in applying the whole of our validity framework to Cambridge Reading tests. We suggest where enhancements and modifications might be considered and implemented over time in order to improve existing Reading tests in terms of each of these validity components. We also indicate where further research into elements of the validity framework might be necessary before such enhancements and modifications can be introduced to the operational testing context. There is no doubt that the identification of such a research agenda could be of considerable value to the wider language testing community as well as to Cambridge ESOL.

8 Conclusions and recommendations

In this volume we have developed a socio-cognitive descriptive framework for validating tests of second language reading ability and applied it through a comprehensive evaluation of Cambridge ESOL's current approach to examining the skill area of reading. The framework has shown itself able to accommodate and strengthen Cambridge ESOL's existing Validity, Reliability, Impact and Practicality (VRIP) approach (see Saville 2003). The new framework seeks to establish similar evidence, but in addition it attempts to describe the constituent parts more fully and explicitly and to reconfigure validity to examine how these parts interact with each other.

We have felt it helpful to conceptualise the validation process in a temporal frame thereby identifying the various types of validity evidence that need to be collected at each stage in the test development and post implementation cycle. Within these broad validity components, criterial individual parameters for helping distinguish between adjacent proficiency levels have also been identified and summarised at the end of each chapter.

The importance of the relationship between the contextual parameters which frame a task and the cognitive processing involved in task performance has been emphasised throughout this volume. Taylor (personal communication) believes it is important in language testing that we give both the socio and the cognitive elements '. . . an appropriate place and emphasis within the whole, and do not privilege one over another. The framework reminds us of language use – and also language assessment – as both a socially situated and a cognitively processed phenomenon. The socio-cognitive framework seeks to marry up the individual psycholinguistic perspective with the individual and group sociolinguistic perspective'.

The results from developing and operationalising the framework in this volume with regard to second language reading ability are encouraging, and evidence to date suggests that where it has been applied to other Cambridge examinations/tests it has proved useful in generating validity evidence in those cases too, e.g. Main Suite Writing tests (see Shaw and Weir 2007), in the International Legal English Certificate (see Corkhill and Robinson 2006 and Thighe 2006), the Teaching Knowledge Test (see Ashton and Khalifa 2005, Harrison 2007 and Novaković 2006), Asset Languages (Ashton

2006 and Jones 2005), the SurveyLang project (see www.surveylang.org and SurveyLang 2008), and BEC and BULATS (see O'Sullivan 2006).

It would be illuminating for other examination boards offering English language tests at a variety of proficiency levels to compare their exams in terms of the validity parameters mapped out in this volume. In this way the nature of language proficiency across 'natural' levels in terms of how it is operationalised through examinations/tests might be better grounded. Similar comparisons across languages may also be worth considering but are likely to be more problematic with regard to certain parameters, for example structural progression (Hardcastle, Bolton and Pelliccia 2008).

In any evidence-based approach to validation it is essential to clearly specify each of the parameters of the validity model first and generate the data appropriate to each of these categories of description. Such data provides the evidential basis for inferential 'interpretative argument' logic. Useful contributions to the conceptualisation of the broad nature of such argument are provided by Toulmin (1958), Kane (1992), Mislevy, Steinberg and Almond (2002 and 2003), Bachman (2004) and Chapelle, Enright and Jamieson (2004 and 2008). These researchers all make a case (in slightly differing ways) for the need for clear, coherent, plausible and logical argument in support of validity claims based on evidence. Saville (2004) argues that this systematic approach to the reporting of a validity argument enables Cambridge ESOL

'to set out our **claims** relating to the usefulness of the test for its intended purpose, explain why each claim is appropriate by giving **reasons** and justifications; and provide adequate **evidence** to support the claims and the reasoning'.

At the heart of any validity argument, though, is the evidence. One potential problem with a number of these logical argument models is that the nature of the evidence to support claims and reasoning is not always clearly, explicitly, or comprehensively specified. The considerable resources, time and effort required to specify and then generate this evidence may partially explain this deficit. This volume has sought to identify the elements of validity we need to collect data on, document what evidence is available in relation to Cambridge ESOL examinations across the range of cognitive, contextual and scoring parameters we have established in our framework, and *begun* to explain their inter-relationships.

Most of the analysis we carried out on context and cognitive validity in Chapters 3 and 4 only covers a small sample of Reading papers from Cambridge ESOL Main Suite examinations and any conclusions drawn from that analysis must be seen as tentative. Additionally the analysis is based on the opinions of a group of expert judges only and findings will need to be more firmly grounded in the future by having students take the various Reading tests and complete verbal protocols on their experiences. An example of such research on IELTS is provided by Weir et al (2008) who comment also on the complexities and time consuming nature of such procedures.

In the remainder of this chapter we attempt to summarise our findings in applying our socio-cognitive validity framework to the Cambridge ESOL Reading examinations we have sampled. We summarise the data that provides the evidence to support the claims and the reasoning for the validity of Cambridge Reading examinations in terms of each element of our socio-cognitive model of validity (context, cognitive, scoring, consequential and criterion related).

Messick (1989) has pointed out, however, that validity is a question of degree, not an all or nothing concept. Validity should be seen as a *relative* concept which examination boards need to work on continually. Much of the substantial validity evidence generated by Cambridge ESOL on its Reading examinations has been brought together in this volume. Additionally, critical evaluation in Chapters 2 to 7 has helped clarify a number of areas in examining reading where further research would be beneficial. As well as drawing conclusions on this data below, we therefore indicate the areas where research will take place at Cambridge ESOL to inform judgements on future revisions to its Reading examinations.

Cognitive validity

There has been limited L2 research to date addressing the cognitive processing dimension and surprisingly little in L2 testing despite the fervour over the criticality of construct validity in the last 30 years. Given our desire to extrapolate from test tasks to real-world behaviour, it is essential to carry out research to establish with greater certainty that the test tasks we employ do indeed activate the types of mental operations that are viewed in the cognitive psychology literature as essential elements of the reading process. To the extent that this is not the case, extrapolation is threatened.

In terms of coverage, the analysis in Chapter 3 indicates that, in general across the suite, the range of careful and expeditious reading types and the various cognitive processes we established in our reading model are covered appropriately, although there are a few anomalies at CAE and CPE that merit consideration. In CPE the first task appears anomalous as the focus is restricted to the process of establishing meaning within the sentence which does not feature in any of the other examinations after PET. Koda (2005) argues that processing at the lexical level predominates among low level proficiency learners whereas the reading of higher level learners is marked by information integration and conceptual manipulation. Part 1 would appear to be somewhat out of place at this level of reading in terms of the processing demands it puts on candidates.

According to the published reading scales we reported in Chapter 1, an expectation of a candidate at the C1 level is that they 'can read quickly enough to cope with an academic course', i.e. they can cope with expeditious global as well as careful global reading demands, adapting their reading style to meet different reading purposes. It does seem odd therefore that there appear to be no tasks which overtly test expeditious global reading at CPE and only a few items at CAE. Further research needs to be carried out into the possibilities of operationalising the testing of expeditious global reading at these levels.

We note elsewhere the practical difficulties of testing expeditious reading; not least the issue of controlling the amount of time candidates spend on a task. The development of computer-based versions of reading tests would eliminate a number of these problems, e.g. time could be strictly controlled and candidates prevented from going back to an expeditious task later for a more careful read if time allowed.

The CPE Reading paper contains no task which requires processing at the whole text level across texts. However, there is a reading task currently located in the Use of English paper, where the candidate has to process and integrate information from two whole texts to form a summary of both (see Use of English paper Part 5 item 5 in CPE Handbook and Weir and Milanovic 2003:251–260; an example is also provided at the end of Appendix A). Moving this task to the Reading paper and moving the selective deletion gap-filling task (current Part 1) into the Use of English paper seems sensible and could be considered in a future revision. Comprehension and integration of main ideas across texts in the CPE Reading paper would establish a clear distinction between CPE and CAE in this skill.

The practical difficulty of including such a constructed response item type into the existing selected response paper obviously complicates matters. However, with the advent of electronic script management (ESM), sending such a task to be marked separately by human markers may become a viable option (see Shaw and Weir 2007 for details of ESM developments within Cambridge Assessment).

Overall in grading the specifications for the five levels of the suite, careful thought has been given to the relative cognitive difficulty both of the tasks and of the texts employed. Text demands are increased only gradually; and the more demanding types of careful global reading, for example reading to comprehend the whole text and integrate information across texts, are reserved for higher levels of the suite.

In general our analysis, according to the panel of judges involved, indicates that the Cambridge ESOL Main Suite examinations correspond closely to what we know of the cognitive processes involved in reading in real life. Further studies involving student retrospection through verbal protocols on their test-taking experiences are needed to confirm these findings (see Weir et al 2008 for an example of a study of the cognitive processing involved in taking the IELTS Reading test). For example, it would be interesting to establish whether students actually read the whole text in selected response careful reading tasks. Evidence that they do would support claims that these tasks encourage cognitive processing similar to real-life reading. It would also be useful to establish if students use the whole text to restore paragraphs into the gapped texts at CAE and CPE and if this differs from the sentence insertion task at FCE. Such research is necessary to provide further support for the relationship between the examination and real-life reading.

The cognitive requirements have been adequately graded in relation to the different levels of the suite. Due consideration has been given both to task demands and to the types of processing that can be deemed to be representative of performance at different stages of proficiency.

Context validity

As we saw in Chapter 4, reading tasks in the Cambridge ESOL examinations are specified in a number of different ways for the purposes of test writing and construction; nevertheless, it is acknowledged that there can be improvements with more comprehensive task specification, particularly in terms of discourse type, timing, and functional, lexical and structural resources.

Response format

Certain task types are introduced at certain levels in Main Suite examinations. For example, Right/Wrong/Doesn't say occurs in KET and True/False in PET, gapped text at the sentence insertion level at FCE, and gapped text at the paragraph level in CAE and CPE. Though not in the Reading paper, there is a task in the Use of English paper at CPE which requires candidates to integrate information across texts. The decision on which task type occurs at which level is based on the interplay between appropriate processing demands, textual parameters, and intended audience.

Critics may query the predominant use of selected as against constructed response format in the Cambridge Main Suite examinations. However, it should be noted that Cambridge ESOL uses variants of selected response formats at all levels in this suite, and these variants in themselves encourage a different approach to completing the different reading tasks. For example, as we saw in Chapter 3, completing a matching gapped-text task (CAE/CPE) involves different levels of processing to answering a set of multiple-choice questions that may only require processing information at the sentence or between sentence levels.

As an examination board, Cambridge ESOL also uses constructed response types, e.g. in BULATS and IELTS. Where such a response type is used, a rigorous marking system has to be in place: a standardised marking scheme is used together with a rater-training manual, an online help desk to answer rater queries is available and close monitoring takes place throughout the process (see Chapter 5 and Appendix E).

Cambridge ESOL's view is that the main advantage of using selected response formats is that they allow a broader range of test focuses than constructed response formats. Furthermore, for examination boards like Cambridge ESOL who are engaged in large scale assessments worldwide, the scoring validity, the practicality of objectively scored formats and the quick turn around of test results are strong arguments in their favour. An argument can also be made that getting candidates to construct their own responses risks muddying the measurement by involving the skill of writing.

Weighting

In cases where two marks are awarded for a correct response to a question/ item, this is due to the linguistic and cognitive demands of text and task. During the review of FCE and CAE, Rose (2006) investigated the amount of time needed for candidates to complete a careful global reading multiple-choice item and an expeditious local multiple-matching item. She found that each careful global reading MCQ item needed more time to answer than each expeditious local reading multiple-matching item, supporting the decision, based on expert views of the processing demands involved, that it was worth more marks.

Knowledge of criteria

This parameter is perhaps less relevant to the Reading papers of Main Suite examinations as the response type adopted to date is a selected one. All answers are mechanically scanned and machine scored.

In other Cambridge ESOL Reading papers such as BEC and IELTS where the response type is a constructed one and in the Use of English papers in FCE, CAE and CPE, trained markers mark candidates' answers (see Chapter 5 on scoring validity). The handbooks inform candidates that, for example, when filling a gap with a word, or a short phrase, spelling should be correct and that answers should be in capital letters to ensure that the word is recognisable and unequivocally the one required. If Intelligent Character Recognition (ICR) methodology is adopted, paving the way for extended use of constructed response formats, such accuracy will be particularly important. Research is necessary to demonstrate that the measurement of the construct of reading is not compromised by the necessity for mechanical accuracy in written responses.

Ordering of items

Questions for careful reading are normally ordered according to the infor-mation in the text although questions addressing overall understanding of gist may occur in initial position and those testing development of an idea/ attitude or summary in the text in final position. In expeditious reading tasks items are not usually in order.

PET Part 3 is the exception which warrants research to examine whether putting the questions out of order (i.e. not following the order of the information in the text) would unacceptably affect the difficulty level of items or bring the cognitive processing of candidates successfully completing the task more in line with such reading in real life.

Text length

In general, the length of the text increases as the examination level increases. This is true for the following adjacent levels: KET/PET, PET/FCE, and FCE/CAE. There is no marked distinction between CAE/CPE in terms of text length, however, CPE has a greater number of different texts normally with a wider coverage of genres.

Time

The amount of time allocated to each level increases as the exam level increases. The allocation of time to any one paper is based on the task and text demands of that paper and includes transfer of answers to the answer sheet.

Cambridge ESOL specifies the total amount of time required for the Reading paper at the planning stage of test development. This specification is then monitored at the pretesting stage (through feedback forms taking account of candidature level) and confirmed prior to the first live administration stage of the test development cycle. Whenever a new task is introduced to a test paper, feedback is gathered on task suitability and on time allotment. This is done via pretesting feedback forms or observation sheets given to test centres where the task is being pretested (see Hawkey 2009 for details).

On the exam paper, time is specified for the whole paper rather than the parts. Ideally, time constraints should be put on tasks to ensure as far as possible that candidates are using the intended reading strategies whether it is careful or expeditious reading. Practically speaking (except in computer-based testing (CBT) mode), an examination board cannot easily force candidates to spend more or less time on a certain task.

What Cambridge ESOL does is provide candidates with guidelines on how they should approach a task and what reading type may be best suited to that task; such guidance is provided through examination reports or information in the handbooks and the websites for teachers and students. Cambridge ESOL practice is to present items in a way that suggests what is intended, e.g. by putting questions intended to test expeditious reading before the text, but this does not control whether students skim, search read, scan or read intensively in practice. The disadvantage of this non-interventionist approach is that items that are intended to test expeditious abilities, such as search reading, may for some candidates become careful reading activities and vice versa if time is running out for the candidate. With the onset of CBT this situation might be reviewed as it is a fairly simple procedure to control the time available for a task in a computerised mode. It would then be interesting to explore how actual cognitive processing in reading is affected by CB delivery and establish the impact of changes in response conditions such as controlling the time available to candidates for task completion.

Text purpose

In looking at text purpose in Main Suite examinations, it becomes apparent that at KET and PET levels, texts are aimed primarily at informing and are limited to the referential in terms of purpose with some emotive texts appearing at PET (see Part 4 in PET). At FCE level, texts with poetic purposes begin to be used; fictional sources begin to have some importance and their primary intentions could be said to be to convey feelings and to entertain. At CAE and CPE levels emotive and poetic language takes on a greater significance. Texts with overall conative purpose also start to be used at these levels. This coincides with the task purposes at CAE and CPE levels as well as the sources and topics used. For example, in CAE, a journal article on social trends where the author is presenting an argument for or against a particular trend may be suitable to assess candidates' understanding of attitude/opinion, text organisation, main idea, or implications.

Writer–reader relationships

The audience for texts in examinations is disparate and it is difficult to make assumptions about what they might or might not know already. However, target age-ranges are known for each examination level from the previous candidate information sheets. At the pre-editing stage, it is decided whether a text is suitable for the age-range of the examination and the global market, and whether it is in accord with the item writer guidelines. The text will be fine tuned at the editing stage and throughout the question paper production stage (see Appendix D for details of this rigorous process).

In Cambridge ESOL practice, Main Suite examination texts are aimed at the general reader. No particular level of education or world knowledge is assumed at lower levels. At higher levels (CAE and CPE) texts assume a certain level of education and understanding of the world as well as of the English language. In general candidates are getting younger, so topics need to be more accessible and interesting to a lower age group too.

The intended effect of writer–reader relationships on performance is a seriously under-researched area (O'Sullivan and Porter 1995) and the way in which this parameter might help to further ground distinctions between FCE, CAE and CPE is worth investigating further.

Discourse mode

Authentic texts from a variety of sources are used throughout the Cambridge examinations. The extent of text adaptation in the examinations decreases as the level of the examination increases. In general, as the exam level increases, more genres are used as well as a greater variety of rhetorical tasks.

The crucial factor in selecting a reading text is whether the text would allow the intended reading activities to be measured. For example, has the text got enough main ideas where extraction of these is the focus of the test or does it have pieces of information that can be linked together where inferencing is the focus of the item? Cambridge ESOL varies the criteria for selecting texts according to the test's intended audience and the test purpose (e.g. Academic English, Business English or General English, i.e. Main Suite examinations). Guidelines to item writers include advice on selecting texts that are coherent, are clearly sequenced or have a clear line of argument running through them.

The effect of discourse mode on performance is another very under-researched area and the way in which this parameter might contribute to further grounding of distinctions between levels in FCE, CAE and CPE needs investigating.

Functional resources

There is a clear functional progression across the first three levels (KET, PET and FCE) in terms of complexity but also in the degree of precision in the grammatical exponents employed to fulfil the function(s). Functions associated with conative purposes and argumentative tasks for language appear at CAE. The functions at CAE and CPE are increasingly diverse and demanding and intended to produce more complex structures or collocations.

Systematic work has been conducted on this key parameter for nearly 40 years by the Council of Europe (Council of Europe 2001) and empirical studies of functional progression have been carried out by North and his associates (North 2000, 2002 and 2004). Coursebook writers (in a more subjective fashion) have similarly operationalised what might be a suitable progression in terms of functions across the range of language ability. As a result we can perhaps be more confident that examinations are better grounded in terms of this parameter than most others. The functional parameter is obviously not a stand-alone element as the structural exponents and the lexis chosen to achieve it will also vary from level to level in those cases where the same functions are being deployed. Research however has indicated a number of functions which seem to occur uniquely for the first time at a particular level. Cambridge ESOL is keen to pursue this research to better ground whether any of these functions is truly implicational, i.e. candidates at the next level down are not capable of realising them adequately even by using less complex structures and lexis.

Recent work by Green (2007a) for English Profile (www.englishprofile. org), a long-term, collaborative programme of interdisciplinary research designed to enhance the learning, teaching and assessment of English, has begun to examine functional progression at the largely neglected upper levels of the CEFR C1–C2. His research suggests that, taken together, the pattern of function words emerging at the C level is suggestive of a shift in focus and points to *rational enquiry* and *exposition, argument* and *suasion* as being of particular relevance to the C level. A similar conclusion was reached by Shaw and Weir (2007) in their retrospective analysis of writing examinations at these levels. More research is needed to help unpack more clearly criterial differences between these higher levels.

Lexis

Invariably as candidates progress up the levels of the Main Suite examinations, the lexical demands that are put upon them are stronger. This shows itself primarily through the number and complexity of the items that they are required to understand. The amount of less frequent, less well known vocabulary increases. Lexis at lower levels is restricted to everyday, literal and factual language. As students advance, they are gradually expected to deal with increasingly subtle uses of the language of feelings and ideas. The senses associated with the words are less concrete and issues of polysemy may arise. More abstract texts will not be presented to candidates until level C1 (CAE) and used to a higher degree in C2 (CPE).

Fiction usually requires a broader receptive vocabulary and this is introduced from FCE onwards. This parallels the opportunity to work on a set text in order to be able to answer an optional task in FCE, CAE and CPE Paper 2 (Writing). Additionally, at higher levels candidates' ability is ascertained by requiring them to handle a much larger number of texts in the exam than at lower levels, covering a wider range of genres as the level moves up.

The research on lexis in Cambridge examinations reported in this volume is illustrative of the value of, the complexities involved in and the effort required for the better grounding of our knowledge of progression in terms of each of our parameters.

Grammatical resources

An analysis of the papers across the five levels shows a clear progression in terms of sentence structure from short, simple sentences to long, complex sentences. This is in line with the structural levels appearing in ELT coursebooks aimed at language levels corresponding to the Council of Europe levels A2 (KET) through to C2 (CPE).

This progression is mirrored in the length of the texts used as very short texts are used at KET level and increasingly longer ones are employed at higher levels. This structural progression does not mean that some short sentences may not pose considerable difficulty and so still have a place in higher level texts. Ellipsis and colloquial use of language may make for short sentences that are hard to process and so only appropriate at more advanced levels.

At KET level, candidates are expected to have control over only the simplest exponents for the Waystage functions at this level. At PET level, candidates show a degree of ability to handle some of the exponents listed at Threshold level. At FCE level, candidates should have a good grasp of Vantage level language. They should have mastered the main structures of the language. CAE candidates must also show that they have a grasp of structures which allow them to understand opinions and feelings written in an appropriate register. By CPE level candidates should have a mastery of the structures needed to understand ideas and attitude expressed in a well-organised and sophisticated manner.

An increasing complexity of verb phrase forms is also noticeable in texts as we move up the Cambridge ESOL levels. The use of modals, conditionals, inversion and other structures becomes more common as the texts used in the examinations become more concerned with conveying feelings and opinions, persuading and hypothesising rather than dealing simply with information as they do at lower levels. As well as sentence length and verb phrase form, referencing is an aspect of structure that becomes noticeably complex in higher level texts where the successful reader needs to appreciate the use of synonymy as well as sophisticated inferencing skills.

Content

At KET level, candidates need to have the language to deal with personal and daily life, i.e. basic everyday situations and communication needs (Van Ek and Trim 1998a). The focus tends to be on topics that are likely to have relevance for teenage candidates since this has traditionally been the predominant age-span of the population to study for and take the KET exam following its introduction in the early 1990s. At PET level, a broader range of general topics relating to the candidate's personal life and experience is covered;

narrative topics also feature at PET level (Van Ek and Trim 1998). FCE candidates may be expected to deal with a wide range of knowledge areas including any non-specialist topic that has relevance for candidates worldwide (Van Ek and Trim 2001). CAE candidates are expected to be able to deal with topics that are more specialised and less personal than those that tend to feature at lower levels. The step up to CAE also involves coping with lexically challenging topic areas (e.g. the environment, the scientific world, traditions). At CPE level more abstract and academic topics appear and the candidate may be expected to be able to read any non-specialist topic. CPE candidates are expected to be able to operate confidently in a wide variety of social, work-related and study-related situations. At all levels topics that might offend or otherwise unfairly disadvantage any group of candidates are avoided.

Empirical research on the effect of knowledge of subject matter contained in the text on performance across levels is noticeably lacking and almost no guidance is available from research on what content is appropriate as one progresses through proficiency levels. Exam board experience is not to be discounted but Cambridge ESOL will be adding to this with more empirically grounded evidence.

Setting: administration

Cambridge ESOL takes considerable care to ensure appropriate physical conditions for taking its exams, to maintain uniform administration across centres and to achieve complete security of tests. The procedures which are currently in place and which are discussed at length in Appendix C will continue to be monitored, evaluated and enhanced to ensure that they do not pose a threat to test reliability and that they safeguard valid measurement of the construct in Reading tests.

Scoring validity

In Chapter 5 we described how the WINSTEPS analysis program (Linacre 2006), supplemented by in-house programs for formatting data and handling output, is used to produce a measurement scale for item-based tests which underpins the Cambridge ESOL Local Item Banking System (LIBS). When Reading Comprehension papers are constructed, every effort is made to ensure that in addition to appropriate cognitive and contextual parameters, the mean difficulty of the paper is as close as possible to the target difficulty set for that paper. For example, a target difficulty of 62 scaled Rasch has been set for the construction of an FCE live Reading Comprehension paper. This helps in achieving equivalent versions of the test over time.

Even though they will be affected by both format and a truncated population, Cambridge ESOL has attempted to apply variance-based estimates to its different papers. The Research & Validation Group routinely calculates Cronbach Alpha when item analysis is carried out at the pretesting stage and after live use. In recent years Cambridge ESOL has set target levels for the internal consistency reliability for the item-based components of the Main Suite examinations – Paper 1 (Reading), Paper 4 (Listening) and, where applicable, Paper 3 (Use of English). Estimates which are obtained operationally in live test administrations typically fall between an acceptable minimum value and the intended target value (which is also sometimes exceeded).

In Main Suite examinations, the expected range of alphas for a Reading paper with 40 items ranges from 0.80 to 0.85. The alphas do vary according to the length of the test paper in terms of number of items. Better reliability scores are obtained if the test has more items. In Chapter 5, we reported 0.84 as an average reliability figure for the FCE Reading paper administered in 2005, 2006 and 2007 thus mirroring Geranpayeh's (2004) findings. This figure is seen as respectable for a test of 35 items, all of which are based on communicative tasks (Weir and Milanovic 2003:107–108). Other examinations exhibit similar levels of reliability. For example, we reported earlier an 0.86 average alpha figure for the IELTS Academic Reading paper (40 items) across different versions in 2007. O'Sullivan (2006:99–100) reports similar levels of reliability for Reading papers at the three levels of the BEC examinations.

Cambridge ESOL is exploring approaches to estimating and reporting on the reliability of the examinations and their components which are appropriate to a level-based system of examinations. Approaches include the application of Generalisability theory (see for example Bachman, Davidson and Milanovic (1996) for the application of G-theory to an FCE Paper 1 data set). Emphasis is placed on identifying and controlling the sources of error in the individual components (papers), and on maximising the dependability of the overall result of the examination in terms of pass/fail and the grade awarded.

The Reading component of the Cambridge Main Suite examinations is an *objectively marked* paper and a reliability of about 0.99 is achieved by the system. However, in other Cambridge ESOL examinations such as BEC or BULATS, where constructed responses are required, the marking of the Reading papers involves the use of certified general markers, i.e. human raters. Throughout the marking period the general marking teams are closely monitored (see Appendix E for details).

Where general marking is involved, there is likely to be a lowering of test reliability. Thighe's (2002) research into IELTS general marking led to the development of the IELTS general marking standardisation manual. Blackhurst and Cope (2007) later investigated the effectiveness of the manual through examining the accuracy and consistency of general markers. They found that there had been a noticeable improvement in the marking accuracy of the Reading paper. The results of the study led them to conclude that the introduction of the manual contributed to an increase in marker reliability. The accuracy of general markers continues to be monitored and similar studies will take place in future.

Routine analysis is carried out on all papers and reports are produced which are used in the Grading and Awards process as well as to feed into the ongoing refinement of test production procedures. The aim is to ensure that the awarding of grades for the examination at each level is as fair as possible and that the examinations continue to be improved over time.

The review of this statistical data enables the subject officers to confirm whether the examination materials 'performed' as predicted by the pretesting and standards fixing activities which were carried out during the question paper production cycle.

The performance of large groups of candidates is compared with cohorts from previous years, and performance is also compared by country, by first language, by age and a number of other factors, to ensure that the standards being applied are consistently fair to all candidates, and that a particular grade 'means' the same thing from year to year and throughout the world. Any requests for special consideration are reviewed at this stage, together with any reports from centres about specific problems that may have arisen during the examination.

After the grading meeting, results in terms of grades are generated. At this stage a procedure known as Awards is carried out to ensure the fairness of the final results before they are issued to candidates. As part of this procedure an Awards Committee looks particularly closely at the performance of candidates who are close to the grade boundaries – particularly the pass/fail boundary.

Post-examination analysis reveals that acceptable levels of reliability are being met and provides the input to ongoing attempts to enhance this aspect of the examinations.

Consequential validity

As detailed in Chapter 6, the need to monitor a test's effects on language materials and on classroom activity (see, for example, Hawkey 2004, Green 2007) and to seek information on the views of a full range of stakeholders (see Taylor 2000) is now accepted by most serious examination boards and it has been the hallmark of Cambridge examinations at least since the modern revisions commenced in the 1980s, and in the case of stakeholder consultation since much earlier according to Weir (2003, and see also Hawkey 2009). In the recent CPE revision and FCE/CAE modifications, conscious efforts were made to elicit feedback on the existing test from test takers and a wide variety of stakeholders contributed to the decisions that were taken concerning changes in the examination (see Weir and Milanovic 2003 for a full account of the CPE revision, Hawkey 2004 for a description of the CELS examination change process and Hawkey 2009 for that in FCE and CAE).

Establishing *a priori* evidence for context and cognitive validity is essential before candidates sit an examination to ensure that no potential sources of bias are allowed to interfere with measurement. Following the test, it is important in post-examination procedures to check that no bias has occurred. As we describe in Chapter 6, this is done statistically in relation to candidate bio data (see Geranpayeh and Kunnan 2007 for an example of Cambridge practice in this area).

It would be useful to see evidence of a lack of bias in all examinations being researched and reported in the public domain.

Criterion-related validity

Evidence of criterion-related validity is routinely generated by Cambridge ESOL. The studies discussed in Chapter 7 show strong links between Cambridge ESOL suites of level-based tests, i.e. Main Suite, BEC, and YLE. These suites are targeted at similar ability levels as defined by a common measurement scale.

Chapter 7 detailed how Cambridge ESOL has linked its examinations closely to the levels laid out in external internationally accepted frameworks such as the CEFR and the ALTE Framework. It is this level system which provides an interpretative frame of reference for all the exams in the suite. These European levels (though currently underspecified for testing purposes, see Weir 2005a) have the advantage of according with the 'natural' proficiency levels familiar to teachers and are supported by the work of the Council of Europe over the last 30 years; this important work is based on a consensus view that adequate coverage is afforded by six broad levels for the purposes of organising language learning, teaching and assessment in the European context (Council of Europe 2001:22–3).

The scale of levels which is used by Cambridge ESOL provides a set of common standards and is the basis of the *criterion-referenced approach* to the interpretation of examination results (see Chapter 1 on the linking of Cambridge Main Suite examinations to the CEFR scale for reading as well as Chapter 7 for more details of this).

Referencing to the criterion is undertaken by means of scalar analyses using the Rasch model to relate the results from the whole range of Cambridge examinations to the global scale of common reference levels of the CEFR (2001:24). In addition, the ALTE 'Can Do' scales provide criterion-related statements at each level in relation to the specified domains which are covered in the examinations (i.e. situated language use for social, tourist, work and study purposes). The criterion scale and the 'Can Do' descriptors provide representations of the external reality, which helps to ensure that the test results are as meaningful and as useful as possible to the key stakeholders (the candidates, their sponsors and other users of examination results). Work to date in this area will be supplemented by the ongoing English Profile programme.

Endnote

The issues of what a language construct is and whether it is possible to identify and measure developmental stages leading towards its mastery are critical for all aspects of language learning, teaching and assessment. Exam boards and other institutions offering high-stakes tests need to demonstrate evidence of the context, cognitive and scoring validity of the test tasks they create to represent the underlying real-life construct. They also need to be explicit as to how they operationalise criterial distinctions between levels in their tests in terms of the various validity parameters discussed above.

Following *Examining Writing* (Shaw and Weir 2007), *Examining Reading* marks the second comprehensive attempt to expose the totality of Cambridge ESOL academic practice in a particular domain to scrutiny in the public arena. As we have demonstrated, much has already been achieved by Cambridge and other researchers towards a better understanding of the nature of second language reading proficiency and how it can be assessed; perhaps not surprisingly, this volume also shows that there are questions still to be answered and a great deal of work still to be done. Future research needs to investigate whether further work on refining the parameters identified in this volume, either singly or in configuration, can help better ground the distinctions in proficiency in reading represented by levels in Cambridge ESOL examinations and its external referent the CEFR, as well as in the level-based tests produced by other language examination boards.

Appendix A

Sample Reading tasks at five levels and answer keys

KET Reading (December 2005)

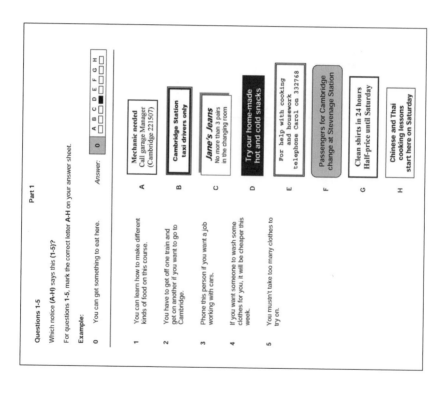

Part 1

Questions 1-5

Which notice (A-H) says this (1-5)?

For questions 1-5, mark the correct letter A-H on your answer sheet.

Example:

0   You can get something to eat here.

Answer:

0	A	B	C	D	E	F	G	H

1   You can learn how to make different kinds of food on this course.

2   You have to get off one train and get on another if you want to go to Cambridge.

3   Phone this person if you want a job working with cars.

4   If you want someone to wash some clothes for you, it will be cheaper this week.

5   You mustn't take too many clothes to try on.

A   **Mechanic needed**
Call garage Manager
(Cambridge 221507)

B   **Cambridge Station**
taxi drivers only

C   *Jane's Jeans*
No more than 3 pairs
in the changing room

D   **Try our home-made**
hot and cold snacks

E   For help with cooking
and housework
telephone Carol on 332768

F   Passengers for Cambridge
change at Stevenage Station

G   **Clean shirts in 24 hours**
Half-price until Saturday

H   **Chinese and Thai**
cooking lessons
start here on Saturday

Appendix A

Part 2

Questions 6-10

Read the sentences about a university student.
Choose the best word (A, B or C) for each space.

For questions 6-10, mark A, B or C on your answer sheet.

Example:

0   Sarah Packer .... to university for the first time on Monday.

A arrived   B went   C was

Answer: 0 [A ☐] [B ■] [C ☐]

6   Sarah is doing a four-year .... in Business Studies.

A class   B lesson   C course

7   The university secretary was there to .... all the new students.

A invite   B speak   C welcome

8   On the first day, Sarah .... some of her new teachers.

A met   B knew   C remembered

9   Today, Sarah is .... reading her business books.

A correct   B useful   C busy

10   Next month, Sarah is hoping to .... the university swimming club.

A play   B join   C become

Part 3

Questions 11-15

Complete the five conversations.
For questions 11-15, mark A, B or C on your answer sheet.

Example:

0   [Where do you come from?]

A New York
B School
C Home

Answer: 0 [A ■] [B ☐] [C ☐]

11   Please answer the phone.

A How are you?
B Why can't you?
C When did he call?

12   Would you prefer lemonade or orange juice?

A Have you got anything else?
B If you like.
C Are you sure about that?

13   The 9.15 train's late again.

A It was never there.
B It often is.
C Will it ever be?

14   Can you help me with my homework?

A I don't understand it.
B It's not ready.
C I can't help it.

15   I thought the play was very boring.

A Yes, I'd like to.
B Which did you think?
C I enjoyed it.

Questions 16-20

Complete the conversation about renting a room.
What does Jack say to Mrs Brown?

For questions **16-20**, mark the correct letter **A-H** on your answer sheet.

Example:

| Mrs Brown: | Good morning. Are you Jack Gomez? |
| Jack: | 0 .... |

Answer:

0	A B C D E F G H
	□□□□□□□■

Mrs Brown:	Come this way. Here it is.
Jack:	16 ....
Mrs Brown:	And it's very warm. The rent is £400 a month.
Jack:	17 ....
Mrs Brown:	There's nothing more to pay. Are you a student?
Jack:	18 ....
Mrs Brown:	It's very quiet here during the day. And the station's not far away.
Jack:	19 ....
Mrs Brown:	Only in the road. I haven't got a garage.
Jack:	20 ....
Mrs Brown:	All right. But before tomorrow.

A   What does the heating cost?

B   I can't decide about the room. Can I phone you later?

C   Can I use the kitchen and bathroom?

D   How near is the bus stop?

E   I like the big window – it's nice and sunny.

F   But is there anywhere to park my car?

G   Yes, I've come about the room.

H   A nurse, so I often have to work at night.

Part 4

Questions 21-27

Read the article about a young girl who plays the violin.
Are sentences **21-27** 'Right' **(A)** or 'Wrong' **(B)**?
If there is not enough information to answer 'Right' **(A)** or 'Wrong' **(B)**, choose 'Doesn't say' **(C)**.

For questions **21-27**, mark **A**, **B** or **C** on your answer sheet.

Chloë Hanslip

Chloë was born in England. Her father works with computers and her mother teaches dance. Chloë began playing the violin when she was two. Her parents bought her a special violin which was small enough for her to use, and, even at this age, she could play without help. Her sister Virginia, who was nineteen at the time, played the piano and after Chloë heard her play something, she tried to play it on her violin. From the age of four, she played at a number of concerts in Britain and America and in 1999 she was a child violinist in the Hollywood film *Onegin*.

Many teachers offered to give Chloë lessons but when she was seven she met Professor Zakhar Bron. She was certain from the beginning that he was the right teacher for her. His work takes him around the world and each year Chloë flies thousands of kilometres to get to his classes.

Chloë was only fourteen when she made her first CD, but she says she is just like any other teenager. 'I have lots of friends and I love pop music. Getting better on the violin is important, but I also make sure I have time for other things.'

235

Example:

0   Chloé's mother gives dance classes.

    A Right   B Wrong   C Doesn't say

Answer:

0	A	B	C
	■	☐	☐

21   Chloé's first violin was the same size as other violins.

    A Right   B Wrong   C Doesn't say

22   To start with, Chloé practised the same music as her sister.

    A Right   B Wrong   C Doesn't say

23   Chloé prefers playing concerts in America to playing in Britain.

    A Right   B Wrong   C Doesn't say

24   When Chloé first met Zakhar Bron, she knew she wanted to study with him.

    A Right   B Wrong   C Doesn't say

25   Chloé travels to other countries for her lessons with Zakhar Bron.

    A Right   B Wrong   C Doesn't say

26   Chloé thinks she has a different life from other people her age.

    A Right   B Wrong   C Doesn't say

27   Chloé plays pop music on the violin for her friends.

    A Right   B Wrong   C Doesn't say

Part 5

Questions 28-35

Read the article about badgers.
Choose the best word (A, B or C) for each space.

For questions **28-35**, mark **A, B** or **C** on your answer sheet.

Badgers

Not many people have **(0)** .... seen a badger. **(28)** .... black and white animals can sometimes **(29)** .... the size of a large dog. They live in underground holes in woods and forests in Europe and many of their homes have been there **(30)** .... centuries. Scientists have even found bones of badgers **(31)** .... 250,000 years ago. The old English word for a badger was 'brock' and a few English villages, for example Brockenhurst and Brockley, have **(32)** .... that name.

(33) .... are lots of children's books about badgers. In **(34)** .... stories badgers are very old and clever, but in others they're not very nice at all. Certainly, badgers are not very friendly and only **(35)** .... out at night. They live on insects and small animals, but also eat young plants and eggs.

KET Reading (December 2005) Answer Key

Part 1		Part 2		Part 3		Part 3		Part 4		Part 5	
1	H	6	C	11	B	16	E	21	B	28	C
2	F	7	C	12	A	17	A	22	A	29	B
3	A	8	A	13	B	18	H	23	C	30	A
4	G	9	C	14	A	19	F	24	A	31	B
5	C	10	B	15	C	20	B	25	A	32	C
								26	B	33	B
								27	C	34	A
										35	B

Example:

| 0 | A | ever | B | still | C | soon | Answer: | 0 | A ■ B ☐ C ☐ |

28	A	That	B	This	C	These
29	A	being	B	be	C	been
30	A	for	B	since	C	during
31	A	after	B	from	C	at
32	A	keeping	B	keep	C	kept
33	A	Here	B	There	C	They
34	A	some	B	any	C	every
35	A	came	B	come	C	comes

237

Appendix A

PET Reading (December 2005)

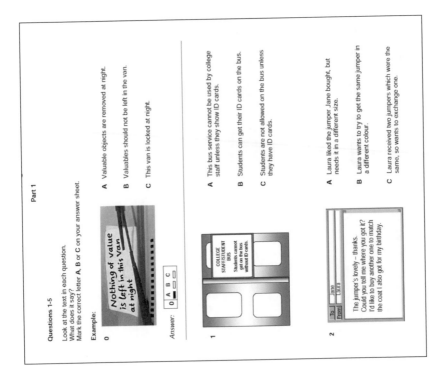

Part 1

Questions 1-5

Look at the text in each question.
What does it say?
Mark the correct letter **A**, **B** or **C** on your answer sheet.

Example:

0

Nothing of value is left in this van at night

A Valuable objects are removed at night.

B Valuables should not be left in the van.

C This van is locked at night.

Answer: 0 | A ▆ | B ☐ | C ☐

1

COLLEGE
STAFF/STUDENT
BUS
Students cannot
get on the bus
without ID cards.

A This bus service cannot be used by college
staff unless they show ID cards.

B Students can get their ID cards on the bus.

C Students are not allowed on the bus unless
they have ID cards.

2

To | Jane
From | Laura

The jumper's lovely – thanks.
Could you tell me where you got it?
I'd like to buy another one to match
the coat I also got for my birthday.

A Laura liked the jumper Jane bought, but
needs it in a different size.

B Laura wants to try to get the same jumper in
a different colour.

C Laura received two jumpers which were the
same, so wants to exchange one.

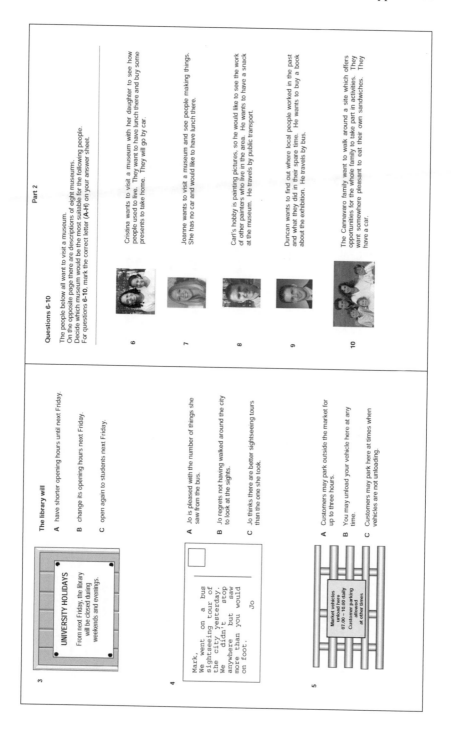

Part 2

Questions 6-10

The people below all want to visit a museum.
On the opposite page there are descriptions of eight museums.
Decide which museum would be the most suitable for the following people.
For questions 6-10, mark the correct letter (A-H) on your answer sheet.

6 Cristina wants to visit a museum with her daughter to see how people used to live. They want to have lunch there and buy some presents to take home. They will go by car.

7 Joanne wants to visit a museum and see people making things. She has no car and would like to have lunch there.

8 Carl's hobby is painting pictures, so he would like to see the work of other painters who live in the area. He wants to have a snack at the museum. He travels by public transport.

9 Duncan wants to find out where local people worked in the past and what they did in their spare time. He wants to buy a book about the exhibition. He travels by bus.

10 The Carnavaro family want to walk around a site which offers opportunities for the whole family to take part in activities. They want somewhere pleasant to eat their own sandwiches. They have a car.

3

UNIVERSITY HOLIDAYS

From next Friday, the library will be closed during weekends and evenings.

The library will

A have shorter opening hours until next Friday.

B change its opening hours next Friday.

C open again to students next Friday.

4

Mark,
We went on a bus sightseeing tour of the city yesterday. We didn't stop anywhere but saw more than you would on foot.
Jo

A Jo is pleased with the number of things she saw from the bus.

B Jo regrets not having walked around the city to look at the sights.

C Jo thinks there are better sightseeing tours than the one she took.

5

Market vehicles unload here
07.00 - 10.00 daily
Customer parking allowed at other times

A Customers may park outside the market for up to three hours.

B You may unload your vehicle here at any time.

C Customers may park here at times when vehicles are not unloading.

MUSEUMS IN THE AREA

A **Stackworth Museum** tells the history of the famous Stackworth family, and gives information about other well-known local people. These include poets, artists and writers. There is an excellent café and a car park.

B **Charberth Museum** is near the main bus station and has a rich collection of objects, 19th-century paintings and photographs showing life in the town over the centuries – the jobs people did and how they entertained themselves. An accompanying book showing the works on display is available from the Museum Shop as well as some attractive gifts. There is no café.

C **Fairley Museum** is arranged like an old-fashioned village. You can see people working at their trades to produce tools, pots and even boats using traditional skills. There is a small picnic area in the car park but most people eat in the excellent café. The museum is on a bus route.

D **Westerleigh Museum** is near the bus station, and contains exhibitions showing the town's development. In a separate room there are works by some well-known artists as well as changing exhibitions of work by local artists. Sandwiches, cakes and hot drinks are on sale in the café.

E The rooms in **Scotwood Manor** are furnished as they were 100 years ago. The staff spend the day as people did then and are happy to explain what it was like. There are activity sheets for children and a shop with books, souvenirs and cards, as well as a good café and car park.

F Freshwater was once an important fishing port. **Freshwater Museum**, inside the old harbour office, shows how the town developed and later became a tourist centre. There is an activity room for young children with DVDs, a large picnic area, car park, and good bus service.

G Set in beautiful countryside, the **Woodlands Museum** is arranged like a village of 100 years ago. To learn more about this period, visitors are encouraged to spend time doing practical things such as making pots and cooking. There is an adventure playground with a picnic area under the trees and parking.

H **Middleworth Museum** is full of objects from the past, which tell the story of different people who worked in the area, from factory workers to the men who built the canal and the railway. There is a Family Folder of things to do. The museum has a café and is near the bus and railway station.

Part 3

Questions 11-20

Look at the sentences below about The Short Story Society.
Read the text on the opposite page to decide if each sentence is correct or incorrect.
If it is correct, mark **A** on your answer sheet.
If it is not correct, mark **B** on your answer sheet.

11 The Short Story Society has existed for over a century.

12 *Short Story Review* publishes work by inexperienced writers.

13 Articles from one of the Society's magazines are available on the internet.

14 Writers entering the National Short Story Competition must choose a subject suggested by the Society.

15 It costs £5 for members of the society to enter the National Short Story Competition.

16 Each year, ten winning writers will be offered contracts to publish their own books.

17 The Short Story Society visits schools to give pupils help with writing.

18 Society members can attend regular events at the Writers' Café.

19 The Writers' Café is situated just outside London.

20 Children from anywhere in the world are able to become members of the Society.

www.shortstorysoc.com

Membership

email enquiries: membership@shortstorysoc.com

The Short Story Society exists to help writers in Britain today. Started in 1899, the Short Story Society is now one of Britain's most active arts organisations.

- Society Magazines
- National Short Story Competition
- Education
- The Writers' Café
- Becoming a Member

Society Magazines

We produce a range of excellent magazines, including the popular *Short Story Review*. This magazine includes short stories by some of Britain's top writers, as well as providing plenty of opportunities for new writers to have their work printed. Another magazine, *Short Story News*, has interviews with writers and is packed with information about events, competitions, festivals and the writing scene in general. To see a selection of articles from recent issues, follow the links on this website.

National Short Story Competition

We run the National Short Story Competition, the biggest competition of its kind. It is open to anyone aged 18 and over and short stories on any topic are accepted. Short stories should be between 1,000 and 1,500 words long. There is no entry fee for anyone belonging to the Society (non-members pay an entry fee of £5). The competition runs from April until the end of October each year. The ten best entries will appear in the Society's annual book of short stories. The actual winner will receive a publishing contract to produce his or her own collection of short stories.

Education

For nearly thirty years the Society has taken writers into classrooms, providing children and teachers with new ideas and building confidence in their own writing. Current projects include the *Young Writer of the Year*, which was started in 1998 and is open to writers aged 11-18. All winners receive book prizes and are invited to study on a five-day course taught by professional writers.

The Writers' Café

The Writers' Café is the social centre of the Society. Relaxed and stylish, with freshly cooked vegetarian food, excellent coffees and cold drinks, it is the ideal place to look through the Society's magazines. The Café also provides monthly exhibitions, short courses and readings. Its location is in the heart of London, and it is open from 11.00 am to 10.00 pm Monday to Friday and 11.00 am to 8.00 pm on Saturday. Society members receive discounts on selected products and events.

Becoming a Member

We have members worldwide, and anyone aged eighteen or over is welcome to join. If you are interested in joining the Short Story Society, click here and fill out a registration form.

Return to Top   Go to **Short Story News**

Part 4

Questions 21-25

Read the text and questions below.
For each question, mark the correct letter A, B, C or D on your answer sheet.

New TV Star

Carolina Fenton talks about her first TV role

'I never expected to spend some of my first year at university filming *The Muldoons*. I'd only ever acted at school, but I'd loved the book since I was eleven. My grandmother used to say I was just like Polly Muldoon and I always imagined myself playing her.

I'd taken a year off to go travelling before university. While I was in Mexico, my mother emailed me to say there were plans to turn the book into a TV drama. I knew I had to go for the part. She was surprised at first, but sent my photograph to the director and persuaded him to meet me. I flew back and got the part.

The outdoor filming started a week into term, so I got permission from the university to be away for three weeks. Once I was back at university, I got up at 6.00 am to write the essays I'd missed. I didn't tell my university friends, but they found out and thought it was great.

It was an amazing experience – I'm so lucky. After university, I definitely want to make acting my career. I'm not from an acting family, though my grandmother was an opera singer. I've tried for other TV parts but haven't received any offers yet.

I don't know how I managed it all, because I had a full social life too. When filming finished, I hardly knew what to do. I've since appeared in two college plays. Unfortunately, I haven't been home much and now my first year at university is over, I'm off to Spain for the summer with friends.'

21   In this text, Carolina Fenton is

    A   advising students to finish studying before taking up acting.

    B   describing how pleased she was about this opportunity to act.

    C   warning other young people that acting is a difficult career.

    D   explaining why she has always wanted to be an actor.

22   Why did Carolina decide to try for a part in *The Muldoons*?

    A   She thought the book would make a great TV drama.

    B   She agreed with her grandmother that she should apply.

    C   She felt she was perfect for the part of Polly.

    D   She was anxious about starting university.

Appendix A

Part 5

Questions 26-35

Read the text below and choose the correct word for each space.
For each question, mark the letter next to the correct word A, B, C or D on your answer sheet.

Example:

0   A most   B more   C very   D too

Answer: 0   A■ B☐ C☐ D☐

Grass

Grass is probably the **(0)** .... successful living plant in the world.

There are over 9,000 different types of grasses and they are
(26) .... in every region on the earth. They are the **(27)** ....
flowering plants that can exist in the freezing **(28)** .... of the Arctic
and the Antarctic.

Grasslands support a wide range of animal life, from tiny insects and
birds to huge animals like cows and lions. All of them **(29)** .... on
grass in one way or another.

Grass **(30)** .... very quickly after it is cut or **(31)** .... Unlike
other plants, the new leaves grow from **(32)** .... the soil, not from
the top of the plant. That is **(33)** .... large families of animals are
able to live together in one area. As **(34)** .... as they have eaten
all the grass there, a fresh meal is always **(35)** .... because the
plants start to grow again.

23   What does Carolina say about her mother?

A   She encouraged Carolina to keep travelling.
B   She felt Carolina would be a good actor.
C   She was sorry she had emailed Carolina.
D   She helped Carolina to get the part.

24   How did Carolina manage to find time to do the filming?

A   She missed lectures and hoped nobody would notice.
B   She delayed going to university until filming was over.
C   She took time off and did her college work later.
D   She asked her friends to help with her essays.

25   Which of the following would Carolina write to a penfriend?

A
I'm going to continue with my
studies, but hope to have the
opportunity to do another TV
programme soon.

B
Now I've finished both the
filming and my first year at
university, I plan to spend
more time with my family.

C
I enjoyed filming the TV drama
but I've missed having a social
life – I don't know what to do
at weekends.

D
Acting is more difficult than
I'd expected, but I've learned a
lot from other members of my
family who work in the
business.

PET Reading (December 2005) Answer Key

Part 1		Part 2		Part 3		Part 4		Part 5	
1	C	6	E	11	A	21	B	26	D
2	B	7	C	12	A	22	C	27	C
3	B	8	D	13	A	23	D	28	A
4	A	9	B	14	B	24	C	29	A
5	C	10	G	15	B	25	A	30	B
				16	B			31	D
				17	A			32	C
				18	A			33	A
				19	B			34	B
				20	B			35	A

	A	B	C	D
26	noticed	realised	caught	found
27	single	one	only	special
28	environment	scene	situation	background
29	depend	build	turn	hang
30	repeats	recovers	reduces	remains
31	hurt	broken	injured	damaged
32	beside	behind	below	beyond
33	why	where	what	when
34	fast	soon	quickly	often
35	available	present	free	complete

Appendix A

FCE Reading (Sample Paper 2007)

You are going to read an extract from a novel. For questions 1 – 8, choose the answer (A, B, C or D) which you think fits best according to the text.

Mark your answers on the separate answer sheet.

I shifted uncomfortably inside my best suit and eased a finger inside the tight white collar. It was hot in the little bus and I had taken a seat on the wrong side where the summer sun beat on the windows. It was a strange outfit for the weather, but a few miles ahead my future employer might be waiting for me and I had to make a good impression.

There was a lot depending on this interview. Many friends who had qualified with me were unemployed or working in shops or as labourers in the shipyards. So many that I had almost given up hope of any future for myself as a veterinary surgeon.

There were usually two or three jobs advertised in the *Veterinary Record* each week and an average of eighty applicants for each one. It hadn't seemed possible when the letter came from Darrowby in Yorkshire, Mr S. Farnon would like to see me on the Friday afternoon; I was to come to tea and, if we were suited to each other, I could stay on as his assistant. Most young people emerging from the colleges after five years of hard work were faced by a world unimpressed by their enthusiasm and bursting knowledge. So I had grabbed the lifeline unbelievingly.

The driver crashed his gears again as we went into another steep bend. We had been climbing steadily now for the last fifteen miles or so, moving closer to the distant blue of the Pennine Hills. I had never been in Yorkshire before, but the name had always raised a picture of a region as heavy and unromantic as the pudding of the same name; I was prepared for solid respectability, dullness and a total lack of charm. But as the bus made its way higher, I began to wonder. There were high grassy hills and wide valleys. In the valley bottoms, rivers twisted among the trees and solid grey stone farmhouses lay among islands of cultivated land which pushed up the wild, dark hillsides.

line 15

Suddenly, I realised the bus was clattering along a narrow street which opened onto a square where we stopped. Above the window of a small grocer's shop I read 'Darrowby Co-operative Society'. We had arrived. I got out and stood beside my battered suitcase, looking about me. There was something unusual and I didn't know what it was at first. Then it came to me. The other passengers had dispersed, the driver had switched off the engine and there was not a sound or a movement anywhere. The only visible sign of life was a group of old men sitting round the clock tower in the centre of the square, but they might have been carved of stone.

Darrowby didn't get much space in the guidebooks, but where it was mentioned it was described as a grey little town on the River Arrow with a market place and little of interest except its two ancient bridges. But when you looked at it, its setting was beautiful. Everywhere from the windows of houses in Darrowby you could see the hills. There was a clearness in the air, a sense of space and airiness that made me feel I had left something behind. The pressure of the city, the noise, the smoke – already they seemed to be falling away from me.

Trengate Street was a quiet little town leading off the square and from there I had my first sight of Skeldale House. I knew it was the right place before I was near enough to read S. *Farnon, Veterinary Surgeon* on the old-fashioned brass nameplate. I knew by the ivy which grew untidily over the red brick, climbing up to the topmost windows. It was what the letter had said – the only house with ivy; and this could be where I would work for the first time as a veterinary surgeon. I rang the doorbell.

Part 2

You are going to read an article about a woman who is a downhill mountain-bike racer. Seven sentences have been removed from the article. Choose from the sentences A – H the one which fits each gap (9 – 15). There is one extra sentence which you do not need to use.

Mark your answers on the separate answer sheet.

Downhill racer

Anna Jones tells of her move from skiing to downhill mountain biking and her rapid rise up the ranks to her current position as one of the top five downhill racers in the country.

At the age of seven I had learnt to ski and by fourteen I was competing internationally. When I was eighteen a close friend was injured in a ski race, and as a result, I gave up competitive skiing. To fill the gap that skiing had left I decided to swap two planks of wood for two wheels with big tyres.

My first race was a cross-country race in 1995. It wasn't an amazing success. [9] After entering a few more cross-country races, a local bike shop gave me a downhill bike to try. I entered a downhill race, fell off, but did reasonably well in the end, so I switched to downhill racing.

I think my skiing helped a lot as I was able to transfer several skills such as cornering and weight-balance to mountain biking. This year I'm riding for a famous British team and there are races almost every weekend from March through to September. [10] In fact, there's quite a lot of putting up tents in muddy fields.

Last season I was selected to represent Great Britain at both the European and World Championships. Both events were completely different from the UK race scene. [11] was totally in awe, racing with the riders I had been following in magazines. The atmosphere was electric and I finished about mid-pack.

Mountain biking is a great sport to be in. People ask me if downhill racing is really scary. I say, 'Yes it is, and I love it.' Every time I race I scare myself silly and then say, 'Yeah let's do it again.'

When you're riding well, you are right on the edge, as close as you can be to being out of control. [12] However, you quickly learn how to do it so as not to injure yourself. And it's part of the learning process as you have to push yourself and try new skills to improve.

Initially, downhill racing wasn't taken seriously as a mountain-biking discipline. [13] But things are changing and riders are now realising that they need to train just as hard for downhill racing as they would do for cross-country.

The races are run all over ground which is generally closer to vertical than horizontal, with jumps, drop-offs, holes, corners and nasty rocks and trees to test your nerves as well as technical skill. At the end of a run, which is between two and three minutes in this country your legs hurt so much they burn. [14] But in a race, you're so excited that you switch off to the pain until you've finished.

A lot of people think that you need to spend thousands of pounds to give downhill mountain biking a go. [15] A reasonable beginner's downhill bike will cost you around £400 and the basic equipment, of a cycle helmet, cycle shorts and gloves, around £150. Later on you may want to upgrade your bike and get a full-face crash helmet, since riders are now achieving speeds of up to 80 kilometres per hour.

---

1 As he travelled, the writer regretted his choice of

A seat.
B clothes.
C career.
D means of transport.

2 What had surprised the writer about the job?

A There had been no advertisement.
B He had been contacted by letter.
C There was an invitation to tea.
D He had been selected for interview.

3 The writer uses the phrase 'I had grabbed the lifeline' (line 15) to show that he felt

A confident of his ability.
B ready to consider any offer.
C cautious about accepting the invitation.
D forced to make a decision unwillingly.

4 What impression had the writer previously had of Yorkshire?

A It was a beautiful place.
B It was a boring place.
C It was a charming place.
D It was an unhappy place.

5 What did the writer find unusual about Darrowby?

A the location of the bus stop
B the small number of shops
C the design of the square
D the lack of activity

6 What did the writer feel the guidebooks had missed about Darrowby?

A the beauty of the houses
B the importance of the bridges
C the lovely views from the town
D the impressive public spaces

7 How did the writer recognise Skeldale House?

A The name was on the door.
B It had red bricks.
C There was a certain plant outside.
D It stood alone.

8 How did the writer's attitude change during the passage?

A He began to feel he might like living in Darrowby.
B He became less enthusiastic about the job.
C He realised his journey was likely to have been a waste of time.
D He started to look forward to having the interview.

Appendix A

Part 3

You are going to read a magazine article about people who collect things. For questions **16 – 30,** choose from the people (A – D). The people may be chosen more than once.

Mark your answers **on the separate answer sheet.**

Which person

had to re-start their collection?	16
has provided useful advice on their subject?	17
was misled by an early success?	18
received an unexpected gift?	19
admits to making little practical use of their collection?	20
regrets the rapid disappearance of certain items?	21
is aware that a fuller collection of items exists elsewhere?	22
has a history of collecting different items?	23
performed a favour for someone they knew?	24
is a national expert on their subject?	25
is aware that they form part of a growing group?	26
insists on purchasing top-quality items?	27
noticed items while looking for something else?	28
has to protect their collection from damage?	29
would like to create a hands-on display of their collection?	30

A   I've fallen off more times than I care to remember.

B   I usually have to stop during practice sessions.

C   The courses were twice as long and the crowds were twice as big.

D   I'm not strong enough in my arms, so I've been doing a lot of upper-body training this year.

E   The attitude was: how much skill do you need to sit on a saddle and point a bike in the same direction for a few minutes?

F   I finished last, but it didn't matter as I really enjoyed it.

G   Nothing could be further from the truth.

H   It's not all stardom and glamour, though.

The World of Collecting

A Ron Barton shares his home with about 200 sewing machines. His passion began when he was searching for bits of second-hand furniture and kept seeing 'beautiful old sewing machines that were next to nothing to buy'. He couldn't resist them. Then a friend had a machine that wouldn't work, so she asked Barton to look at it for her. At that stage he was not an authority on the subject, but he worked on it for three days and eventually got it going.

Later he opened up a small stand in a London market. 'Most people seemed uninterested. Then a dealer came and bought everything I'd taken along. I thought, "Great! This is my future life." But after that I never sold another one there and ended up with a stall in another market which was only moderately successful.'

Nowadays, he concentrates on domestic machines in their original box containers with their handbooks. He is often asked if he does any sewing with them. The answer is that, apart from making sure that they work, he rarely touches them.

B As a boy, Chris Peters collected hundreds of vintage cameras, mostly from jumble sales and dustbins. Later, when the time came to buy his first house, he had to sell his valuable collection in order to put down a deposit. A few years after, he took up the interest again and now has over a thousand cameras, the earliest dating from 1860.

Now Peters 'just cannot stop collecting' and hopes to open his own photographic museum where members of the public will be able to touch and fiddle around with the cameras. Whilst acknowledging that the Royal Camera Collection in Bath is probably more extensive than his own, he points out that so few of the items are on show there at the same time that I think my own personal collection will easily rival it.

C Sylvia King is one of the foremost authorities on plastics in Britain. She has, in every corner of her house, a striking collection of plastic objects of every kind, dating from the middle of the last century and illustrating the complex uses of plastic over the years.

King's interest started when she was commissioned to write her first book. In order to do this, she had to start from scratch; so she attended a course on work machinery, maintaining that if she didn't understand plastics manufacture then nobody else would.

As she gathered information for her book, she also began to collect pieces of plastic from every imaginable source: junk shops, arcades, and the cupboards of friends. She also collects 'because it is vital to keep examples. We live in an age of throw-away items: tape-recorders, cassettes, hair dryers – they are all replaced so quickly.'

King's second book, Classic Plastics: from Bakelite to High Tech, is the first published guide to plastics collecting. It describes collections that can be visited and gives simple and safe home tests for identification.

King admits that 'plastic is a mysterious substance and many people are frightened of it. Even so, the band of collectors is constantly expanding.'

D Janet Pontin already had twenty years of collecting one thing or another behind her when she started collecting 'art deco' fans in 1966. It happened when she went to an auction sale and saw a shoe-box filled with them. Someone else got them by offering a higher price and she was very cross. Later, to her astonishment, he went round to her flat and presented them to her. 'That was how it all started.' There were about five fans in the shoe-box and since then they've been exhibited in the first really big exhibition of 'art deco' in America. The fans are not normally on show, however, but are kept behind glass. They are extremely fragile and people are tempted to handle them. The idea is to have, one day, a black-lacquered room where they can be more easily seen.

Pontin doesn't restrict herself to fans of a particular period, but she will only buy a fan if it is in excellent condition. The same rule applies to everything in her house.

FCE Reading (Sample Paper 2007) Answer Key

Part 1		Part 2		Part 3	
1	A	9	F	16	B
2	D	10	H	17	C
3	B	11	C	18	A
4	B	12	A	19	D
5	D	13	E	20	A
6	C	14	B	21	C
7	C	15	G	22	B
8	A			23	D
				24	A
				25	C
				26	C
				27	D
				28	A
				29	D
				30	B

Appendix A

CAE Reading (Sample Paper 2008)

Part 1

You are going to read three extracts which are all concerned in some way with scientific research. For questions 1 – 6, choose the answer (A, B, C or D) which you think fits best according to the text.

Mark your answers **on the separate answer sheet.**

YOUNG ENVIRONMENTAL JOURNALIST COMPETITION

HOW TO ENTER:

- If you're aged 16–25, we're looking for original articles of 1,000 words (or less) with an environmental or conservation theme. The closing date for entries is 30 December 2006.

- Your article should show proof of investigative research, rather than relying solely on information from the internet and phone interviews. You don't have to go far; a report on pollution in a local stream would be as valid as a piece about the remotest rainforest.

- Your article should show you are passionate and knowledgeable about environmental issues. It should also be objective and accurate, while being creative enough to hold the reader's interest. We are not looking for 'think pieces' or opinion columns.

- Your aim should be to advance understanding and awareness of environmental issues. You should be able to convey complex ideas to readers of this general interest magazine in an engaging and authoritative manner.

- Facts or information contained in short-listed articles will be checked.

- Read the rules carefully.

1 Before entering for the competition, young people must have

- A conducted some relevant research in their local area.
- B gained a qualification in environmental research.
- C uncovered some of the evidence in their research themselves.
- D consulted a number of specialists on the subject under research.

2 The articles submitted must

- A focus on straightforward concepts.
- B include a range of views.
- C be accessible to non-specialists.
- D reveal the writer's standpoint.

EXTRACT FROM A NOVEL

Chapter One

The landing cupboard is stacked high with what Glyn calls low-use material: conference papers and research papers including, he hopes, a paper that he needs right now for the article on which he is working. All of these go back to his postgraduate days, in no convenient sequential order but all jumbled up. A crisp column of *Past and Present* magazine is wedged against a heap of tattered files. Forgotten students drift to his feet as he rummages, and he reproachful on the floor: 'Susan Cochrane's contributions to my seminar have been perfunctory' … labelled boxes of aerial photographs showing archaeological sites are squeezed against a further row of files. To remove one will bring the lot crashing down, like an ill-judged move in that game involving a tower of balanced blocks. But he has glimpsed behind them a further cache which may well include what he is looking for.

On the shelf above he spots the gold-lettered spine of his own doctoral thesis, its green cloth blotched brown with age. On top of it sits a 1985 run of the *Archaeological Journal.* Come to think of it, the contents of the landing cupboard are a nice reflection of his profession – it is a landscape in which everything co-exists requiring expert deconstruction. But he does not dwell on that, intent instead on this increasingly irritating search.   line 12

3 The writer mentions a game in line 12 in order to emphasise

- A the difficulty in accessing some material stored in the cupboard.
- B the poor condition of much of the contents of the cupboard.
- C Glyn's approach to locating items stored in the cupboard.
- D Glyn's skill in manoeuvring the material in the cupboard.

4 In the second paragraph, the writer makes a comparison between the cupboard and

- A the development of Glyn's academic career.
- B Glyn's particular area of work.
- C Glyn's way of life.
- D the current state of Glyn's research.

THE THEORY OF EVERYTHING

Time was when physicists dreamed of a final theory of fundamental physics, a perfect set of equations that would describe every force and particle in nature. Today that dream is being overtaken by the suspicion that there is no such thing. Some even fear that all attempts at a deeper understanding of nature are dead ends. This will lend support to those who have long claimed that research into fundamental physics is a waste of time and money; that at best it provides answers to obscure questions which few people understand or care about.

So do these reservations undermine pure physics as a scientific pursuit? Surely, it makes no difference if the truths that physicists seek turn out to be more complex and messy than they once hoped. It could even make the search more intriguing. There are as many profound questions out there as there have ever been, and to answer them physicists need the

kind of hard experimental evidence that can only come from pure research.

Can we, therefore, justify spending the huge sums of money that such research demands? What it boils down to is whether we think the search for fundamental truths is important. This quest for knowledge is a defining human quality, but it's hard to quantify how our lives have been 'improved' by it. There have been plenty of technological spin-offs from the space race and other experiments. But all the spin-offs are not the point. In showing us how the universe works, fundamental physics could also tell us something profound about ourselves. And for that, a few billion dollars would be a small price to pay.

5   According to the writer, technological 'spin-offs' from scientific research

   A   do not justify the sums invested in it.
   B   reveal the true aims of those promoting it.
   C   should convince the public of the value of it.
   D   should not be the main reason for pursuing it.

6   In this piece, the writer is generally

   A   distrustful of those who doubt the value of pure research.
   B   supportive of those wishing to carry out pure research.
   C   sceptical about the long-term benefits of pure research.
   D   optimistic about the prospects of funding for pure research.

You are going to read an extract from a magazine article. Six paragraphs have been removed from the extract. Choose from the paragraphs **A–G** the one which fits each gap (**7–12**). There is one extra paragraph which you do not need to use. Mark your answers **on the separate answer sheet.**

THE HONEY GUIDE

The message most frequently declared by one species to another is simple and straightforward – 'Go away!'. But inter-species communications can be more complicated than that and can, on occasion, even be co-operative. The honey-guide is a good example of this.

The honey-guide is a lark-sized bird that lives in East Africa. Its diet is insects of all kinds and it has a particular liking for the grubs of honey-bees. Getting them is not easy, however. Wild African bees build their nests in hollow trees or clefts in rocks. The honey-guide's beak is slender and delicate so the bird cannot cut away wood, still less chip stone. It it to procure its favourite food, it has to recruit a helper, usually a man.

In northern Kenya, where honey-guides still live in some numbers, the men of the semi-nomadic Boran tribe specialise in collecting honey. Indeed, their standing within the tribe will depend on the frequency and quality of their honey collecting.

7

As soon as the two have registered one another's presence, the bird flies off with a peculiar low swooping flight, spreading its tail widely as it goes so that the white feathers on each side of it are clearly displayed. The man follows, whistling and shouting to reassure the bird that he understands its summons and is following.

8

It is now up to the man to take the initiative. If the day is hot, a stream of bees may be buzzing in and out of the entrance. Something has to be done to pacify them if the man and the bird are not both to get badly stung. The man lights a fire close to the

nest and, if possible, pushes burning sticks into holes beneath it so that smoke swirls up around the nest itself.

9

The honey-guide can in turn get its share. It flies to the remains of the wrecked nest and pulls out the fat while bee-grubs from the cells of the combs. It also, very remarkably, feeds enthusiastically on the wax. It is one of the very few animals that can digest it. The bird does not find its bees' nests by accident. It has a detailed knowledge of its territory and knows the exact location and state of every bee colony within it.

10

When the bird starts guiding the man, it does not wander about at random but leads him directly to the nearest nest. And the reason it leaves him for a short period just after their initial meeting is because it makes a quick flight to the nest it has in mind, perhaps to check that it is still flourishing.

11

There is ample evidence to suggest that the bird has been plundering bees' nests for a very long time and that, therefore, the relationship with man is an ancient one. Human beings have certainly been collecting honey in this part of the world for some

Appendix A

Part 3

Groomed for TV

You are going to read a newspaper article. For questions 13 – 19, choose the answer (A, B, C or D) which you think fits best according to the text.

Mark your answers on the separate answer sheet.

Martyn Harris looks back on his experience of being trained to appear on TV.

I am terrible on TV. I slouch, sneer, stammer, fidget, forget my lines and swallow the ends of my words. It rankles, because I know inside I am scintillating, sensitive and sincere. Television can make any fool look like an intellectual. Newsreaders can contrive to look nice and even the worst presenters can seem sensible, but I come over as a shifty subversive. The single television programme I have presented was so awful that even my mother couldn't find a good word for it. After a catastrophic radio chat show last year, when I addressed the interviewer by the wrong name throughout, I swore I'd never do broadcasting again.

Until now, that is. I have my first novel out next month, which is called *Do It Again*, and the PR people inform me you just have to get out there and promote it. Scotland one day, the south coast of England the next. It's going to be hectic and I have to get my act together. Which is how I find myself being scrutinised for televisual potential by two svelte creatures from Public Image Ltd, while cameraman Alastair focuses on my trembling upper lip. Public Image is the outfit which has been teaching MPs how to look good on TV. They also groom executives from major companies in everything from corporate presentations to handling broadcast interrogation, but as far as I'm concerned, if they can make politicians look like real people, they are good enough for me.

'He blinks a lot, doesn't he?' says Diana, the speech specialist, studying my image on a video monitor. 'And the crossed legs look defensive. But the voice isn't bad.' Jeannie, who is introduced to me as Public Image's 'charisma consultant', takes a step backwards to study the general posture. 'Needs to get his bottom back in the sofa. And the jacket makes him look a bit deformed. Where *does* he get his clothes from?'

'Honesty is the most important thing,' says Diana. 'We don't want to turn people into actors. We want to bring out the personality. And of course speech is most important too. Lots of politicians don't breathe properly, so they have to shout. They give themselves sore throats and polyps on the vocal chords. Breathe from the diaphragm and you can speak quite loudly and for quite a long time without strain. Then most importantly, there are the three

E's: Energy, Enthusiasm and Enjoyment. And do try to stop blinking.'

And so, as I breathe from the diaphragm, clench my eyelids apart and desperately try to project honesty as well as the three Es at once, the camera rolls. 'Today we are visiting the home of Martyn Harris,' says Diana dishonestly, 'a journalist who has recently published his first novel *Do It Again*. So, what can you tell us about the novel, Martyn?' 'Umm …' A long pause. 'Errr …' A longer pause. 'Tee hee, hargh …' An asinine giggle. 'All right Alastair,' says Diana patiently, 'we'll try that again.'

We try it again, many, many times, each time chipping away at another tic and mannerism and gaucherie. On the second run-through, my crossed legs keep bobbing up and down, which makes me look as if I want to run away (I do, I do). On the third run they are uncrossed, but my hands are clenched in my lap. On the fourth I have wrenched my hands from my lap, but now they are fiddling with my ears. On the fifth, I'm throwing away the ends of my sentences, which sounds as if I think my audience is thick (I don't really).

Television does cause curious things to your face, dragging it towards the edges of the screen. If you have a long face, as I have, it makes you look like a cadaverous mule. It emphasises the darkness of lipstick and eyeshadow, so make-up should be minimal and used mainly to soften facial shadows. Does Diana think it is wicked, I wonder, to mould politicians in this way? 'As soon as anyone gets on telly these days, we expect them to be as good as the professionals, because that's where we get our standards from. It's unfair, but that's the way of the world. As for the ethics, I leave that to others and get on with my job.'

And it's a job she does very well, because on the final run-through, after three hours or so, I really don't look too bad. Steady gaze, breathing from the diaphragm, no twitches, no blinking. Not a consummate professional in the business, but not bad.

I'm brimming with honesty, energy, enthusiasm and enjoyment and I'm talking a lot of twaddle, but you'd hardly notice. When you watch politicians on TV, you'll see a lot more just like me.

---

twenty thousand years, as is proved by rock paintings that show them doing so. Perhaps the partnership was forming as far back as then.

12 ☐

It is a powerful digger with strong forelegs and it can squeeze into very narrow openings. It can even

A But the bird probably had other honey-hunting helpers even earlier still. The ratel, a badger-sized relative of the skunk, is also a lover of honey. A honey-guide encountering one will behave in just the same way as it does towards the man. When they reach the bees' nest, the ratel tackles it with great efficiency.

B Nomadic tribesmen like this spend most of the year travelling across a vast area in search of a variety of food. Their way of life is clearly illustrated in the rock paintings found in East Africa.

C The bird may now disappear for several minutes. When it comes back, it perches some distance away, calling loudly and waiting for the man. As the two travel together, the bird stops and calls frequently until its song changes into one that is low and less agitated. It then falls silent and flutters to a perch, where it stays. Beside it will be a bees' nest.

rival a man in pacifying the bees. Like its cousins, it has a large scent gland below its tail which it rubs all round the nest entrance so that the wood or rock is smeared with scent. The smell is so powerful that the bees are stupefied, and human beings who have peered inside a plundered nest after a visit by one of these animals have said that they were made almost as dizzy as the bees themselves.

D Furthermore, if, having reached the nest, the man for some reason does not open it, the bird, after a pause, will once more give its 'follow-me' call and lead him to another.

E Watchers in camouflaged hides have observed a bird visiting every one of its bees' nests, day after day, as though mapping them out and checking on their condition. On a cold day, when the bees are quiescent, it may hop onto the lip of the entrance and peer inquisitively inside.

F When one of them sets out to do so, he begins by walking into the bush and whistling in a very penetrating way. If he is within the territory of a honey-guide, the bird will appear within minutes, singing a special chattering call that it makes on no other occasion.

G With the bees partially stupefied, he now opens up the tree with his bush knife or pokes out the nest from a rock cleft with a stick and extracts the combs, dripping with rich, deep-brown honey.

Appendix A

Part 4

You are going to read an article containing reviews of crime novels. For questions 20 – 34, choose from the reviews (A – F). The reviews may be chosen more than once.

Mark your answers **on the separate answer sheet.**

In which review are the following mentioned?

a book successfully adapted for another medium	20
characters whose ideal world seems totally secure	21
a gripping book which introduces an impressive main character	22
a character whose intuition is challenged	23
the disturbing similarity between reality and fiction within a novel	24
an original and provocative line in storytelling	25
the main character having a personal connection which brings disturbing revelations	26
the completion of an outstanding series of works	27
the interweaving of current lives and previous acts of wickedness	28
a deliberately misleading use of the written word	29
a rather unexpected choice of central character	30
an abundant amount of inconclusive information about a case	31
a character seeing through complexity in an attempt to avert disaster	32
a novel which displays the talent of a new author	33
the characters' involvement in a crime inevitably leading to a painful conclusion	34

---

13 The writer believes that one reason he is terrible on TV is that

A he doesn't make enough effort to perform well.
B he can't help being rude to interviewers.
C his personality seems unappealing to viewers.
D his personality differs from that of newsreaders and presenters.

14 The writer has become involved with Public Image Ltd because

A he wants to find out what such companies do.
B he has been told that it is in his interests to do so.
C he is intrigued by the work they do for politicians.
D he has been told that the company is good at promoting novels.

15 Diana and Jeannie both say that one of the writer's problems when appearing on TV concerns

A the way he sits.
B the clothes he wears.
C the way his eyes move.
D the way he moves.

16 What does Diana tell the writer about politicians?

A They are usually reluctant to tell the truth.
B They often fail to realise that they are shouting.
C They are frequently nervous when they appear on TV.
D They frequently speak in a way that is harmful to them.

17 The writer believes that his response to Diana's first question sounds

A insincere.
B silly.
C rude.
D predictable.

18 When the writer asks Diana about her job, she

A says that she is only interested in doing it well.
B admits that sometimes it results in people looking foolish.
C says that it frequently involves frustrations.
D agrees that it is hard to justify it.

19 In the final paragraph, the writer concludes that

A he has underestimated how challenging appearing on TV can be for politicians.
B he has learnt how to sound convincing without saying anything meaningful.
C some people can be trained to do absolutely anything.
D viewers are more perceptive than is generally believed.

Updated CAE Reading (Sample paper 2008) Answer Key

Part 1		Part 2		Part 3		Part 4	
1	C	7	F	13	C	20	B
2	C	8	C	14	B	21	E
3	A	9	G	15	A	22	C
4	B	10	E	16	D	23	D
5	D	11	D	17	B	24	F
6	B	12	A	18	A	25	B
				19	B	26	C
						27	E
						28	E
						29	B
						30	A
						31	F
						32	E
						33	D
						34	D

CHILLING READS TO LOOK OUT FOR
Some recommendations from the latest batch of crime novels

A Zouache may not be the obvious heroine for a crime novel, but November sees her debut in Fidelis Morgan's wonderful Restoration thriller *Unnatural Fire*. From debtor to private eye, this Countess is an aristocrat, fleeing for her life through the streets of 17th-century London. Featuring a colourful cast of misfits and brilliantly researched period detail, *Unnatural Fire* has a base in the mysterious world of alchemy, and will appeal to adherents of both crime and historical fiction.

B Minette Walters is one of the most acclaimed writers in British crime fiction whose books like *The Sculptress* have made successful transitions to our TV screens. Preoccupied with developing strong plots and characterisation rather than with crime itself, she has created some disturbing and innovative psychological narratives. *The Shape of Snakes* is set in the winter of 1978. Once again Walters uses her narrative skills to lead the reader astray (there is a clever use of correspondence between characters), before resolving the mystery in her latest intricately plotted bestseller which is full of suspense. Once again she shows why she is such a star of British crime fiction.

C Elizabeth Woodcraft's feisty barrister heroine in *Good Bad Woman*, Frankie, is a diehard Motown music fan. As the title suggests, despite her job on the right side of the law, she ends up on the wrong side – arrested for murder. No favourite of the police – who are happy to see her go down – in order to prove her innocence she must solve the case, one that involves an old friend and some uncomfortable truths a bit too close to home. *Good Bad Woman* is an enthralling, fast-paced contemporary thriller that presents a great new heroine to the genre.

D *Black Dog* is Stephen Booth's hugely accomplished debut, now published in paperback. It follows the mysterious disappearance of teenager Laura Vernon in the Peak District. Ben Cooper, a young Detective Constable, has known the villagers all his life, but his instinctive feelings about the case are called into question by the arrival of Diane Fry, a ruthlessly ambitious detective from another division. As the investigation twists and turns, Ben and Diane discover that to understand the present, they must also understand the past – and, in a world where none of the suspects is entirely innocent, misery and suffering can be the only outcome.

E Andrew Roth's deservedly celebrated Roth Trilogy has drawn to a close with the paperback publication of the third book, *The Office*, set in a 1950s cathedral city. Janet Byfield has everything that Wendy Appleyard lacks – she's beautiful, she has a handsome husband, and an adorable little daughter, Rosie. At first it seems to Wendy as though nothing can touch the Byfields' perfect existence, but old sins gradually come back to haunt the present, and new sins are bred in their place. The shadows seep through the neighbourhood and only Wendy, the outsider looking in, is able to glimpse the truth. But can she grasp its twisted logic in time to prevent a tragedy whose roots lie buried deep in the past?

F And finally, Reginald Hill has a brilliant new Dalziel and Pascoe novel, *Dialogues*, released in the spring. The uncanny resemblance between stories entered for a local newspaper competition and the circumstances of two sudden disappearances attracts the attention of Mid-Yorkshire Police. Superintendent Andy Dalziel realises they may have a dangerous criminal on their hands – one the media are soon calling the Wordman. There are enough clues around to weave a tapestry, but it's not clear who's playing with whom. Is it the Wordman versus the police, or the criminal versus his victims? And just how far will the games go?

CPE Reading (June 2005)

Part 1

For questions **1-18**, read the three texts below and decide which answer (**A**, **B**, **C** or **D**) best fits each gap. Mark your answers **on the separate answer sheet**.

Listing

In Britain the badge of distinction awarded to historic buildings is unheroically called 'listing'. When a building is listed it is **(1)** .... for preservation and it is expected to stand more or less indefinitely – nobody expects it to be demolished, ever. But what is the **(2)** .... expectancy of, **(3)** .... a nineteenth-century terraced house? A few years ago most people assumed that such houses would eventually wear out and be replaced – and millions were demolished in slum **(4)** ..... But about 2.5 million of these terraces survive, and in some towns they are being given 'conservation area' **(5)** .... so don't expect the bulldozers there. The very low rates of demolition and construction in the UK **(6)** .... that the building stock as a whole is ageing, and this has enormous implications for the long-term sustainability of housing.

	A		B		C		D	
1	A	branded	B	earmarked	C	minted	D	tagged
2	A	time	B	age	C	strength	D	life
3	A	say	B	imagine	C	think	D	look
4	A	removal	B	riddance	C	clearance	D	dispatch
5	A	quality	B	class	C	rank	D	status
6	A	mean	B	convey	C	explain	D	determine

Shopping in Europe

The first self-service stores opened in America in the 1920s but they didn't catch on in Europe until later, when the French forged ahead with their massive hypermarkets. Britain **(7)** .... behind. Although the first self-service shop and the first supermarket were opened in the early 1940s, it was thought that British housewives did not particularly want efficiency and speed. Surveys showed that while American shoppers complained most about delays in check-out queues, British ones objected to being pushed and **(8)** .... by other customers.

The **(9)** .... of supermarket shopping is impersonality, with no mediating salesman between shopper and goods, only the 'silent persuaders' of packaging and display. However, there is a current **(10)** .... towards 'boutiques', with personal service, within supermarkets – the butcher, the baker, the fishmonger – and small specialist shops and farmers' markets are making a **(11)** .... in Britain. In France, where every **(12)** .... provincial town, ringed by supermarkets, retains its specialist food shops and weekly street market, the traditional co-exists with the new.

	A		B		C		D	
7	A	dwelled	B	clung	C	deferred	D	lagged
8	A	thrust	B	shoved	C	heaved	D	jerked
9	A	crux	B	key	C	gist	D	essence
10	A	momentum	B	trend	C	craze	D	vogue
11	A	comeback	B	rebound	C	rally	D	pick-up
12	A	self-regarding	B	self-appointed	C	self-respecting	D	self-conscious

Appendix A

Teeth

Smile at yourself in the mirror. Do you like what you see? If not, cosmetic dentistry could be the answer. 'Dentistry has (13) .... a long way since the days of simple fillings and extractions,' says London dental surgeon Dr Phil Stemmer, whose client list at his Teeth For Life clinic (14) .... pop stars, actresses and even royalty, although his lips are tightly (15) .... on names. 'More and more people are turning to dentistry as a way of improving appearance,' he says. 'Shape, form, colour and alignment all make noticeable differences to a smile, and by creating an improved smile I can dramatically alter a person's whole (16) .... of themselves.' Top actress Julia Roberts seems to be universally (17) .... as the 'gold standard' in smiles, and, following her lead, one of the first things top models invest in is a perfect set of teeth to improve their chances of becoming cover-girl (18) ....

13	A	gone	B	been	C	come	D done
14	A	proclaims	B	brags	C	trumpets	D boasts
15	A	closed	B	glued	C	sealed	D shut
16	A	perception	B	observation	C	discernment	D consciousness
17	A	cheered	B	hailed	C	saluted	D exalted
18	A	stuff	B	substance	C	material	D matter

Part 2

You are going to read four extracts which are all concerned in some way with advertising and publicity. For questions 19-26, choose the answer (A, B, C or D) which you think fits best according to the text.

Mark your answers on the separate answer sheet.

Advertising in the US

A kind of creeping illiteracy invaded advertising in the US in the 1950s, to the dismay of many. By 1958 Ford was advertising that you could 'travel smooth' in a Thunderbird Sunliner and the maker of Ace Combs was urging buyers to 'comb it handsome' - a trend that continues today with other linguistic manglings too numerous and disputing to dwell on.

We may smile at the advertising ruses of the past but in fact such manipulation still goes on, albeit at a more sophisticated level. The *New York Times Magazine* reported in 1990 how an advertising copywriter had been told to come up with some impressive labels for a putative hand cream. She invented the arresting and healthful-sounding term 'oxygenating moisturizers', and wrote the accompanying text with references to 'tiny

bubbles of oxygen that release moisture into your skin'. This done, her work was turned over to the company's research and development department, which was instructed to come up with a product that matched the text.

Truth has seldom been a particularly visible feature of American advertising. And has all this deviousness led to a tightening of the rules concerning what is allowable in advertising? Hardly. In 1986, as William Lutz relates in *Doublespeak*, the insurance company John Hancock launched an ad campaign in which 'real people in real situations' discussed their financial predicaments with remarkable candour. When a journalist asked to speak to these real people, a company spokesman conceded that they were actors and 'in that sense they are not real people'.

19 What is the writer's point about the advertisement for a hand cream?

A It existed before the product was created.
B It inaccurately described the product.
C It caused controversy when it came out.
D It made the product sound interesting.

20 Which of these words is used to express disapproval on the part of the writer?

A dismay (line 3)
B manglings (line 9)
C putative (line 17)
D candour (line 36)

254

A New Copywriter

Mr Bredon had been a week with Pym's publicity, and had learnt a number of things. He learned the average number of words that can be crammed into four inches of copy; that the word 'pure' was dangerous, because if lightly used, it laid the client open to prosecution by the Government inspectors, whereas the words 'highest quality', 'finest ingredients', 'packed under the best conditions' had no legal meaning, and were therefore safe; that the most convincing copy was always written with the tongue in the cheek, since a genuine conviction of the commodity's worth produced – for some reason – poverty and flatness of style, that if, by the most far-fetched stretch of ingenuity, an indecent meaning could be read into a headline, that was the meaning that the great British Public would infallibly read into it; that the great aim and object of the studio artist was to crowd the copy out of the advertisement and that, conversely, the copywriter was a designing villain whose ambition was to cram the space with verbiage and leave no room for the sketch; that the layout man, a meek ass between two burdens, spent a miserable life trying to reconcile these opposing parties; and further, that all departments alike united in hatred of the client, who persisted in spoiling good layouts by cluttering them up with coupons, free-gift offers, lists of local agents and realistic portraits of hideous and uninteresting cartons, to the detriment of his own interests and the annoyance of everybody concerned.

21 Mr Bredon learnt that there was tension between artists and copywriters because

A they each felt that the other exerted too much influence on the layout man.

B no attempt was made to get them to work together.

C decisions about the final content of advertisements kept changing.

D they each felt that their individual contribution was the most important.

22 Mr Bredon learnt that clients were unpopular because

A they directly caused advertisements for their products to be unappealing.

B they were conservative in their approach to what advertisements should contain.

C they demanded that the content of advertisements should be re-arranged.

D they treated the people who produced their advertisements with contempt.

Nick Drake and his record company

Island Records had as much faith in Nick Drake as anyone, but in those antediluvian times before videos, the only way an audience got to see an act whose record they liked was in performance. And playing live was something which Nick was beginning to have a serious problem with. For him, the very idea of 'promoting product' was probably anathema; but it was essential for acts to be seen, not just heard. Nick's reluctance to perform effectively cut off the prime avenue of exposure for any new act, a fact which did not escape his record label. David Sandison explains: 'There was interest from a few people but it was limited. It was "Yeah, that's nice, but so what?" ... And that's understandable. There wasn't any profile. There wasn't anything to grab on to. There wasn't even explaining the songs in interviews. There wasn't any gigging so that you could make that live connection.'

In the light of frequent allegations of his record company's indifference, it is interesting that Gabrielle feels strongly that Island could not have been more supportive of her brother. 'Island was not where the problem lay. I read about Nick ruling that he wasn't more famous, but in the end, you jolly well have to set about becoming famous. As a young artist of any sort, you have to push. I think he was very lucky – he was also extraordinarily talented – but he found somewhere like Island who were prepared to support him, nurture him, and not mind that he didn't do the publicity.'

23 What does David Sandison say about Nick Drake?

A Some people began to lose patience with him.

B His image was wrong.

C He wasn't a very appealing person.

D People didn't have much to say about him.

24 What view is expressed by Nick Drake's sister?

A He was much misunderstood.

B He wasn't aware of how great his talent was.

C He had opportunities that he didn't take.

D He never wanted to be popular.

Part 3

You are going to read an article about a jazz record. Seven paragraphs have been removed from the extract. Choose from the paragraphs A-H the one which fits each gap (27-33). There is one extra paragraph which you do not need to use. Mark your answers on the separate answer sheet.

Kind of Blue

As two books celebrate Miles Davis's Kind of Blue, *Martin Gayford salutes a towering achievement*.

What is the greatest jazz album ever made? Perhaps it's an impossible question, but there is a strong candidate in *Kind of Blue*, recorded by the Miles Davis Sextet in the spring of 1959. It is the one jazz album owned by many people who don't really like jazz at all.

27

And for many who do love jazz, this is the one record that they would choose to take with them to a desert island. If he had to select one record to explain what jazz is, producer and arranger Quincy Jones has said, this would be it (he himself plays it every day – 'It's my orange juice').

28

What is so special about *Kind of Blue*? First, it was made by a magnificent band. Apart from Davis himself, *Kind of Blue* features John Coltrane on tenor saxophone, Cannonball Adderley on alto, and Bill Evans on piano – all among the finest performers of that era, and at the height of their powers. And, unlike many all-star recordings, the players were at ease in each other's musical company, as this was a working group (or almost).

29

Everybody was on the most inspired form. That does not happen every day, and is particularly unlikely to happen in the tense and clinical atmosphere of the recording studio. Other jazz performers, for example the saxophonist Sonny Rollins and the trumpeter Roy Eldridge, have spoken of rare days on which some external force seems to take over their instrument, and they can do no wrong.

30

Evans wrote about that spur-of-the-moment freshness in his original notes for the album. Each of the five

pieces on the album, he claimed, was recorded in a single take, and the musicians had never seen the music before, as Miles was still working on it hours before the recording sessions. Davis was credited with all the compositions.

31

The key to *Kind of Blue* lies in the enigmatic personality of Davis, who died in 1991. He was an irascible, contrary, foul-mouthed, aggressive man who, it seems, sheltered within an extremely sensitive soul. 'Miles talks rough,' claimed trumpeter Dizzy Gillespie, 'but his music reveals his true character ... Miles is shy. He is super-shy.' As a young man, playing with Charlie Parker, Davis was so paralysed with terror that he sometimes had to be pushed on stage. At that time he seriously considered forsaking music for dentistry.

32

'I think,' he said in 1958, 'that a movement in jazz is beginning, away from a conventional string of chords – a return to an emphasis on melodic rather than harmonic variations. There will be fewer chords, but infinite possibilities as to what to do with them.'

'Classical composers,' he went on, 'some of them have been working that way for years. Indeed, Davis's feeling for European music – Ravel, Khachaturian, Rachmaninov – colours *Kind of Blue*. He disliked most attempts to blend classical and jazz – so-called 'third stream music'.

33

It is a completely integrated, freely improvised album of unhackneyed, moving music. Davis never sounded better – and in his heart, he knew it.

Advertising agencies and their clients

Advertising agencies have long been viewed by their clients with a mixture of wariness and envy. Fat pay cheques and fast cars remain an enduring image. But things have changed. British advertising agencies are turning to training: not just for their own staff but for their clients as well. Role reversal has become a novel way of educating companies which use advertisements in the advertising agency's darkest arts.

The agency LHS last month staged its first role reversal course. It involved 19 managers from 15 different companies and their task was to plan and create an entire campaign within 48 hours, culminating in a pitch for the £5m advertising business for a fictitious product launch. Participants were divided into groups of five or six. Their first job was to create a brief to advertise a new ice cream bar. Briefs were then swapped and

each group became an 'agency'. The agencies' first task was to interpret the brief. 'These were of decidedly mixed quality,' Kevin Duncan of LHS said. 'Clear briefs elicit no questions. Poor briefs generate many – and no answers.' They then had to decide their strategy. They were given market and media data, though some of this was erroneous, 'to illustrate how a good brand manager sifts information in advance'.

The next step was to develop a creative approach and by the end of the first full day the agencies were expected to be in a position to test their ideas with research groups made up of members of the public. Interpreting the results of qualitative research is critical, Mr Duncan said. 'People wilfully interpret research findings to rationalise their ideas.'

25 On the LHS agency's course, what did participants have to do?

A design a new product
B try to win a contract
C move from group to group
D negotiate a budget

26 What is said about research groups?

A People in advertising get confused by what they say.
B People in advertising pay too much attention to them.
C People in advertising pretend that they have been proved right by them.
D People in advertising change their strategies as a result of what they say.

Part 4

You are going to read an extract from a book about the United States. For questions **34-40**, choose the answer (**A, B, C** or **D**) which you think fits best according to the text. Mark your answers **on the separate answer sheet.**

Sound and Fury

If I had to instruct a stranger on the contrasts between the United States and Britain, I would start with some televised weather reports from the two countries.

In Britain, the weather is presented in a mild, diffident, terribly-sorry-for-the-inconvenience manner. There's not much variety or excitement. The typical British weatherman appears in front of the camera with his head lowered, shoulders hunched, hands clasped and jacket buttoned. He speaks softly, almost meekly, as if telling a child's bedtime story. He points to curvy isobars that bend into the country from the sea. They all seem to mean the same thing. He might talk positively about 'sun and showers' or 'sunny spells' but usually the day will be 'dull'. In Britain the weather is so lacking in spirit that it is reported apologetically.

In America, on the other hand, the weather is pitched with the verve customarily reserved for a used-car lot. American weathermen report the next day's outlook as if they were trying to sell it to you. There's always a lot to talk about and big things are happening. Most prognostications are delivered in a you're-not-going-to-believe-me tone of voice. There are heatwaves in one part of the country and blizzards in another. Hot fronts and cold fronts march across the map. A freeze oozes ominously down from the Canadian wastes, and a tropical storm builds up in the Caribbean. American weather is raucous, and so are American weathermen.

American weather is also intimidating in a manner you hardly ever see in the equable British climate. Americans know their weather and they watch it warily. In my wife's home town in South Carolina, for example, the heat comes early in the year, balmy and lulling at the start of spring. But by the summer high it spreads out across the land like a heavy duvet. You can almost cup the humidity in your hands, and it's impossible to take more than a few steps without breaking into a glistening sweat. There is no relief at night. And when it rains there, it rains apocalyptically. The heat gathers itself up in a darkening sky, and by the afternoon there is a still, humid anticipation that something epic is about to burst. The trees rustle and the land goes quiet until a sudden split of lightning streaks across the black heaven and a cracking slip of thunder makes the clouds rumble. The earth shakes and the rain comes down as if the bottom of the sky had collapsed under its weight. It beats against the land in fat, hammering drops, filling the streets with torrents.

line 74

As runny as it is in Britain, it never rains this way. Here, the sky looks like a grey veil. It often seems about to rain but it takes for ever to get on with it. And when the rain finally comes, it sprays down as if the sky had sprung a couple of small leaks, and you think more of nourishment than calamity.

The American climate can be so quixotic and so destructive that the federal government and the National Weather Service have established a network of 450 radio transmitters across the nation to beam warnings of potential hazards to unwary communities, and commercial radio stations are required to test their civil emergency systems at regular intervals. An American cable television channel offers twenty-four-hour coverage of the weather. The Federal Emergency Management Agency is geared to respond to the natural disasters that regularly afflict the nation, and a president or state governor runs major political risks if he fails to react swiftly enough to a civil calamity.

The moderation of British weather fit naturally with the character of the two countries. The climate in Britain is hardly ever out of sorts. A wind storm or drought are major aberrations. Except for the swings of daylight, it's sometimes difficult to tell one season from another, so subtle are the shifts in pattern.

American weather is the opposite. A meteorological study once concluded that there were two places on earth which could boast the world's worst weather, the Gobi Desert and Amarillo, Texas. For extremes of heat, cold, wind, rain and so forth, it's hard to beat Amarillo. But what is true of Texas is more or less true of the rest of the country as well. In 1995, a heatwave incinerated the Midwest and East Coast with temperatures as high as 43°C reported daily for a week. On average there are 106 complete days of fog in the appropriately named Cape Disappointment, Washington, and in nearby and inappropriately named Paradise 3, 109 cm of snow fell in the winter of 1972. And in the winter of 1993, the wind chill temperature in Devil's Lake, Wisconsin touched –33°C.

Drizzle and sunny spells in Britain. The climate is moderate and restrained, with no extremes of anything, and so the isle is green and providential. Fire and ice in America. The climate is fearsome and doesn't work by half-measures.

A Over the years he developed a tough carapace. But in a music characterised by extroversion and ostentatious virtuosity, he developed a style that became ever more muted, subtle, melodic and melancholy.

B Firstly, most of Davis' albums were largely recorded in one take per tune. He seems to have believed that first thoughts were the freshest (the alternative, adopted by Bill Evans and Coltrane on their own recordings, is to do takes by the dozen in a search for perfection.) And the other point about *Kind of Blue* is its musical novelty. As revered pianist Chick Corea has put it, 'It's one thing to play a tune or a programme of music, but it's another to practically create a new language of music, which is what *Kind of Blue* did.'

C Now comes another sign of renown. How many jazz recordings are the subject of even one book? This spring, not one but two are being published on the subject of *Kind of Blue*. There is *Kind of Blue: The Making of a Jazz Masterpiece* by Ashley Kahn and, published in the US, *The Making of Kind of Blue: Miles Davis and his Masterpiece*.

D On closer examination, these celebrated facts, which make *Kind of Blue* seem almost supernatural, are only partially true. Two tracks, *So What* and *All Blues*, had been played previously by the band, on the road, which Evans, not having been with them, probably didn't realise. And Evans himself was largely responsible for the two mesmerisingly beautiful slow pieces, *Blue in Green* and *Flamenco Sketches* – a fact that he modestly suppressed at the time, and then seems to have been quietly resentful about.

E But did he do it himself on *Sketches of Spain*, and he loved the playing of Bill Evans, which uniquely combined the feeling of classical piano and the freshness of jazz. The partnership of Davis and Evans is at the heart of *Kind of Blue*, and gives it a wonderful unity of mood – romantic, delicate, hushed on the slow pieces, more exuberant elsewhere.

F The contemporary guitarist John Scofield remembers knocking on strangers' doors when he was a student in the 1970s, and asking if he could borrow their copy. The point was, he knew they would have one.

G On *Kind of Blue*, all the principals seem to feel like that. Davis and Evans, I would say, never played better. The result is something close to the philosopher's stone of jazz: formal perfection attained with perfect spontaneity.

H In fact, Evans had actually resigned the previous November– *Kind of Blue* was made on March 2, and April 22, 1959 – and was invited back for the recording (this replacement, Wynton Kelly, appears on one track).

Appendix A

CPE Reading (June 2005) Answer Key

Part 1		Part 2		Part 3		Part 4	
1	B	19	A	27	F	34	B
2	D	20	B	28	C	35	A
3	A	21	D	29	H	36	D
4	C	22	A	30	G	37	C
5	D	23	D	31	D	38	A
6	A	24	C	32	A	39	C
7	D	25	B	33	E	40	B
8	B	26	C				
9	D						
10	B						
11	A						
12	C						
13	C						
14	D						
15	C						
16	A						
17	B						
18	C						

34 It is the writer's opinion that British weathermen
A are not aware that they are being patronising to viewers.
B talk as if they are personally responsible for the weather.
C do not feel that weather reports ought to be entertaining.
D have little enthusiasm for presenting weather reports on TV.

35 The writer says that US weather reports
A are intended to impress viewers.
B tend to exaggerate the real situation.
C are often rather confusing for viewers.
D tend to be entertaining rather than informative.

36 What does the writer seek to illustrate by mentioning the weather in his wife's home town?
A the tendency of American people to complain about the weather
B how unpleasant he finds certain weather conditions
C the unpredictable nature of the weather in certain parts of America
D why Americans treat the climate with such respect

37 What does the writer say about rain in Britain?
A He looks forward to it.
B There is less of it than people think.
C It gives no cause for anxiety.
D It depresses people living there.

38 The writer mentions the US federal government to illustrate
A how important an issue the weather is in America.
B past failures to deal efficiently with problems caused by the weather.
C how complicated the situation is concerning the weather in America.
D the public's annoyance when terrible weather conditions suddenly affect them.

39 What does the writer mean when he says that the climate in Britain is 'hardly ever out of sorts' (line 74)?
A that it has a calming influence
B that it is virtually unique
C that it is mostly very predictable
D that people seldom remark on it

40 The writer includes Cape Disappointment in his list of places in the United States because
A it is a place that got its name as a result of the weather conditions there.
B it has bad weather conditions a great deal of the time.
C it has extreme weather conditions that are not typical in America.
D it is a place with a bad reputation among Americans on account of its weather.

CPE Use of English Paper (June 2008)

Part 5

For questions **40-44**, read the following texts on robots. For questions **40-43**, answer with a word or short phrase. You do not need to write complete sentences. For question **44**, write a summary according to the instructions given.

Write your answers to questions **40-44 on the separate answer sheet.**

Of all the 20th century science fiction predictions that are yet to be realised in the new millennium – including cities on the moon and time machines – few are as frustrating as the lack of good robot servants. Yet while the arrival of robots to cater for our every whim remains several years in the future, more basic robots are now entering our lives, from lawn mowers and vacuum cleaners to the two-legged robots emerging from universities across the world. Computer power is leaping ahead every year and researchers are busy developing hands, feet, eyes and ears that will one day be stitched together to make a functioning humanoid.

Many experts question whether this is wise; one has warned that robots may one day contribute to the demise of humans. However, most scientists guarantee that they will be able to keep their mechanical creations in check, and believe that if these robots are ever to integrate fully into our world, they will need to have a human form and to relate benignly to humans.

Japanese industrialists and academics have produced a two-legged robot which can change direction and shift its centre of gravity while maintaining steady balance. It walks, climbs stairs, negotiates corners and turns out the lights. An American researcher has produced a robot which can change its facial expression and respond to human emotions. If humans engage with it, then it looks happy; if they ignore it, it goes looking for something more interesting to do.

line 2

40 Explain in your own words what the writer means by 'good robot servants' in this context. (line 2)

....

41 Which four-word phrase in this text anticipates the idea of mankind's 'own species' doom' in the final line of the **second text**?

....

With a hiss and a clank, one of the world's first predatory robots seized its metal prey, plunged a claw into its electronic heart and whirred off to a computerised mate to 'breed'. I was watching the preview of an exhibition being staged by the head of a creative robotics unit. 'This behaviour represents pure survival of the fittest,' he said, happily preparing another combatant for the arena.

line 3

In the near future, the public will be able to watch as predators and prey do battle for limited supplies of electronic power.

line 5

These experiments are designed to develop robotic 'thinking', which will allow machines to adapt and survive in extreme conditions. A robot's success will depend on its ability to store the lessons of victory and defeat and learn from the experiences. The most successful will be bred. That involves taking half of each machine's set of 'artificial genes' – actually electronic chips which record the robot's actions – and joining them together. These will then be installed in a new robot and the resulting composite machine tested in further struggles.

In the demonstrations, small solar-powered robots, having topped up their energy levels under a powerful lamp, strove to evade larger, predator robots. The predators were fitted with power-draining units but, if defeated in their attempts to drain power from their victims, they died of electronic starvation. Eventually, the public will be encouraged to enter into the spirit of competition by cheering on their favourites, although there is a danger that humans will be cheering on their own species' doom.

42 In your own words, describe what is referred to by 'This behaviour' in line 3.

....

43 Which word used later in the text means the same as the word 'prey' in line 5?

....

44 In a paragraph of **50-70** words, summarise **in your own words as far as possible** the ways in which, according to the writers of **both** passages, scientists are trying to make their robots like humans. Write your summary **on the separate answer sheet.**

Appendix A

CPE Use of English Paper (June 2008)
Part 5

Answer Key

40	paraphrase of 'cater for our every whim',
	e.g. • capable of responding to **any** and **every** human's needs and requirements
	• serving humans and obeying their **every** order
	• doing **everything** for somebody

| 41 | (the) demise of humans |

| 42 | one robot killing / destroying / defeating another |

| 43 | victim(s) |

Content Points

(i)	make them look like humans / give them a human form
	Text A
(ii)	give them the ability to move around like humans.
	Text A
(iii)	idea of, change its facial expression AND/OR respond to human emotions
	Text A
(iv)	get them to learn from experience / remember events
	Text B
(v)	in the ability to be replicated / reproduced
	Text B

CPE Use of English Paper (June 2008)
Part 5

Mark Scheme

Band 5	Outstanding realisation of the task set:
	• Totally relevant
	• Concise and totally coherent
	• Skilfully organised, with effective use of linking devices
	• Skilfully re-worded, where appropriate
	• Minimal non-impeding errors, probably due to ambition
	Clearly informs and requires no effort on the part of the reader.

Band 4	Good realisation of the task set:
	• Mostly relevant
	• Concise and mostly coherent
	• Well organised, with good use of linking devices
	• Competently re-worded, where appropriate
	• Occasional non-impeding errors
	Informs and requires minimal or no effort on the part of the reader.

Band 3	Satisfactory realisation of the task set:
	• Generally relevant, with occasional digression
	• Some attempt at concise writing and reasonably coherent
	• Adequately organised with some appropriate use of linking devices
	• Adequately re-worded, where appropriate
	• Some errors, mostly non-impeding
	Adequately informs, though may require some effort on the part of the reader.

Band 2	Inadequate attempt at the task set:
	• Some irrelevance
	• Little attempt at concise writing, so likely to be over-length and incoherent in places OR too short
	• Some attempt at organisation, but only limited use of appropriate linking devices and may use inappropriate listing or note format
	• Inadequately re-worded and/or inappropriate lifting
	• A number of errors, which sometimes impede communication
	Partially informs, though requires considerable effort on the part of the reader.

Band 1	Poor attempt at the task set:
	• Considerable irrelevance
	• No attempt at concise writing, so likely to be seriously over-length and seriously incoherent OR far too short
	• Poorly organised, with little or no use of appropriate linking devices and/or relies on listing or note format
	• Poorly re-worded and/or over-reliance on lifting
	• Numerous errors, which distract and impede communication
	Fails to inform and requires excessive effort on the part of the reader.

Band 0	Negligible or no attempt at the task set:
	• Does not demonstrate summary skills
	• Incomprehensible due to serious error
	• Totally irrelevant
	• Insufficient language to assess
	• Totally illegible

Appendix B
Candidate Information Sheet

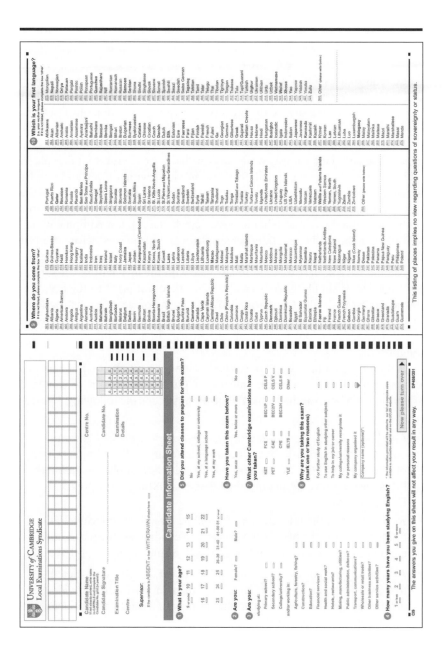

Appendix C
Administrative setting

The circumstances under which an examination takes place can significantly affect candidate performance. Test-taking conditions need to be equivalent across administration sites or the processing involved in completing test tasks may well differ in important respects and unreliable results may occur.

Precise steps must be laid down to ensure that the test is administered in exactly the same efficient way whoever is in charge or wherever it takes place. This requires that exam invigilators are provided with a clear and precise set of instructions and are familiar and comfortable with all aspects of the test before administering it; test settings should be of equivalent standards with appropriate facilities (chairs, desks, clock etc. ...); test equipment, e.g. CD players should be carefully screened for any problems before the test is administered; procedures for dealing with any candidates caught cheating should have been sorted out in advance with the invigilators; all administrative details should have been clearly worked out prior to the exam, in particular ground rules for late arrivals, the giving of clear test instructions, ensuring candidates have properly recorded their names and other necessary details (see Khalifa 2003 for a comprehensive approach to this aspect of test validity).

Within the Cambridge ESOL context, there are a number of publications dealing with the general requirements for the administration of standard Cambridge ESOL examinations. Publications include the following:

- *Cambridge ESOL Centre Registration Information Booklet* gives an outline of the responsibilities of centres in regard to the administration of Cambridge ESOL exams, particularly with new applicants in mind: https://www.esolcentrenet.org/digitalAssets/208148_CentreRegBklt_Exams__2008.pdf
- *Regulations* for the relevant year (available on www.CambridgeESOL. org) specify, for the benefit of schools and candidates, the terms and conditions under which Cambridge ESOL examinations are offered
- *Handbook for Centres* (available on CentreNet, a website restricted to Centre Examinations Managers and their support staff) provides detailed general information on the running of a centre and guidelines on the administration of the examinations:

https://www.esolcentrenet.org/digitalAssets/207954_Handbook_for_centres_2008.pdf

- the *Examination Instruction Booklets* provide detailed instructions and guidelines to supervisors and invigilators on the conduct of each examination in separate booklets: https://www.esolcentrenet.org/digitalAssets/207926_PET_2008_v4.pdf

All centre documentation is regularly updated by the Cambridge ESOL Centre Support Unit.

These publications, issued to Centre Examinations Managers, are supplemented by promotional materials for specific examinations such as exam specific handbooks or leaflets.

The administrative elements of the assessment, which may be centralised (i.e. Cambridge ESOL) or local (i.e. centre-based), include: ensuring that the candidates have information on what to expect when they are examined (the experiential dimension discussed in Chapter 2); making all necessary arrangements for the administration of papers under secure, standardised or special conditions (see Chapter 2 also for full discussion of Special Arrangements); providing the candidates with their results, with the means to interpret them and, if there are grounds, to have their results checked; and – to those candidates who have gained appropriate grades – issuing their certificates. Responsibility for these elements of carrying out assessment is shared between Cambridge ESOL administrative staff based in Cambridge and the centres where examinations take place (Centre Examinations Managers, their supervisors, invigilators, etc.)

A number of Cambridge ESOL candidates have special requirements (including those with a permanent or long-term disability or those with short-term difficulties) which make it difficult for them to demonstrate their ability in English. In such cases the appropriate action is to make special arrangements for these candidates so that, insofar as possible, they are then able to take the examination on an equal footing with other candidates (see Chapter 2 on test-taker characteristics in relation to Special Arrangements made before the candidate sits the examination and during the examination). Responsibilities for dealing with Special Requirements are distributed across a number of groups within Cambridge ESOL. One of those responsibilities is to give advice on the most appropriate arrangements for any given candidate. Special Arrangements fall into two main categories: those involving the provision of modified material (often in conjunction with administrative arrangements), and those involving administrative arrangements only.

Examination requirements and arrangements

Requirements of the place where the examination is held are such as to ensure that the range of Cambridge ESOL examinations is administered under secure conditions in circumstances conducive to the candidates performing to their best ability. To facilitate the carrying out of inspections, Centre Examinations Managers must complete and return at the earliest opportunity, a Venue Details form to the Cambridge ESOL Centre Inspections Officer, giving details of examination venues where these differ from the centre's main postal address.

All candidates (except for the YLE tests) are informed that they are required to provide evidence of identity at each separate paper, by passport, identity card, etc. Ensuring that candidates' identities are checked against photographic evidence – a key responsibility for Centre Examinations Managers – provides confidence regarding a candidate's true identity.

Cambridge ESOL has clear rulings on examination supervision. The purpose of supervision and invigilation is to ensure that all candidates are under surveillance for every moment of each examination period. Supervision and invigilation arrangements for the examinations are entrusted to the Centre Examinations Manager, who ensures that these tasks are carried out by suitably qualified people. Relatives of candidates in the examination room are specifically not eligible to serve as a supervisor or invigilator.

The supervisor is the person appointed at each centre or separate hall to be responsible for overseeing the general conduct of the examination sessions. The invigilator is the person in the examination room responsible for the conduct of a particular paper. In large centres, for example, with 100 candidates or more, Cambridge ESOL advises that the supervisor has an assistant. Sufficient invigilators are appointed to ensure that each examination paper is conducted in accordance with certain requirements, including having at least one invigilator for every 30 candidates, being able to observe each candidate at all times, the facility for lone invigilators to be able to summon assistance easily and so on. In the case of external venues, Cambridge ESOL may request centres to appoint an external supervisor, i.e. one not connected with the venue.

Centres keep signed records of the invigilation arrangements for each examination paper which are made available to Cambridge ESOL on request.

Supervisor and invigilator familiarity with the relevant notices and requirements relating to the specific Reading examination is assured through a document entitled Examination Instructions – a copy of which is kept in every examination room. It is also a requirement for a copy of the *Handbook for Centres* to be available in each examination venue.

Physical conditions

In Cambridge ESOL examinations the selection of venues must take into account a number of factors including general ambience, accessibility of location and suitability of rooms. Cambridge ESOL ensures that any room in which the examination is conducted, whether on centre premises or in an external venue, provides candidates with appropriate conditions in which to take the examination. Matters such as general cleanliness, air temperature, lighting, ventilation and the level of external noise are taken into careful consideration.

Candidates who do not comply with instructions which prohibit eating, drinking, smoking, carrying of digital recording equipment and possession of mobile phones during the examination, may be disqualified from taking the examination. Incidents of disqualification and malpractice are reported to Cambridge ESOL on the Report on Suspected Malpractice During Examinations form (see https://www.esolcentrenet.org/digitalAssets/207370_MALESOL_Form_-_Nov_2007.pdf).

Cambridge ESOL insists upon rooms offering certain facilities. A board must be visible to all candidates showing the centre number, the actual time that each component will start and the time at which it will finish. Moreover, the provision of a reliable clock – made visible to all candidates in the room – is regarded as essential.

The seating arrangements for all Cambridge ESOL examinations are such as to prevent candidates from overlooking, intentionally or otherwise, the work of others. Cambridge ESOL stipulates very exact seating arrangements. Each candidate is provided with adequate space for a reading question paper and answer sheet and at least 1.25 metres must be allowed between the centre of the desk assigned to any candidate and the centre of the desk assigned to the next candidate in any direction. Special care is taken to ensure distances are adequate, and are increased as necessary, for example, where some candidates are sitting higher than others. The use of chairs with side flaps is not permitted where these impede the candidate from being able to work with reading question papers and answer sheets side by side as in the case of full-size desks. The sharing of desks is discouraged. However, if desks are to be shared, the minimum distance between candidates is still observed. Candidates are seated in column layout in candidate number order, facing the same direction and their numbers are displayed clearly on each desk.

During the examination, a simple sketch plan is completed for each room which accompanies the answer sheets and/or question papers being returned to Cambridge ESOL. The plan indicates the position of each candidate by candidate number, the direction in which candidates are facing, and the distance between the rows of candidates and between the candidates in each row. The room plan also indicates the number and base position of invigilators. Each room plan is signed by the supervisor.

Uniformity of administration

A constant testing environment where the test is conducted according to detailed rules and specifications so that testing conditions are the same for all test takers is essential. If the uniformity rule is broken, for example by one centre giving extra time for a task, then the cognitive validity of the test is compromised because processing may as a result differ markedly across testing sites.

General conduct (for all examinations) covers starting the examination, supervision of candidates, completing the attendance register, late arrival of candidates, completing the room plan, leaving the examination room, irregular conduct, emergency procedures, Special Consideration (for candidates who have been disadvantaged), concluding the examination, collection of candidate answers and collection of question papers. In addition, detailed instructions for individual papers are provided in the instructions. Every supervisor in each centre is required to follow specific procedures for each of the respective examination papers.

The conduct of the Reading examinations

Cambridge ESOL question papers remain sealed so that they may be opened by the invigilator in the examination room in the presence of the candidates. Papers are not normally opened more than 10 minutes before the time at which the test is set to begin. Before candidates are permitted to start, the invigilator ensures that candidates are seated according to prescribed arrangements and that they conform to the regulations of the examination. At this point candidates will have their attention drawn to any Reading test instructions and are helped to complete any administrative requirements such as entering their names, candidate numbers and so on. Candidates are also informed as to when they may begin to answer with the time allowed for the paper specified.

A candidate who arrives late for a Reading paper may be admitted at the discretion of the supervisor or the Centre Examinations Manager who takes into account reason for lateness (normally not later than half way through the time allowed for the paper concerned) and possible disruption to the exam schedule. Late arrivals have separate invigilation and are given full instructions as issued to other candidates and are allowed the full schedule time for completion of the paper. However, if the candidate arrives for the Reading paper after any candidate has been released from the examination room, that candidate is not admitted nor are they accommodated in a separate sitting for the same paper but are recorded as an absentee.

According to the *Handbook for Centres* (UCLES 2008), where a candidate is admitted late into the examination any work done after the scheduled finishing time must be indicated, taking particular care where questions may have been answered non-sequentially. In cases where candidates are late for a good reason, for example, sudden illness or transport difficulties, so long as Cambridge ESOL is satisfied that there has been no breach of examination security, the work completed in the whole of the examination period will normally be accepted. The same applies in cases where candidates are late because of negligence or oversight, including over-sleeping and misreading of the timetable. The work completed in any additional time allowed to compensate for the late arrival, however, is not normally accepted.

All cases of irregularity or misconduct in connection with the examination are reported to Cambridge ESOL Results (Special Circumstances) by the Centre Examinations Manager, who is empowered to exclude or expel a candidate if the behaviour is considered disruptive to the other candidates. Any infringement of the regulations or any irregularity, misconduct or dishonesty may lead to the disqualification of the candidate. The decision on disqualification rests with Cambridge ESOL.

At the conclusion of the Reading test, candidates' scripts, answer sheets, etc., whether being returned to Cambridge ESOL or retained at the centre for safe destruction, are collected and accounted for before candidates leave the examination room. After collation, the attendance register, room plan and all answer materials are handed immediately to the person responsible for packing and despatching them to Cambridge ESOL or ensuring their security. All question papers for the Reading test – used and unused – are returned to Cambridge ESOL or destroyed securely by the centre. Scripts and answer sheets are packed in accordance with the instructions and despatched to Cambridge ESOL by the fastest means within five calendar days of the paper having been taken.

Cambridge ESOL reserves the right to visit centres unannounced during the period of the examinations to inspect the arrangements made for the security of confidential examination material and for the conduct of examinations. Inspections are intended to ensure that arrangements are in order, but can also offer opportunity to capture first-hand knowledge of any problems from the centre's point of view. Centre Examinations Managers are expected to point out the security facilities and examination rooms to visiting inspectors who may visit any Reading test being conducted. A copy of the inspector's report is left with the centre and any shortcomings identified in the report are invariably rectified immediately. In the case of an adverse report which indicates cause for concern, the Cambridge ESOL Centre Inspections Officer will write to the centre requesting written assurance that appropriate remedial action is being taken.

Security

This involves limiting access to the specific content of a test to those who need to know it for test development, test scoring, and test validation. In particular, test items of secure tests are not published; unauthorised copying is forbidden by any test taker or anyone otherwise associated with the test. If tests are not secure then some candidates would be able to prepare their answers in advance and their processing will be of an entirely different nature, i.e. solely reliant on memory.

Examination reading materials

Confidential examination materials, at both pre and post examination stage, are locked away in a place of high security such as a safe or non-portable, lockable, reinforced metal cabinet or other similar container. Cambridge ESOL requests that the safe or container is held in a securely locked room with access restricted to a small number of authorised persons. The room should preferably be windowless and on an upper floor; windows, whether internal or external, should be fitted with safety devices. Moreover, the door to the room is expected to be of a solid construction, have secure hinges and be fitted with a secure lock. If the security of the question papers or confidential ancillary materials is put at risk by fire, theft, loss, damage, unauthorised disclosure, or any other circumstances, Cambridge ESOL is informed immediately.

All materials – packed separately to ensure that question paper packets do not need to be opened before the test date – required for Cambridge ESOL examinations are despatched to centres according to the dates listed in the relevant administrative calendar, which is available to Centre Examinations Managers on CentreNet. On receipt of the materials, the Local Secretary is required to check the contents of the despatch carefully, giving particular attention to the question paper packets. This is done under strict security conditions. Question paper packets are checked against the timetable and arranged in timetable order so as to reduce the possibility of opening a packet of question papers at the wrong time.

Standard procedures for the production of examination materials

Cambridge ESOL employs a set of systems, processes and procedures for designing, developing and delivering its examinations (Reading papers included). This appendix provides a brief description of the standard procedures for the production of examination materials. They are reported in greater detail, though, in the *Handbook for Chairs, Routine Test Production Process* document, the *Production of Examination Materials Standard Operating Procedure* document and included in item writer guidelines as appropriate.

The appendix focuses on the process of question paper production (QPP) and the standard procedures employed in this process. It should be noted that these procedures and processes are certified as meeting the internationally recognised ISO 9001:2000 standard for quality management.

The key objectives of the QPP process are:

* production of valid tests to a defined timescale
* production of items and test papers that are of a consistently high quality and appropriate difficulty
* ensuring item banks contain the appropriate number of test items
* co-ordinating test production schedules to the appropriate time scales
* keeping an accurate record of items and test usage.

The production of exam material for any given paper is the responsibility of the subject officer for the paper, who is a Cambridge ESOL member of staff, and the chair of the Item Writing team, who is an external consultant. The subject manager, who is also a staff member, has the overall responsibility for all the papers in his/her suite of examinations.

The role of the chair is principally concerned with the technical aspects of writing the examination materials and ensuring that the item writers on the team are fully equipped to produce material to the best of their ability. The chair, in conjunction with the subject officer and other members of the team, ensures that tasks for their paper are appropriate in terms of topic, content and level and that they comply fully with the Specifications for the paper and item writer guidelines. The subject officer is responsible for managing the production of the examination material through the various stages, ensuring that sufficient material is produced to the agreed schedule and that test papers are produced to schedule and of the appropriate quality. Both the chair and the subject officer also bring expertise to the partnership from their experience of teaching and assessment.

Stages in QPP process

There are several stages in the production of an exam paper: commissioning, pre-editing, editing, pretesting, pretest review, paper construction and exam overview. Below, we provide a brief description of these stages/procedures.

Figure 1 opposite provides a visual representation of the question paper production (QPP) process.

Commissioning

Commissioning of item writers is the first stage of the QPP process and is a task that has been centralised for Cambridge ESOL exams. The aims of centralised commissioning are:

- to co-ordinate the timing of commissions
- to plan well in advance across all Cambridge ESOL examinations
- to co-ordinate and utilise effectively the item writer resource
- to standardise commissioning procedures across examinations.

The subject officer for each paper, in consultation with the subject manager and chair, determines the number of commissions and the amount of materials required for the forthcoming year in accordance with current banks of material and future requirements.

Pre-editing

Pre-editing takes place when commissioned tasks are received by Cambridge ESOL for the first time. The pre-editing stage is intended to select material which will progress in the production process and to improve the quality and maximise the quantity of material available for editing.

The aims of pre-editing are:

- To suggest appropriate changes to material requiring amendments or re-writing.
- By reference to the item writer guidelines, to reject unsuitable, problematic or weak material.
- To comment on the item writer's proposed exploitation of a text and suggest possible alternatives (where appropriate). However, it is not intended that material is edited or rewritten by the pre-editing team, as this is not a function of this stage.

Figure 1 Question paper production process

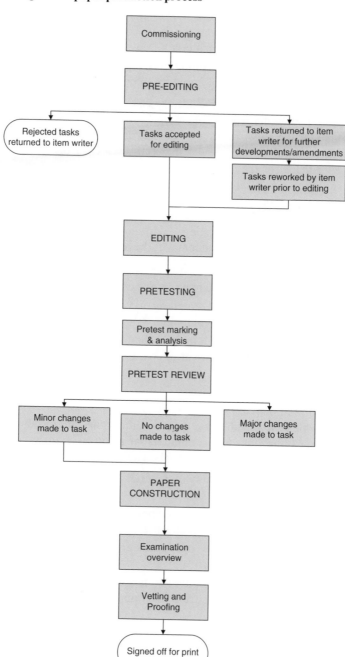

- To carry out an initial check on the descriptive system information provided on the Task Description form.
- To speed up the editing process (i.e. item writers will not have to spend time working on unsuitable material).
- To increase the efficiency of editing since rejection at editing of tasks accepted at pre-editing is not normally an option.

Participants in pre-editing include the chair, the subject officer, and an experienced item writer who is not currently on the team but has experience of working on the paper or on a similar paper at the same level. The pre-editing meeting attendees consider material, decide on the outcome, and prepare feedback for the item writers. Decisions are made on the basis of the quality of the material and conformity to the item writer guidelines. All decisions are based on or justifiable by reference to the item writer guidelines. Feedback to item writers is communicated on a form and/or notes on text completed at the pre-editing meeting.

The following are possible outcomes of the pre-editing stage:

- Material passes straight to the editing stage.
- Material is returned to the item writer for fine-tuning of items.
- Material requiring extensive re-writing may be re-submitted for pre-editing as part of a future commission.
- The material may be rejected. In this case it may be used for item writer training, item writer guidelines or offered to another suitable exam.

Editing

Materials which successfully pass the pre-editing stage are re-submitted for editing. The editing stage ensures that, as far as possible, material is of an acceptable standard for inclusion in trials. The aims of editing are:

- to check or re-check the quality of material against specifications and item writer guidelines
- to make any changes necessary to submitted materials so that they are of an acceptable standard for pretesting
- to ensure that the answer key and rubrics are appropriate and comprehensive
- to further develop the skills of item writers in order to improve the quality of materials submitted and the input of item writers to future editing sessions.

Each editing group meeting consists of the chair, the subject officer and members of the item writing team. Before the meeting writers send in all material for editing. Chairs check the material, as appropriate, to make sure all materials are ready for editing. The expectation at the meeting is that material should require minimal changes only. However, re-writing of items will sometimes be necessary, and may be an important part of training. Material is not usually rejected at editing on the grounds that it is of unacceptable quality or does not correspond with current guidelines relating to quantity, length, subject matter, level, etc. These aspects have been dealt with at the pre-editing stage. The final decisions on acceptability of material rest with the subject officer and chair.

Edited material is entered into the appropriate bank in LIBS (local item banking system), i.e. the edited bank. Attributes such as question type and text length are added according to the information on the task description form. The tasks are then sent to the chair, who checks them against the editing meeting copy for both content and typographical errors and makes any necessary amendments.

Pretesting

After the editing meeting the edited materials are checked by the chair in readiness for pretesting. The chair then combines tasks into pretests, which, as far as possible, mirror the format of the live test. The aims of pretesting are:

- to establish measurement characteristics
- to fine-tune rubrics
- to check that visual prompts are clear and accessible (where appropriate)
- to ensure that tasks are at an appropriate level, and
- to establish, as far as possible, that tests are equivalent in terms of difficulty of the question and output (vocabulary, functions and structures that candidates will need to use) in order to enable tests of comparable difficulty to be constructed and to confirm that material is of a suitable quality to be used in a live examination.

Edited material is pretested at selected centres/schools around the world on a large representative sample using anchor materials. Careful writing and editing should result in a high proportion of materials which are good enough to go into a live examination. To ensure the most effective use of the pretesting resource, experimental/new item types are normally trialled on smaller samples rather than fully pretested on large groups. The aim of pretesting is, therefore, to confirm that the materials are of a suitable quality to be used in a live examination.

Pretest review

After pretesting, a meeting is held to review the performance of materials. It aims at:

- reviewing pretested material in the light of candidate performance and feedback from candidates and centres, as appropriate; and evaluating the measurement characteristics of tasks and items
- finalising and ensuring that the material is acceptable for use in paper construction
- decision making, e.g. whether to bank the material for paper construction, rewrite or reject
- making essential adjustments to tasks so that, as far as possible, no editing will need to take place at the paper construction stage
- expanding and finalising the mark scheme where appropriate.

The review meeting takes place as soon as possible after the pretesting session. The chair, the subject officer, and an item writer participate in the meeting. Systematic feedback to item writers is provided either in writing after pretest review or as part of a separate item writer training/feedback day.

Paper construction

Paper construction aims to construct sufficient question papers to meet ongoing requirements and to ensure that question papers meet required standards in terms of level, coverage, content and comparability. Depending on the nature of the paper concerned, the chair may make a proposal for paper content in advance of the paper construction meeting. This meeting usually consists of the subject officer, the chair, an experienced item writer and a validation officer (as required). The chair initially and subsequently the teams at the meeting check that:

- a range of topics/tasks is maintained on each paper, bearing in mind the range of cultural perspectives desirable
- there is no obvious overlap in content either within a paper or historically
- the paper is at the right level (especially parallel tests)
- keys (where applicable) are accurate and comprehensive
- no two keys are the same (same thing not tested twice)
- options or vocabulary items do not appear twice
- the rubrics are correct.

The draft papers and Attribute reports are circulated to those attending in advance of the paper construction meeting for preliminary consideration of content, range of items, and statistical features such as the level of difficulty and range of discrimination. After the meeting, draft papers are amended by the paper administrator, any necessary amendments are made to LIBS keys and the subject officer checks all the material.

Examination overview

The aims of examination overview are:

• to review content of the examination in order to confirm earlier decisions made at paper construction
• to ensure the examination as a whole possesses the required continuity
• to check topics across the examination and historically
• to enable subject officers to communicate across papers and across examinations and to inform other subject officers of the content of the examination.

The examination overview meeting includes all subject officers working on the examination as a whole and the subject manager. Chaired by the subject manager, draft question papers are circulated and reviewed at the meeting. Decisions taken at paper construction or pretest review are looked at again, decisions are made on remedial action to be taken (if necessary) and the overall level of the paper is checked.

After the meeting, the subject manager checks any remedial action taken by the subject officers. Final copies of question papers are passed to the QPP Unit. Papers are sent out by secure post to the appropriate chairs and content vetters for content checking. Following this, subject officers review papers in the light of the feedback from chairs and content vetters. The papers are given a final check by two proof readers before being signed off for print.

Appendix E
General marking: performance management

1. Introduction

This document describes quality control procedures in the performance management of General Marking staff.

General Markers may be deployed on Scheduled, On-Demand or Pretesting assignments. The management of temporary General Marking (GM) staff is shown below:

Scheduled General Marking (GM):

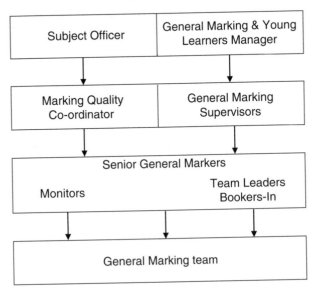

Permanent Cambridge ESOL staff, through the Team Leader and Booker-In, are responsible for administrative and procedural aspects of the marking, including script management and the monitoring of throughput to ensure that scheduled targets are met. The Marking Quality Co-ordinator (MQC), through the Monitor, is responsible for the content of the mark scheme and for ensuring that quality standards are met in terms of marking accuracy.

For On-Demand/Pretesting GM, the mark scheme is not subject to amendment during the earlier stages of marking. Therefore a Marking Quality Co-ordinator is not used.

2. General markers

2.1 Recruitment

General markers are employed on short- or mid-term fixed-period contracts. Initial contact is sometimes by newspaper advertisement, though a high proportion of returning seasonal workers often makes this unnecessary. Where General Markers have previous experience in the role, recruitment is based on performance history.

All new prospective General Markers are interviewed by Cambridge ESOL Human Resources staff. At interview, evidence is sought of the candidate's attitude and ability to express themselves clearly. Grade C GCSE English or equivalent is the required English-language standard. In addition to this, all applicants are required to complete (and pass at 80%) an aptitude test designed to provide evidence of attention to detail and language awareness at CEFR B2–C1 level.

References are taken up prior to the start of employment and all referees are asked to comment on the following qualities:

* reliability
* punctuality and attendance
* attitude to work and colleagues
* inter-personal skills
* honesty and integrity.

2.2 Training and co-ordination

The training of General Markers takes place on the first morning of the marking assignment.

Training in procedure is delivered by permanent members of Cambridge ESOL staff (typically the General Marking Supervisor). This is supported by work instructions describing the General Marker role.

Training in marking issues is delivered by the General Marking Supervisor in the case of On-Demand and Pretesting General Marking, and by the Marking Quality Co-ordinator in the case of Scheduled General Marking. This is supported by documentation on component-specific marking issues.

Co-ordination (i.e. version-specific training and the marking of non-live practice scripts) is delivered by the General Marking Supervisor or Marking Quality Co-ordinator immediately after training.

2.3 Monitoring and evaluation

General Markers are monitored on a daily basis by senior General Marking staff (Monitors). Feedback is given on both throughput and marking accuracy. Action may be taken in the case of General Markers who fail to meet the required standard of marking accuracy. This may consist of remedial training and co-ordination, or re-deployment to a simpler assignment.

At the end of the assignment, the performance of General Markers is appraised and graded according to the following performance descriptors:

Performance of an exceptional standard
Clear and consistent exceptional performance. A reasonable observer would recognise this performance as significantly above average.

Performance of a high standard
The job holder's performance was of a consistently very high standard. The job holder has achieved the set objectives well; some were exceeded in their requirement. The job holder made a significant contribution to the work of the team.

Performance of a good standard
The job holder's performance was of a good standard. The post holder contributed well to the work of the team, took responsibility for more than his/her work, and required little supervision.

Performance of an acceptable standard
The job holder achieved the set objectives to an acceptable standard. The job holder generally took responsibility for his/her own work and required only normal supervision.

Incomplete performance
Performance varied from the standards expected. Objectives were not always achieved. The post holder required more than normal supervision, and did not always take responsibility for his/her work. The post holder did not always contribute well to the work of the team.

Performance of an unacceptable standard
The job holder's performance fell well short of that which was acceptable. Objectives were not achieved. The job holder's performance was in general significantly below the expected level of competence for the grade. The work of the team suffered, or other members of the team had to 'carry' the job holder.

---

3 Senior General Markers

3.1 Recruitment

Senior General Markers (Team Leaders, Bookers-In and Monitors) are employed on short- or mid-term fixed-period contracts. The cadre is drawn, on the recommendation of the General Marking Supervisor, from experienced former members of the General Marking team with excellent performance history in terms of both procedural reliability and marking accuracy and speed. A very considerable majority of senior General Markers are highly experienced returning seasonal workers.

3.2 Training and co-ordination

The training, or re-training, of senior General Markers takes place on the first day of their assignment. This is typically one or two days before the team on which they are deployed start marking.

Training is delivered by the General Marking Supervisor. This is supported by work instructions describing the roles of Team Leader, Booker-In and Monitor.

For Monitors on Scheduled General Marking assignments, co-ordination (i.e. version-specific training and the marking of non-live practice scripts) is delivered by the Marking Quality Co-ordinator immediately after training. On-Demand and Pretesting Monitors are permanent members of ESOL staff.

3.3 Monitoring and evaluation

Senior General Markers are monitored on a daily basis by the General Marking Supervisor or Marking Quality Co-ordinator (in the case of Monitors). Feedback is given on performance and action may be taken in the case of senior General Markers who fail to meet the required standard. This may consist of remedial training and co-ordination, or re-deployment to a simpler assignment or to basic marking duties.

At the end of the assignment, the performance of senior General Markers is appraised and graded according to the same performance descriptors used for General Markers (see section 2.3 above).

4 Marking Quality Co-ordinators

4.1 Recruitment

Marking Quality Co-ordinators are contracted by a subject officer. It is also part of the subject officer's responsibility to manage the performance of Marking Quality Co-ordinators across all Scheduled General Marking components. Where vacancies occur, applications are invited from suitably qualified and experienced ELT professionals to take up short-term marking consultancies. Minimum professional requirements for the role are:

* education to Degree level or equivalent
* recognised TESOL qualification

- ability to carry out administrative tasks efficiently and to established deadlines
- good written and spoken communication skills.

All prospective Marking Quality Co-ordinators are interviewed by a panel of Assessment staff and complete a marking task, designed to measure marking accuracy and attention to detail. The task is used in interview as a platform for the discussion of professional issues arising from marking. References are taken up. Successful applicants are contracted on a session-by-session basis. A very high proportion of repeat consultancies are offered, resulting in a small cadre of Marking Quality Co-ordinators with a wealth of experience both individually and as a team.

4.2 Training and co-ordination

Marking Quality Co-ordinators are provided with documentation (the *Handbook for MQCs*) to provide both self-access training and reference. This describes all General Marking procedures and gives guidance in the interpretation of mark schemes. Newly contracted Marking Quality Co-ordinators are, where possible, given the opportunity to shadow experienced MQCs and are encouraged to discuss issues both with permanent Cambridge ESOL staff and with their peers.

Marking Quality Co-ordinators undergo co-ordination in version-specific marking issues as part of standard pre-marking procedures. They analyse a sample of live candidate responses and are responsible, with the subject officer, for producing the initial version of the mark scheme.

4.3 Monitoring and evaluation

The performance of MQCs is monitored on an ongoing basis by permanent members of Cambridge ESOL staff. There are also typically at least two progress meetings during the session, where issues brought up either by Marking Quality Co-ordinators or permanent members of Cambridge ESOL staff are discussed and addressed. MQCs work in partnership with ESOL administrative staff at marking venues and are in close daily contact with ESOL staff at Cambridge ESOL headquarters.

Marking Quality Co-ordinators' performance is evaluated at the end of each session by the subject officer responsible for MQC management, in consultation with colleagues. MQCs considered to have performed to a satisfactory level are likely to be asked to take on future contracts. Those whose performance is considered to be in need of improvement receive remedial feedback and are monitored especially closely in subsequent sessions. Those whose performance is considered to be unsatisfactory are not invited to take on subsequent contracts.

Computer-based (CB) reading tests versus paper-based (PB) versions: some issues and directions

Computer-delivered or computer-based (CB) language tests are becoming available in many areas of the world. At the same time, conventional paper-based (PB) testing continues to be the norm for many, thus CB and PB testing are likely to co-exist for some time. This situation of relying on two different modes of delivering a test calls for research into the comparability of CB and PB testing, and the research activity should provide answers to whether and when a test given in two modes can be comparable as well as what characteristics of the test and the test takers can threaten the equivalence between these two modes of testing. Although these issues apply to the testing of any language area, the present survey focuses on the testing of reading ability.

The research literature

As part of the ongoing research into the equivalence of actual and potential computer-based (CB) and paper-based (PB) versions of its Reading tests, a number of background reviews of the research literature have been commissioned by Cambridge ESOL. The first reported below is a general review of the literature on using CB and PB formats in the testing of reading by Shiotsu and Weir (2005). They were asked to establish what is known about the equivalence of testing reading in the two modes. This is followed by a second study by Salamoura and Brett (2007) who looked specifically at issues related to scrolling reading texts and the use of text highlighters in CB reading tests where lengthy passages are used as one means of making the experience in both modes more comparable. Both papers illustrate the commitment of Cambridge ESOL to achieving fairness in its testing operations.

This work is ongoing and a number of small scale empirical studies have also taken place to establish the equivalence of CB and PB formats (see Chapter 7 for an extended discussion of test equivalence). The reports on CB PET and CB IELTS in the section on Cambridge ESOL practice below provide details of the results of some of this research as well as other research in the area of CB/PB comparability.

Paper 1: Equivalence of PB and CB testing of reading in a second language: focus on the test outcomes and the test-taking processes

Introduction

The present paper attempts to review the past research studies that are relevant to the issue of the cross-mode equivalence of CB and PB testing of L2 reading ability, with an intent to identify adequate methodologies and potentially significant variables to be considered for a future empirical study in this area.

Cross-mode equivalence has been investigated in several different ways, and it is possible to view the work in this area as either focusing on the test outcomes or on the test-taking processes involved in the two modes of testing. The paper will first discuss research that employed test outcomes as evidence. Of the available research in this area, studies producing correlations and comparing score means across modes will be examined first. Those studies that shed light on the effects of some test-taker characteristics will then be examined, followed by those testing the factor structures underlying the observed performances on the tests administered in the two modes. After the analysis of the outcome-based research, emerging work addressing some process variables will be reviewed.

Focus on test outcomes

Considerable attention has been paid to establishing or investigating equivalence between PB and CB testing in terms of their psychometric outcomes.

A well-quoted guideline published by the APA (1986) on the psychometric equivalence of the computerised and conventional tests is most concerned with the test outcomes as measured via computer or paper. It states:

> When interpreting scores from the computerized versions of conventional tests, the equivalence of scores from computerized versions should be established and documented before using norms or cutting scores obtained from conventional tests. Scores from conventional and computer administrations may be considered equivalent when (a) the rank orders of scores of individuals tested in alternative modes closely approximate each other, and (b) the means, dispersions, and shapes of the score distributions are approximately the same, or have been made approximately the same by rescaling the scores from the computer mode (APA 1986:18).

Without explicitly referring to these conditions, a number of studies have published empirical data related to the equality of the rank orders or that of the means.

Cross-mode correlations as evidence of equivalence

Equality of rank orders can be established through cross-mode correlation, and it is reported in many studies researching cross-mode equivalence of cognitive abilities testing. Mead and Drasgow (1993) conducted a meta-analysis of past studies with adult L1 (English) test takers which addressed the comparability of computerised and PB cognitive ability tests, some of which involved reading comprehension explicitly and/or other abilities which seem partly related to reading (e.g. verbal reasoning). Based on 159 correlations corrected for measurement error, they estimated the cross-mode correlation in timed power tests to be .95 and that in speeded tests to be .72. Results of their moderator analysis indicated that speededness was a factor that affected the cross-mode correlation coefficient. Although the moderator analysis also suggested that the correlations varied depending on the test battery analysed, even the lowest coefficient obtained for any power test battery was .90. Based on this data, Mead and Drasgow concluded that 'there is no medium effect for carefully constructed power tests' (1993:457).

Mead and Drasgow's findings suggest that it is relatively easier to make PB and CB power tests comparable than speed tests and that some test takers may be advantaged or disadvantaged depending on the test mode if the test involved an element of speededness. Speededness as typically employed in the assessment of clerical skills or cognitive development seldom features in L2 reading tests and may seem unrelated to the language learners. Nevertheless, presence of any time limit can present the test taker with time pressure, and test takers are expected to vary in their actual processing speed and thus their sense of speededness of the test. Therefore, in addition to the obvious test duration, information on the test taker's sense of speededness of the test, or at least whether they had enough time to complete the test, should be collected for analysis when comparing cross-mode test performances.

More recently, there have been several studies which included a correlational analysis of reading or a closely related skill tested in the CB and PB modes with fairly large samples (de Beer and Visser 1998, Neuman and Baydoun 1998, Taylor et al 1998, Choi, Kim and Boo 2003). While most of these studies also compared the score means in the two modes of testing, such comparisons will be discussed separately in a later section, and the present section concentrates on their correlational data.

De Beer and Visser (1998) administered to more than 600 16-year-olds in South Africa both PB and CB versions of an identical scholastic aptitude test, which contained a verbal ability subsection. The participants took the test in two modes, otherwise identical in contents. The order of testing was varied, and the Verbal section scores from the two versions correlated at .91 and .96 depending on the order of testing.

A study by Neuman and Baydoun (1998) was concerned with the cross-mode equivalence of a timed clerical test, which included a 13-item paragraph reading subsection. With their more than 400 university students, they obtained a cross-mode correlation of .84 for this subsection, whose contents were identical across modes.

Taylor et al's (1998; see also Eignor, Taylor, Kirsch and Jamieson 1998 and Kirsch, Jamieson, Taylor and Eignor 1998) study involved more than 1,000 individuals taking the TOEFL CBT, and their PB TOEFL scores were available for correlational analyses. The cross-mode correlation for the Reading subsection was .69. Unlike de Beer and Visser (1998) and Neuman and Baydoun (1998) studies, the two TOEFL versions for Taylor et al's study differed in content. It is unknown whether all the examinees received a common set of items within the PB and CB modes or whether they varied across the examinees.

Choi, Kim and Boo's (2003) research involved EFL learners at Korean universities (n = 258) and their test content differed between CB and PB modes. Reading was one of four areas tested in both modes, and its cross-mode correlation was .63. When corrected for measurement error, the coefficient improved to .93.

Of the four studies just referred to, the first two studies (de Beer and Visser 1998, Neuman and Baydoun 1998), in which a common set of items were used across the two test modes, produced correlations in the .80s and .90s, whereas the last two (Taylor et al 1998, Choi et al 2003), in which the items differed across the modes, resulted in correlations in the .60s. It is notable that correcting for measurement error in Choi et al's (2003) study raised the cross-mode correlation to the .90s. Although this correction was not attempted by Neuman and Baydoun (1998) nor by Taylor et al (1998), it is possible that correcting for measurement error can improve the cross-mode correlations significantly. Along with Mead and Drasgow's (1993) meta-analysis of the correlations on timed power tests from earlier research, these relatively recent studies give indications that reading test scores from CB and PB modes can correlate quite substantially, especially after correcting for measurement error (see also Blackhurst 2005, Green and Maycock 2004 and 2005 for further evidence of this in relation to Cambridge ESOL examinations).

Where reading is a subset of several different skills measured in CB and PB modes, it is possible to assess the degree to which the reading test given in one mode correlates more strongly with another reading test given in the opposite mode than with a test of another skill given in the same mode. Such a case would strengthen the notion that a common construct is measured by the two different modes of testing reading, whereas the reverse would weaken it. Neuman and Baydoun (1998), Taylor et al (1998), and Choi et al's (2003) research design allowed this type of analysis.

In Neuman and Baydoun's (1998) study, Reading ability was assessed along with nine other subskills (e.g., Grammar, Punctuation, Spelling, Vocabulary), and the cross-mode correlation for Reading ($r = .84$) was stronger than any of the correlations between Reading and non-Reading skills ($r = .33$ to $.68$). Taylor et al's (1998) TOEFL data generally produced a similar pattern, with a Reading in one test mode showing stronger correlation with its cross-mode counterpart ($r = .69$) than with any other subskills measured in the same mode ($r = .64$ and $.67$). One exception was that in the PB mode, Reading correlated with PB Structure subsection at .76, which exceeded the Reading cross-mode correlation. The study by Choi et al (2003) included Listening, Grammar, and Vocabulary measures together with Reading in CB and PB modes, and the cross-mode correlation for Reading ($r = .63$) was lower than many correlations between two subscores from the same mode (e.g., $r = .71$ between CB Reading and Vocabulary, $r = .70$ between PB Reading and Grammar). Among the three studies reviewed here, Neuman and Baydoun (1998) is the only study which used a common set of items across the two modes. This may be one reason their results showed a clear advantage in terms of cross-mode correlations.

Comparisons of cross-mode correlations for several different subscores were also possible in the three studies referred to above (Neuman and Baydoun 1998, Taylor et al 1998, Choi et al 2003). Neuman and Baydoun's (1998) data showed their cross-mode correlation for Reading subsection ($r = .84$) to be comparable with such subsections as Spelling ($r = .84$), Grammar ($r = .83$), and Vocabulary ($r = .80$) but lower than others such as Punctuation ($r = .92$) and Oral Directions ($r = .91$). Taylor et al (1998) found a lower cross-mode correlation for the Reading section ($r = .69$) than for other subsections in TOEFL ($r = .71$ and $.73$), and the same pattern emerged in Choi et al's results, with the cross-mode correlation for Reading ($r = .63$) exceeded by those for other subskills tested ($r = .67$ to $.76$). Taylor et al (1998) and Choi et al (2003) both revealed the relative but clear weakness of cross-mode correlations in the test of reading compared with other language skills.

Though not directly related to CB testing, there has been a report on a correlational analysis in which any of the multiple versions of a reading test correlated more strongly with a grammar test score than any other versions of a reading test (Alderson 1993 and see also Weir 1983 for a similar finding), and this was the case when the tests were given in the PB mode alone. It is thus a possibility that it is relatively more difficult to achieve similarities in the rank orders across different versions of a reading test regardless of the test mode. If that is the case, cross-mode correlation for a reading test should be evaluated in light of correlations achieved between reading tests in the same test mode. It is thus recommended that not only non-reading skills be added in the test battery in both PB and CB modes, multiple measures of reading ability should also be included so that cross-mode correlation in the area of reading ability can be assessed within a reasonable frame of reference.

In addition to the surface-level bivariate correlations of the reading outcome measures across modes, Neuman and Baydoun (1998) and Choi et al (2003) were both able to submit their data to confirmatory factor analysis, which will be discussed in a separate section.

Equivalence of score means as evidence

Another common approach to investigating cross-mode equivalence is comparing the reading test outcomes in terms of score means across the two modes.

Previous reviews

A number of reports with L1 readers as test takers are available, many of which are already reviewed elsewhere (Dillon 1992, Bugbee 1996, Sawaki 2001, McDonald 2002).

Dillon (1992) reviewed studies published mostly in the 1980s and stated that 'it would seem as if reading from VDU (Visual Display Unit = computer screen) does not negatively affect comprehension rates, though it may affect the speed with which readers can attain a given level of comprehension (p. 1304).' Together with Mead and Drasgow's (1993) finding above, of the weaker relationship for speeded measures, Dillon's conclusion seems to add support to the view that a speed factor needs to be accounted for when investigating cross-mode comparability of reading tests.

Several other reviews pertaining to the issue of equivalence between CB and PB testing are available (Mazzeo and Harvey 1988; Bunderson, Inouye, and Olsen 1989; Wise and Plake 1989; Bugbee 1996; Sawaki 2001; McDonald 2002). Among these, one that was concerned with an L2 reading test and is thus directly relevant to the present paper is Sawaki (2001), in which a section is devoted to nine selected studies on the comparability of reading tests in CB and PB modes (Belmore 1985; Heppner, Anderson, Farstrup and Weiderman 1985; Reinking and Schreiner 1985; Reinking 1988; Fish and Feldmann 1987; Feldmann and Fish 1988 and McKnight, Richardson and Dillon 1990; McGoldrick, Martin, Bergering and Symons 1992), and they are compared in depth.

According to Sawaki (2001), though there are a number of unresolved issues to be kept in mind in evaluating these studies, '(i)n terms of the level of reading comprehension, six studies out of the nine reported that comprehension level was similar across the modes . . . while one favored paper . . ., and two showed interactions . . . (p. 47)'. As with the studies reviewed by Dillon (1992), evidence from the comprehension performance seems to be more in favour of equivalence, rather than discrepancy, across modes. Findings on the reading speed are more mixed. Six of the nine studies additionally compared the test takers' reading speed, and three of them reported longer reading time on screen than on paper while the other three demonstrated no significant difference in reading time across modes. Of note is the gain observed in two of the six studies in CB reading speed as the experiments proceeded, which suggests the possible effect of mode familiarity. While computer familiarity needs proper treatment in the cross-mode comparability studies, possible effects of test order must also be accounted for by counter-balancing the order of testing.

Those empirical studies reviewed in Dillon (1992) and Sawaki (2001) were typically based on computer devices that were common in the 1980s, and it is reasonable to assume that advances in technology have brought changes to not only the qualities of the devices for CB testing but also access of the wider population of people, including prospective CB test examinees, to such devices. It is therefore necessary to update the research base in this area to account for this dynamic relationship between the state of the CB test devices currently available and the current state of the test-taking population. The present paper thus focuses on the relatively recent development in the empirical investigations of test comparability across the CB and PB modes.

Specific research studies

The last decade saw a number of additional research studies on the comparability of CB and PB testing, some of which included a reading comprehension component. These studies compared the score means across test modes, and they either used the test mode as a between-subjects factor or a within-subject factor. In the former case, different individuals are assigned to each of the two test conditions, while in the latter, the same individuals are tested in both conditions. The equal rank order condition can only be assessed in the latter case, and the former case requires a prior test of equivalence of the compared groups on a baseline reading ability measure such as a common PB test. This section focuses on score mean comparisons in studies of within-subject design and those of between-subjects design which demonstrated baseline equality of the compared groups.

Studies such as de Beer and Visser (1998), Neuman and Baydoun (1998), and Choi et al (2003) adopted the within-subject design, which allows for cross-mode correlations (see above) as well as score mean comparisons between the modes.

De Beer and Visser (1998) compared performances on PB and CB versions of an identical scholastic aptitude test for South African L1-English students, which contained a verbal section. Of their two fairly large participant groups ($n = 242$ and 371), the first initially took the CB version and subsequently the PB version and did significantly better in the PB mode, and the means for the other group, who took the two versions in the reverse order, were not significantly different. The lower mean on the CB version for the first subgroup can be attributable to their unfamiliarity with CB testing. De Beer and Visser's data remind us of the need to introduce means for minimising the impact of test mode unfamiliarity.

Neuman and Baydoun (1998) administered both CB and PB versions of an identical clerical skills test that included a paragraph reading subsection to more than 400 university students. The reading score means were very similar across modes, and the results of item bias analysis on the whole test battery identified only a few out of their entire 400 items as marginally but significantly different between the two versions. The authors interpreted this to indicate that overall the items 'did not function differently across formats' (p. 78), with the implication that the paragraph reading measures did not function differently across modes.

Unlike the two studies just reviewed, Choi, Kim and Boo's (2003) research involved L2 learners (of English at Korean universities; n = 258) and their test contents differed across modes. Reading was one of four areas tested in both modes, and care was taken to avoid topic bias across modes. No order effect was evident though a significant mode effect indicating relative diffi-culty in CB mode was. The authors partly attribute the lower scores and reli-ability (alpha = .60) in this mode to test mode unfamiliarity, reflected in their students' self-reported 'eye fatigue' during CB testing. Blackhurst (2005) also points to the possibility that some candidates may experience fatigue when reading extended passages on computer. He notes Wolfe and Manalo's (2004) recommendation that test designers 'think seriously about providing examinees with a choice of composition medium . . . particularly when high-stakes decisions will be made based upon the test results' (p. 61).

The three fairly recent and large scale research studies that were just reviewed (de Beer & Visser 1998, Neuman and Baydoun 1998, Choi et al 2003) seem to provide support for cross-mode comparability, although concerns remain in the case of some L2 readers unfamiliar with CB testing. Further improvements in ergonomic features, including display quality, are expected to reduce the effects of computer unfamiliarity, which nevertheless constitutes an important research variable today (cf. Taylor et al 1998).

Studies reviewed so far have adopted the within-subject design, which enables not only the comparison of the score means but also that of the rank orders across modes by means of correlational analysis (see the section on correlation above). In contrast, studies adopting between-subjects design do not permit cross-mode correlation, thus no evidence will be collected on the equality of rank orders. Nevertheless, this less-than-ideal method is employed rather frequently and some studies appear to merit our review.

Between-group comparison for testing cross-mode equivalence requires a baseline measure of the compared groups so that the equivalence of their abili-ties can be established or, in the case of non-equivalence, cross-mode compari-son can take account of the variance on the baseline measure. Two studies that included such measures are Russell and Haney (1997) and Russell (1999).

Russell and Haney's (1997) study involved 86 secondary school students responding to instruments containing 'Language Arts' sections. The group means were not significantly different on a baseline measure nor were they on the criterion Language Arts scores. However, when the criterion measure was subjected to separate *post hoc* analyses on multiple-choice and short-answer items, significant difference was found on the Short Answer items favouring the CB group. Although it was not possible to tease out the student performance on reading, the results of Russell and Haney's study imply that test mode and test method might interact and affect test performance under certain conditions.

In his later study, Russell (1999) tested over 100 secondary school students in several subject areas including 'Language Arts' in one of PB and CB testing conditions. Russell's Language Arts measures consisted of both reading and writing tasks in open-ended format and no reading subscore was presented. The group means did not differ significantly on the baseline reading achievement measure nor on their composite Language Arts measures. In addition to test mode, Russell also explored the possible effects of the test takers' past computer experiences and their keyboarding skills and found that, when subgroups of faster typists from the two modes were compared, the score mean was higher for the CB group than the PB group. Although the impact of this variable is likely to be less significant on a reading measure than on writing, it points to the need to consider variables like keyboarding skills in any investigation of cross-mode equivalence.

It has to be remembered that Russell and Haney (1997) and Russell (1999) are based on the between-subjects comparison and do not address the rank order side of the equivalence conditions (APA 1986). To those of us interested in the effects of test mode on reading test performance in particular, their results are confounded and difficult to interpret as it was obviously not their goal to address reading test performance exclusively. Nevertheless, their studies usefully underscore the need to consider factors that might interact with the test mode to influence the cross-mode equivalence of reading test performance, such as item format and keyboarding skills. Sawaki (2001) discusses previous research on the interaction of examinee characteristics and testing conditions and concludes that it should be covered in future comparability studies for L2 reading tests. In the context of examining comparability of CB and PB testing, test-taker characteristics have been considered in some studies, to which we will now turn.

Test-taker characteristics

Attention to the possible effects of test-taker characteristics on the equivalence of CB and PB testing is not a new phenomenon. The review by Wise and Plake (1989) is one of those which Bugbee (1996) labels 'ancient reviews' of comparability research, and they concluded that neither computer anxiety nor computer inexperience significantly affected performance differences. That conclusion certainly did not stop other researchers investigating these variables, and an extensive review by McDonald (2002) still identifies computer familiarity, along with computer anxiety and computer attitudes, as having an impact on the equivalence of the two modes of testing. This section discusses some additional studies, including a computer-based assessment of reading ability, that also address test-taker characteristics (Vogel 1994; Taylor, Jamieson, Eignor and Kirsch 1998; Shermis and Lombard 1998; Clariana and Wallace 2002), and attempts to identify test-taker characteristics that deserve further attention in future research.

Vogel (1994) explored how some types of trait anxiety, computer anxiety and computer experience affected the equivalence of scores on the verbal section of CB and PB Graduate Record Examination (GRE) and found a cross-mode correlation of .66 and no significant test version or mode order effect. Vogel's main findings based on separate ANOVAs showed the following: students in the low computer anxiety subgroup scored higher on CB than those with mid or high computer anxiety; the mid computer anxious subgroup scored higher on CB than on PB; introverts scored higher on CB than on PB, and they outperformed extroverts on CB; computer experience did not interact with test mode. Computer anxiety and introversion/extroversion are shown to be potentially significant and are worth our further research efforts. If these test-taker characteristics interact with test mode among university students reading in L1, their impact on L2 reading can be even more significant.

Aside from trait and computer anxiety, one test taker variable that has repeatedly been mentioned in the context of cross-mode comparability is familiarity with or experience in computer use (Wise and Plake 1989, de Beer and Visser 1998, Russell 1999, Sawaki 2001, McDonald 2002). A study involving more than 1,000 TOEFL examinees by Taylor et al (1998) was concerned exactly with this variable. Unlike the studies reviewed so far, Taylor et al did not focus on score mean equivalence across modes, but instead they compared the CB test performances of computer-familiar and computer-unfamiliar groups, using their PB TOEFL score as the covariate; they found no meaningful relationship between level of computer familiarity and level of CB test performance.

Shermis and Lombard (1998) attempted to compare the effects of several personal characteristics of their university students on computer-delivered tests in three skill areas including reading, and they identified age and computer anxiety as significant, since older students and students with lower computer anxiety performed better than their counterparts on the CB reading test. It has to be pointed out that since the test was only conducted in the CB mode, the question remains whether the same or different pattern would have emerged had the researchers collected data on the PB mode as well.

A study by Clariana and Wallace (2002) was designed to consider the effects of such test-taker variables as content familiarity and computer familiarity on the outcomes of their end-of-term test of the course contents in a computer fundamentals class at a university. They found the main effect of test mode favouring the CB testing group as well as a significant interaction of test mode and content familiarity, which they operationalised as the students' final course grade. The researchers' use of between-subjects design without any attempt to control for inherent group differences and their rather coarse operationalisation of the content familiarity variable are some sources of concern, especially given that the students had just undergone a heavily computer-oriented course prior to the test. It is also difficult to assess the degree to which reading of text was required in their test of content knowledge. It should still be interesting to consider the effects of content familiarity on the equivalence of CB and PB tests of reading if it is indeed possible to operationalise it with more rigour.

Studies reviewed so far identified such test-taker characteristics as age, computer anxiety, computer experience and familiarity, introversion/extroversion, and content familiarity as potential sources of threat to equivalence of CB and PB test scores.

Taylor et al (1998) argued, based on a large dataset, that whether the test taker was computer-familiar or not was not a determining factor on CB test performance after an adequate tutorial on CB test procedure is completed. Similarly, studies by Vogel (1994) and Clariana and Wallace (2002) did not find any obvious effect of computer familiarity or experience. On the other hand, Russell's (1999) data indicated that the keyboarding skills of the test takers can interact with test mode. Effect of familiarity with computer or CB testing is suspected by some as possible explanations for the lower CB scores in their comparisons (de Beer and Visser 1998, Choi et al 2003). Even with the widespread use of personal computers in our daily lives, individual differences in basic computer operation skills including keyboarding skills are expected to remain to some degree. Tutorials and practice sessions should serve to narrow these individual differences, but it is certainly premature to dismiss this variable as unworthy of investigation.

Another test-taker characteristic addressed in some studies above is computer anxiety. Both Vogel's (1994) and Shermis and Lombard's (1998) results suggested that computer anxiety does have an impact on CB test performance or the equivalence of CB and PB testing. However, the details of their results differed considerably, making any generalisation extremely difficult. It is thus necessary to continue to address the test takers' computer anxiety in future comparability studies.

Variables suggested as significant in some contexts are age (Shermis and Lombard 1998), introversion/extroversion (Vogel 1994), and content familiarity (Clariana and Wallace 2002). Work on these variables is still very limited and any generalisations from them need to wait for further development of research in this area.

Evidence of equivalence based on factor structures

Most past studies on the comparability of CB and PB tests compared the score means in the two modes with some additionally evaluating cross-mode correlations. In addition to such focus on the differences in and interrelationships among observed performance measures, attention also needs to be paid to the pattern of score relationships in terms of factor structures as recommended by Steinberg, Thissen and Wainer (1990), Mead and Drasgow (1993), and Sawaki (2001). Two of the studies on the comparability issue that examined such factor structures were Neuman and Baydoun (1998) and Choi et al (2003) reviewed in earlier sections.

In Neuman and Baydoun's (1998) study, reading skill was one of 10 constructs measured on both CB and PB modes of testing, and they submitted their data from their more than 400 examinees to confirmatory factor analysis (CFA) to test if the two scores on the different modes of testing for each of the 10 constructs are best accounted for by a common underlying factor. Therefore, their model included a total of 10 underlying factors each of which was thought to account for the examinee performances on the two modes of testing a particular skill like reading. Their results supported this model and the notion that a common underlying ability is elicited through the CB and PB testing.

Choi et al's (2003) CFA followed a similar procedure to Neuman and Baydoun's (1998) and tested a model in which each of their four target constructs of Listening, Grammar, Vocabulary, and Reading abilities accounts for scores from both modes of testing those distinct skills. Choi et al's data fits sufficiently well with their model, thus the notion that a common underlying ability is responsible for the observed performances in both CB and PB modes was supported. As reviewed earlier, cross-mode correlation for the Reading subtest was the lowest ($r = .63$) among their four subskills tested, and this also coincided with the lowest factor loadings of the two Reading scores on the Reading ability factor (.79 each).

Despite the relatively lower cross-mode correlations reported for the reading tests in an earlier section, both of the factorial studies reviewed here supported the hypothesis that a common underlying ability is assessed whether it is in the CB mode or in the PB mode. The approach taken in these studies provides an additional perspective in the analysis of cross-mode equivalence, and it should be employed in future comparability studies whenever feasible.

Focus on test-taking process

Studies reviewed so far were concerned with the equivalence of test outcomes or identifying test-taker characteristics that might threaten the equivalence of test outcomes. The latent variables in the confirmatory factor analyses were derived from the observed test outcomes as well. The focus of the research activities was thus the outcomes in the two test modes rather than the processes involved in taking the reading test on computer and paper or how comparable these processes might be. While examination of such processes is expected to offer additional windows through which the nature of different test modes can be researched, there is a clear lack of work in this area, which is in stark contrast with the abundance of reports on the CB and PB test outcomes. Three studies which consider process-oriented data from CB and PB test of reading are reviewed below (Mayes, Sims and Koonce 2001; Noyes and Garland 2003; Noyes, Garland and Robbins 2004).

Mayes, Sims and Koonce (2001) conducted two studies in which university students were assessed on their reading comprehension in either CB or PB mode. The researchers were also interested in the mental workload involved in the processes of taking a reading test on computer or paper and administered a questionnaire called NASA-TLX (Task Load Index; Hart and Staveland 1988), which was designed for rating 'the workload of a task immediately after task completion' (Mayes et al 2001:372). In the first of their two experiments, no effect of test mode was found, but their correlational data indicated that those who reported experiencing more mental workload tended to perform poorly on reading comprehension regardless of the test mode. In their second experiment, the researchers added an increased workload condition by having half of the participants in each test mode hear a meaningless string of consonants during the passage reading and recall them afterwards. While the participants' perception of workload as monitored through TLX was not influenced by the addition of the letter string recall task, 'those reading from a VDT (visual display text) were found to have somewhat lower comprehension scores when a working memory load was present, $F(1, 47) = 3.66$, $p = 0.06$' (p. 376). Use of between-subjects design makes us cautious in interpreting Mayes et al's results, but their analysis of workload shows promise in capturing an aspect of the test-taking process which might differ across the test modes.

Noyes and Garland (2003) attempted to address the memory processes that might take place when responding to a reading task on paper and computer. On the assumption that knowledge can be in one of the four states of 'Remember', 'Know', 'Familiar', or 'Guess' (Conway, Gardiner, Perfect, Anderson and Cohen 1997), they had university students report the perceived state of their knowledge when answering the post-reading comprehension questions. They found no main effect of test mode on the comprehension scores, but they discovered that different test modes resulted in slightly different states of knowledge about the points tested. Namely, the CB mode elicited many more 'Remember' responses than 'Know' responses, whereas the PB mode provoked almost the same number of 'Remember' and 'Know' responses. Based on these results, Noyes and Garland concluded that 'there are differences in cognitive processing taking place when learning from VDT (computer screen) and paper' (p. 421). Unfortunately, Noyes and Garland too adopted a between-subjects design, which complicates the interpretation of the results. A within-subject comparison of the memory conditions between the CB and PB modes needs to be conducted to eliminate the possibility of inherent group differences in future studies if the knowledge states are to be further researched.

Another study by Noyes, Garland and Robbins (2004) was similar in intent to Mayes et al's (2001) study quoted above. They had university students read a text of over 1,800 words in either CB or PB mode and respond to NASA-TLX to assess their mental workload after the reading. Although no main effect of the test mode was found on their comprehension scores, the two test mode groups differed in one of the TLX subscales, 'perceived effort', meaning that more mental effort was felt to be involved in completing the reading task by those in the CB condition than their PB counterparts. Their correlational data replicated Mayes et al's (2001) findings in that comprehension performances were negatively related to the perceived mental workload. Again, their study was of the between-subjects design and requires caution. Following the similar results obtained in Mayes et al (2001) and Noyes et al (2004), it seems worth the effort to collect data on the mental workload required in completing the reading tasks in the two modes of testing the students' reading comprehension.

The three studies just reviewed above all adopted the between-subjects design, which is not truly capable of evaluating the effects of test mode. The suggested relationships between perceived workload and test mode should be examined with data from the same individuals performing the tasks in both modes. If the findings above are replicated in such within-subject studies, then these process variables must be examined more fully. Asking the examinee's state of knowledge on each item as done by Noyes and Garland (2003) is not easily possible and requires a dedicated effort by the researchers. If feasible, however, the approach has the potential of revealing some differences in the process of taking the reading test in CB and PB modes. As seen above, process-related research is extremely limited, and there is an obvious need for expanding research in this area (Sawaki 2001). Both quantitative and qualitative data must be collected through questionnaires, interviews, and recall or online protocols to complement the emerging findings of the types introduced in this section.

Summary of the findings

The previous sections have reviewed past research which addressed the comparability of a reading test in CB and PB modes in terms of test outcomes and cognitive processes involved. The bulk of the work compared the test outcomes in the form of score means in the two modes of testing, with some of them additionally examining cross-mode correlations.

Achieving similar rank orders and means across modes is said to be one of two necessary conditions of equivalence between the test modes (APA 1986), and a cross-mode correlation can serve as evidence of similarity in rank orders. From a meta-analysis of a large number of previously published correlational analyses (Mead and Drasgow 1993), it was found that speeded tests generally produced a much lower level of cross-mode correlation than did timed power tests. It is thus much more difficult to achieve equivalence between two speeded tests than between two power tests. Reading tests which are meant to be timed power tests can in fact require L2 learners' speeded processing, and the sense of speededness must vary depending on the learner. It is therefore recommended that the test taker's sense of speededness of the test and whether they felt they had sufficient time should be recorded.

More recent test mode comparability studies producing cross-mode correlations were also reviewed. Cross-mode correlations were high when tests in the two modes contained the same items (de Beer and Visser 1998, Neuman and Baydoun 1998), but they were somewhat lower when they did not (Taylor et al 1998, Choi et al 2003). Nevertheless, correction for measurement errors is likely to improve the cross-mode correlation to an adequately high level. Therefore, data available on cross-mode correlation is generally supportive of the similarity of the rank orders. However, our database on cross-mode correlation for a reading test is still limited and more work in this area is necessary.

Studies employing other skill variables along with reading were able to examine the correlations between reading and non-reading variables in the same mode, which should be lower than the cross-mode correlation for reading to be evidence of discriminant validity. This was the case in Neuman and Baydoun (1998) and largely so in Taylor et al (1998) but not in Choi et al (2003). These studies also allowed for comparisons of various cross-mode correlations, and in both Taylor et al (1998) and Choi et al's (2003) studies, the cross-mode correlations for reading were lower than those for other subscores such as Listening, Grammar/Structure, or Vocabulary. There is a possibility that in passage based reading tests it is relatively more difficult to obtain high correlations between different versions regardless of the test mode. As well as the different features of presentation conditions, text and item characteristics should be made available for evaluation of the results, and it is recommended that a baseline correlation between the different versions of the passage reading test in the PB mode be obtained before these versions are used in cross-mode studies so that it can be evaluated in light of that baseline correlation.

Another criterion of test equivalence is equal score means and distributions. In the studies using the test mode as the within-subjects factor, the two modes produced comparable means when the item contents were constant across modes and when the PB version was given before the CB version (Neuman and Baydoun 1998, de Beer and Visser 1998). However, the only study available involving L2 learners (Choi et al 2003) found a significant advantage for the PB condition, indicating negative effect of computerisation. We are still too limited in available research evidence and are in urgent need of further research preferably focusing on L2 learners.

The effects of test-taker characteristics on the CB test outcomes or the equivalence of CB and PB test outcomes were considered by a number of researchers, and data from several studies (Vogel 1994, Taylor et al 1998, Clariana and Wallace 2002) suggest that, after adequate CB test tutorials, the test takers' computer familiarity does not unduly affect their CB scores. However, possible effects of computer or test mode familiarity are implicated in a few studies as well (de Beer and Visser 1998, Russell 1999, Choi et al 2003), and more research addressing this variable should be conducted.

Other test-taker variables that may be worth our investigation in future comparability studies include computer anxiety (Vogel 1994, Shermis and Lombard 1998), introversion/extroversion (Vogel 1994), keyboarding skills (Russell 1999), and content familiarity (Clariana and Wallace 2002). Little is known about the effects of these variables on the test score equivalence of CB and PB L2 reading tests so far.

The few studies that subjected the data to confirmatory factor analysis obtained results which support the view that a common underlying factor is responsible for the test performances in both the CB and PB modes. Such results can strengthen the comparability argument. The analysis usefully complements the data on score means and simple cross-mode correlation. It is recommended for future research where possible to obtain a large sample size and multiple variables measured in both modes about all test takers.

Research on the cognitive processes involved in taking a reading test in CB and PB modes is extremely scarce. The little work available addressed the mental workload required in taking a reading test in CB and PB modes and indicated that a reading test in the CB mode can be perceived to require more mental efforts than in the PB mode. Increased mental workload is expected to pose challenges to L2 learners taking a reading test. By observing not only the score means but also these indices of mental workload, we may begin to uncover the similarities or differences in the processes of taking a reading test in CB and PB modes.

Conclusions

The present paper has reviewed the past research pertaining to the comparability of CB and PB testing of L2 reading ability with some emphasis on relatively recent studies that were based on more current computer devices.

Although both the test outcomes and processes need to be considered, the majority of the available evidence was concerned with the test outcomes alone. Reading test outcomes from the CB and PB modes yielded high correlations, and the score means were either comparable across modes or lower in the CB mode. Familiarity with computers and CB testing is suggested as a possible explanation for the poorer performance on the CB mode where the gap was observed, but in studies that specifically set out to address this variable, no significant effect was observed. What is clear is that we must continue to address computer familiarity in our future studies of this issue. Some of the test outcomes were also submitted to confirmatory factor analysis for evidence of a common underlying ability being responsible for observed performances in the two modes of testing, and the research base using this methodology should be expanded.

The outcome-based evidence such as correlations, score mean differences, and factor structures were mostly in favour of the equivalence notion. The paucity of the process-oriented research in this area defies any generalisations, and there is an urgent need to expand research on the test-taking processes in the two modes. For instance, the research on mental workload should be followed up so that more definitive answers can be found on this promising variable.

In conclusion, test mode equivalence must not only be demonstrated on the basis of score means and rank orders but also be explored by considering the test-taker characteristics, underlying factor structures, and the processes required to complete the various tasks in the two test modes. More rigorous research on the comparability of the tests of L2 reading in the CB and PB modes must be conducted addressing these areas. Such an effort has the potential of untangling not simply the equivalence issue but also the construct of the L2 reading ability measured via the two modes of testing this ability.

Evidence of equivalence from the studies on performance on CB and PB versions of Cambridge ESOL examinations (see studies described in sections on PET and IELTS below), and the evidence from the above review of the reading research literature notwithstanding, Cambridge commissioned a further internal study to explore how the experiences of candidates taking the test in CB mode could be made more similar to those for PB candidates. This second study by Salamoura and Brett (2007) is included below as an example of ongoing work in this area in pursuit of test fairness.

Paper 2: Scrolling reading texts and use of text highlighters in CB tests

Introduction

This paper examines the extent to which the use of electronic text navigational tools in CB reading texts, in particular text highlighters and text scrolling versus pagination, may improve their comparability with PB reading texts. In a recent review of the literature on comparability studies between CB and PB tests, Paek (2005) argues that results from studies conducted from 1993 hitherto show CB reading tests to be equivalent or slightly easier than PB tests (e.g. Choi et al 2003; Choi and Tinkler 2002; Neuman and Baydoun 1998; Nichols and Kirkpatrick 2005; Pommerich 2004; Pomplun, Frey and Becker 2004; Wang 2004). Reasons for this include the fact that computers have become much more common these days and many recent CB tests have better navigational tools than they would have had in the past.

Scrolling reading texts and text highlighters

An exception to the above general rule may be reading tests that involve extensive reading passages. A number of studies have shown that CB tests with long reading passages appear to be more difficult than their PB counterparts (Choi and Tinkler 2002; Mazzeo and Harvey 1988; Murphy, Long, Holleran and Esterly 2000; O'Malley, Kirkpatrick, Sherwood, Burdick, Hsieh and Sanford 2005; Rawson and Quinlan 2002). Some insights as to why students find CB reading of long texts harder than PB reading are provided by studies that collected student feedback. A survey evaluating the features of a computer program designed to assist medical students in their study of acid/base physiology indicated that students found it easier to read from paper, especially when texts were lengthy, primarily because it was not possible to 'mark up' text on screen. Students explained that they liked to interact with the text by highlighting and annotating it (Rawson and Quinlan 2002). Rawson and Quinlan also noted that people tend to skim or read quickly and cursorily on screen, whereas they have a slower pace, and hence a more thorough understanding, with a paper version where they can mark, annotate and take notes.

Another likely explanation is that candidates use different reading comprehension strategies depending on the test mode (Paek 2005). For example, in PB tests candidates can – if they wish – highlight parts of text or employ visual awareness techniques to remember where a piece of information is located in a passage. It has been suggested that the use of scrolling to read texts may impede the use of this 'visual learning' because the sense of placement on the page is lost (Paek 2005:18).

Indeed, studies have indicated lower performance for CB tests involving lengthy texts that require scrolling as against pagination (Bridgeman, Lennon and Jackenthal 2001; Choi and Tinkler 2002; CTB/McGraw-Hill 2003; Higgins, Russell and Hoffmann 2005; O'Malley et al 2005; Pommerich 2004; Ricketts and Wilks 2002; Way, Davis and Fitzpatrick 2006). For instance, Pommerich's (2004) comparability studies demonstrated test mode effects for different types of passage-based tests and different forms of scrolling. Choi and Tinkler (2002) argue that students' test-taking behaviour is intercepted by having to scroll reading passages on computer screens – this being especially true for younger students. Similarly, Higgins et al (2005) claim that although no statistically significant differences were found in reading comprehension scores based on the computer fluidity and computer literacy of candidates, test takers were disadvantaged by the scrolling test mode. Other studies have suggested that paper-based reading of lengthy passages may 'facilitate construction of spatial memory about discrete pieces of information included in a reading passage' (Sawaki 2001:51; see also Matthew 1997, Piolat, Roussey and Thunin 1997).

However, these findings have not been unanimously accepted. Pomplun, Frey and Becker (2002) maintained that difficulties in reading on computer screens were related to primitive technology. Dillon (1992) conceded that, in a long text that does not fit into one screen and therefore requires scrolling or paging, other factors such as the quality of the visual image presented to readers as well as the availability and quality of text manipulation facilities (e.g. text search facilities) play a significant role.

In relation to Cambridge ESOL exams, a recent study that trialled the CB version of PET (Hackett 2005) argues that scrolling was preferred more than pagination as a text navigation method. It is likely that this later finding reflects a trend of changing reading comprehension strategies as candidates become more and more familiar with reading on a computer or the web by means of scrolling.

Choi and Tinkler (2002), postulate that the provision of an electronic marker, which allows students to highlight parts of a passage as they wish, will both mimic the paper-and-pencil test-taking behaviour and attenuate any test mode effects. In a similar vein, Higgins et al (2005) recommend text highlighters and review markers as useful tools in CB reading tests but, at the same time, they also point out that such tools may not be the preferred way of dealing with on-screen reading texts for all candidates. Their study included a tutorial which showed students how to electronically highlight text in passages but a post-tutorial survey indicated that fewer than 20% of the test takers had actually used the highlighting feature during the CB test.

Conclusion

In summary, the literature in this area suggests that comparability between PB and CB Reading tasks is maximised when questions and text are presented

on a single screen. There is some concern that having to scroll lengthy passages may disadvantage candidates taking the test on screen. However, there
appears to be a consensus that this effect is eliminated when appropriate electronic navigational tools are provided (e.g. text highlighters) that allow candidates to 'mark up' text if they so wish, as they could on a paper test. It is
therefore recommended that a reading text highlighter tool is made available
for CB tests that contain lengthy reading passages in order to maximise the
comparability between PB and CB formats.

Computer-based assessment: Cambridge ESOL practice

Cambridge ESOL has been engaged in computer-based assessment for
a number of years, offering several computer-based tests; among them,
the computer-adaptive CB BULATS since 1995; and since May 2005, CB
IELTS. Both of these CB assessments are delivered offline via CD-ROM and
are offered alongside their paper-based counterparts.

In November 2005, Cambridge ESOL launched its first CB test (CB
PET) delivered by means of a specially developed CB test delivery engine,
Cambridge Connect. CB PET has since been followed by several other
Cambridge ESOL examinations: CB KET, CB BEC Preliminary, CB BEC
Vantage, CB BEC Higher, CB Skills for Life Reading, CB Skills for Life
Writing and CB TKT.

Cambridge Connect is Cambridge Assessment's internally developed
online test delivery engine, which allows a range of secure, online assessments

**Figure 1 Cambridge Assessment's online delivery engine (Cambridge
Connect)**

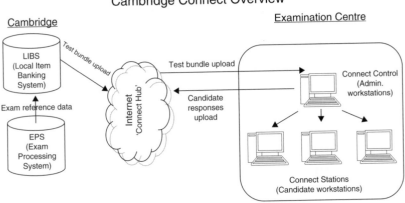

to be delivered to candidates. Connect has been developed in response to an increasing demand for computer-based assessment and all the advantages it has to offer. Apart from delivering computer-based tests at test venues, Connect also ties in to the 'backend' systems that drive Cambridge ESOL examinations and assessments, including the Local Item Banking System (LIBS) and the Examination Processing System (EPS), as well as Online Entries and Online Return of Results initiatives (see Fig 1).

We will report below on two of Cambridge ESOL's computer-based assessments: CB PET and CB IELTS.

CB PET

CB PET, the first Main Suite examination to be delivered online was officially launched in November 2005 and offered as an alternative to the paper-based format. The reasons for its introduction are clear. The candidature for PET had grown rapidly and there had been demand for PET sessions outside the standard exam timetable. Moreover, over 70% of PET candidates were aged 20 or under, and this was an age group likely to cope well with keyboard technology.

Prior to its launch, the ESOL CBT Development Unit engaged in a series of trials relating to the CB PET project. The first task in the project was to assess the suitability of PET task types for use in a computer test and to identify any potential problems and their likely impact on test design or candidate performance. There were four key stages of development:

- feasibility study
- task design and trialling
- navigation design and trialling
- equivalence trialling.

It was agreed upon at an early stage that CB PET would retain the same exam format for the Writing (Reading/Writing) component. That is, the task types would be the same as in paper-based PET and candidate results would report on the same scale. This would allow schools to follow the same preparation course for both forms of the examination.

Feasibility study, task design and trialling

The aim of the feasibility study was to look at the suitability of the tasks for on-screen adaptation and to propose designs for trialling. Cambridge ESOL has produced computer-based tests in CD-ROM format since 1999, for example CB BULATS (Business Language Testing Service) and QPT (the Quick Placement Test, which is distributed and marketed by Oxford University Press). Experience with developing such tests has enabled a body of knowledge and expertise to be established. One key difference between the majority of paper-based tests and on-screen display is 'aspect': most test papers are in portrait view (with candidates being able to view two pages at one time) whereas computer screens are in landscape.

An initial phase of the feasibility study was to identify those task types successfully used in previous Cambridge ESOL CB products and to undertake a risk assessment on any remaining task types in order to determine particular features of the processing of items that might raise problems for on-screen display and impact on the manner in which the candidate processes the task. The layout of previously used task-types was also reviewed in the hope that advances in technology would engender opportunities for improvement.

Navigation design and trialling

Following on from task template trialling and design modification, the navigation system was more fully developed: the primary aim being to allow candidates to progress through the PET test as they would in the more conventional format, selecting which questions to attempt first and re-visiting questions at any time throughout the test. Navigation trialling was tested on a mixed-nationality group of CEFR A2/B1 level non-PET students from a UK language school in April 2004 (it was believed that if candidates with little or no knowledge of the PET test format were successful at navigating through the test, this should present few difficulties for real PET candidates). Findings from navigation trialling were very encouraging: all candidates were able to work their way through the test without instruction. Nevertheless, the Reading and Writing component contains a brief tutorial, available to candidates prior to starting the main test screen in line with British Standard BS:7988.

Equivalence trialling

Analysis of results from equivalence trials (where participating candidates scheduled to enter for the computer-based PET session soon after the trial also took a paper-based anchor test) found performance consistent in both forms of the test, replicating earlier studies in CB/PB equivalence (Jones 2000a, Green and Maycock 2004, Blackhurst 2005).

Candidate reaction to task design and navigation usability was garnered through questionnaire responses and post-test focus groups. An overwhelming proportion of candidates rated the test navigation easy to use, with 96% giving ratings of three or above on a scale of 1 to 5, where five indicates total agreement. A number of specific questions relating to candidates' reactions to reading and writing on computer were asked in order to gauge the general suitability of taking the test on computer as opposed to on paper. In response to the question 'Did you find reading on computer easier than reading on paper?' 46% found it easier, whereas only 25% preferred reading on paper. This perhaps reflects an increasing familiarity with on-screen reading, at home, in school or at work. Typing written answers on computer was significantly more popular than writing by hand, with 67% showing a preference for typing and only 25% expressing a preference for handwriting. In general, a preference for taking CB PET was expressed by the majority of candidates: 63% preferred taking the Reading and Writing test on computer (as opposed to 20% preferring the paper-based version). These findings were corroborated by candidate comments obtained from the focus groups. Whilst there was general satisfaction with the screen layout and navigation toolbars, a few candidates expressed a desire to be able to use a *highlighting tool* in the Reading section of the test, mirroring the function of underlining text on paper.

CB PET appears to have been well suited to a sizeable proportion of the PET candidature and it is anticipated that it will become increasingly popular with centres looking for greater flexibility and faster turnaround times. However, it is appreciated that not all centres are equipped to deliver computer-based products and some candidates will still prefer to take the paper-based version, so CB PET has been developed as an additional service rather than a replacement for traditional PB PET sessions.

CB IELTS

Test delivery mode

Before launching CB IELTS in 2005, Cambridge ESOL needed to be confident that the introduction of a new test mode would not affect candidates' test performance in any significant way. Initial studies (Shaw, Jones and Klux, 2001, Thighe, Jones and Geranpayeh 2001), carried out to investigate the equivalence of PB and CB forms of IELTS Listening and Reading, were encouraging. The Shaw et al (2001) study involved 192 candidates taking a trial version of CB IELTS before taking their live PB test a short time later. Item difficulties for reading correlated highly (.90) between both modes of the test, and test format therefore seemed to have little or no influence on the test scores. This research and that of Thighe et al (2001) concluded that the test delivery mode did not have any significant effect on test scores. However, these studies called for further research to be carried out to account for the possibility that these conclusions were somewhat 'muddied' by a motivational effect, candidates seemingly performing better on the live test than on the trial practice test. These recommendations led to further large scale studies being carried out between 2002 and 2005 where subjects were given two tests, one computer-based and one paper-based, but were not told which test would generate their final result. These studies are referred to below as Trial A (Green and Maycock 2004) and Trial B (Blackhurst 2005).

In Trial A, 627 candidates took a computer-based version of IELTS as well as a paper-based version, half the candidates taking the CB version a week before the PB version and half taking the PB version a week before the CB version. Candidates were assumed to be equally motivated to achieve in both versions as they would not know which would give them their final score. Candidates were also assumed to be equally prepared for both test formats as a condition of participation was that they were exposed to test practice in both formats. The results of Trial A showed that nearly 30% of candidates achieved an identical band score for the PB Reading test and the CB Reading test, and 72% achieved a score that differed by just half a band, which correlated well with the rate of agreement from one paper-based IELTS version to another (Thighe et al 2001). Trial B, which was an extension of Trial A, conducted on 785 candidates during 2004–5, produced very similar findings and concluded: 'The rates of agreement between paper-based IELTS and CB IELTS are satisfactorily similar, when compared with the agreement rates for live candidates taking two paper-based IELTS versions' (Blackhurst 2005:15).

Blackhurst (2005) provides the following account: 'CB IELTS is a linear computer-based test, designed to provide as similar experience as possible to the paper-based (PB) IELTS examination, using source texts and questions, drawn from the same pool of previously- trialled material.'

He concludes that 'the evidence gathered since 1999 provides support for using CB IELTS interchangeably with PB IELTS, and indicates that candidates, given adequate computer familiarity, will perform equally well on either version of the test. In reporting results, no distinction is made between candidates who have taken the test in one mode or the other: from the point of view of receiving institutions the results may be considered equally valid, whichever form is taken'. To support IELTS's claim to fairness he notes:

> There are important considerations involved in providing an established test in different formats: not all candidates will have adequate computer familiarity; some candidates may experience fatigue when reading extended passages on computer. Accordingly, Wolfe and Manalo (2004) recommended that test designers "think seriously about providing examinees with a choice of composition medium . . . particularly when high-stakes decisions will be made based upon the test results" (61). The IELTS partners have always recognised that it is important that candidates should be able to take the test in the form with which they feel comfortable: the pen and paper test will continue to be available, so only those candidates who feel confident in their ability to use a computer need do so . . . In this way, as the new form of the test becomes more widely available, IELTS will be able to ensure that candidates will have the option of taking the test that suits them best (Blackhurst 2005:16–17)

Test-taker characteristics

The effects of computer familiarity and competence were also a concern in research into CB IELTS prior to its launch. All candidates who took part in Trial A (Green and Maycock 2004) and Trial B (Blackhurst 2005) referred to earlier, were also given a questionnaire which addressed among other issues, computer familiarity and competence. Like the CB TOEFL candidates in Taylor et al's (1998) study, all candidates had been given a training tutorial before taking the test (though this tutorial was only 3–4 minutes in length), and CB IELTS candidates were also provided with sample materials in advance of taking the test. The questionnaires showed that the majority of candidates were computer-literate (perhaps not surprising since all candidates were self-selecting): only 1% put their ability as 'zero'. Interestingly, although candidates themselves believed that those with better computer skills would perform better than those with less good computer skills, analysis of test scores and questionnaire responses showed that candidates' ability and experience in using computers did not have any significant impact on test scores for reading or any of the other skills tested.

There has been less research carried out into the effects of age, gender and computer anxiety, although conclusions formed on the effects of computer familiarity will often be applicable to these variables too. It would not be unreasonable to assume, for example, that younger candidates, who are likely to be more familiar with using computers, may outperform older candidates on CB tests and may themselves find that they perform better on a CB test than a PB test. Neither is it unreasonable to assume that those who are less familiar with computers may be more anxious about taking a test on computer. Some of the studies mentioned earlier (Blackhurst 2005, Maycock and Green 2005, Taylor et al 1998) found no evidence to suggest any gender bias between CB and PB modes.

Reading speed

As mentioned in the above literature review (Paper 1) reading speed and preferences for reading on paper are issues that come up in CB/PB comparability research. Anecdotal evidence suggests that people generally prefer to read on paper than on screen, and usually print out to read. However, this is something which may well change in the future as technology develops. L1 reading research shows that reading rates drop 10–30% when moving from on-paper to on-screen reading (Anderson 2003), and researchers like Kruk and Muter (1984) and Muter and Maurutto (1991) all found that reading speed is affected by mode of delivery and that it takes longer to read a text on computer. The evidence from Trial A and Trial B of CB IELTS, however, did not conclude that candidates found it took longer or was more difficult to read in either mode (Maycock and Green 2005), demonstrating perhaps that increasingly improved screen resolutions and changes in test-taker characteristics may already be making a difference, and may be resulting in less of a difference between taking a test in CB and PB modes.

References

Adolphs, S and Schmitt, N (2003) Lexical coverage of spoken discourse, *Applied Linguistics* 24 (4), 425–38.

Alderman, D L and Holland, P W (1981) Item performance across native language groups on the Test of English as a Foreign Language, *TOEFL Research Report* 9, Princeton, NJ: Educational Testing Service.

Alderson, J C (n.d.) *Waystage and Threshold. Or does the emperor have any clothes?* unpublished mimeo, University of Lancaster.

Alderson, J C (1978) *A Study of the Cloze Procedure with Native and Non-Native Speakers of English*, PhD thesis, University of Edinburgh.

Alderson, J C (1990) Testing Reading Comprehension Skills (Part One), *Reading in a Foreign Language* 6 (2), 425–38.

Alderson, J C (1990a) Testing Reading Comprehension Skills: Getting Students to Talk about Taking a Reading Test (Part Two), *Reading in a Foreign Language* 7 (1), 465–503.

Alderson, J C (1993) The relationship between grammar and reading in an English for academic purposes test battery, in Douglas, D and Chappelle, C (Eds) *A New decade of Language Testing Research*, Washington: TESOL, 203–214.

Alderson, J C (1996) The Testing of Reading, in Nuttall C, *Teaching reading skills in a foreign language* (Second Ed), Oxford: Heinemann English Language Teaching, 221–229.

Alderson, J C (2000) *Assessing reading*, Cambridge: Cambridge University Press.

Alderson, J C (Ed) (2002) *Common European Framework of Reference for Languages: learning, teaching, assessment: Case Studies*, Strasbourg: Council of Europe.

Alderson, J C (2005) *Diagnosing foreign language proficiency: the interface between learning and assessment*, London: Continuum.

Alderson, J C (2007) Judging the Frequency of English Words, *Applied Linguistics* 28 (3), 383–409.

Alderson, J C and Banerjee, J (1996) *How might Impact study instruments be validated?*, unpublished paper commissioned by UCLES as part of the IELTS Impact Study.

Alderson, J C and Hamp-Lyons, L (1996) TOEFL preparation courses: a study of washback, *Language Testing* 13 (3), 280–97.

Alderson, J C and Urquhart, A H (Eds) (1984) *Reading in a Foreign Language*, London: Longman.

Alderson, J C and Wall, D (1993) Does washback exist? *Applied Linguistics* 14 (2), 115–29.

Alderson, J C and Wall, D (1996) Special Issue: Washback, *Language Testing* 13 (3).

Alderson, J C, Clapham, C and Wall, D (1995) *Language test construction and evaluation*, Cambridge: Cambridge University Press.

References

Alderson, J C, Figueras, N, Kuijper, H, Nold, G, Takala, S and Tardieu, C (2004) *The development of specifications for item development and classification within The Common European Framework of Reference for Languages: Learning, Teaching, Assessment: Reading and Listening: Final report of The Dutch CEF Construct Project.* Project Report. Lancaster University, Lancaster, UK (Unpublished).

American Educational Research Association, American Psychological Association, and National Council on Measurement in Education (1974, 1985 and 1999) *Standards for educational and psychological testing*, Washington, DC.

American Psychological Association (APA) (1986) *Guidelines for Computer-based Tests and Interpretations*, Washington, DC: APA.

Anastasi, A (1988) *Psychological Testing* (6th edition), New York: Macmillan.

Anderson, N (2004) 'Scrolling, Clicking and Reading English: Online Reading Strategies in a Second/Foreign Language'. Retrieved January 9th 2007 from <http://www.readingmatrix.com/articles/anderson/article.pdf>.

Anderson, N J, Bachman, L F, Perkins, K, and Cohen, A D (1991) An Exploratory Study into the Construct Validity of a Reading Comprehension Test: Triangulation of Data Sources, *Language Testing* 8 (1), 41–66.

Anderson, R C (1974) Concretization in sentence learning, *Journal of Educational Psychology* 66 (2), 179–83.

Angoff, W H and Sharon, A T (1974) A comparison of scores earned on the Test of English as a Foreign Language by native American college students and foreign applicants to US colleges, *TESOL Quarterly* 5 (2), 129–36.

Ashton, K (2006) Can Do self-assessment: investigating cross-language comparability in reading, *Research Notes* 24, 10–14.

Ashton, M (1998) *An investigation into the task types used in the reading paper of the Certificate of Advanced English Examination (CAE)*, unpublished MA dissertation, University of Reading.

Ashton, M (2003) The change process at the paper level, Paper 1 Reading, in Weir, C J and Milanovic, M (Eds) Continuity and Innovation: Revising the Cambridge Proficiency in English Examination 1913–2002, *Studies in Language Testing* 15, Cambridge: UCLES/Cambridge University Press, 121–64.

Ashton, M and Khalifa, H (2005) Opening a new door for teachers of English: Cambridge ESOL Teaching Knowledge Test, *Research Notes* 19, 5–7.

Association of Language Testers in Europe (1994, 2000) *ALTE Code of Practice and Quality Assurance Checklists*, <www.alte.org>.

Association of Language Testers in Europe (1998) *ALTE Handbook of European Language Examinations and Examination Systems*, Cambridge: University of Cambridge Local Examinations Syndicate.

Association of Language Testers in Europe (1998a) Multilingual glossary of language testing terms, *Studies in Language Testing* 6, Cambridge: UCLES/ Cambridge University Press.

Bachman, L F (1990) *Fundamental Considerations in Language Testing*, Oxford: Oxford University Press.

Bachman, L F (2004) *Building and supporting a case for test utilization*, paper presented at LTRC, Temecula, California, March 2004.

Bachman, L F (2004a) *Statistical Analyses for Language Assessment*, Cambridge: Cambridge University Press.

Bachman, L F and Palmer, A S (1996) *Language Testing in Practice*, Oxford: Oxford University Press.

Bachman, L F, Kunnan, A J, Vanniarajan, S, and Lynch, B (1988) Task and ability analysis as a basis for examining content and construct comparability in two EFL proficiency test batteries, *Language Testing* 5 (2), 128–59.

Bachman, L F, Davidson, F, Ryan, K and Choi, I-C (1995) An investigation into the comparability of two tests of English as a foreign language, *Studies in Language Testing* 1, Cambridge: UCLES/Cambridge University Press.

Bachman, L F, Davidson, F and Milanovic, M (1996) The Use of Test Method Characteristics in the Content Analysis and Design of EFL Proficiency Tests, *Language Testing* 13 (2), 125–50.

Bailey, K M (1996) Working for Washback: A review of the washback concept in Language Testing. *Language Testing* 13(3), 257–279.

Bailey, K M (1999) Washback in Language Testing, *TOEFL Monograph Series* 15, Princeton, NJ: Educational Testing Service.

Ball, F (2002) Developing wordlists for BEC, *Research Notes* 8, 10–13.

Banerjee, J V (1996) *The Design of the Classroom Observation Instruments*, Cambridge: UCLES internal report.

Banks, C (1999) An investigation into age bias in PET, *Cambridge ESOL Internal Research and Validation Report* 22.

Barker, F (2004) Using Corpora in Language Testing: Research and validation of language tests, *Modern English Teacher* 13 (2), 63–7.

Barnett, M A (1989) *More than Meets the Eye*, Englewood Cliffs, NJ: Prentice Hall Regents.

Barr, P, Clegg, C and Wallace, C (1981) *Advanced Reading Skills*, London: Longman.

Barr, R, Kamil, M L, Mosenthal, P and Pearson, P D (Eds) (1991) *Handbook of Reading Research* 2, London: Longman.

Beard, R (1972) *Teaching and Learning in Higher Education*, Harmondsworth: Penguin Books.

Belmore, S M (1985) Reading computer-presented text, *Bulletin of the Psychonomic Society* 23 (1), 12–14.

Bensoussan, M and Ramraz, R (1984) Testing EFL reading comprehension using a multiple choice rational cloze, *Modern Language Journal* 68 (3), 230–39.

Bergstrom, B (1992) *Ability measure equivalence of computer adaptive and pencil and paper tests: A research synthesis*, paper presented at the annual meeting of the American Educational Research Association, San Francisco, CA, 20–24 April 1992.

Berman, R A (1984) Syntactic Components of the Foreign Language Reading Process, in Alderson, J C and Urquhart, A H (Eds) *Reading in a Foreign Language*, London: Longman, 139–59.

Bernhardt, E B (1991) Reading Development in a Second Language: Theoretical, Empirical and Classroom Perspectives, Norwood, NJ: Ablex.

Bernhardt, E B (2005) Progress and procrastination in second language reading, *Annual Review of Applied Linguistics* 25, 133–150.

Berry, V (1995) Current assessment issues and practices in Hong Kong: A preview [Introduction to Colloquium on Assessment and change in the classroom], in Nunan, D, Berry, R and Berry, V (Eds) *Bringing about change in language education*, Proceedings of the 2nd ILE Conference, Hong Kong: Dept. of Curriculum Studies, The University of Hong Kong, 31–34.

References

Berry, V (1997) *Gender and personality as factors of interlocutor variability in oral performance tests*, paper presented at the Language Testing Research Colloquium, Orlando, Florida.

Birch, M (2007) English L2 Reading: *Getting to the Bottom*, Mahwah: Lawrence Erlbaum Associates.

Blackhurst, A (2005) Listening, Reading and Writing on computer-based and paper-based versions of IELTS, *Research Notes* 2, 14–17.

Blackhurst, A and Cope, L (2007) IELTS Clerical marking review: Phase 8, *Cambridge ESOL Internal Research and Validation Report* 1070.

Block, E (1986) The Comprehension Strategies of Second Language Readers, *TESOL Quarterly* 20 (3), 463–94.

Bond, T G and Fox, C M (2001) *Applying the Rasch model*, NJ: Lawrence Erlbaum Associates.

Bonkowski, F (1996) *Instruments for the Assessment of Teaching Materials*, unpublished MA assignment, Lancaster University.

Bridgeman, B, Lennon, M L and Jackenthal, A (2001) Effects of screen size, screen resolution, and display rate on computer-based test performance, *ETS RR-01-23*, Princeton, NJ: Educational Testing Service.

Britt, M A and Aglinskas, C (2002) Improving student's ability to use source information, *Cognition and Instruction* 20 (40), 485–522.

Britt, M A and Sommer, J (2004) Facilitating textual integration with macro-structure focusing tasks, *Reading Psychology* 25, 313–339.

Brown, A and Iwashita, N (1998) The role of language background in the validation of a computer-adaptive test, in Kunnan, A J (Ed.) *Validation in Language Assessment*, selected papers from the 17th language Testing Research Colloquium, Mahweh, NJ: Lawrence Erlbaum Associates, 195–208.

Buck, G (1988) Testing Listening comprehension in Japanese University entrance examinations, *JALT Journal* 10 (1), 15–42.

Buck, G (2001) *Assessing Listening*, Cambridge: Cambridge University Press.

Bugbee, A C (1996) The equivalence of paper-and-pencil and computer based testing, *Journal of Research on Computing in Education* 28 (3), 282–99.

Bunderson, C V, Inouye, D K, and Olsen, J B (1989) The four generations of computerized educational measurement, in Linn, R L (Ed.) *Educational Measurement* (3rd edition), New York: American Council on Education/ Macmillan, 367–407.

Calver, L and Khalifa H (2008) Demographic Variables and performances on Main Suite Reading Papers, *Cambridge ESOL Internal Validation Report* 1153.

Camilli, G and Shepard, L (1994) *Methods for identifying biased test items*, Thousand Oaks, CA: Sage.

Canale, M (1983) From communicative competence to communicative language pedagogy, in Richards, J C and Schmidt, R (Eds) *Language and communication*, London and New York: Longman.

Canale, M and Swain, M (1980) Theoretical Bases of Communicative Approaches to Second Language Teaching and Testing, *Applied Linguistics* 1 (1), 1–47.

Carrell, P L (1984) The Effects of Rhetorical Organisation on ESL Readers, *TESOL Quarterly* 18 (3), 441–69.

Carrell, P L and Grabe, W (2002) Reading, in Schmitt, N (Ed.) *An introduction to Applied Linguistics*, London: Arnold, 233–50.

Carson, J G (2001) A task analysis of reading and writing in academic contexts, in Belcher, D and Hirvela, A (Eds) *Linking literacies: Perspectives on L2 reading-writing connections*, Ann Arbor: The Michigan University Press, 43–83.

Carver, R P (1985) How Good are Some of the World's Best Readers?, *Reading Research Quarterly* 20 (4), 389–419.

Carver, R P (1992) Reading Rate: Theory, Research and Practical Implications, *Journal of Reading* 36 (2), 84–95.

Chamot, A U and El-Dinary, P B (1999) Children's learning strategies in language immersion classrooms, *Modern Language Journal* 83 (3), 319–38.

Chapelle C A and Douglas, D (Eds) (1993) *A New Decade of Language Testing Research*, Alexandria, VA: TESOL.

Chapelle, C A, Enright, M K and Jamieson, J (2004) *Issues in developing a TOEFL validity argument*, draft paper presented at LTRC, Temecula, California, March 2004.

Chapelle, C A, Enright, M K and Jamieson, J (2008) *Building a validity argument for the test of English as a foreign language*, New York: Routledge.

Chen, Z and Henning, G (1985) Linguistic and cultural bias in language proficiency tests, *Language Testing* 2 (2), 155–63.

Cheng, L (1997) How does washback influence teaching? Implications for Hong Kong. *Language and Education* 11(1), 38–54

Cheng, L (2005) Changing Language Teaching through Language Testing: A washback study, *Studies in Language Testing* 21, Cambridge: UCLES/Cambridge University Press.

Cheng, L and Watanabe, Y (Eds) (2004) *Washback in Language Testing: Research Contexts and Methods*, NJ: Lawrence Erlbaum Associates.

Chikalanga, I W (1991) *Inferencing in the reading process: a cross cultural study*, unpublished PhD thesis, University of Reading.

Chikalanga, I W (1992) A suggested taxonomy for inferences for the reading teacher, *Reading in a Foreign Language* 8 (2), 697–709.

Chishold, W, Vanderheiden, G and Jacobs, I (1999) *Web content accessibility guidelines*, Madison, WI: University of Wisconsin, Trace R and D Center, retrieved from: <http://www.w3.org/TR/1999/WAI-WEBCONTENT-19990505>.

Choi, I-C, Kim, K and Boo, J (2003) Comparability of a paper-based language test and a computer-based language test, *Language Testing* 20 (3), 295–320.

Choi, S W and Tinkler, T (2002) *Evaluating comparability of paper and computer-based assessment in a K-12 setting*, paper presented at the annual meeting of the National Council on Measurement in Education, New Orleans, LA, 1–5 April 2002.

Clapham, C (1996) The development of IELTS: A study in the effect of background knowledge on reading comprehension, *Studies in Language Testing* 4, Cambridge: UCLES/Cambridge University Press.

Clariana, R B and Wallace, P E (2002) Paper-based versus computer-based assessment: key factors associated with the test mode effect, *British Journal of Educational Technology* 33 (5), 593–602.

Cohen, A D (1994) *Assessing Language Ability in the Classroom* (2nd edition), Boston, MA: Heinle and Heinle.

Cohen, A D (2006) The Coming of Age of Research on Test-Taking Strategies, *Language Assessment Quarterly* 3 (4), 307–32.

Cohen, A D and Upton, T A (2006) Strategies in responding to the new TOEFL reading tasks, *Monograph* 33, Princeton, NJ: Educational Testing Service.

References

Coltheart, M (1978) Lexical access in simple reading tasks, in Underwood, G (Ed.) *Strategies in information processing*, London: Academic Press, 151–216.

Conway, M A, Gardiner, J M, Perfect, T J, Anderson, S J and Cohen, G (1997) Changes in memory awareness during learning: the acquisition of knowledge by psychology undergraduates, *Journal of Experimental Psychology: General* 126 (4), 393–413.

Corkill, A J, Glover, J A and Bruning, R H (1988) Advance organizers: Concrete versus abstract, *Journal of Educational Research* 82 (2), 76–81.

Corkhill, D and Robinson, M (2006) Using the global legal community in the development of ILEC, *Research Notes* 25,10–11.

Council of Europe (2001) *Common European Framework of Reference for Languages: learning, teaching, assessment*, Cambridge: Cambridge University Press.

Council of Europe (2003) *Relating language examinations to the Common European Framework of Reference for Languages: learning, teaching, assessment (CEF), Manual: Preliminary Pilot Version*, DGIV/EDU/LANG 2003, 5, Strasbourg: Language Policy Division.

Council of Europe (2004) *Reference supplement to the Preliminary Pilot Version of the Manual for Relating language examinations to the CEFR*, DGIV/EDU/LANG (2004) 13, Strasbourg: Language Policy Division.

Coxhead, A (2000) A new academic word list, *TESOL Quarterly* 34 (2), 213–38.

Crick, J E and Brennan, R L (1983) Manual for GENOVA: a generalized analysis of variance system, *ACT Technical Bulletin* 43, Iowa City, IA: American Testing Program.

Crocker, L and Algina, J (1986) *Introduction to classical and modern test theory*, Orlando, FL: Harcourt Brace Jovanovitch.

Cromer, W (1970) The difference model: a new explanation for some reading difficulties, *Journal of Educational Psychology* 61 (6) Pt 1, 471–83.

CTB/McGraw-Hill (2003) *The Computer-Based or Online Administration of Paper-and-Pencil Tests*, retrieved from: <http://www.ctb.com/media/articles/pdfs/AssessmentRelated/Computer_Based_or_Online_Admin_of_P_P_Tests.pdf?FOLDER%3C%3Efolder_id=1408474395222381>.

Davey, B and Lasasso, C (1984) The interaction of reader and task factors in the assessment of reading comprehension, *Experimental Education* 52 (4), 199–206.

David, G (2007) *A Case Study: Euro examinations, Budapest*, paper presentation given at the Council of Europe Colloquium, Cambridge, December 2007.

Davies, A (Ed.) (1997) Special Issue: Ethics in Language Testing, *Language Testing* 14 (3).

Davies, A (2008) Assessing Academic English: Testing English proficiency 1950–1989 – the IELTS solution, *Studies in Language Testing* 23, Cambridge: UCLES/Cambridge University Press.

Davies, A, Brown, A, Elder, C, Hill, K, Lumley, T and McNamara, T (1999) Dictionary of Language Testing, *Studies in Language Testing* 7, Cambridge: UCLES/Cambridge University Press.

Davies, E and Whitney, N (1981) *Strategies for Reading*, London: Heinemann.

Davis, F B (1968) Research in Comprehension in Reading, *Reading Research Quarterly* 3 (4), 499–545.

De Beaugrande, R (1981) Design Criteria for Process Models of Reading, *Reading Research Quarterly* 16 (2), 261–315.

De Beer, M and Visser, D (1998) Comparability of the paper-and-pencil and computerised adaptive versions of the General Scholastic Aptitude Test (GSAT) Senior, *South African Journal of Psychology* 28 (1), 37–42.

De Bello, T (1990) Comparison of eleven major learning styles models: Variables, appropriate populations, validity of instrumentation, and the research behind them, *Reading and Writing Quarterly* 6, 203–222.

De Groot, A (1966) Perception and Memory Versus Thought: Some Old Ideas and Recent Findings, in Kleinmumtz, B (Ed.) *Problem Solving*, New York: Wiley.

Dillon, A (1992) Reading from paper versus screens: A critical review of the empirical literature, *Ergonomics* 35 (10), 1297–326.

Douglas, D (2000) *Assessing Language for Specific Purposes: Theory and practice*, Cambridge: Cambridge University Press.

Drum, P A, Calfee, R C and Cook, L K (1981) The effects of surface structure variables on performance in reading comprehension tests, *Reading Research Quarterly* 16 (4), 486–514.

Dunn, R, Beaudry, J and Klavas, A (1989) Survey of research on learning styles, *Educational Leadership* 46 (6), 50–58.

Eamon, D B (1978–79) Selection and recall of topical information in prose by better and poorer readers, *Reading Research Quarterly* 14 (2), 244–57.

Ede, L and Lunsford, A (1984) Audience addressed, audience invoked: The role of audience in composition theory and pedagogy, *College Composition and Communication* 35 (2), 155–71.

Edgeworth, F Y (1888) The statistics of examinations, *Journal of the Royal Statistical Society* 51, 599–635.

Eignor, D, Taylor, C, Kirsch, I S and Jamieson, J (1988) Development of a Scale for Assessing the Level of Computer Familiarity of TOEFL Examinees, *TOEFL Research Report* 60, Princeton, NJ: Educational Testing Service.

Engelhard, G (2001) Historical views of the influences of measurement and reading theories on the assessment of reading, *Journal of Applied Measurement* 2 (1), 1–28.

Enright, M K and Schedl, M (2000) *Reading for a reason: using reader purpose to guide test design*, unpublished manuscript in preparation.

Enright, M K, Grabe, W, Koda, K, Mosenthal, P, Mulcahy-Ernt, P and Schedl, M (2000) TOEFL 2000 Reading Framework: A Working Paper, *TOEFL Monograph Series* 17, Princeton, NJ: Educational Testing Service.

ETS (2000) *ETS Standards for Quality and Fairness*, Princeton, NJ: Educational Testing Service.

ETS (2003) *Task Specifications for Next Generation TOEFL reading test*, unpublished manuscript.

Faerch, C and Kasper, G (1986) The Role of Comprehension in Foreign Language Learning, *Applied Linguistics* 7 (3), 257–74.

Farr, R and Carey, R F (1986) *Reading: What can be measured?*, Newark, DE: International Reading Association.

Farr, R, Pritchard, R and Smitten, B (1990) A description of what happens when an examinee takes a multiple-choice reading comprehension test, *Journal of Educational Measurement* 27 (3), 209–26.

Feldmann, S C and Fish, M C (1988) Reading comprehension of elementary, junior high, and high school students on print vs. microcomputer-generated text, *Journal of Educational Computing Research* 4 (2), 159–66.

References

Feldt, L S and Brennan, R L (1989) Reliability, in Linn, R L (Ed.) *Educational Measurement* (3rd edition), New York: American Council on Education/ Macmillan.

Ferne, T and Rupp, A A (2007) A Synthesis of 15 Years of Research on DIF in Language Testing: Methodological Advances, Challenges, and Recommendations, *Language Assessment Quarterly* 4 (2), 113–48.

Field, J (2004) *Psycholinguistics: the Key Concepts*, London: Routledge.

Field, J (forthcoming) Cognitive Validity, in Taylor, L (Ed) Examining Speaking, *Studies in Language Testing* 30, Cambridge: UCLES/Cambridge University Press.

Fish, M C and Feldmann, S C (1987) A comparison of reading comprehension using print and microcomputer presentation, *Journal of Computer-Based Instruction* 14 (2), 57–61.

Foulke, E (1991) Braille, in Heller M, Schiff, W (Eds) *The Psychology of Touch*, Hillsdale NJ: Lawrence Erlbaum Associates, 219–33.

Fry, E (1963) *Teaching Faster Reading: A Manual*, Cambridge: Cambridge University Press.

Fulcher, G (2003) *Testing Second Language Speaking*, London: Longman/ Pearson Education.

Galaczi, E and Ffrench, A (2007) Developing revised assessment scales for Main Suite and BEC Speaking tests, *Research Notes* 30, 28–31.

Geranpayeh, A (2001) Country bias in FCE listening comprehension, *Cambridge ESOL Internal Research and Validation Report* 271.

Geranpayeh, A (2004) Reliability in First Certificate in English objective papers, *Research Notes* 15, 21–33.

Geranpayeh, A (2007) Using Structural Equation Modelling to facilitate the revision of high stakes testing: the case of CAE, *Research Notes* 30, 8–12.

Geranpayeh, A and Kunnan, A J (2007) Differential Item Functioning in Terms of Age in the Certificate in Advanced English Examination, *Language Assessment Quarterly* 4 (2), 190–222.

Gernsbacher, M A (1990) *Language comprehension as structure building*, Hillsdale, NJ: Lawrence Erlbaum Associates.

Gervasi, V and Ambriola, V (2002) Quantitative assessment of textual complexity, in Merlini Barbesi, L (Ed.) *Complexity in Language and Text*, Pisa: PLUS-University of Pisa, 197–228.

Goh, S T (1990) The Effects of Rhetorical Organisation in Expository Prose on ESL Readers in Singapore, *RELC Journal* 21 (2), 1–13.

Goldman, S R (1997) Learning from text: Reflections on the past and suggestions for the future, *Discourse Processes* 23, 357–398.

Goldman, S R (2004) Cognitive aspects of constructing meaning through and across multiple texts, in Shuart-Faris N and Bloome D (Eds) *Uses of intertextuality in classroom and educational research*, Greenwich, Connecticut: Information Age Publishing, 317–51.

Goodman, K S (1967) Reading: A Psycholinguistic Guessing Game, *Journal of the Reading Specialists* 6 (4), 126–35.

Gough, P B (1972) One Second of Reading, *Visible Language* 6 (4), 291–320.

Grabe, W (2004) Research on teaching reading, *Annual Review of Applied Linguistics* 24, 44–69.

Grabe, W and Kaplan, R B (1996) *Theory and Practice of Writing: An Applied Linguistic Perspective*, London: Longman.

Grabe, W and Stoller, F L (2002) *Teaching and Researching Reading*, London: Longman.

Graddol, D (2006) *English Next: Why global English may mean the end of English as a Foreign Language*, London: The British Council.

Granger, S (2004) Computer learner corpus research: current status and future prospects, in Connor, U and Upton, T A (Eds) *Applied Corpus Linguistics: A Multidimensional Perspective*, Amsterdam and Atlanta: Rodopi.

Graves, M F, Prenn, M C, Earle, J, Thompson, M, Johnson, V and Slater, W H (1991) Improving Instructional Texts: Some Lessons Learned, *Reading Research Quarterly* 26 (2), 110–32.

Green, A B (2007) IELTS Washback in Context: Preparation for academic writing in higher education, *Studies in Language Testing* 25, Cambridge: UCLES/Cambridge University Press.

Green, A B (2007a) Functional Progression at the C level of the CEFR, *Cambridge ESOL internal report.*

Green, A B and Maycock, L (2004) Computer based IELTS and paper based versions of IELTS, *Research Notes* 18, 3–6.

Green, A B and Maycock, L (2005) The effects on performance of computer familiarity and attitudes towards CB IELTS, *Research Notes* 20, 3–8.

Grellet, F (1987) *Developing Reading Skills*, Cambridge: Cambridge University Press.

Guthrie, J T and Kirsch, I S (1987) Distinctions Between Reading Comprehension and Locating Information in Text, *Journal of Educational Psychology* 79 (3), 220–27.

Guthrie, J T and Mosenthal, P (1987) Literacy as multidimensional: locating information and reading comprehension, *Educational Psychologist* 22 (3&4), 279–97.

Gutteridge, M (2006) *ESOL Special circumstances in 2006: a review of Upper Main Suite provision,* downloadable from: <http://www.cambridgeesol.org/exams/exams-info/special-circumstances/index.html>.

Hackett, E (2005) The development of a computer-based version of PET, *Research Notes* 22, 9–13.

Hale, G, Taylor, C, Bridgeman, B, Courson, J, Kroll, B, and Kantor, R (1996) A study of writing tasks assigned in academic degree programs. TOEFL Research Report 54, Princeton, NJ: Educational Testing Service.

Hambleton, R K, Swaminathan, H and Rogers, H J (1991) *Fundamentals of Item Response Theory*, Newbury Park, CA: Sage.

Hamp-Lyons, L (1990) Second Language Writing: Assessment issues, in Kroll, B (Ed.) *Second Language Writing: Research Insights for the Classroom*, Cambridge: Cambridge University Press, 69–87.

Hamp-Lyons, L (1997) Washback, Impact and Validity: Ethical concerns, *Language Testing* 14 (3), 295–303.

Hamp-Lyons, L (2000) Social, professional and individual responsibility in language testing, *System* 28 (4), 579–91.

Hardcastle, P, Bolton, S and Pelliccia, F (2008) Test comparability and construct compatibility across languages, in Taylor, L and Weir, C J (Eds) *Multilingualism and Assessment, Studies in Language Testing* 27, Cambridge: UCLES/Cambridge University Press, 130–146.

Hargreaves, P (2000) How Important is Collocation in Testing the Learner's Language Proficiency? in Lewis, M (Ed) *Teaching Collocation – further developments in the Lexical Approach,* Hove: Language Teaching Publications.

Harrison, C (2007) Teaching Knowledge Test update – adoptions and courses, *Research Notes* 29, 30–32.

References

Hart, S G and Staveland, L E (1988) Development of NASA-TLX (Task Load Index): results of empirical and theoretical research, in Hancock P A and Meshakati, N (Eds) *Human Mental Workload*, New York: Elsevier, 5–39.

Hartman, D K (1995) Eight readers reading: The intertextual links of proficient readers reading multiple passages, *Reading Research Quarterly* 30 (3), 520–561.

Hawkey, R (2004) *CPE Textbook: Washback Study*, UCLES internal paper.

Hawkey, R (2004a) An IELTS Impact Study: implementation and some early findings, *Research Notes* 15, 12–16.

Hawkey, R (2005) A modular approach to Testing English Language Skills: The development of the Certificates in English Language Skills (CELS) examinations, *Studies in Language Testing* 16, Cambridge: UCLES/ Cambridge University Press.

Hawkey, R (2006) Impact theory and practice: studies of the IELTS test and Progetto Lingue 2000, *Studies in Language Testing* 24, Cambridge: UCLES/ Cambridge University Press.

Hawkey, R (2009) Examining FCE and CAE, *Studies in Language Testing* 28, Cambridge: UCLES/Cambridge University Press.

Haynes, M and Carr, T H (1990) Writing system background and second language reading: a component skills analysis of English reading by native speakers of Chinese, in Carr, T H and Levy, B A (Eds) *Reading and its Development: Component Skills Approaches*, San Diego, CA: Academic Press, 375–421.

Hazenberg, S and Hulstijn, J H (1996) Defining a minimal receptive second language vocabulary for non-native university students: An empirical investigation, *Applied Linguistics* 17 (2), 145–63.

Hegarty, M and Just, M A (1989) Understanding Machines From Text and Diagrams, in Mandl, H and Levine, J (Eds) *Knowledge Acquisition from Text and Picture*, Amsterdam: North-Holland.

Hegarty, M, Carpenter, P A and Just, M A (1991) Diagrams in the Comprehension of Scientific Texts, in Barr, R, Kamil, M L, Mosenthal, P and Pearson, P D (Eds) *Handbook of Reading Research* 2, London: Longman.

Henning, G (1987) A Guide to Language Testing Development, *Evaluation and Research*, Cambridge, MA: Newbury House.

Heppner, F H, Anderson, J G R, Farstrup, A E and Weiderman, N H (1985) Reading performance on a standardized test is better from print than from computer display, *Journal of Reading* 28 (4), 321–25.

Herington, R (1996) *Test-taking strategies and second language proficiency: Is there a relationship?* unpublished MA dissertation, Lancaster University.

Hess R (2000) *Web Workshop – More or Less: Can Color-Blind Users See Your Site?* retrieved from: <http://msdn.microsoft.com/workshop/design/color/ hess10092000.asp>.

Hetter, R D, Segall, D O and Bloxom, B M (1994) A comparison of item calibration media in computerized adaptive testing, *Applied Psychological Measurement* 18 (3), 197–204.

Higgins J, Russell, M and Hoffmann, T (2005) Examining the Effect of Computer-Based Passage Presentation on Reading test Performance, *Journal of Technology, Learning and Assessment* 3 (4), 1–35.

Hindmarsh, R (1980) *Cambridge English Lexicon*, Cambridge: Cambridge University Press.

Hinofotis, F B (1983) The structure of oral communication in an educational environment: A comparison of factor-analytic rotation procedures, in Oller, J W (Ed) *Issues in language testing research*, Rowley, MA: Newbury House, 170–87.

Holliday, W G, Brunner, L L and Donais, E L (1977) Differential Cognitive and Affective Responses to Flow Diagrams in Science, *Journal of Research in Science Teaching* 14 (2), 129–38.

Hoover, W A, and Tunmer, W E (1993) The components of reading, in Thompson, G B, Tunmer, W E and Nicholson, T (Eds), *Reading acquisition processes*, Clevedon, PA: Multilingual Matters, 1–19.

Horak, T (1996) *IELTS Impact Study Project*, unpublished MA assignment, Lancaster University.

Hosenfeld, C (1977) A Preliminary Investigation of the Reading Strategies of Successful and Nonsuccessful Second Language Learners, *System* 5 (2), 110–23.

Hudson, T (1996) Assessing second language academic reading from a communicative competence perspective: Relevance for TOEFL 2000, *TOEFL Monograph Series* MS-4, Princeton, NJ: Educational Testing Service.

Hughes, A (1989) *Testing for language teachers*, Cambridge: Cambridge University Press.

Hughes, A (1993) Testing the ability to infer when reading in a second or foreign language, *Journal of English and Foreign Languages* 10 (11), 13–20.

Hughes, A (2003) *Testing for language teachers* (2nd edition), Cambridge: Cambridge University Press.

Huhta, A, Luoma, S, Oscarson, M, Sajavaara, K, Takala, S and Teasdale, A (2002) *A diagnostic language assessment system for adult learners*, in Alderson (Ed.) 2002, 130–46.

Hyland, K (2002) Teaching and Researching Writing, *Applied Linguistics in Action Series*, London: Longman.

Hymes, D (1972) On communicative competence, in Pride, J and Holmes, A (Eds) *Sociolinguistics*, Harmsworth and New York: Penguin, 269–93.

Hyona, J and Nurminen, A M (2006) Do adult readers know how they read? Evidence from eye movement patterns and verbal reports, *British Journal of Psychology* 97 (1), 31–50.

Ingham, K (2008) The Cambridge ESOL approach to item writer training: the case of ICFE Listening, *Research Notes* 32, 5–8.

International Language Testing Association (2000) *Code of Ethics*, <www.ilta.org>.

International Test Commission (2001) International Guidelines for Test Use, *International Journal of Testing* 1 (2), 93–114.

Jackobson, R (1960) Linguistics and Poetics, in Seboek, T A (Ed.) *Style in language*, New York: John Wiley.

Jenkins, J R, Fuchs, L S, van den Broeck, P, Espin, C and Deno, S L (2003) Sources of individual difference in reading comprehension and reading fluency, *Journal of Educational Psychology* 95 (4), 719–29.

Jones, N (2000) Background to the validation of the ALTE Can Do Project and the revised Common European Framework, *Research Notes* 2, 11–13.

Jones, N (2000a) BULATS: A case study comparing computer-based and paper-and-pencil tests, *Research Notes* 3, 10–13.

Jones, N (2001) Reliability as one aspect of test quality, *Research Notes* 4, 2–5.

Jones, N (2001a) The ALTE Can Do Project and the role of measurement in constructing a proficiency framework, *Research Notes* 5, 5–8.

References

Jones, N (2002) Relating the ALTE Framework to the Common European Framework of Reference, in Alderson, J C (Ed.) *Case Studies in applying the Common European Framework*, Strasbourg: Council of Europe, 167–83.

Jones, N (2005) Raising the Languages Ladder: constructing a new framework for accrediting foreign language skills, *Research Notes* 19, 15–19.

Jones, N and Hirtzel, M (2001) The ALTE Can Do Project, English Version: Articles and Can Do statements produced by the members of ALTE 1992–2002, Appendix D in Council of Europe (2001) *Common European Framework of Reference for Languages*, Cambridge: Cambridge University Press.

Jones, N and Saville, N (2008) Scales and Frameworks, in Spolsky, B and Hult, F M (Eds) *The Handbook of Educational Linguistics*, Malden, MA: Blackwell, 495–509.

Just, M A and Carpenter, P A (1980) A theory of reading: from eye fixations to comprehension, *Psychological Review* 87 (4), 329–54.

Just, M A and Carpenter, P A (1987) *The Psychology of Reading and Language Comprehension*, Boston, MA: Allyn and Bacon.

Kaftandjieva, F (2004) *Standard setting, Section B, Reference Supplement to the Preliminary Pilot version of the Manual for Relating Language examinations to the Common European Framework of Reference for Languages: learning, teaching, assessment*, Strasbourg: Council of Europe, Recovered from: <http://www.coe.int/t/dg4/linguistic/Manuel1_EN.asp>.

Kane, M T (1992) An argument-based approach to validity, *Psychological Bulletin* 112 (3), 527–35.

Keddle, J S (2004) The CEF and the secondary school syllabus, in Morrow, K (Ed.) *Insights from the Common European Framework*, Oxford: Oxford University Press, 43–54.

Keefe, J W and Monk, J S (1986) *Learning style profile examiners' manual*, Reston, VA: National Association of Secondary School Principals.

Khalifa, H (1997) *A study in the Construct Validation of the Reading Module of an EAP Proficiency test Battery: Validation from a variety of Perspectives*, unpublished PhD thesis, University of Reading.

Khalifa, H (2003) Student Achievement Test Development Manual: Training Resource in English Language Testing. Academy for Educational Development/United States Agency for International Development (AED/USAID).

Khalifa, H (2005) Are test taker characteristics accounted for in Main Suite Reading papers?, *Research Notes* 21, 7–10.

Khalifa, H and Pike, N (2006) *English Benchmarking Test*, unpublished project report submitted to the Colombian Ministry of Education.

Khalifa, H, Robinson, M, and Geranpayeh, A (2005) *English Diagnostic Test*, unpublished project report submitted to the Chilean Ministry of Education.

Kim, M (2001) Detecting DIF across the different language groups in a speaking test, *Language Testing* 18 (1), 89–114.

Kintsch, W and van Dijk, T A (1978) Toward a Model of Text Comprehension and Production, *Psychological Review* 85 (5), 363–94.

Kintsch, W and Yarborough, J C (1982) Role of rhetorical structure in text comprehension, *Journal of Educational Psychology* 74 (6), 828–34.

Kirsch, I, Jamieson, J, Taylor, C and Eignor, D (1998) Computer familiarity among TOEFL examinees, *TOEFL Research Report* 59, Princeton, NJ: Educational Testing Service.

Klare, G (1984) Readability, in Pearson, P D, Barr, R, Kamil, M and Mosenthal, P (Eds) *Handbook of reading research*, New York: Longman, 681–744.

Kobayashi, M (1995) *Effects of Text Organisation and Test Format on Reading Comprehension Test Performance*, unpublished PhD thesis, Thames Valley University.

Koda, K (2005) *Insights into second language reading*, New York: Cambridge University Press.

Koenig, A J (1992) A framework for understanding the literacy of individuals with visual impairments, *Journal of Visual Impairment and Blindness* 86, 277–284.

Kong, D (1996) *An Empirical Study of the Strategies Adopted by EFL Readers While Reading EAP Materials for Main Ideas–Implications for Teaching and Testing Reading*, unpublished MA TEFL dissertation, University of Reading: CALS.

Koran, M L and Koran, J (1980) Interaction of Learner Characteristics with Pictorial Adjuncts in Learning From Science Text, *Journal of Research in Science Teaching* 17 (5), 477–83.

Kruk, R S and Muter, P (1984) Reading of Continuous Text on Video Screens, *Human Factors* 26 (3), 339–345, Retrieved May 13th 2005 from: <http://psych.utoronto.ca>.

Kunnan, A J (1990) DIF in native language and gender groups in an ESL Placement test, *TESOL Quarterly* 24 (4), 740–46.

Kunnan, A J (1994) Modelling relationships among some test-taker characteristics and performance on EFL tests: An approach to construct validation, *Language Testing* 11 (3), 225–52.

Kunnan, A J (1995) Test taker characteristics and test performance: A structural modelling approach, *Studies in Language Testing* 2, Cambridge: UCLES/Cambridge University Press.

Kunnan, A J (2000) Fairness and justice for all, in Kunnan, A J (Ed.) Fairness and validation in language assessment, *Studies in Language Testing* 9, Cambridge: UCLES/Cambridge University Press, 1–13.

Kunnan, A J (2004) Test fairness, in Milanovic, M and Weir, C J (Eds) European language testing in a global context, *Studies in Language Testing* 18, Cambridge: UCLES/Cambridge University Press, 27–48.

Kunnan, A J (2008) Towards a model of test evaluation: using the Test Fairness and Test Context Frameworks, in Taylor, L and Weir, C J (Eds), Multilingualism and assessment: Achieving transparency, assuring quality sustaining diversity, *Studies in Language Testing* 27, Cambridge: UCLES/Cambridge University Press, 229–251.

LaBerge, D and Samuels, S D (1974) Towards a Theory of Automatic Information Processing in Reading, *Cognitive Psychology* 6 (2), 293–323.

Lacroix, N (1999) Macrostructure construction and organisation in the processing of multiple text passages, *Instructional Science* 27, 221–33.

Lado, R (1961) *Language Testing: The Construction and Use of Foreign Language Tests*, London: Longman.

Larkin, J H and Simon, H A (1987) Why a Diagram is Sometimes Worth Ten Thousand Words, *Cognitive Science* 11 (1), 65–99.

Laufer, B (1988) What percentage of text-lexis is essential for comprehension? in Lauren, C and Nordmann, M (Eds) *Special language: From humans to machines*, Clevedon: Multilingual Matters, 316–23.

Laufer, B (1997) What's in a word that makes it hard or easy?: Some intralexical factors that affect the learning of words, in Schmitt, N (Ed.) *Vocabulary: Description, Acquisition, and Pedagogy*, Cambridge: Cambridge University Press.

References

Laufer, B (1998) The development of passive and active vocabulary in a second language: same or different?, *Applied Linguistics* 19 (2), 255–71.

Lave, J and Wenger, E (1991) *Situated Learning, Legitimate peripheral participation*, Cambridge: Cambridge University Press.

Legge, G E, Madison, C and Mansfield, J S (1999) Measuring Braille reading speed with the MNREAD test, *Visual Impairment Research* 1 (3), 131–45.

Lewkowicz, J (1997) *Investigating authenticity in language testing*, unpublished PhD thesis, University of Lancaster.

Linacre, J M (2006) *Winsteps Rasch measurement computer program*, Chicago: Winsteps.com.

Lipson, M Y and Wixson, K K (1991) *Assessment and instruction of reading disability: An interactive approach*, New York: Harper Collins.

Lumley, T (1993) The notion of subskills in reading comprehension tests: An EAP example, *Language Testing* 10 (3), 211–34.

Luoma, S (2004) *Assessing Speaking*, Cambridge: Cambridge University Press.

McDonald, A (2002) The impact of individual differences on the equivalence of computer-based and paper-and-pencil educational assessments, *Computers and Education* 39 (3), 299–312.

McGoldrick, J A, Martin, J, Bergering, A J and Symons, S (1992) Locating discrete information in text: Effects of computer presentation and menu formatting, *Journal of Reading Behavior* 14 (1), 1–20.

McKnight, C, Richardson, J and Dillon, A (1990) A comparison of linear and hypertext formats in information retrieval, in McAleese, R and Green, C (Eds) *Hypertext: State of the Art*, Oxford: Intellect, 10–19.

McKoon, G (1977) Organisation of information in text memory, *Journal of Verbal Learning and Verbal Behavior* 16, 247–60.

Malvern, D D, and Richards, B J (1997) A new measure of lexical diversity, in Ryan, A and Wray, A (Eds), *Evolving models of language*, papers from the Annual Meeting of the British Association of Applied Linguists held at the University of Wales, Swansea, September 1996, Clevedon: Multilingual Matters, 58–71.

Markham, P (1985) The Rationale Deletion Cloze and Global Comprehension in German, *Language Learning* 35 (3), 423–30.

Marshall, H (2006) The Cambridge ESOL Item Banking System, *Research Notes* 23, 6–8.

Martyniuk, W (2008) Relating language examinations to the Council of Europe's Common European Framework of Reference, in Taylor, L and Weir C J (Eds) Multilingualism and Assessment, *Studies in Language Testing* 27, Cambridge: UCLES/Cambridge University Press, 9–20.

Masi, S (2002) The literature on complexity, in Merlini Barbesi, L (Ed) *Complexity in Language and Text*, Pisa: PLUS-University of Pisa, 197–228.

Matthew, K (1997) A comparison of the influence of interactive CD-ROM storybooks and traditional print storybooks on reading comprehension, *Journal of Research in Computing in Education* 29 (3), 263–75.

Maycock, L and Green, A B (2005) The effects on performance of computer familiarity and attitudes to CB IELTS, *Research Notes* 20, 3–8.

Mayers, D K, Sims, V K and Koonce, J M (2001) Comprehension and workload differences for VDT and paper-based reading, *International Journal of Industrial Ergonomics* 28 (6), 367–78.

Mazzeo, J and Harvey, A L (1988) The equivalence of scores from automated and conventional educational and psychological tests: A review of the literature, *ETS RR-88-21*, Princeton, NJ: Educational Testing Service.

Mead, A D and Drasgow, F (1993) Equivalence of computerized and paper-and-pencil cognitive ability tests: A meta-analysis, *Psychological Bulletin* 114 (3), 449–58.

Melka, F (1997) Receptive vs productive aspects of vocabulary, in Schmitt, N and McCarthy, M (Eds) *Vocabulary: Description, Acquisition, and Pedagogy*, Cambridge: Cambridge University Press, 84–102.

Messick, S A (1989) Validity, in Linn, R L (Ed.) *Educational Measurement* (3rd edition), New York: Macmillan, 13–103.

Messick, S A (1994) The interplay of evidence and consequences in the validation of performance assessments, *Educational Researcher* 23 (2), 13–23.

Messick, S A (1996) Validity and washback in language testing, *Language Testing* 13 (3), 241–256.

Meyer, B J F (1975) *The Organisation of Prose and its Effect on Memory*, Amsterdam: North-Holland.

Meyer, B J F and Freedle, R O (1984) Effects of Discourse Type on Recall, *American Educational Research Journal* 21 (1), 121–43.

Milanovic, M and Saville, N (1996) *Considering the impact of Cambridge EFL examinations*, Cambridge: UCLES internal report.

Miller, M D and Linn, R L (1988) Invariance of Item Characteristic Functions with Variations on Instructional Coverage, *Journal of Educational Measurement* 25 (3), 205–19.

Mislevy, R J (1992) *Linking Educational Assessments: Concepts, Issues, Methods, and Prospects*, Princeton, NJ: Educational Testing Service.

Mislevy, R J, Steinberg, L S and Almond, R G (2002) Design and analysis in task-based language assessment, *Language Testing* 19 (4), 477–96.

Mislevy, R J, Steinberg, L S and Almond, R G (2003) On the structure of educational assessments, *Measurement: Interdisciplinary Research and Perspectives* 1 (1), 3–62.

Moe, E (2008) Juggling numbers and opinions: an attempt to set CEFR standards in Norway for a test of reading in English, in Taylor, L and Weir C J (Eds) Multilingualism and Assessment, *Studies in Language Testing* 27, Cambridge: UCLES/Cambridge University Press, 67–78.

Morrow, K (1979) Communicative Language testing: revolution or evolution? in Brumfit, C and Johnson, K (Eds) *The communicative approach to language teaching*, Oxford: Oxford University Press.

Morrow, K (Ed) (2004) *Insights from the Common European Framework*, Oxford: Oxford University Press.

Munby, J (1978) *Communicative Syllabus Design*, Cambridge: Cambridge University Press.

Murphy, P K, Long, J, Holleran, T and Esterly, E (2000) *Persuasion online or on paper: A new take on an old issue*, paper presented at the annual meeting of the American Psychological Association, Washington DC, 4–8 August 2000.

Murray, S (2007) Broadening the cultural context of examination materials, *Research Notes* 27, 19–22.

Muter, P and Maurutto, P (1991) Reading and skimming from computer screens and books: the paperless office revisited?, *Behaviour and Information Technology* 10 (4) 257–66. Retrieved May 13th 2005 from: <http://psych.utoronto.ca>.

Nation, P (2001) *Learning Vocabulary in Another Language*, Cambridge: Cambridge University Press.

Nation, P and Gu, P Y (2007) *Focus on Vocabulary*, Sydney: NCELTR.

References

Neuman, G and Baydoun, R (1998) Computerization of paper-and-pencil tests: When are they equivalent?, *Applied Psychological Measurement* 22 (1), 71–83.

Nevo, N (1989) Test-taking strategies on a multiple-choice test of reading comprehension, *Language Testing* 6 (2), 199–215.

Nichols, P and Kirkpatrick, R (2005) *Comparability of the computer-administered tests with existing paper-and-pencil tests in reading and mathematics tests*, paper presented at the AERA Division D Graduate Student Seminar, Montreal, Canada, April 2005.

Noijons, J and Kuijper, H (2006) *Mapping the Dutch Foreign Language State Examinations onto the Common European Framework of Reference*, Arnhem, The Netherlands: National Institute of Educational Measurement.

North, B (2000) *The Development of a Common Framework Scale of Language Proficiency*, New York: Peter Lang.

North, B (2000a) Linking Language Assessments: an example in a low-stakes context, *System* 28 (4), 555–77.

North, B (2002) Developing Descriptor Scales of Language Proficiency for the CEF Common Reference Levels, in Alderson, J C (Ed) *Case Studies in applying the Common European Framework*, Strasbourg: Council of Europe.

North, B (2002a) A CEF-based self-assessment tool for university entrance, in Alderson, J C (Ed.) *Case Studies in applying the Common European Framework*, Strasbourg: Council of Europe.

North, B (2004) Relating assessments, examinations, and courses to the CEF, in Morrow, K (Ed.) *Insights from the Common European Framework*, Oxford: Oxford University Press, 77–90.

North, B (2006) *The Common European Framework of Reference: Development, Theoretical and Practical Issues*, paper presented at the symposium 'A New Direction in Foreign Language education: The Potential of the Common European Framework of Reference for Languages', Osaka University of Foreign Studies, Japan, March 2006.

North, B (2008) *The educational and social impact of the CEFR in Europe and beyond: a preliminary overview*, paper presented at the 3rd ALTE Conference, Cambridge, April 2008.

North, B and Schneider, G (1998) Scaling descriptors for language proficiency scales, *Language Testing* 15 (2), 217–62.

Novaković, N (2006) TKT – a year on, *Research Notes* 24, 22–24.

Noyes, J and Garland, K (2003) VDT versus paper-based text: Reply to Mayers, Sims and Koonce, *International Journal of Industrial Ergonomics* 31 (6), 411–23.

Noyes, J, Garland, K and Robbins, L (2004) Paper-based versus computer-based assessment: Is workload another test mode effect? *British Journal of Educational Technology* 35 (1), 111–13.

Nuttall, C (1996) *Teaching Reading Skills in a Foreign Language*, London: Heinemann.

Nystrand, M (1989) A social interactive model of writing, *Written Communication* 6 (1), 66–85.

Oakhill, J and Garnham, A (1988) *Becoming a Skilled Reader*, Oxford: Blackwell.

Oates, T (2006) *Codes of practice: Consolidating best practice or putting a brake on innovation?* plenary presentation at ALTE Conference on Codes of Practice in Language Testing, University of Sofia, Bulgaria; November 2006.

Oltman, P K, Stricker, L J and Barrows, T (1988) Native Language, English Proficiency and the Structure of the Test of English as a Foreign Language, *TOEFL Research Report* 27, Princeton, NJ: Educational Testing Service.

O'Malley, J M and Valdez Pierce, L (1996) *Authentic Assessment for English Language Learners*, New York: Addison Wesley.

O'Malley, K J, Kirkpatrick, R, Sherwood, W, Burdick, H J, Hsieh, M C and Sanford, E E (2005) *Comparability of a Paper Based and Computer Based Reading Test in Early Elementary Grades*, paper presented at the AERA Division D Graduate Student Seminar, Montreal, Canada, April 2005.

O'Sullivan, B (2000) *Towards a Model of Performance in Oral Language Testing*, unpublished PhD thesis, University of Reading.

O'Sullivan, B (2006) Issues in Testing Business English: The revision of the Cambridge Business English Certificates, *Studies in Language Testing* 17, Cambridge: UCLES/Cambridge University Press.

O'Sullivan, B (2008) *Modelling Performance in Tests of Spoken Language*, Frankfurt: Peter Lang.

O'Sullivan, B and Porter, D (1995) *The importance of audience age for learner-speakers and learner-writers from different cultural backgrounds*, paper presented at the RELC conference, Singapore.

Pae, T I (2004) DIF for examinees with different academic backgrounds, *Language Testing* 21 (1), 53–73.

Paek, P (2005) Recent Trends in Comparability Studies, *Pearson Research Report* 05–05, August 2005.

Partnership for Accessible Reading Assessment (PARA) (2005) *Reading and Students with Visual Impairments or Blindness*: <www.readingassessment.info/resources/publications/visualimpairment.htm>.

Pearson, I (1988) Tests as levers for change, in Chamberlain, D and Baumgartner, R (Eds) *ESP in the Classroom: Practice and Evaluation*, ELT Documents 128, London: Modern English Publications.

Pearson, P D, Barr, R, Kamil, M L and Mosenthal, P (1984) *The Handbook of Reading Research* 1, London: Longman.

Perera, K (1984) *Children's Writing and Recording*, Oxford: Basil Blackwell.

Perfetti, C A (1985) *Reading Ability*, New York: Oxford University Press.

Perfetti, C A (1994) Psycholinguistics and reading ability, in Gernspacher, M (Ed) *Handbook of Psycholinguistics*, San Diego, CA: Academic Press, 849–94.

Perfetti, C A (1997) Sentences, individual differences, and multiple texts: three issues in text comprehension, *Discourse Processes* 23 (3), 337–55.

Perfetti, C A (1999) Comprehending written language: a blueprint for the reader, in Brown, C M and Hagoort, P (Eds) *The neurocognition of language*, New York: Oxford University Press, 167–208.

Perfetti, C A, Rouet, J F and Britt, M A (1999) Toward a theory of document representation, in Van Oostendorp, H and Goldman, S R (Eds) *The construction of mental representations during reading*, London: Lawrence Erlbaum Associates Publishers, 99–122.

Phakiti, A (2003) A Closer Look at the Relationship of Cognitive and Metacognitive Strategy Use to EFL Reading Achievement Test Performance, *Language Testing* 20 (1), 26–56.

Piolat, A, Roussey, J Y and Thunin, O (1997) Effects of screen presentation on text reading and revising, *International Journal of Human-Computer Studies* 47 (4), 565–89.

Poggio, J, Glassnapp, D R, Yang, X and Poggio, A J (2005) A comparative evaluation of score results from computerized and paper and pencil mathematics testing in a large scale state assessment program, *The Journal of Technology, Learning, and Assessment* 3 (6), 1–30.

References

Pollitt, A and Ahmed, A (2000) *Comprehension failures in educational assessment*, paper presented at the European Conference for Educational Research, Edinburgh.

Pollitt, A and Taylor, L (2006) Cognitive psychology and reading assessment, in Sainsbury, M, Harrison, C and Watts, A (2006) *Assessing Reading: from theories to classrooms*, Slough: NFER, 38–49.

Pommerich, M (2004) Developing computerized versions of paper tests: Mode effects for passage-based tests, *The Journal of Technology, Learning, and Assessment* 2 (6), 1–44.

Pomplun, M, Frey, S and Becker, D F (2002) The score equivalence of paper and computerized versions of a speeded test of reading comprehension, *Educational and Psychological Measurement* 62 (2), 337–54.

Popham, W J (1990) *Modern Educational Measurement* (2nd edition), Englewood Cliffs, NJ: Prentice-Hall.

Powers, D E (2001) Test anxiety and test performance: comparing paper-based and computer-adaptive versions of the Graduate Record Examinations (GRE) General Test, *Journal of Educational Computing Research* 24 (3), 249–73.

Pressley, M and Afflerbach, P (1995) *Verbal Protocols of Reading: The Nature of Constructively Responsive Reading*, Hillsdale, NJ: Lawrence Erlbaum Associates.

Pring, L (1994) Touch and go: Learning to read Braille, *Reading Research Quarterly* 29 (1), 67–74.

Pugh, A K (1978) *Silent Reading*, London: Heinemann.

Purpura, J (1999) *Learner Strategy Use and Performance on Language Tests*, Cambridge: Cambridge University Press.

Rawson, R E and Quinlan, K M (2002) Evalaution of a computer-based approach to teaching acid/base biology, *Advances in Physiology Education* 26 (2), 85–97.

Rayner, K and Pollatsek, A (1989) *The Psychology of Reading*, Englewood Cliffs, NJ: Prentice Hall.

Read, J M (2000) *Assessing Vocabulary*, Cambridge: Cambridge University Press.

Reinking, D (1988) Computer-mediated text and comprehension differences: The role of reading time, reader preference, and estimation of learning, *Reading Research Quarterly* 23 (4), 484–500.

Reinking, D and Schreiner, R (1985) The effects of computer-mediated text on measures of reading comprehension and reading behaviour, *Reading Research Quarterly* 20 (5), 536–52.

Resnick, L B and Resnick, D P (1992) Assessing the thinking curriculum: New tools for educational reform, in Gifford, B G and O'Conner M C (Eds), *Changing Assessments: Alternative views of aptitude, achievement and instruction*, Boston: Kluwer Academic Publishers, 37–75.

Richards, J C, Platt, J and Platt, H (1992) *Dictionary of Language Teaching and Applied Linguistics*, London: Longman.

Ricketts, C and Wilks, S (2002) Improving student performance through computer-based assessment: insights from recent research, *Assessment and Evaluation in Higher Education* 27 (5), 475–79.

Rixon, S (2007) Cambridge ESOL YLE tests and children's first steps in reading and writing in English, *Research Notes* 28, 7–14.

Roach, J O (1944) *The Cambridge Examinations in English, A Survey of their History*, Cambridge Assessment Archives: PP JOR 1/1a xxi.

Rose, D (2006) *Report on Observations of FCE and CAE Time Trials*, Cambridge ESOL internal report.

Rosenshine, B V (1980) Skill Hierarchies in Reading Comprehension, in Spiro, R J, Bruce, B C and Brewer, W F (Eds), *Theoretical issues in reading comprehension*, Hillsdale, NJ: Lawrence Erlbaum, 535–59.

Rothkopf, E Z (1982) Adjunct aids and the control of mathemagenic activities during purposeful reading, in Otto, W and White, S (Eds) *Reading Expository Material*, New York: Academic Press, 109–38.

Rouet, J F, Vidal-Abarca, E, Bert-Erboul, A and Millogo, V (2001) Effects of information search tasks on the comprehension of instructional text, *Discourse Processes* 31(2), 163–86.

Ruddell, R B and Speaker, R (1985) The Interactive Reading Process: A Model, in Singer, H and Ruddell, R B (Eds) *Theoretical Models and Processes of Reading* 3rd edition, Newark, Delaware: International Reading Association, 751–93.

Rupp, A A, Ferne, T and Choi, H (2006) How assessing reading comprehension with multiple-choice questions shapes the construct: A cognitive processing perspective, *Language Testing* 23 (4), 441–74.

Russell, M and Haney, W (1997) Testing writing on computers: an experiment comparing student performance on tests conducted via computer and via paper-and-pencil, *Educational Policy Analysis Archives* 5 (3).

Russell, M (1999) Testing on computers: a follow-up study comparing performance on computer and on paper, *Education Policy Analysis Archives* 7 (20).

Ryan, K and Bachman, L F (1992) DIF on two tests of EFL proficiency, *Language Testing* 9 (1), 12–29.

Salamoura, A and Brett, T (2007) Use of Reading text highlighters in CB tests. *Cambridge ESOL Internal Research and Validation Report 1087.*

Saville, N (2000) Developing Language Learning Questionnaires (LLQs), *Research Notes* 1, 6–7.

Saville, N (2001) Investigating the impact of international language examinations, *Research Notes* 2, 4–7.

Saville, N (2003) The process of test development and revision within UCLES EFL, in Weir, C J and Milanovic, M (Eds) Continuity and Innovation: Revising the Cambridge Proficiency in English Examination 1913–2002, *Studies in Language Testing* 15, Cambridge: UCLES/Cambridge University Press, 57–120.

Saville, N (2004) *The ESOL Test Development and Validation Strategy*, UCLES internal discussion paper.

Saville, N (2009) *Developing a model for investigating the impact of language assessment within educational contexts by a public examination provider*, unpublished PhD thesis: University of Bedfordshire.

Saville, N and Hawkey, R (2004) The IELTS Impact Study: Investigating Washback on Teaching Materials, in Cheng, L and Watanabe, Y (Eds) *Washback in Language Testing: Research Contexts and Methods*, NJ: Lawrence Erlbaum Associates, 97–112.

Sawaki, Y (2001) Comparability of conventional and computerized tests of reading in a second language, *Language Learning and Technology* 5 (2), 38–59.

Sawilowsky, S S (2000) Psychometrics versus datametrics: comment on Vacha-Haase's "reliability generalization" method and some EPM editorial policies, *Educational and Psychological Measurement* 60 (2), 157–73.

References

Scardamalia, M and Bereiter, C (1987) Knowledge telling and knowledge transforming in written composition, in Rosenberg, S (Ed) *Advances in Applied Psycholinguistics, Volume 2: Reading, writing and language learning,* Cambridge: Cambridge University Press.

Schedl, M, Gordon, A, Carey, P A and Tang, K L (1996) An Analysis of the Dimensionality of TOEFL Reading Comprehension Items, *TOEFL Research Report* 53, Princeton, NJ: Educational Testing Service.

Schulte, A G, Elliott S N, and Kratchowill, T R (2001) Effects of testing accommodations on students' standardized mathematics test scores: An experimental analysis, *School Psychology Review* 30, 527–47.

Shaw, S and Weir, C J (2007) Examining Writing: Research and practice in assessing second language writing, *Studies in Language Testing* 26, Cambridge: UCLES/Cambridge University Press.

Shaw, S, Jones, N and Flux, T (2001) CBIELTS – a comparison of computer-based and paper versions. *Cambridge ESOL Internal Research and Validation Report 216.*

Shermis, M and Lombard, D (1998) Effects of computer-based test administration on test anxiety and performance, *Computers in Human Behavior* 14 (1), 111–23.

Shi, L (2004) Textual borrowing in second-language writing, *Written Communication* 21 (2), 171–200.

Shih, M (1992) Beyond Comprehension Exercises in The ESL Academic Reading Class, *TESOL Quarterly* 26 (2), 289–318.

Shiotsu, T (2003) *Linguistic knowledge and processing efficiency as predictors of L2 reading ability: a component skills analysis,* unpublished PhD thesis, University of Reading.

Shiotsu, T and Weir, C J (2005) *Equivalence of the Paper-Based and Computer-Based Testing of Reading in a Second Language: Focus on the Test Outcomes and the Test Taking Processes,* Cambridge ESOL internal commissioned report.

Shiotsu, T and Weir, C J (2007) The Relative Significance of Syntactic Knowledge and Vocabulary Breadth in the Prediction of Second Language Reading Comprehension Test Performance, *Language Testing* 24 (1), 99–128.

Shohamy, E (2001) *The Power of Tests: A critical perspective on the uses of language tests,* Harlow: Pearson Education.

Sireci, S G, Scarpati, S and Li, S (2005) Test accommodations for students with disabilities: An analysis of the interaction hypothesis, *Review of Educational Research* 75 (4), 457–90.

Skehan, P (1998) Task-based instruction, *Annual Review of Applied Linguistics* 18, 268–86.

Smith, J (2004) IELTS Impact: a study on the accessibility of IELTS GT Modules to 16–17 year old candidates, *Research Notes* 18, 6–9.

Spiegel, D L and Fitzgerald, J (1990) Textual Cohesion and Coherence in Children's Writing Revisited, *Research in the Teaching of English* 24 (1), 48–64.

Spivey, N and King, J R (1989) Readers as writers composing from sources, *Reading Research Quarterly* 24 (1), 7–26.

Spolsky, B (1981) Some ethical questions about language testing, in Klein-Braley, C and Stevenson, D K (Eds) *Practice and problems in language testing,* Frankfurt am Main, Verlag: Peter D Lang, 5–30.

Spolsky, B (1995) *Measured Words,* Oxford: Oxford University Press.

Spray, J A, Ackerman, T A, Reckase, M D and Carlson, J E (1989) Effect of the medium of item presentation on examinee performance and item characteristics, *Journal of Educational Measurement* 26 (3), 261–71.

Stahl, S A, Hynd, C R, Britton, B K, McNish, M M and Bosquet, D (1996) What happens when students read multiple source documents in history?, *Reading Research Quarterly* 31 (4), 430–456.

Stanovich, K E (1980) Toward an Interactive Compensatory Model of Individual Differences in the Development of Reading Fluency, *Reading Research Quarterly* 16 (1), 32–71.

Stanovich, K E (1991) Word recognition: changing perspectives, in Barr, R, Kamil, M L, Mosenthal, P and Pearson, P D (Eds) (1991) *Handbook of Reading Research* 2, London: Longman, 418–52.

Steinberg, L S, Thissen, D and Wainer, H (1990) Validity, in Wainer, H, Dorans, N J, Flaughter, R, Green, B F, Mislevy, R J, Steinberg, L S and Thissen, D (Eds) *Computerized Adaptive Testing: A Primer*, Hillsdale, NJ: Lawrence Erlbaum Associates, 187–232.

Sticht, T G and James, J H (1984) Listening and reading, in Pearson, P D, Barr, R, Kamil, M and Mosenthal, P (Eds) *Handbook of Reading Research*, New York: Longman, 293–317.

Stromso, H I and Braten, I (2002) Norwegian law students' use of multiple sources while reading expository texts, *Reading Research Quarterly* 37 (2), 208–27.

SurveyLang (2008) *Inception report for the European Survey on Language Competence*, Submitted to Directorate General Education and Culture of the European Commission.

Swinton, S S and Powers, D E (1980) Factor Analysis of the Test of English as a Foreign Language for Several Language Groups, *TOEFL Research Report* 6, Princeton, NJ: Educational Testing Service.

Szabo, G (2007) *Potential problems concerning the empirical validation of linking exams to the CEFR*, paper presentation given at the Council of Europe Colloquium, Cambridge, December 2007.

Tan, S H (1990) The Role of Prior Knowledge and Language Proficiency as Predictors of Reading Comprehension among Undergraduates, in de Jong, J H A L and Stevenson, D K (Eds) *Individualising the Assessment of Language Abilities*, Clevedon, PA: Multilingual Matters.

Tannebaum, R J and Wylie, E C (2004) *Mapping Test Scores onto the Common European Framework*, Princeton, NJ: Educational Testing Service.

Taylor, C, Jamieson, J, Eignor, D and Kirsch, I S (1998) The Relationship between Computer Familiarity and Performance on Computer-Based TOEFL Test Tasks, *TOEFL Research Report* 61, Princeton, NJ: Educational Testing Service.

Taylor, L (2000) Stakeholders in Language Testing, *Research Notes* 2, 2–4.

Taylor, L (2004) Issues of test comparability, *Research Notes* 15, 2–5.

Taylor, L (2004a) IELTS, Cambridge ESOL examinations and the Common European Framework, *Research Notes* 18, 2–3.

Taylor, L (2006) The changing landscape of English: implications for language assessment, *ELT Journal* 60 (1), 51–60.

Taylor, L (2008) *The Cambridge Colloquium (6–7 December 2007) – Summary of discussion*, draft paper.

Taylor, L (2009) Developing assessment literacy, *Annual Review of Applied Linguistics* 29 (1), 21–36.

References

Taylor, L (Ed) (forthcoming) Examining Speaking: Research and practice in assessing second language speaking, *Studies in Language Testing* 30, Cambridge: UCLES/Cambridge University Press.

Taylor, L and Barker, F (2008) Using corpora for language assessment, in Shohamy, E and Hornberger, N (Eds) *Language Testing and Assessment, Encyclopedia of Language and Education* Vol. 7, New York: Springer, 1–14.

Taylor, L and Gutteridge, M (2003) Responding to diversity: providing tests for language learners with disabilities, *Research Notes* 11, 2–4.

Taylor, L and Jones, N (2006) Cambridge ESOL exams and the Common European Framework of Reference (CEFR), *Research Notes* 24, 2–5.

Taylor, L and Weir, C J (Eds) (2008) Multilingualism and Assessment, *Studies in Language Testing* 27, Cambridge: UCLES/Cambridge University Press.

Taylor, S E (1965) Eye Movements in Reading: Facts and Fallacies, *American Educational Research Journal* 2 (November), 187–202.

Teasdale, A (1989) *Introspection and Judgemental Approaches to Content Validation: A Study Using the Test In English For Educational Purposes*, unpublished MA dissertation, University of Reading.

Thighe, D (2002) IELTS remarking Project Phase 6: marker reliability, *Cambridge ESOL Internal Research and Validation Report* 355.

Thighe, D (2006) Placing The International Legal English Certificate on The CEFR, *Research Notes* 24, 5–7.

Thighe, D, Jones, N, Geranpayeh, A (2001) IELTS PB and CB Equivalence: A comparison of equated versions of the Reading and Listening components of PB IELTS in relation to CB IELTS. *Cambridge ESOL Internal Research and Validation Report 288*.

Thompson, S J, Blount, A and Thurlow M L (2002) *A summary research on the effects of test accommodations: 1999 through 2001 [Techincal Report 34]*, Minneapolis: University of Minnesota, National Centre on Educational Outcomes.

Thorndike, R L (1973) Reading as Reasoning, *Reading Research Quarterly* 9 (2), 135–47.

Thurlow, M L, Thompson, S J and Lazarus, S (2006) Considerations for the Administration of Tests to Special Needs Students: Accommodations, Modifications, and More, in Downing, S and Haladyna, T (Eds), *Handbook of test development*, Mahwah, NJ: Lawrence Erlbaum Associates, 653–73.

Tittle, C K (1990) Test bias, in Walberg, H J and Haertel, G D (Eds) *The International Encyclopedia of Educational Evaluation*, Oxford: Pergamon, 128–33.

Toulmin, S E (1958) *The uses of argument*, Cambridge: Cambridge University Press.

Trabasso, T and Bouchard, E (2002) Teaching Readers How to Comprehend Text Strategically, in Block, C C and Pressley, M (Eds) *Comprehension Instruction: Research-Based Best Practices*, New York: The Guilford Press, 176–200.

Tuokko, E (2008) *What levels do 9th graders reach in terms of CEFR and Finnish National Core Curriculum*, paper presented at the 3rd ALTE Conference, Cambridge, April 2007.

Unaldi, A (forthcoming) *Investigating the levels of careful reading for academic purposes: practice, process and product*, unpublished PhD thesis, University of Bedfordshire.

University of Cambridge ESOL Examinations (2005) *BEC Handbook for teachers*, UCLES.

University of Cambridge ESOL Examinations (2008) *BEC Handbook for teachers*, UCLES.

University of Cambridge ESOL Examinations (2005) *CAE Handbook for teachers*, UCLES.

University of Cambridge ESOL Examinations (2008) *CAE Handbook for teachers*, UCLES.

University of Cambridge ESOL Examinations (2005) *CPE Handbook for teachers*, UCLES.

University of Cambridge ESOL Examinations (2008) *CPE Handbook for teachers*, UCLES.

University of Cambridge ESOL Examinations (2005) *FCE Handbook for teachers*, UCLES.

University of Cambridge ESOL Examinations (2007) *FCE Handbook for teachers*, UCLES.

University of Cambridge ESOL Examinations, British Council, IDP Australia: (2005) *IELTS Handbook*, UCLES.

University of Cambridge ESOL Examinations, British Council, IDP Australia: (2007) *IELTS Handbook*, UCLES.

University of Cambridge ESOL Examinations (2005) *KET Handbook for teachers*, UCLES.

University of Cambridge ESOL Examinations (2008) *KET Handbook for teachers*, UCLES.

University of Cambridge ESOL Examinations (2005) *PET Handbook for teachers,* UCLES.

University of Cambridge ESOL Examinations (2007) *PET Handbook for teachers*, UCLES.

University of Cambridge ESOL Examinations (2008) *Handbook for Centres*, UCLES.

Urquhart, A H (1984) The Effect of Rhetorical Ordering on Readability, in Alderson, J C and Urquhart, A H (Eds) *Reading in a Foreign Language*, London: Longman, 160–75.

Urquhart, A H and Weir, C J (1998) *Reading in a Second Language: Process, Product and Practice*, New York: Longman.

Vahapassi, A (1982) On the specification of the domain of school writing, in Purves, A C and Takala, S (Eds) *An international perspective on the evaluation of written composition*, Oxford: Pergamon, 265–89.

Van Ek, J and Trim, J (1998) *Threshold 1990*, Cambridge: Cambridge University Press.

Van Ek, J and Trim, J (1998a) *Waystage 1990*, Cambridge: Cambridge University Press.

Van Ek, J and Trim, J (2001) *Vantage*, Cambridge: Cambridge University Press.

Vipond, D (1980) Micro- and Macro-processes in Text Comprehension, *Journal of Verbal Learning and Verbal Behaviour* 19 (3), 276–96.

Vogel, L A (1994) Explaining performance on P&P versus computer mode of administration for the verbal section of the Graduate Record Exam, *Educational Computing Research* 11 (4), 369–83.

Wagner, R and Stanovich, K E (1996) Expertise in Reading, in Ericsson, K A (Ed) *The road to excellence*, Mahwa, NJ: Lawrence Erlbaum Associates, 189–225.

Wall, D (1997) Test Impact and Washback, *Language Testing and Evaluation* Vol. 7: *Kluwer Encyclopaedia of Language Education*, 291–302.

References

Wall, D (2005) The Impact of a High-Stakes Examination on Classroom Teaching: A Case Study Using Insights from Testing and Innovation Theory, *Studies in Language Testing* 22, Cambridge: UCLES/Cambridge University Press.

Wang, S (2004) *Online or paper: Does delivery affect results? Administration mode comparability study for Stanford diagnostic Reading and Mathematics tests*, San Antonio, Texas: Harcourt.

Way, W, Davis, L L and Fitzpatrick, S (2006) *Score Comparability of Online and Paper Administration of the Texas Assessment of Knowledge and Skills*, paper presented at the annual meeting of the National Council on Measurement in Education, San Francisco, CA, 6–10 April 2006.

Weakley, S (1993) *Procedures in the Content Validation of an EAP Proficiency Test of Reading Comprehension*, unpublished MA TEFL dissertation, University of Reading: CALS.

Weigle, S C (2002) *Assessing Writing*, Cambridge: Cambridge University Press.

Weir, C J (1983) *Identifying the language problems of overseas students in tertiary education in the United Kingdom*, unpublished PhD thesis, University of London.

Weir, C J (1990) *Communicative Language Testing*, Englewood Cliffs, NJ: Prentice Hall.

Weir, C J (1993) *Understanding and Developing Language Tests*, New York: Prentice Hall.

Weir, C J (2001) The formative and summative uses of language test data, in Elder, C et al (Eds) *Experimenting with Uncertainty* 2001: Cambridge University Press, 117–26.

Weir, C J (2003) A survey of the history of the Certificate of Proficiency in English (CPE) in the twentieth century, in Weir, C J and Milanovic, M (Eds) Continuity and Innovation: Revising the Cambridge Proficiency in English Examination 1913–2002, *Studies in Language Testing* 15, Cambridge: UCLES/ Cambridge University Press, 1–56.

Weir, C J (2005) *Language Testing and Validation: An Evidence-Based Approach*, Basingstoke: Palgrave Macmillan.

Weir, C J (2005a) Limitations of the Council of Europe's Framework of reference (CEFR) in developing comparable examinations and tests, *Language Testing* 22 (3), 281–300.

Weir, C J and Milanovic, M (Eds) (2003) Continuity and Innovation: Revising the Cambridge Proficiency in English Examination 1913–2002, *Studies in Language Testing* 15, Cambridge: UCLES/Cambridge University Press.

Weir, C J and Porter, D (1994) The Multi-Divisible or Unitary Nature of Reading: The language tester between Scylla and Charybdis, *Reading in a Foreign Language* 10 (2), 1–19.

Weir, C J and Wu, J R W (2006) Establishing Test Form and Individual Task Comparability – A Case Study of a Semi-direct Speaking Test, *Language Testing* 23 (3), 167–97.

Weir, C J, Yang, H and Jin, Y (2000) An Empirical Investigation of the Componentiality of L2 Reading in English for Academic Purposes, *Studies in Language Testing* 12, Cambridge: Cambridge University Press.

Weir, C J, Devi, S, Green, A B, Hawkey, R, Maniski, T , Unaldi A, and Zegarac, V (2006) *The relationship between the academic reading construct as measured by IELTS and the reading experiences of students in the first year of their courses at a British University*, unpublished Research Report, British Council/ IELTS.

Weir, C J, Green, A B, Hawkey, R and Unaldi, A (2008) *The cognitive processes underlying the academic reading construct as measured by IELTS*, unpublished Research Report, British Council/IELTS.

Wenger, E (1999) *Communities of practice: Learning, meaning and identity*, Cambridge: Cambridge University Press.

Wilkins, D A (1973) The Linguistic and Situational Content of the Common Core in a Unit/Credit System, in Trim, J L M, Richterich, R, van Ek, J A and Wilkins, D A (Eds) *Systems Development in Adult Language Learning*, Strasbourg: Council of Europe, 129–45.

Wilkins, D A (1976) *Notional Syllabuses*, Oxford: Oxford University Press.

Williams, E and Moran, C (1989) Reading in a foreign language at intermediate and advanced levels with particular reference to English, *Language Teaching* 22 (4), 217–28.

Winetroube, S (1997) *The design of the teachers' attitude questionnaire*, Cambridge: UCLES internal report.

Winn, W D (1987) Charts, Graphs and Diagrams in Educational Materials, in Williams, D M and Houghton, H A (Eds) *The Psychology of Illustrations*, New York: Springer-Verlag.

Wise, S L and Plake, B S (1989) Research on the effects of administering tests via computers, *Educational Measurement: Issues and Practice* 8 (3), 5–10.

Wolfe, E and Manalo, J (2004) Composition medium comparability in a direct writing assessment of non-native English speakers, *Language Learning and Technology* 8 (1), 53–65.

Wood, R (1993) *Assessment and Testing: A survey of research*, Cambridge: Cambridge University Press.

Wright, B D and Stone, M H (1979) *Best Test Design*, Chicago, IL: MESA Press.

Wu, J R W and Wu, R Y F (2007) *Using the CEFR in Taiwan: the perspective of a local examination board*, The Language Training and Testing Center, Taipei: Taiwan, paper presented at EALTA conference, Sitges: Spain, July 2007.

Wu Yi'an (1998) What do tests of listening comprehension test? – A retrospection study of EFL test-takers performing a multiple-choice task, *Language Testing* 15 (1), 21–44.

Yang, H and Weir, C J (1998) *Validation Study of the College English Test*, Shanghai: Shanghai Foreign Language Education Press.

Yue, W (1997) *An investigation of textbook materials designed to prepare students for the IELTS test: a study of washback*, unpublished MA dissertation, Lancaster University.

Zhou, S, Weir, C J and Green, R (1998) *The Test for English Majors Validation Project*, Shanghai: Foreign Language Education Press.

Zumbo, B D (2007) Three Generations of DIF Analyses: Considering Where It Has Been, Where It Is Now, and Where It Is Going, *Language Assessment Quarterly* 4 (2), 223–33.

Author index

Author index

Hargreaves, P 127, 206
Harrison, C 217
Hart, S G 293
Hartman, D K 54
Harvey, A L 286, 298
Hawkey, R 8, 26, 66, 104, 170–172, 174, 175,
  177–182, 184, 185, 223, 230, 231
Haynes, M 50, 102
Hazenberg, S 126
Hegarty, M 98, 99
Henning, G 144, 171, 186
Heppner, F H 286
Herrington, R 183
Higgins, J 299
Hill, K 146
Hindmarsh, R 125
Hinofotis, F B 35
Hirtzel, M 205
Hoffmann, T 299
Holland, P W 19
Holleran, T 298
Holliday, W G 98
Hoover, W A 45
Horak, T 183
Hosenfeld, C 75
Hsieh, M C 298
Hudson, T 47
Hughes, A 51, 90, 96, 138, 154, 156, 171–174
Huhta, A 124
Hulstijn, J H 126
Hyland, K 106
Hymes, D 104
Hynd, C R 54
Hyona, J 55

I
IDP Australia 16
Ingham, K 199
Inouye, D K 286
International Language Testers Association
  20
International Test
Commission 20
Iwashita, N 19

J
Jackenthal, A 299
Jackobson, R 105
James, J H 54
Jamieson, J 290
Jenkins, J R 41, 42, 48
Jin, Y 36
Johnson, V 82
Jones, N 9, 150, 195, 203–205, 213, 214, 218,
  302
Just, M A 41, 98

K
Kaftandjieva, F 211
Kane, M T 218
Kaplan, R B 106
Kasper, G 42
Keddle, J S 119
Keefe, J W 25
Khalifa, H 19, 22, 32, 138, 217, 262
Kim, K 283, 284, 288
Kim, M 171, 186
King, J R 54, 61
Kintsch, W 36, 41, 45, 52, 53, 57, 82, 89
Kirkpatrick, R 298
Kirsch, I S 36, 284, 290
Klare, G 122
Klavas, A 25
Kobayashi, M 82, 89
Koda, K 44, 53, 66, 68, 219
Koenig, A J 21
Kong, D 45
Koonce, J M 293
Koran, J 98
Koran, M L 98
Kratchowill, T R 21
Kruk, R S 305
Kuijper, H 83, 212
Kunnan, A J 18, 32, 39, 171, 175, 184,
  186–188, 231

L
LaBerge, D 41
Lacroix, N 45, 53, 61
Lado, R 144
Larkin, J H 99
Lasasso, C 75
Laufer, B 126, 127, 135, 136
Lave, J 199
Lazanis, S 20
Lennon, M L 299
Lewkowicz, J 91
Li, S 21
Linacre, J M 147, 228
Linn, R L 146
Lipson, M Y 40
Lombard, D 290, 291, 296
Long, J 298
Lumley, T 39
Lunsford, A 106
Luoma, S 124, 154
Lynch, B 39

M
Malvern, D D 101
Manalo, J 288, 304
Maniski, T 66
Markham, P 89

Author index

Rose, D 61, 95, 222
Rosenshine, B V 36, 59
Rothkopf, E Z 56
Rouet, J F 53
Roussey, J Y 299
Ruddell, R B 41
Rupp, A A 83, 84, 171, 187
Russell, M 288–291, 296, 299
Ryan, K 186

S
Sajavaara, K 124
Samuels, S D 41
Sanford, E E 298
Saville, N 3, 26, 151, 164, 170, 171, 174–179,
    181–183, 188, 193, 195, 213, 214, 217,
    218
Sawaki, Y 286, 287, 289, 290, 292, 294, 299
Sawilowsky, S S 151, 152
Scardamalia, M 54
Scarpati, S 21
Schedl, M 36, 44, 53, 88
Schmitt, N 126, 131
Schneider, G 211
Schreiner, R 286
Schulte, A G 21
Sharon, A T 19
Shaw, S 1, 25, 54, 93, 113, 210, 212, 215, 217,
    220, 226, 232, 303
Shepard, L 171, 187
Shermis, M 290, 291, 296
Sherwood, W 298
Shi, L 91
Shih, M 97
Shiotsu, T 50, 118, 281
Shohamy, E 172, 175
Simon, H A 99
Sims, V K 293
Sireci, S G 21
Skehan, P 101
Slater, W H 82
Smith, J 181
Smitten, B 84
Sommer, J 54, 61
Speaker, R 41
Spiegel, D L 82
Spivey, N 54, 61
Spolsky, B 174
Stahl, S A 54, 61
Stanovich, K E 41, 42, 48
Staveland, L E 293
Steinberg, L S 292
Sticht, T G 54
Stoller, F L 39, 90, 150
Stone, M H 147, 194
Stricker, L J 19

Stromso, H I 45, 53, 54
SurveyLang 202, 218
Swain, M 104
Swaminathan, H 146
Swinton, S S 19
Symons, S 286
Szabo, G 202

T
Takala, S 83, 124
Tan, S H 138
Tang, K L 36
Tannenbaum, R J 212
Tardieu, C 83
Taylor, C 283–285, 288, 290, 291, 295, 296,
    305
Taylor, L 41, 90, 126, 177, 178, 180, 181,
    191–193, 198, 199, 203, 214–217
Taylor, S E 102
Teasdale, A 39, 124
Thighe, D 160, 217, 229, 303, 304
Thissen, D 292
Thompson, M 82
Thompson, S J 21
Thorndike, R L 36
Thunin, O 299
Thurlow, M L 20
Tinkler, T 298, 299
Toulmin, S E 218
Trabasso, T 57
Trim, J 111, 116, 120, 128, 130, 141, 203,
    204
Tunmer, W E 45
Tuokko, E 202

U
Unaldi, A 54, 61
University of Cambridge ESOL
    Examinations 14, 15, 16
Upton, T A 39, 41, 44, 60, 61, 69, 86, 88, 100,
    109
Urquhart, A H 39, 44, 46, 47, 54–58, 107,
    109, 124, 138, 150

V
van den Broeck, P 41
van Dijk, T A 36, 41, 45, 52, 53, 57
Van Ek, J 111, 116, 120, 128, 130, 141, 203,
    204
Vahapassi, A 104
Valdez Pierce, L 41
Vanniarajan, S 39
Vipond, D 45
Visser, D 283, 284, 287, 288, 290, 291, 295,
    296
Vogel, L A 290, 291, 296

336

Author index

Subject index

338

Subject index

Knowledge of the world 41, 43, 51–52, 57, 68, 107, 224

L

L1 reading 43, 48, 305
Learning strategies 26
Lexical
  Access 5, 41, 43, 45, 49, 55, 58, 59, 70, 72, 75, 89, 103
  Analysis 131
  Density 131
  Development 78
  Resources 5, 82, 124–128, 131
  Variation 101, 131, 136
Lexico-grammatical 114, 126, 203
Lexicon 43, 49, 125, 127, 130
Lexis 15, 35, 49, 76–78, 106, 114, 118, 124–130, 132, 135, 226
Linguistic demands 5, 7, 80–82, 104

M

Main Suite 9, 14, 19, 22–24, 26–28, 30, 32, 34, 44, 61–63, 67–70, 74–78, 80, 91–93, 95–98, 101, 103, 105, 107, 109–110, 114–116, 119–123, 127–128, 131, 133, 135, 140–141, 150–152, 157, 163–164, 167–168, 181–182, 191–192, 196, 203–206, 210, 213, 217–218, 220–222, 224–226, 229, 231, 301
Malpractice 265
Marker reliability 5, 83, 144, 156–157, 160, 230
Matching 47, 48, 58–59, 61, 63, 70–71, 85–87, 221
Meaning representation 41, 43, 52, 55, 57, 59, 64, 71, 73
Measurement scale 146, 147, 191, 194, 195, 211, 228, 231
Mental model 5, 35, 43, 49, 51–52, 58–60, 70–71, 74–75, 84, 88–89, 100–101, 106
Monitoring 4–5, 26, 32, 52, 55, 60, 94, 157, 159, 178, 179, 198–199, 207, 209, 221, 276, 278–280
Multiple-choice question 61, 67, 83–85, 92–93, 95, 126, 150–151, 158, 221, 222, 289
Multiple matching 61, 67, 85–86, 92, 95, 145, 222

N

Nature of information 5, 82, 137

O

Order of items 5, 65, 82, 96–98

P

Parallel forms 148, 193, 195, 197, 200
Patterns of exposition 109

PET 14, 24, 28, 30–32, 63–66, 68, 70–72, 76–78, 84, 86–87, 91–92, 95, 97–99, 101, 103, 105, 110–111, 114–122, 128–137, 140–141, 151, 165, 167, 192, 194, 196, 203–204, 210, 219, 221, 223–225, 227–228, 238, 243, 263, 281, 297, 299–303
Physical conditions 5, 16, 228, 264
Point-biserial correlation 144–145
Post-exam analysis 167
Practicality 35, 67, 68, 81, 93, 151, 222
Pretesting 31, 103–104, 117, 120–121, 129–130, 142, 147, 152, 158–159, 184, 194–195, 197, 199–201, 211, 223, 229–230, 270–274, 276–277, 279
Processes
  Bottom-up/Top-down 41–42, 96–97, 100
Propositional meaning
  Macro-proposition 45–46, 52, 56–58, 60, 65, 73, 97
  Micro-proposition 45, 52, 58, 60, 65
Purpose 2, 5, 7, 9, 14–16, 25, 30–31, 34, 36, 40, 44–45, 47, 53, 55–56, 60, 62, 69, 72, 78, 82, 90, 95, 96, 98, 100, 104–106, 109, 111, 119, 161–162, 164, 167, 169, 179, 187, 210, 213–215, 218, 224, 225

Q

Question paper production 31, 107, 194, 198, 201, 224, 230, 269–271
Questions
  Textually explicit 45
  Textually implicit 75

R

Rasch analysis 66, 146, 200, 213
Readability 123
Readers
  Good/Poor 41, 75, 102
  Skilled/Unskilled 41, 46, 48, 55, 68–69
Readership 106
Reading
  Ability 1, 3, 9, 17, 35, 62, 73–74, 86, 90, 93, 150, 217, 281–282, 284–285, 287, 290, 292, 296–297
  Construct 3, 11, 36, 40, 186, 215
  Process 37, 39, 40–41, 43–44, 46, 50, 54, 94, 96, 219
  Skills/Subskills 3, 16, 34, 36, 48, 76, 103, 126, 185, 285, 292
  Strategies 47, 104, 223
  Tasks 6, 9, 41–43, 61, 68–69, 74, 80, 84, 88, 93, 97, 102, 118, 220–221, 223, 233, 293–294, 299

Subject index

Tests 1, 7, 14, 16–17, 21, 34–37, 42, 57, 63, 65, 75, 201, 215–216, 218, 220, 228, 281, 283, 285–286, 289, 292, 295–296, 298–299

Texts 79, 122, 131–132, 281, 298, 299

Topics 12, 15, 25, 31–32, 43, 45–46, 57–58, 68, 76–77, 92–98, 100, 105, 107, 109, 125–130, 138–141, 182–183, 185, 198, 200–201, 210, 224, 227–228, 269, 274–275, 288

Types 34, 61–62, 64, 79–81, 87, 90, 94, 97, 100, 104, 223, 219

Real life 6, 8–9, 16, 18, 34, 41, 43, 51, 55, 71, 79–81, 84, 90–91, 97, 101, 104, 206, 220–221, 223, 232

Reliability
  Estimates 149, 151, 154, 167
  Inter-rater 156, 208
  Intra-rater 156, 208

Response method/response format 5–6, 21, 67, 82–83, 86–88, 91–93, 221–222

Results

Reporting 163, 165, 187, 304

Statement 163–166

Right/Wrong/Doesnít say items 85, 91–92, 221

S

Scanning 16, 35, 46, 47, 56, 58–59, 62–67, 71, 87, 94, 97, 157–158, 185

Scores 4, 6–7, 20–21, 33, 88, 90, 138, 142–143, 145, 148–150, 152, 154–156, 161–163, 167–168, 171, 177–178, 181, 186, 188, 190–193, 197, 211–212, 214–215, 229, 282–285, 288–296, 299, 303, 305

Scoring criteria 143

Scoring validity 4, 5, 7–8, 11, 16–17, 35, 93, 96, 142–168, 222, 228, 232

Search reading 35, 45–47, 56–59, 63–65, 67, 87, 97, 99–100, 104, 185, 224

Security 5, 100, 163, 228, 266–268

Selected response 21, 83, 88, 93, 145, 148, 156–157, 220–222

Sentence length 77, 79,122, 124, 227

Short answer question 87–89

Skimming 16, 43, 45–47, 55–58, 63, 67, 69, 87, 96–97, 99–100, 104, 185, 224, 298

Socio-cognitive approach 4, 178

Stakeholders 2, 4, 26, 164–165, 167, 171, 173, 176–180–181, 183, 193, 199, 203, 205, 208, 210, 216, 230, 232

Standard error of measurement 154–155

Standard setting 160, 203, 206, 208, 211

Standardised testing 84, 176, 186

Structural equation modelling 118

Structural resources 79, 221

Structure 14–16, 35–36, 43–46, 49–50, 52–61, 65–66, 70, 72, 74, 76–79, 83, 85–86, 89–90, 95, 97, 107, 109, 110, 114, 118–121, 123–124, 127, 150, 198, 225–227, 273, 282, 285, 292, 295, 297

Syntactic
  Knowledge 43, 118
  Parsing 5, 43, 45, 49, 55, 70, 72, 75, 89, 103
  Processing 59

T

Task
  Construction 31
  Rhetorical 25, 43, 45, 53, 60–61, 106–107, 109–111, 119–121, 225
  Type 66, 85, 88, 91, 141, 182, 197, 221, 301, 302

Test
  Bias 5, 7, 22, 31–33, 88, 90, 100, 139–140, 160, 169–171, 186–189, 197, 200, 231, 288
  Comparability 5, 14, 25, 31, 190–191, 196, 201–203, 281, 283, 286–292, 294–300, 305
  Conditions 20, 38, 177, 191, 287
  Consequences 7, 95, 169, 171, 174, 176
  Development (model) 26, 178
  Equivalence 5, 7, 25, 149, 190, 193–194, 197, 200–201, 281–284, 286–287, 288–292, 295–297, 301–303
  Mode 283, 285, 287–291, 293–299, 303
  Scores 4, 7, 17, 20–21, 138, 143, 145, 149, 154, 156, 167–168, 171, 177, 181, 186, 188, 190, 193, 212, 213–215, 284–285, 291, 296, 303, 305

Test-taker characteristics
  Experiential 4–6, 18, 25–26, 32–33, 181, 263
  Physical/physiological 4–6, 18–19, 22–23, 25
  Psychological 4–6, 18, 25–26, 33

Test-taker profile
  Age 27–28, 30–31
  Educational level 27–28, 30–31
  Exam preparation 27–28, 30
  Gender 27–28, 30–31
  L1 27–28, 30–31

Test task performance 81

Text
  Complexity 34, 61–62, 68, 76–77, 91, 94, 101, 118, 122, 141
  Length 5, 6, 40, 48, 77–79, 82, 99–102, 109–110, 124, 141, 198, 200, 223, 227, 273, 298–299
  Level representation 5, 52, 72–73, 75, 100

Subject index